Identity-Based Brand Management

Christoph Burmann · Nicola-Maria Riley
Tilo Halaszovich · Michael Schade

Identity-Based Brand Management

Fundamentals—Strategy—
Implementation—Controlling

Springer Gabler

Christoph Burmann
Chair of innovative Brand Management (LiM®)
University of Bremen
Bremen, Germany

Nicola-Maria Riley
Chair of innovative Brand Management (LiM®)
University of Bremen
Bremen, Germany

Tilo Halaszovich
Chair in International Management and
   Governance
University of Bremen
Bremen, Germany

Michael Schade
Chair of innovative Brand Management (LiM®)
University of Bremen
Bremen, Germany

ISBN 978-3-658-13560-7   ISBN 978-3-658-13561-4   (eBook)
DOI 10.1007/978-3-658-13561-4

Library of Congress Control Number: 2017931579

Translation from the German language edition: *Identitätsbasierte Markenführung, 2nd ed.* by Christoph Burmann, Tilo Halaszovich, Michael Schade and Frank Hemmann, © Springer Fachmedien Wiesbaden 2015. Springer Fachmedien Wiesbaden is a part of Springer Science+Business Media. All Rights Reserved.

Lektorat: Barbara Roscher

Printed on acid-free paper

This Springer Gabler imprint is published by Springer Nature
The registered company is Springer Fachmedien Wiesbaden GmbH
The registered company address is: Abraham-Lincoln-Str. 46, 65189 Wiesbaden, Germany

Preface

Strong brands are critical for the success of a company, and there are numerous academic and practitioners' texts on the art and science of branding. Identity-based brand management has been one of the most widely adopted management models. The concept was developed in different parts of the world during the 1990s by David Aaker, Jean-Noel Kapferer, as well as Christoph Burmann and Heribert Meffert. It complements the external view of the brand held by customers, competitors and others with managers' and employees' internal perspectives. Its major strength emanates from the fact that it draws on the widely used "competence-based theory of the firm" in strategic management research.

Why publish a new brand management textbook? The short answer is that the first two German editions have been extremely positively received and we have been asked time and again for an international edition of the book. So we took up the challenge of writing an equally practical and theoretically sound textbook for an international audience. The English and Chinese versions have now been published and will be followed in due course by French, Portuguese and Arabic translations.

This first English edition would not have been possible without the talent and dedication of various members of the Chair of Innovative Brand Management, Bremen. In particular, we would like to express our gratitude to Corinna S. Beckmann, Julia Sinnig, Stephan Hanisch, Dr. Ines Nee, Patrick Roßmann and Ayla Rößler. Furthermore, we thank our student assistants Jana Johannsen and Philip Werner for their work and dedication. We were fortunate to have Pippa Dobson's support in ensuring that this book balances contextual accuracy with idiomatic fluency.

Finally, we thank the team of Springer Gabler for their helpful support. In particular, we would like to offer our special thanks to Ms. Birgit Borstelmann and Ms. Barbara Roscher.

Identity-based brand management has been further explored in almost 70 doctoral theses at the Chair of Innovative Brand Management and Marketing at the University of Bremen. Almost all of them have been published in the Springer Gabler book series "*Innovatives Markenmanagement*" (in German and English).

We hope that this text will prove useful to and inspire discussions between theoreticians and practitioners alike.

Bremen, Germany   Christoph Burmann
                                                                   Nicola-Maria Riley
                                                                   Tilo Halaszovich
                                                                   Michael Schade

Contents

1   The Foundations of Identity-Based Brand Management   1
    1.1   Current Challenges Facing Brand Management   2
    1.2   Theoretical Foundations of Branding   6
           1.2.1   The Market-Based View   6
           1.2.2   The Resource-Based View   8
           1.2.3   The Competence-Based View   9
           1.2.4   Linking the Market-Based View
                   with the Competence-Based View   14
    1.3   Conclusion   14
    References   15

2   The Concept of Identity-Based Brand Management   17
    2.1   Development of an Identity-Based Brand Management   18
    2.2   Identity-Based Brand Definition   26
    2.3   The Fundamental Concept of Identity-Based Brand Management   27
    2.4   Comparison of Brand Management Approaches   29
    2.5   The Current Status of Identity Research   32
           2.5.1   Socio-Scientific Approaches to Identity Research   33
           2.5.2   Socio-Scientific Identity Research and Brand Identity   35
           2.5.3   Economic Approaches of Identity Research   40
    2.6   Conceptual Design of Brand Identity   42
           2.6.1   Brand Identity as an Internal Management Concept   42
           2.6.2   Dimensions of Brand Identity   44
    2.7   The Brand Image Concept   56
           2.7.1   The Brand Image Concept in Identity-Based
                   Brand Management   57
           2.7.2   Associative Neural Brand Networks
                   as the Product of Stimulus Processing in the Brain   60
           2.7.3   Storage of Brand-Related Information in the Memory   65

2.7.4   Neuroscientific Implications for Identity-Based
        Brand Management   67
2.8   Brand Trust in Identity-Based Brand Management   70
      2.8.1   Relevance of Brand Trust   70
      2.8.2   Components of Brand Trust   71
      2.8.3   Implications for Identity-Based Brand Management   75
2.9   Brand Authenticity in Identity-Based Brand Management.   76
      2.9.1   The Relevance of Brand Authenticity   76
      2.9.2   The Object of Brand Authenticity   77
      2.9.3   Implications for Identity-Based Brand Management   78
2.10 The Process of Identity-Based Brand Management   81
References   83

3   **Strategic Brand Management**   91
3.1   Situational Analysis   93
      3.1.1   Objectives of Internal Brand Management   93
      3.1.2   Objectives of External Brand Management   102
3.2   Brand Identity   106
3.3   Brand Positioning   106
      3.3.1   Classifying and Demarcating Brand Positioning   106
      3.3.2   The Positioning Process in Identity-Based Brand Management. . .   109
      3.3.3   Brand Repositioning as a Special Form of Positioning.   113
      3.3.4   Analysing Brand Positioning by Means of Positioning Models . . .   115
      3.3.5   Choosing Appropriate Positioning Strategies   118
      3.3.6   Multi-sensual Brand Positioning.   119
3.4   Brand Architecture   122
      3.4.1   Definition.   122
      3.4.2   The Process of Brand Architecture Design   124
3.5   Brand Evolution   140
      3.5.1   Definition and Overview   140
      3.5.2   Brand Dynamisation   140
      3.5.3   Brand Restructuring   149
3.6   Brand Budgeting.   162
      3.6.1   The Purpose of Brand Budgeting   162
      3.6.2   The Budgeting Process   163
References   165

4   **Operational Brand Management**   173
4.1   Operational Internal Brand Management   175
      4.1.1   Moderators of the Relationships with Brand
              Citizenship Behaviour.   175
      4.1.2   Instruments to Influence Brand Understanding
              and Brand Commitment   177

4.2   Operational External Brand Management   189
        4.2.1   Brand Offering Policy   190
        4.2.2   Brand Price Policy   191
        4.2.3   Brand Distribution Policy   191
        4.2.4   Brand Communication Policy   194
4.3   Identity-Based Brand Management in the Digital Context   195
        4.3.1   Challenges for Brand Management by Digitalization   195
        4.3.2   Instruments of Online Communication   198
        4.3.3   Special Position of Social Media in Identity-Based
                Brand Management   200
References   225

5   **Identity-Based Brand Controlling**   233
5.1   Internal and External Brand Performance Measurement   235
        5.1.1   Main Features of Identity-Based Brand Controlling   235
        5.1.2   Operationalisation of the External and Internal Brand Strength . . .   241
5.2   Customer Equity Versus Brand Equity as Key Performance
        Indicator of Brand Controlling   245
5.3   Necessity for an Identity-Based Brand Valuation Approach   245
        5.3.1   Deficits of Brand Valuation to Date in Theory and Practice   245
        5.3.2   Requirements and Purposes of Identity-Based Brand Valuation . . .   249
        5.3.3   Financial General Conditions of Brand Valuation   253
5.4   Systematisation of Brand Valuation Approaches   254
        5.4.1   Financial Approaches   255
        5.4.2   Behavioural Approaches   255
        5.4.3   Combined Approaches   259
        5.4.4   Stakeholder-Oriented Approaches   264
        5.4.5   Identity-Based Brand Valuation   268
References   277

6   **Identity-Based Trademark Protection**   281
6.1   Integral Identity-Based Trademark Protection   282
6.2   Developing a Trademark Protection Strategy   283
6.3   Legal Trademark Protection   284
        6.3.1   Determining the Territoriality of Trademark Protection   284
        6.3.2   Obtaining Trademark Protection   285
6.4   Extra-Legal Trademark Protection   285
        6.4.1   Enhancing Innovation Capabilities   285
        6.4.2   Cooperating with Authorities   285
        6.4.3   Consumer- and Sales-Oriented Measures   286
        6.4.4   Supplier- and Production-Oriented Measures   287
6.5   Internal Requirements for Integrated Trademark Protection   287
        6.5.1   Organisational Anchoring   287

6.5.2   Recourse to Local Knowledge 288
6.5.3   Channel Monitoring 288
References 289

7 International Identity-Based Brand Management..................... 291
7.1   Standardisation Versus Differentiation in International Marketing 292
7.2   Important Influences of Consumer Behaviour
       on Brands in International Markets............................. 293
       7.2.1   National Culture 293
       7.2.2   Stage of Economic Development 296
       7.2.3   Socio-Demographic Characteristics 297
       7.2.4   Brand Origin 297
7.3   Strategic and Operational Aspects
       of International Brand Management............................ 299
       7.3.1   Timing of Market Entry................................ 299
       7.3.2   Positioning Brands in an International Context 300
       7.3.3   International Brand Architecture........................ 301
       7.3.4   Specifics of Internal Brand Management
                in an International Context 306
References 308

Index... 313

The Foundations of Identity-Based Brand Management

1

Contents

1.1	Current Challenges Facing Brand Management	2
1.2	Theoretical Foundations of Branding	6
	1.2.1 The Market-Based View	6
	1.2.2 The Resource-Based View	8
	1.2.3 The Competence-Based View	9
	1.2.4 Linking the Market-Based View with the Competence-Based View	14
1.3	Conclusion	14
References		15

Structure and Learning Objectives of This Chapter

This first chapter focuses on the foundations of brand identity and addresses the two key questions in this area, namely:

– Which challenges does brand management face today, and how can they be tackled most effectively?
– How can identity-based brand management help to create competitive advantages?

To begin with, an overview of the present challenges facing brand managers will reveal how the waning, or in some markets, non-existent, differentiating power of many brands results in enormous price pressures. After that the creation of competitive advantage will be examined from three different perspectives: the market-based view, the resource-based perspective, and the competence-based position of the firm. The findings of these analyses will then form the basis upon which the management of brand identity will be introduced.

© Springer Fachmedien Wiesbaden GmbH 2017
C. Burmann et al., *Identity-Based Brand Management,*
DOI 10.1007/978-3-658-13561-4_1

1.1　Current Challenges Facing Brand Management

Brand management and brand leadership have been pivotal topics for corporate management strategies for many years.

The relevance of brand management is reflected in the mere number of new brand registrations: 2.99 million brands were registered in 2013 alone, 2.4% more than in the previous year. Summed up herein are registrations that were submitted directly to the national or regional offices (Paris route), or in designated offices via the Madrid System (WIPO 2014). The magnitude of this figure proves that brands are significant in terms of their economic value. Their value stems primarily from their relevance to potential customers and other reference groups (i.e. the "demand side" of market transactions). For instance, the brand value of "Google" has been estimated to amount to 158 bn US dollars in 2011 (cf. Millward Brown 2014). The economic and managerial significance of brands stems from three brand functions for consumers and other reference groups (see Fig. 1.1).

Firstly, from a **behavioural perspective**, the brand offers **orientation**. It increases market transparency, which in turn enables the buyer to choose the most suitable offering

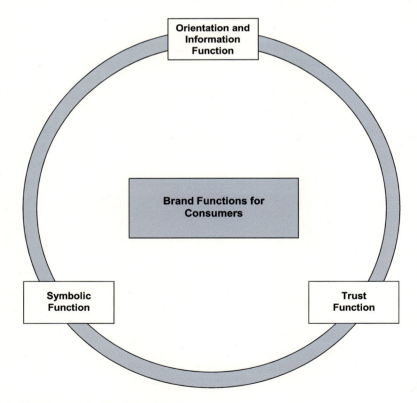

Fig. 1.1　Functions of the brand for potential customers

faster and with more ease. Due to the large number of interchangeable brands ("brand inflation") this function is seldom fulfilled. However, there are a few strong brands whose power is predominantly based on an orientation function (e.g. Google). From a **transaction-theoretical perspective**, brands reduce the cost of product and information searches. Hence, a brand can be "cheaper" than a "brandless" offering, as the sum of the price and transaction costs proves relevant for purchasing behaviour (cf. Williamson 1985).

Secondly, a brand can create trust based on awareness and perceived competence (**trust function**): The transaction between seller and buyer often leads to information asymmetries, which in turn results in behavioural insecurities (cf. Williamson 1983). Trust dissolves such asymmetries and hence facilitates market transactions. In general, the larger the subjectively perceived risks of a purchasing decision are, the greater is the trust function of a brand.

In addition, a brand can fulfil a prestige function for potential customers: As early as in the 19th century, William James recognised that human beings tend to use objects over and above their functional role as an expression of their personality: "A man's self is the sum total of all that he can call his, not only his body and his psychic power, but his clothes and house, his wife and children, his ancestors and friends, his reputation and works, his lands and yacht and bank account. All these things give him the same emotions." (James 1890, p. 291). Therefore, brands can become a means of communicating one's own identity to other people. In addition, brands can contribute to the development of a sense of identity by offering the buyer the opportunity to transfer brand attributes from the brand onto themselves (self-image). Over and above the enjoyment of identifying and living in accordance with one's own personality (self-realisation), this process can express the buyer's affiliation to a group. In such cases the brand is a symbol of the important motivational factors for the buyer. Today, this third, **symbolic function** of the brand tends to be the predominant factor.

The functions detailed above present corporations with numerous opportunities: a successful brand contributes towards top line growth and hence the economic value of the entire company. Professional brand management is thus expected to create preferences for the company's offering, and hence to differentiate it from competing offerings. In order to achieve this potential for success, it is necessary to master the challenges of brand management.

The key challenge for brand managers is the **perceived interchangeability** of brands on the demand side. For brands in a B2C or B2B market, in which there is a high degree of interchangeability, it is increasingly difficult to highlight and uniquely differentiate a brand from the mass of competing offerings (cf. Dolak 2005; Wiedmann and Ludewig 2014; Bruhn 2005). Hence, 64% of Germans cannot identify any significant differences between brand offerings (BBDO 2009).

Figure 1.2 shows the positioning of insurance companies in Germany as an example in case and based on multidimensional scaling. The study is based on a representative survey of 6666 people in Germany from 2009, who just covered insurance. Almost all

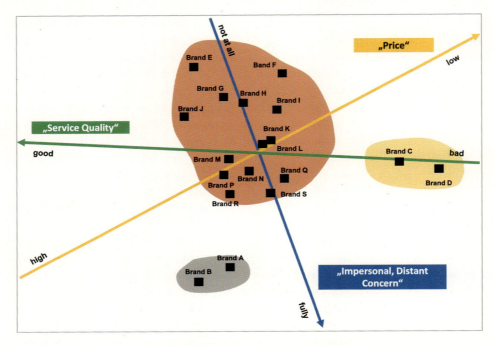

Fig. 1.2 Lack of differentiation of corporate brands in the German Insurance Market 2009

insurance companies were assigned to one large undifferentiated group by the consumers (see red area in Fig. 1.2). Only two companies distinguished themselves positively or negatively as "affordable with low service" and as "expensive and impersonal".

These analyses show the lack of differentiation power of many brands. This lack leads to the comparison of the different offers on a pure price level. In consequence, only that provider will prevail in the market that is able to achieve a sufficient margin even at constant price erosion.

One of several solutions to this problem is the development of "experience orientation" (cf. Pine and Gilmore 1999; Freundt 2006). Therefore, research is being increasingly devoted to the construct of brand experience. However, there is no agreement in the literature on the exact definition of the term "experience". As a matter of fact, the English term "experience" is unhelpful in describing the concept as it tends towards a rather undifferentiated understanding of experience: it conveys the dimension of "accumulated knowledge" as well as that of a singular noteworthy or exciting experience. In contrast, the German language differentiates between the terms "Erfahrung" and "Erlebnis". Whilst "Erfahrung" can broadly be translated by the term "experience", the concept of "Erlebnis" is much wider and encompasses a considerably stronger emotional factor, with connotations of adventure, fun and often more existential, personal involvement. Therefore, based on the German term "Erlebnis", the brand experience for the purpose

Fig. 1.3 Experiential differentiation of starbucks. (Source: www.blogs.starbucks.com)

of this book is defined along four brand experience ("Erlebnis") dimensions: sensory (the brand addresses the senses), affective (the brand prompts emotions), intellectual (the brand stimulates thought and reflection) and a behavioural dimension (the brand offers opportunities for physical interaction) (cf. Brakus et al. 2009).

The targeted design of the brand experience along these four dimensions can help to differentiate a brand—even in the context of highly standardised brand performance. The international success of Starbucks, for instance, is largely based on their experience orientation. In a market where differentiation between competitive products is negligible, Starbucks distinguishes itself through a skilful application of all four brand experience dimensions (see Fig. 1.3).

A second major challenge for manufacturer brands is the penetration of private label brands. Formerly brands were manufactured exclusively by specialized producers and afterwards sold through retail. Nowadays retailers often act in direct competition with the manufacturer brands, by offering their own private label brands. The less a manufacturer brand differentiates itself from competitors, the more it gets under pressure by the private labels.

Digitalization is the third important challenge for brands. It initially intensifies competition because internet and e-commerce enable new competitors to enter the market. Furthermore, market transparency is increased for the buyers (e.g. by comparing products online). Simultaneously, the consumer demands are increasing. They expect the contemporaneous presence of brands in several distribution channels (e.g. physical stores, online-shops and electronic retailers such as Amazon). Under such tough market conditions brands are only successful if their identity provides special benefits, both internally (employees) and externally (consumers). These benefits must create meaning and go beyond the technical and functional products and services of a brand.

1.2 Theoretical Foundations of Branding

A company needs to possess one or several competitive advantages in order to differentiate itself from its competitors. The question as to how competitive advantage is created, maintained and defended has been considered in strategic management theory by different schools of thought. The major approaches are detailed below (for a more in-depth discussion see Meffert et al. 2015).

1.2.1 The Market-Based View

The creation of competitive advantage is often explained by the company's market orientation. The term "**market orientation**" refers to the company's strategy of exclusively focussing on the market rather than on company-specific factors (cf. Narver and Slater 1990).

This market orientation is based on an all-encompassing market focus which is reflected in the "**market-based**" view (MbV) (cf. Teece et al. 1997). The MbV purports that the focus of the company has to be geared towards competitive advantage, which in turn is seen as a necessary condition for long-term above-average returns. The MBV explains competitive advantage exclusively from an "outside-in" perspective (cf. Hannan and Freeman 1977). Competitive advantage is created by a two-step process: while the first step comprises the correct selection of a specific market using market characteristics as the selection tool, the second step deals with the creation of a dominant, superior market position in the selected market (cf. Burmann 2002).

This approach reflects the paradigm of "**structure-conduct-performance**" (**S-C-P**) (cf. Bain 1959). It states that the structure of an industry influences the behaviour of the companies, which in turn influences the overall performance of the industry. Accordingly, the success of a brand and the behaviour of the leading players in its market can be traced back to the characteristics of the specific market concerned. The resources and the

Fig. 1.4 The positioning of European passenger airline brands at the beginning of the 1980s

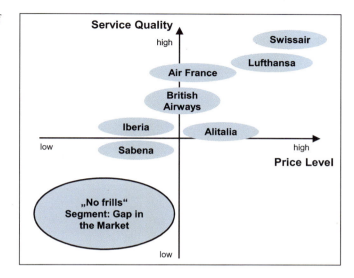

level of competence within a company are not considered relevant as this view assumes that all strategic resources are mobile and can be traded (cf. Nolte and Bergmann 1998).

This fundamental assumption leads to the conclusion that the free tradability of resources always leads to resource homogeneity amongst all market players (cf. Zahn et al. 2000). This market-oriented paradigm dominated strategic management research during the 1970s and 1980s, with Porter (1980, 1985) as its key proponent.

This strict focus on the environment in which the firm operates inevitably excludes any company-internal factors which may contribute to the success of a company. Hence, exclusively focusing on the market runs the risk of not being able to position a brand on a promising footing because the company may lack the necessary internal expertise, and it additionally hinders progressive brand management. Henry Ford summarised this succinctly at the beginning of the 20th century: "If I had asked people what they wanted, they would have said faster horses". This quotation reveals the greatest danger of pure market orientation: consumers are, for the most part, incapable of thinking outside their current status quo, nor can they formulate their future needs and desires.

The European passenger air traffic industry at the beginning of the 1980s is a good example of this predicament: the positioning of each established airline is shown in Fig. 1.4. The low-cost, "no frills" airline industry did not exist at that time. Then, in the 1990s, more than a dozen low-cost airlines attempted to replicate the success of the American airline "Southwest" in Europe and enter into the aviation sector (e.g. European Belgian Airlines, Go, easyJet, Ryanair, Hapag-Lloyd Express, Germanwings).

To date, only Ryanair and easyJet have been able to operate profitably in the "no frills" airline sector. Most of the other participants exited the market, incurring large losses or becoming insolvent: they lacked the necessary resources and expertise to establish a successful business in this sector.

1.2.2   The Resource-Based View

The **resource-based view (RbV)** was developed in response to the shortcomings of the market-based approach. The RbV views the tangible and intangible assets of the firm as the reason for its success or failure (cf. Freiling 2001). The RbV questions the importance of external market factors and proposes that company performance is predominantly due to internal aspects of the firm. These differ from company to company and, seen from the outside, represent a "black box".

Input items, which, in principle are the same for all companies operating in the market, constitute the first stepping stones for success. The company then develops these input items further into resources by means of internal refining processes. These processes are an important step towards achieving heterogeneity and competitive advantage. However, they can also lead to an uncompetitive market position if "incorrect" **refinement processes** are applied. This is the case if, for instance, the input is not refined in accordance with market requirements.

In a third step, complementary resources are combined to create a potentially unique customer benefit. This requires a certain amount of competence on the part of the internal side of the company. "**Competence**" is therefore defined as the application of repeatable skills which are based on knowledge and governed by target-driven rules as well as organisational expertise. Thus, competence serves to maintain competitiveness and to create competitive advantage (cf. Gersch et al. 2005).

The market always judges the economic relevance of resources and competencies. Long-term company success is thus based on the "correct" use of the resources, which are "correctly" made available and refined so as to generate a **relative net advantage** for the customer compared to the offerings of competitors (cf. Meffert et al. 2015). The net advantage for the customer is defined as the gain from the expected product benefit minus the costs of purchasing and usage. Hence competencies are crucial for the generation of competitive advantage.

In order to be able to define competence as an organisational rather than individual ability, there has to be **collective activity** (by two or more people), as well as an existing complementarity. If the result of the behaviour of each person is independent of that of the other members of the group (i.e. lacking complementarity), then it is impossible for the collective expertise of the firm to lead to any form of competitive advantage: the sum of all individual activity in the firm can be easily copied (e.g. by recruiting the relevant employees). Furthermore, if the sum of the work performed does not create additional returns over and above the value created by each individual, the value will be completely paid out to the employees with their individual compensation (cf. Burmann 2002).

The RbV has been justifiably criticised because of its static perspective as well as its inability to explain how a company establishes a unique resource profile and how it can successfully respond to changes over time (cf. Rasche and Wolfrum 1994). It is therefore far from the ideal theory to explain the creation of competitive advantage.

1.2.3   The Competence-Based View

The **competence-based view (CbV)** is based on the RbV and develops it further, hence constituting the most advanced perspective on how competitive advantage can be explained. The CbV emphasises the fact that resources alone are insufficient to establish competitive advantage. In contrast to resources, competence can only be grasped from the perspective of dynamic processes (see Fig. 1.5). **Competence** is always intangible and the result of expertise based on experience (cf. Freiling 2004). Furthermore, competence is the result of an interactive process over time, which has been codified into rules and processes, explaining how competencies can create competitive advantage for a company (cf. Burmann 2002).

There are three different kinds of competence (cf. Gersch et al. 2005): refinement competence, market supply competence and meta-competence, which potentially supports and, if necessary, alters the other two forms of competence.

Refinement competence offers the possibility of identifying those input goods which are potentially relevant for market success. These input goods can then be altered so that they become required resources for the company. The company's employees manage this process of alteration. An example of this process in the area of marketing would be to rent a shop at a suitable location (input). The empty shop would then be equipped and furnished as required (the refinement process).

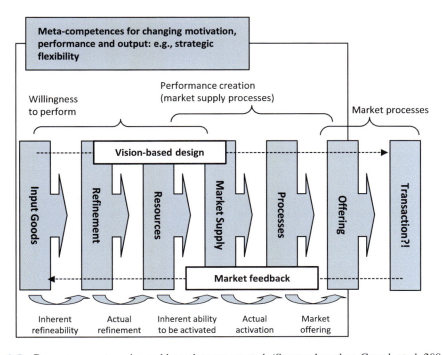

Fig. 1.5 Competence categories and how they are created. (Source: based on Gersch et al. 2005)

Market supply competence is the organisational expertise of the company. It converts the company's abilities into actual market offerings and market transactions. Thus input goods and resources are combined in order to create a market-relevant offering. An example of this would be the expertise required to establish and maintain a retail branch network, which subsequently achieves the aspired volume of transactions. Activities in this domain include, for example, managing training requirements, motivating the sales force, and managing optimal point-of-sale communications.

Meta-competence represents the company's overall framework. It takes precedence over the operational performance and affects all input goods, resources, competencies and processes. Meta-competence is crucial for a company's ability to adjust to changing market conditions (e.g. updating the product range in order to compensate for changing customer requirements and preferences).

Figure 1.5 should not give the impression that CbV perceives this process as an activity which can be planned and predicted in its entirety. Rather, the development of company competences and resources requires entrepreneurial talent and is always accompanied by uncertainty (cf. Freiling 2004). Collective competence as such is always based on the individual abilities of the employees. This methodological individualism (cf. Schumpeter 1970) forms the basis of modern research into competence (cf. Gersch et al. 2005).

Employees, therefore, need to learn from new information in order to create new individual knowledge which, in turn, has to be integrated into the firm's collective competence base (cf. Burmann 2002; Lierow and Freiling 2006). Hence competencies of the firm are always the sum of the individual capabilities on a company level (see Fig. 1.6).

From the first step, i.e. information acquisition and processing, the difficulty arises that individuals cannot access all information necessary for effective and efficient learning. Secondly, most knowledge is implicit, i.e. it consists of individual expertise, which is difficult or impossible to verbalise (cf. Polanyi 1967). Thirdly, the flow of information between individuals is heavily influenced by an **organisation's culture**, with the term "organisational culture" defined as a system in which the long-term values and convictions are shared by all of its members (cf. Fichtner 2008).

The flow of information is hindered by the fact that not every employee shares the entirety of his or her knowledge with his or her colleagues. Sharing one's expertise often

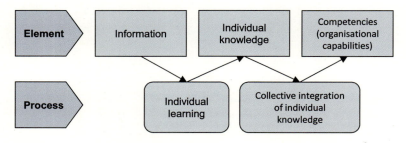

Fig. 1.6 The process of creating competencies. (Source: based on Lierow 2006, p. 128)

creates a feeling of being easily replaceable, or at the very least of giving up a personal advantage in the job market. The willingness to learn as a team and to share knowledge depends to a large extent on the culture of the company as well as suitable incentive schemes (cf. Burmann 2002). Both are important constituents of internal brand management, which will be discussed in more depth in Sect. 4.2.

Generating competence is a never-ending process. Teece et al. (1997) have examined this process in their "**Dynamic Capabilities Approach**" which tries to explain a company's ability to **change its competitive advantage**. Organisational changes are modelled as path-dependent development processes (cf. Arthur 1988; van Driel and Dolfsma 2009) which lead to the acquisition of new competencies based on old, existing competencies (cf. Burmann 2002). The existence of "dynamic capabilities" ensures that these path-dependent processes can be mastered. Whether or not these processes are mastered well depends on the quality of these "dynamic capabilities".

The most important hypothesis of the "dynamic capabilities" approach is to be found in the linking of competence development with the historical development of the company (see Fig. 1.7): existing resources and competencies ("**evolutionary paths**") heavily influence the way new solutions to problems are searched for. Hence, combining different resources is seen as the only way competencies can be created and therefore the historical resource set-up of the company ("firm-specific resource positions") has a crucial influence on the creation of new competencies.

According to Teece et al. (1997), as well as Burmann (2002), dynamic capabilities can be subdivided into several processes, as follows.

Replication processes offer an effective and efficient means of coordinating resources and refer to tasks which are well known and well established in the firm. **Replication competence** is the organisational ability of the company to multiply operative process abilities in day-to-day business. The importance of replication competence is twofold: on the one hand, it enables the company to grow more quickly and more efficiently, on the other hand, the quality of the replication competence reveals the degree to which the firm is capable of comprehending the structure and function of its organisational abilities. The latter is a key starting point for improving and developing organisational capabilities. Thus replication competence is based on the precise and comprehensive codification and transferral of existing competencies within the company.

Reconfiguration processes lead to extensive changes within a company's set of resources and competencies. In order to control reconfiguration processes, it is necessary to recognise the need for change as early as possible. The earlier the need for change is recognised, the less expensive the reconfiguration process becomes. Secondly, the company must be in a position to be able to learn the requisite new resources and competencies. Hence it presupposes a willingness and ability to learn on the part of the employees.

Replication and **reconfiguration competence** can be combined to form a **meta-competence**: both refer to dynamic changes which take place over a distinct period of time. Meta-competence can also be termed "strategic flexibility" (see Fig. 1.8). It is not possible to increase the dynamics of identity-based brand management without strategic flexibility.

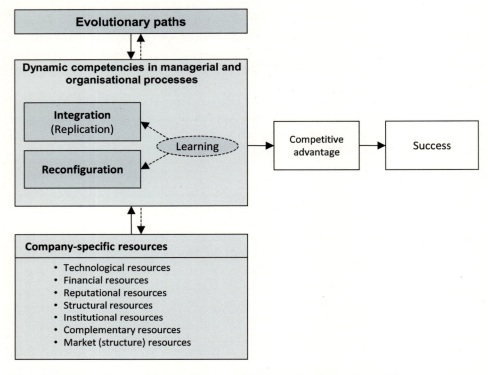

Fig. 1.7 The dynamic capabilities approach. (Source: based on Teece et al. 1997)

Replication competence describes the speed with which action is taken. It is determined by the quality of knowledge codification and the ability of the company to transfer knowledge. The knowledge employees have acquired is individual, implicit knowledge. It is only accessible by the employees themselves. In order for the organisation to be able to utilise and ensure that this knowledge is not lost if the employee leaves the company, implicit knowledge has to be transformed into explicit knowledge. This process is called the "codification of knowledge". Employees have to be motivated to codify their knowledge. Motivation to participate in this process tends to arise from the employees' expectation that they will be able to acquire their colleagues' knowledge through the same process, thus increasing their own value to the firm and to the wider market (cf. Szulanski 1996; Hauschild et al. 2001). Codification is the necessary requirement for efficient learning processes throughout the company (cf. Coriat 2000; Chen et al. 2009).

The codification of knowledge makes sense if, and only if, the codified knowledge is transferred to other employees. This transfer of knowledge is of particular importance for companies with a high turnover of staff (sometimes caused by acquisitions) and in a cooperative agreement context (cf. Capron 1999). The faster a company is able to codify and transfer knowledge, the higher the speed of action with which it will be able to manage its brands (cf. Boisot 1999; Burmann 2002).

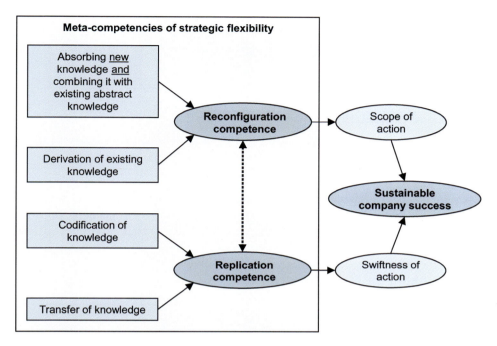

Fig. 1.8 The nature and consequences of strategic flexibility. (Source: based on Burmann 2002, p. 276)

In contrast, the reconfiguration competence denotes a company's scope for action, enabling it to develop new organisational capabilities. The development of new competencies depends on the skilful utilisation of existing knowledge in the company. For this, two processes are necessary: the processes of deriving and absorbing knowledge.

Knowledge derivation reduces knowledge to elementary cause and effect relationships. Hence it is a form of pattern recognition (cf. Boisot 1999). By deriving knowledge, a company seeks to identify the routines upon which employees' knowledge is based and which ultimately form the basis of its set of competencies. **Knowledge absorption** can be interpreted as an internalisation process of new knowledge. This process requires the application of new knowledge time and again, as well as direct experience of this new knowledge and its application (cf. Boisot 1995). The extent to which employees are receptive to new information and knowledge is very much dependent upon the culture of the firm; hence the culture of a company represents its crucial strategic flexibility (cf. Meffert 1969).

If only one of the two competencies (replication and reconfiguration, cf. Fig. 1.8) is well developed, a company is limited in its strategic flexibility: it might find itself in a situation where it encounters several courses of action, but is not in a position to realise these as quickly as required. As a result, it will lose a portion or all of its sales potential to competitors that pre-empt the company's move. Similarly, a company whose pro-

Fig. 1.9 Synthesising the competence- and market-based perspectives helps to better explain the success of a company or brand. (Source: based on Zentes et al. 2010)

cesses are predominantly standardised, and hence very fast and efficient, may not be able to exploit potential new sales opportunities since it does not possess the necessary scope for action.

1.2.4   Linking the Market-Based View with the Competence-Based View

These two approaches (RbV and CbV) do not represent opposites, but rather are inter-dependent. Neither the MbV nor the CbV are capable of explaining company success in a market in its entirety. Competence management in a company always has to integrate information emanating from the market in order to develop valuable competencies; otherwise the company would risk building up competencies which are not relevant for potential customers (see Fig. 1.9).

An exclusively market-oriented alignment of corporate behaviour would lead to the company following every market trend without being able to fulfil the market's requirements as the organisational competencies would be missing. The integration of both sides, i.e. looking at the outside-in, as well as the inside-out, perspective in parallel is the basis of identity-based brand management.

1.3   Conclusion

Given the difficulty of brand differentiation in most markets, the development and maintenance of a unique market position for a specific brand is a major challenge for most companies. Such a project requires specific competitive advantages.

This chapter has shown the limitations of the market-oriented view, which is not capable of creating and maintaining competitive advantage. In order to achieve this goal, the market-based view has to be combined with the specific competencies of the individual firm. Hence the **outside-in view** is supplemented by the **inside-out perspective**: only the combination of both perspectives can lead to competitive advantage. Insights into the status quo and the likely future developments of the market are combined with an internal view of the brand: its identity is the key driving force that, in the long run, enables the management to differentiate its offering from those of all other competitors. The combination of the outside-in and inside-out perspectives represents the core of identity-based brand management.

References

Arthur, B. (1988). Competing technologies: An overview. In G. Dosi, C. Freeman, R. Nelson, G. Silverberg, & L. Soete (Hrsg.), *Technical change and economic theory* (S. 590–607). London.

Bain, J. (1959). *Industrial organization*. New York: Wiley.

BBDO Consulting GmbH. (2009). Brand parity studie 2009. Düsseldorf.

Boisot, M. H. (1995). *Information space. A framework for learning in organizations, institutions and culture*. London: Routledge.

Boisot, M. H. (1999). *Knowledge assets. Securing competitive advantage in the information economy*. Oxford: Oxford University Press.

Bruhn, M. (2005). *Unternehmens- und Marketingkommunikation*. Munich: Vahlen.

Burmann, C. (2002). *Strategische Flexibilität und Strategiewechsel als Determinanten des Unternehmenswertes (zugl. Habilitationsschrift Universität Münster)*. Wiesbaden: Dt. Univ.-Verlag.

Capron, L. (1999). The long-term performance of horizontal akquisitions. *Strategic Management Journal, 20*, 631–661.

Chen, H.-H., Lee, P.-Y., & Lay, T.-J. (2009). Drivers of dynamic learning and dynamic competitive capabilities in international strategic alliances. *Journal of Business Research, 62*(12), 1289–1295.

Coriat, B. (2000). The "Abominable Ohno Production System". Competences, monitoring, and routines in Japanes production systems. In G. Dosi, R. R. Nelson, & S. Winter (Hrsg.), *The nature and dynamics of organizational capabilities* (S. 213–243). Oxford.

Dolak, D. (2005). *How to brand and market a commodity*. http://www.brandchannel.com/papers_review.asp?sp_id=570. Zugegriffen: 27. Oktober 2014.

Fichtner, H. (2008). *Wirkungsmechanismen der Unternehmenskultur im strategischen Kompetenzmanagement*. Bremen: Dissetationsschrift an der Universität Bremen.

Freiling, J. (2001). *Resource-based View und ökonomische Theorie – Grundlagen und Positionierung des Ressourcenansatzes*. Wiesbaden: Dt. Univ.-Verlag.

Freiling, J. (2004). Competence-based view der Unternehmung. Die Unternehmung. *Schweizerische Zeitschrift für betriebswirtschaftliche Forschung u. Praxis, 58*, S. 5–25.

Freundt, T. C. (2006). *Emotionalisierung von Marken: Inter-industrieller Vergleich der Relevanz emotionaler Markenimages für das Konsumentenverhalten*. Wiesbaden: Dt. Univ.-Verlag.

Gersch, M., Freiling, J., & Goeke, C. (2005). Grundlagen einer, competence-based theory of the firm. *Arbeitsbericht, Institut für Unternehmensführung*, Nr. 100, Ruhr Universität Bochum, Bochum.

Hannan, M. T., & Freeman, J. (1977). The population ecology of organizations. *American Journal of Sociology, 82*, 929–964.

Hauschild, S., Licht, T., & Stein, W. (2001). Creating a knowledge culture. *McKinsey Quarterly*, Nr. 1.

James, W. (1890). *The principles of psychology*. New York.

Lierow, M. A. (2006). *Competence building und Internationalisierungserfolg – Theoretische und empirische Betrachtung deutscher Unternehmen*. Wiesbaden: Dt. Univ.-Verlag.

Lierow, M., & Freiling, J. (2006). Determinanten der Bildung von Kompetenzen und ihr Einfluss auf den Internationalisierungserfolg. In: C. Burmann, J. Freiling, M. Hülsmann (Hrsg.), *Neue Perspektiven des Strategischen Kompetenz-Managements* (S. 123–148). Wiesbaden: Dt. Univ.-Verlag.

Meffert, H. (1969). Zum Problem der betriebswirtschaftlichen Flexibilität. *Zeitschrift für Betriebswirtschaft, 39*(12), 779–800.

Meffert, H., Burmann, C., & Kirchgeorg, M. (2015). *Marketing: Grundlagen markorientierter Unternehmensführung*. Wiesbaden: Springer.

Millward Brown. (2014). *BrandZ Top 100 Most valuable global brands*. http://www.millwardbrown.com/brandz/2014/Top100/Docs/2014_BrandZ_Top100_Chart.pdf. Zugegriffen: 27. Oktober 2014.

Narver, J. C., & Slater, S. F. (1990). The effect of a market orientation on business profitability. *Journal of Marketing, 54*(4), 20–34.

Nolte, H., & Bergmann, R. (1998). Ein Grundmodell des ressourcenorientierten Ansatzes der Unternehmensführung. In H. Nolte (Hrsg.), *Aspekte ressourcen- orientierter Unternehmensführung* (S. 1–27). Munich [u.a.]: Hampp.

Pine, B. J., & Gilmore, J. H. (1999). *The experience economy—Work is theatre and every business a stage*. Boston: Harvard Business School Press.

Polanyi, M. (1967). *The tacit dimension*. New York: Doubleday.

Porter, M. E. (1980). *Competitive strategy: Techniques for analyzing industries and competitors*. New York: Free Press.

Porter, M. E. (1985). *Competitive advantage: Creating and sustaining superior performance*. New York: Free Press.

Rasche, C., & Wolfrum, B. (1994). Ressourcenorientierte Unternehmensführung. *DBW, 54*, 501–517.

Schumpeter. (1970). *Das Wesen und der Hauptinhalt der theoretischen Nationalökonomie*. Berlin: Duncker & Humblot.

Szulanski, G. (1996). Exploring internal stickiness: Impediments to the transfer of best practices within the firm. *Strategic Management Journal, 17 (special issue)*, 27–43.

Teece, D. J., Pisano, G., & Shuen, A. (1997). Dynamic capabilities and strategic management. *Strategic Management Journal, 18*, 509–533.

van Driel, H., & Dolfsma, W. (2009). Path dependence, initial conditions, and routines in organizations The Toyota production system re-examined. *Journal of Organizational Change Management, 22*(1), 49–72.

Wiedmann, K.-P., & Ludewig, D. (2014). Commodity branding. In: M. Enke, & M. Reimann (Hrsg.), *Commodity Marketing – Grundlagen und Besonderheiten* (S. 73–99). Wiesbaden: Springer Gabler.

Williamson, O. E. (1983). Credible commitments: Using hostages to support exchange. *The American Economic Review, 73*(7), 519–540.

Williamson, O. E. (1985). *The economic institutions of capitalism*. New York/London.

WIPO. (2014). *World intellectual property indicators*. WIP Publication No. 941E/14, Genf.

Zahn, E. O. K., Foschiani, S., & Tilebein, M. (2000). Wissen und Strategiekompetenz als Basis für die Wettbewerbsfähigkeit von Unternehmen. In: P. F. J. Hammann (Hrsg.), *Die Ressourcen- und Kompetenzperspektive des strategischen Managements* (S. 47–68). Wiesbaden: Dt. Univ.-Verlag [u.a.].

Zentes, J., Swoboda, B., & Schramm-Klein, H. (2010). *Internationales marketing*. Munich: Vahlen.

The Concept of Identity-Based Brand Management

2

Contents

2.1   Development of an Identity-Based Brand Management   18
2.2   Identity-Based Brand Definition   26
2.3   The Fundamental Concept of Identity-Based Brand Management   27
2.4   Comparison of Brand Management Approaches   29
2.5   The Current Status of Identity Research   32
    2.5.1   Socio-Scientific Approaches to Identity Research   33
    2.5.2   Socio-Scientific Identity Research and Brand Identity   35
    2.5.3   Economic Approaches of Identity Research   40
2.6   Conceptual Design of Brand Identity   42
    2.6.1   Brand Identity as an Internal Management Concept   42
    2.6.2   Dimensions of Brand Identity   44
2.7   The Brand Image Concept   56
    2.7.1   The Brand Image Concept in Identity-Based Brand Management   57
    2.7.2   Associative Neural Brand Networks as the Product of Stimulus Processing
            in the Brain   60
    2.7.3   Storage of Brand-Related Information in the Memory   65
    2.7.4   Neuroscientific Implications for Identity-Based Brand Management   67
2.8   Brand Trust in Identity-Based Brand Management   70
    2.8.1   Relevance of Brand Trust   70
    2.8.2   Components of Brand Trust   71
    2.8.3   Implications for Identity-Based Brand Management   75
2.9   Brand Authenticity in Identity-Based Brand Management   76
    2.9.1   The Relevance of Brand Authenticity   76
    2.9.2   The Object of Brand Authenticity   77
    2.9.3   Implications for Identity-Based Brand Management   78
2.10 The Process of Identity-Based Brand Management   81
References   83

© Springer Fachmedien Wiesbaden GmbH 2017
C. Burmann et al., *Identity-Based Brand Management*,
DOI 10.1007/978-3-658-13561-4_2

Structure and Learning Objectives of This Chapter

The second chapter focuses on the concept of identity-based brand management. The design of the brand identity as the internal side of a brand and the resulting external brand image for the consumers constitute the foundation of every brand that is successful in the long term. A unique and differentiating positioning is a great challenge in mature markets. Without such a positioning, the long-term retention of consumers by the brand is significantly impeded. Therefore, subsequently this chapter deals with the following questions:

– Which brand management concept is suitable for conquering the current challenges in the markets?
– What is the brand identity based on and how can it be designed?
– How do strong brands form in the minds of consumers? What conclusions can brand management draw from neuroeconomics?
– How can brand authenticity and brand trust be established and how do these two factors contribute to the success of the brand?

To answer these questions, the reader is first of all provided with an overview of the development of brand management. Subsequently, the concept of identity is deduced and operationalised. The brand image is presented as an action model of the brand identity and its components are explained. For a deeper understanding of consumer behaviour, current findings of neuroeconomics are referenced. The second chapter will conclude with the concepts of brand trust and brand authenticity, which are pivotal for successful brand management.

2.1   Development of an Identity-Based Brand Management

Since the development of the classic branded product concept in the early 20th century, the understanding of the essence of a brand has changed due to radical changes in the market and in environmental conditions. The changed general conditions have led to different brand definitions and various approaches to brand management. In highly simplified terms, within this context we can define five stages of brand development and identify their implications for brand management (see Table 2.1).

The incipient industrialisation and, with it, the mass production of many consumer goods that had been manually produced to date, led to a loss of the personal business relations between manufacturing companies and the end consumer from the mid-19th century onwards (cf. Leitherer 1955, 2001). Personal relations were replaced by the anonymous mass market. Manufacturers lost their direct contact with the consumer. The production technology, which was still immature in many industries, implicated that the quality of industrially manufactured goods was often subject to significant variations. Furthermore, the rudimentary production and coordination know-how limited the size of the manufacturers' companies. Therefore, the structure of the goods on offer maintained

Table 2.1 Development stages of brand management

Period	Mid-19th century to early 20th century	Early 20th century to mid-1960s	Mid-1960s to mid-1970s	Mid-1970s to late 1980s	1990s
Environment	Industrialisation and mass production	Economic growth, "demand pull"	Recession/1st oil crisis	Mature markets	Information society, brand management on the Internet
	Quality fluctuations	Numerous technical innovations	Abolition of price-fixing (1967)	Fast pace of imitations	Tight positioning
	Unbranded products (staple goods) predominant	Seller's markets	Buyer's markets	"Information overload"	Shift of responsibility from individual brands to (corporate) umbrella brands
				Quality as the deal maker/deal breaker	
Retailer–manufacturer relationships	Personal customer relationships of manufacturers and retailers	Sidekick role of the retailers	Introduction of trade brands	Increasing commercial power of retailers and exacerbation of the conflict	"Information monopoly" of the retailers
	strong position of the retailers	Opinion monopoly of the manufacturers' brands	"Popularisation of marketing"	Introduction of generic brands, increasing brand know-how of the retailers	Marketing leadership of the retailers in many areas
		Leaps in retail productivity	Asymmetry in brand know-how in favour of the manufacturer		Trade brands are crowding out manufacturer's brands
		Massive expansion of classic manufacturer's brands			Intensification of the direct channel between manufacturers and customers

(continued)

Table 2.1 (continued)

Period	Mid-19th century to early 20th century	Early 20th century to mid-1960s	Mid-1960s to mid-1970s	Mid-1970s to late 1980s	1990s
Brand understanding	Brand as a symbol of ownership and proof of origin	Product focus	Production and marketing methods	Acquisition of consumers	Bundle of benefits with sustainable differentiation potential
		Brand as a catalogue of characteristics	Determined by the form of marketing	Subjective determination of the brand	Brand identity as the self-perception of the brand
					Brand image as the public image of the brand
"Modern" brand management		Instrumental "branding" approach	Function-oriented approach	Behaviour- and image-oriented approach	Integrated, identity-based brand management
				Technocratic, policy-driven approach	Fractal brand management

a highly regional character. Unbranded products dominated the picture in almost all product groups. In the early days of the last century a growing price competition emerged in the area of trade through department stores, chains and co-operatives as innovative types of business (cf. Berekhoven 1978). During this time, the branding of goods was used primarily as a symbol of ownership and **proof of origin** (cf. Linxweiler 2001). The understanding of a brand was characterised by the mere process of labelling or branding. Brand management as a business management concept was as yet non-existent.

The development and the rapid propagation of the **classic branded product concept**, which has been shaped primarily by Domizlaff, must be seen against the background of these general conditions (cf. Domizlaff 1939). This concept provided manufacturers of consumer goods with the opportunity to indirectly establish contact with the consumer again and to significantly increase their influence on the sale of their goods in the market. These objectives of the manufacturers were supposed to be achieved by means of a high and, above all, consistent product quality, uniform packaging, marketing in a large nationwide market and, in particular, advance sales of the products through classic advertising. For the most part, the numerous technical innovations which had developed during the course of industrialisation and mass production constituted the quintessence for successful brand communication and branding. Strong economic growth and the prevalence of a seller's market in most product lines facilitated the rapid diffusion of the classic branded product concept. Under these market conditions, the promise of a reliably high level of quality, a high degree of awareness established through advertising and a previously unknown level of convenience (price parity and availability in all major commercial transactions) were the key factors for market success.

Among retailers, the classic branded product concept initially also met with approval as price fixing and selected distribution prevented cut-throat competition. Furthermore, significant progress in retail productivity was made by introducing the concept of self-service and generally transferring design, packaging, quality assurance and information functions to the manufacturers (cf. Meffert and Burmann 1991). Along with the expansion of the manufacturing companies through mass production, this development ultimately resulted in the branded product manufacturers holding a strong position of power. Soon the retailers complained that they had been downgraded to vicarious agents and accused manufacturers of holding the "**opinion monopoly of branded products**" (cf. Berekoven 1978).

Brand management and brand leadership were pivotal topics for corporate management strategies for many years.

During this second stage of development, the understanding of the essence of a brand was characterised by a consumer goods-oriented product focus and the search for constitutive qualities. The brand definition was identified by a catalogue of characteristics which always related to physically tangible consumer goods. Services, investment goods and preliminary products did not constitute brands according to the understanding at that time (cf. Mellerowicz 1963). Consequently, in everyday business life, in science and even on the side of the legislator, people exclusively referred to branded products or branded merchandise. For instance, Mellerowicz defines brands as "… manufactured goods for private demand, which are available in a larger sales area under a specific characteristic (brand) indicating their origin, in uniform packaging, the same quantity and consistent or improved quality and which, due to this as well as the advertising carried out for them, have acquired the recognition of the business community involved (consumers, retailers and manufacturers)" (Mellerowicz 1963, p. 39). If this characteristic-oriented understanding is interpreted strictly, a branded product definitely needs to fulfil all of these requirements (cf. Leitherer 1955).

In brand management, an **instrumental understanding** prevailed (cf. Findeisen 1925; Goldack 1948; Domizlaff 1951; Mellerowicz 1963; Hartmann 1966). This instrumental approach was reflected in the term "branding", which primarily dealt with brand naming and design, the type of packaging and the use of classic advertising. Irrespective of the company's position and the market situation, basic rules were established which, if followed, should supposedly result in success (cf. Domizlaff 1951). For instance, Domizlaff—who is regarded as one of the fathers of professional branding policy—drafted the "**22 basic laws of natural branding**" in 1939. These basic laws take up the constitutive characteristics of the brand and describe instruments to establish and cultivate them.

Whilst this perception of brand management may to some extent appear strange from a present-day perspective, it must be taken into account that, due to the macroeconomic circumstances during that time, this type of brand management actually frequently met with success.

The **third development** stage, which began around the mid-1960s, was characterised macroeconomically by the first recessionary trends and, later on, by the first oil crisis. At the same time, the situation changed from a seller's to a buyer's market in numerous product lines. The range of goods on offer expanded tremendously and, for the time being, many basic needs in the fields of both commodities and durable consumer goods were met.

Sales developed into the key area and increasingly became the focus of attention (cf. Meffert 1994). This was also due to the fact that the most reliable factor in sales so far, the stable unit price, was turned into an apparently incalculable sales variable by the abolition of statutory resale price-fixing in 1967. As a result of this change, the manufacturers of branded products increasingly engaged in a **methodical design of the sales segment**. This led to a popularisation of the marketing know-how developed in the USA in German companies and subsequently, to an asymmetrical distribution of knowledge between manufacturers and retailers. The manufacturers used this gap in marketing know-how as a tool for the quality-oriented profiling of their branded products, thus consolidating their market position.

The retailers attempted to counteract the manufacturers' drive to stand out from the rest with "**me-too**" **strategies**, by **introducing trade brands** (cf. Schenk 1994). These copies of successful manufacturer brands were based on the understanding of a brand of that time, according to which branded products were characterised primarily by consistent quality and packaging, as well as availability across a large sales area. However, on this basis the retailers were unable to effectively establish strong brands. Trade brands were only able to maintain their position in the market due to their significantly lower prices.

During this stage, the **product range-related understanding of a brand** was geared to the production and marketing methods of the time (cf. Dichtl 1978). The branded product was defined as a "closed marketing system" (Hansen 1970, p. 64) with the aim of getting into direct contact with the consumer and attaining the highest possible degree of proximity to the customer. The branded product was now understood as a specific form of marketing and not just as a bundle of characteristics (cf. Alewell 1974).

In brand management, a **function-oriented approach** emerged. In contrast to the instrumental approach, the scope of brand management was now significantly broader. Whilst the representatives of the instrumental approach had not included market research, product development, pricing and distribution policy in brand management (cf. Hartmann 1966), these areas were integrated in the function-oriented approach (cf. Angehrn 1969; Hansen 1970). Here, the question of how to organise all operational functions in such a way as to ensure the success of a branded product took centre stage. In contrast, the representatives of the instrumental approach to brand management had been interested in identifying the marketing tools that would turn unbranded products into branded products.

In the function-oriented approach to brand management developing the various marketing functions is regarded as a crucial competitive advantage. Among these functions, distribution is seen as a key factor for the success of the branded product (cf. Dubber 1969; Hansen 1970). In contrast, the instrumental approach focused on the branding and packaging design.

In the **fourth stage of development**, approximately from the mid-1970s until the late 1980s, the macroeconomic circumstances were characterised by pronounced saturation trends in numerous markets, by more critical and in particular more price-sensitive consumers, by the rapid imitation of technical innovations and an increasing "information overload" of the consumers as a result of brand inflation (cf. Kroeber-Riel 1988).

Accordingly, the manufacturers of branded products attempted to develop new forms of addressing target groups in addition to classic advertising for the branded product (sponsoring, event marketing etc.). Due to the fast pace of imitations, technical innovations, which had traditionally represented the essence of a brand, could often only be used for the short-term profiling of brands. Consistently high quality as a characteristic for differentiating branded products became less important because high quality was taken for granted by most consumers when purchasing a product. The high level of intensity in both vertical and horizontal competition, in conjunction with consumer saturation trends, led to the rapid development of strategic marketing know-how, especially by manufacturers. This know-how was deployed to defend the market position in the face of an ever more confident presence of the retail sector in the branded products segment.

Increasing concentration in the retail sector turned the intermediaries into "gatekeepers" that controlled the path of a branded product from the manufacturer to the consumer (cf. Lewin 1963). At the same time the retailers responded to the consumers' increased price consciousness with the introduction of generic brands (cf. Meffert and Bruhn 1984). The scarce shelf space led to the retailers demanding listing fees and other hidden discounts in exchange for including new brands in the product range, resulting in the exacerbation of the conflict between retailers and manufacturers.

During this stage, the understanding of a brand was characterised by a **demand-related, subjective perception**. According to this approach, those products and services were to be identified as branded products which were perceived as such by the consumers (cf. Berekoven 1978; Meffert 1979). This understanding of a brand deliberately left behind all objectively definable product characteristics or specific production and marketing methods. Instead, it focused on the acquisition of customers and their perception of the brand.

The subjective understanding of a brand was also reflected by the contemporary brand management. During this stage, the **behaviour- and image-oriented approach** to brand management became wide-spread, both in theory and in practice (cf. Berekoven 1978; Murphy 1987; Aaker and Keller 1990; Trommsdorff 1992). This approach was based on the results of extensive research on the significance, the development and the components of the brand image (cf. Keller 1993). Based on these studies, recommendations for action were developed in order to influence the brand image as perceived by the consumer in a specific way.

In contrast to the function-oriented approach, which understood brand management merely as a part of branded product marketing, the image-oriented approach demands the equal treatment of marketing and brand management. This concept is based on the belief that all marketing parameters are generally relevant for the brand image. Despite this fundamentally wide scope of brand management, the distinct image focus of this approach led to an overemphasis on methodical aspects (e.g. operationalisation of the brand image) and to the neglect of the necessary integration of all brand management measures.

Parallel to the image-oriented approach, a **technocratic, policy-driven approach** to brand management emerged (cf. Meffert 1988; Brandmeyer and Schulz 1989; Franzen et al. 1994; Haedrich et al. 2003). This approach attempted to eliminate the integration deficits of the image-oriented approach by shifting from the behaviourial level to the corporate management level. The planning, control and coordination of all brand design measures directed at the sales market were the focus of attention. The preoccupation with the economic brand equity that had started in the 1980s led to a further popularisation of this strategic approach of brand management. However, the highly formalised interpretation of branding subsequently resulted in a very technocratic and mechanistic conception of the goals and responsibilities of brand management.

The **fifth stage of development**, from the early 1990s onwards, is characterised by a further approximation of the objective technical qualities of products. This is primarily the result of the increasing modularisation of product concepts, e.g. for computers, household appliances and automobiles, as well as the associated standardisation. Due to cost and flexibility considerations outsourcing became increasingly popular and contributed to a rising level of homogeneity of the branded products due to the use of identical suppliers and mounting parts, while in the past all manufacturers had developed their parts independent of one another.

The growing international interrelation and globalisation of competition led to the ever faster dissemination of new technological know-how. In addition, this development also promoted the approximation of the technical product characteristics of competing brands. The increasing homogenisation of the quality and the substitutability of the offers extended not only to consumer goods, but also to services and investment goods. This explains why service providers, manufacturers of investment goods and suppliers have recently also resorted to developing their own brands in order to differentiate their services (cf. Simon 1994).

The proliferation of corporate brands is also to be seen against this background. On the one hand, corporate brands are generally more advantageous for service companies (cf. Meffert and Bruhn 2012). On the other hand, corporate brands facilitate positioning in the "jungle" of brand inflation. Due to the tight positioning and the increased costs of brand management as a result of the high minimum advertising presence companies more and more refrain from individual brand concepts when launching new products. This is also in accordance with the consumers' requirements. Due to their greater economic knowledge, today's consumers define the responsibility of companies much more broadly than before, shifting responsibility from individual brands to the company as a whole (cf. Goodyear 1994).

Another general condition that is important for branding is the coalescence of the information and communication technologies and the existence of global communication networks. The Internet, in conjunction with social media, has led to a significant increase in market transparency. It enables the consumer to get a comprehensive overview of the market, without great effort, before making a buying decision. Thus, consumers can compare prices and procure services from providers who, until a few years ago, were not part of the consumer's "evoked set" due to their physical distance.

These changes in the relationship between manufacturers and retailers have led to a tremendous gain in influence and know-how on the part of the retailers. Profiting from the customers' trust in large retail chains and the margin benefits of their trade brands, they further expand their brand programme. The availability of free production capacity on the part of the manufacturers strongly supports this development. The nation-wide prevalence of scanning cash registers and the customer data obtained this way put the trade in the position of an information monopolist vis-à-vis the manufacturers. The retailers are attempting to use this information advantage to strengthen their own brands by expanding their brand know-how, for instance by poaching brand specialists from manufacturers. If nothing else, the introduction of category management is an outcome of this development (cf. Steiner 2007).

With growing brand know-how, retailers increasingly proceed to take over functions that previously resided with the manufacturer (cf. Meffert and Burmann 1991). The ever-increasing concentration in the retail trade is another factor that strengthens the position of the retailers vis-à-vis the manufacturers. In the light of this, only the strongest manufacturer brands of a product line (so-called A-brands) are likely to have a realistic chance of a trade listing in the future (cf. Steffenhagen 2008).

In turn, these changes in the general conditions have led to a modified understanding of brands since the 1990s. Today, a brand is primarily considered under **social and psychological aspects**. While the highly formalised perception of branding associated with the ("hard") technocratic, policy-driven approach to brand management did not fully meet the requirements of "soft" brand management, which is characterised by subjective influences and emotional aspects, these factors are emphasised more strongly within the context of an **identity-based approach to brand management**.

Just as the market perspective and the competence perspective were synthesised into strategic corporate management (cf. Meffert et al. 2015), brand management also needs to be reoriented. While until the 1990s the statements of marketing science with regard to brand management were based on the **outside-in perspective** (demand or image orientation), today this view must be supplemented with an identity-based **inside-out perspective** (employee and competence orientation). Ultimately, brand management can only be successful in the long term if both perspectives are taken into consideration.

2.2   Identity-Based Brand Definition

The use of the term "brand" from an identity-based brand management perspective originates from Meffert, Burmann and Keller (cf. Meffert 1974; Meffert and Burmann 1996; Keller 1993). They define a **brand** as "a bundle of functional and non-functional benefits which, from the target groups' point of view, differentiate the brand from competing offers in a sustainable way."

The above definition integrates cause and effect mechanisms, i.e. an internal and an external perspective of the brand (cf. Keller 2015). The **internal perspective** describes the process by which target groups link specified benefits to the brand itself. This distinct bundle of benefits is determined by the brand owner and communicated to its external target groups through **brand touch points**. In contrast, the actual brand perceptions are captured by the **external perspective**. Ideally, the perceived bundle of benefits matches the internally defined bundle of benefits. In order to be of behavioural relevance in an external target group, the perceived bundle of benefits must satisfy some of their important needs. The perceived degree of differentiation between a brand and the competitors' brands is another component of the external perspective (see Fig. 2.1).

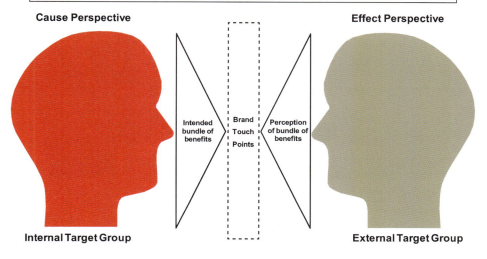

Fig. 2.1 The structure of identity-based brand management

The identity-based definition of brands described above can be clearly differentiated from other approaches which also adopt an internal perspective. For example, Kapferer (1992) does not provide a clear definition of the brand concept; Aaker (1996) defines the brand merely as a symbol (cf. Welling 2006); and for Esch (2003) a brand is a purely subjective image in the consumers' minds, which leads him to use the terms "brand" and "brand image" synonymously and to neglect the management perspective.

2.3   The Fundamental Concept of Identity-Based Brand Management

Our concept of identity-based brand management is in line with Meffert and Burmann (1996) and supplements the "classic" outside-in perspective by an inside-out perspective: The self-perception of the brand (e.g. accessible resources, competences) is determined by the internal target groups of the institution which owns the trademark. This self-perception represents the **brand identity**, and comprises all spatiotemporally homogeneous characteristics which, from the viewpoint of the **internal target groups**, determine the character of that brand.

While the brand identity is designed by the company itself, the external, i.e. public, image among various external target groups develops only over time. Hence the resulting brand image is an indirect reaction to internal brand management efforts (cf. Meffert and

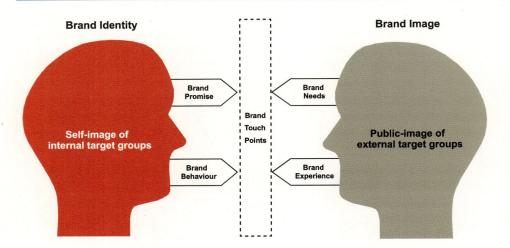

Fig. 2.2 The fundamental concept of identity-based brand management

Burmann 1996). Hence, the **brand image** is a condensed concept which is firmly rooted in the minds of the relevant **external target groups** (cf. Burmann et al. 2003). The relationship between brand identity and brand image is illustrated in Fig. 2.2.

The first step towards establishing a strong brand is to formulate the **brand promise** (Burmann et al. 2007). This comprises all benefits which are relevant for the purchase decision and are offered to the external target groups. To arrive at the brand promise the constituents of the usually more broadly formulated **brand identity** are condensed into a few concise and easily understood statements. Moreover, the brand promise should ensure brand differentiation as well as address the most significant brand-related needs of the target group. These **brand needs** primarily depend on the perceptions of the target group and what its members expect the ideal brand to be. Furthermore, they depend upon experiences with the brand and competing brands in the past.

Brand behaviour is determined by the fundamental types of products and services offered by a brand, by the behaviour of all its employees (e.g. customer service staff) and by all other points of contact between the consumer and the brand (e.g. advertising). Brand behaviour is directly correlated with the consumers' actual **brand experience**, i.e. their interactions with the brand at various **brand touch points**. These experiences are then reflected in the **brand image**.

To fulfil the needs and expectations of the external target groups at all brand touch points (brand experience), the actual brand behaviour must match the communicated brand promise (i.e. it must convey a high degree of brand authenticity). Without this match, the brand image will deteriorate, negative word of mouth will spread and customers are likely to shift to competing brands.

2.4 Comparison of Brand Management Approaches

Keller's approach to brand management is among the most well-known (1993, 2013). It focuses on external target groups (**outside-in perspective**) and constructs **customer-based brand equity** (CBBE) as the core of its theory. Thus Keller defines CBBE "as the differential effect that brand knowledge has on consumer response to the marketing of that brand" (Keller 2013, p. 69). With this definition, a brand has positive CBBE if consumers react more favourably to a product when the brand is identified compared to when it is not. These favourable reactions result from the consumers' knowledge about the brand. Therefore, **brand knowledge** is key to creating brand equity. Keller (2013) distinguishes two dimensions of brand knowledge: whereas "**brand awareness** is related to the strength of the brand node or trace in memory", **brand image** is the "consumers' perception about a brand, as reflected by the brand associations held in consumer memory" (Keller 2013, p. 72).

The first dimension of brand knowledge (**brand awareness**) consists of **brand recognition** (consumers' ability to confirm prior exposure to the brand when cued with the brand) and **brand recall** (consumers' ability to retrieve the brand from memory when given a cue such as the product category) (cf. Keller 2013). With a sufficient level of brand awareness, brand managers can start to strengthen the **brand image**. A brand enjoys a strong image when associations with it are strong, favourable and unique. These associations (brand image) can be further distinguished into product and non-product-related brand attributes (i.e. features that characterise a product or service) and brand benefits (i.e. meanings that consumers attach to product or service attributes). Keller (2013) differentiates **brand benefits** as functional, symbolic and experiential. Figure 2.3 depicts the components of brand knowledge (cf. Keller 2013).

As Fig. 2.3 shows, Keller's (2013) brand management approach only considers the external perspective (brand knowledge) and neglects the internal perspective. However, the external perspective is insufficient, because employees are responsible for fulfilling the brand promise through their brand-related behaviour. Consideration of the internal perspective thus is necessary for brand management. Several brand management methods adopt this internal perspective, so the following section explores two well-established approaches, i.e. the one introduced by Aaker (1996, 2010) and Kapferer (1992, 2012).

Brand identity is central to **Aaker's** brand management approach (1996, 2010): brand identity is defined as "a unique set of brand associations that the brand strategist aspires to create or maintain. These associations represent what the brand stands for and they imply a promise to customers from the members of its organisation" (Aaker 1996, p. 68). This concept of brand identity consists of four dimensions: (1) the "brand-as-product" (product scope, product attributes, quality/value, uses, users, country of origin), (2) the "brand-as-organisation" (organisational attributes such as innovation or trustworthiness, local vs. global), (3) the "brand-as-person" (brand personalities such as

Internal perspective   **External perspective**

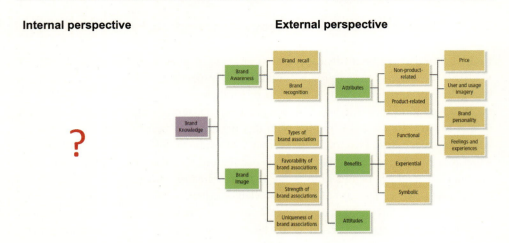

Fig. 2.3   A Summary of brand knowledge by Keller (2013, p. 548)

tolerant or rugged, brand–customer relationships), and (4) the "brand-as-symbol" (visual imagery/metaphors, brand heritage) (cf. Aaker 1996). A brand should consider all these perspectives and use the ones which are most helpful in communicating what the brand should stand for in the consumer's mind. According to Aaker (1996), brand identity should help establish a relationship between the brand and external target groups by generating a value proposition, or "a statement of the functional, emotional and self-expressive benefits delivered by the brand that provide value to the customer" (Aaker 1996, p. 95). Figure 2.4 depicts the brand management approach by Aaker (1996, 2010).

As Fig. 2.4 reveals, this approach focuses on brand identity as an internal statement (i.e. what the brand stands for). A detailed conceptualisation of the external perception of the transmitted brand identity (i.e. brand image) is missing. Furthermore, the interaction between internal and external target groups is neglected.

In contrast, the identity-based brand management approach proposed in this textbook regards brand image as the external perception of the transmitted brand identity. It considers the interaction between internal and external target groups by incorporating an inside-out perspective (brand promise, brand behaviour) as well as an outside-in perspective (customer needs, customer experiences).

Kapferer's (1992, 2012) approach focuses on brand identity and brand image: brand identity represents the sender's side and specifies the meaning of the brand, its aim and self-image (cf. Kapferer 2012). In contrast, brand image emanates from the receiver's side and refers to how certain external target groups perceive a brand. Therefore, Kapferer (2012) concludes that brand identity precedes brand image. Hence "before projecting an image to the public, we must know exactly what we want to project" (Kapferer 2012, p. 151). The brand identity is transmitted by various messages in the form of the

**Internal perspective
(Sender)**

**External perspective
(Receiver)**

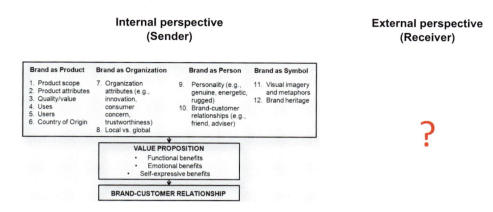

Fig. 2.4 A summary of the brand management approach by Aaker (1996, 2010)

brand name, visual symbols, products, advertisements, sponsoring and/or patronage. The brand image results from decoding these messages.

Furthermore, Kapferer (2012) defines six facets of brand identity in a so-called brand identity prism:

1. Physical specificity and quality of the brand ("physique").
2. "Personality", i.e. how the brand "speaks" about its products or services, showing what kind of person the brand would be as a human (cf. Kapferer 2012).
3. "Culture", which Kapferer considers the most important facet of brand identity because it spells out the ideology and vision of the brand.
4. A brand is also a "relationship" because it is often the crux of transactions and exchanges between people (cf. Kapferer 2012).
5. As customer "reflections", most brands build an image of their buyers or users, such as when a particular brand is "for young people" (cf. Kapferer 2012).
6. Brands also contribute towards the self-image of consumers. For instance, for some owners of a Porsche, purchasing a Porsche proves that they can afford to buy such a car (cf. Kapferer 2012).

Fig. 2.5 summarises the brand management approach by Kapferer (2012).

In line with the identity-based brand management approach presented in this textbook, Kapferer (2012) also considers internal and external target groups. However, Kapferer's approach predominantly focuses on the inside-out perspective: the brand, as a sender, transmits the brand identity through messages to the receiver; the receiver then decodes these messages, which results in the formation of a brand image. Thus, the interaction between internal and external target groups is mostly neglected (i.e. a synthesis of the inside-out and outside-in perspectives is missing). In addressing these interactions, the proposed identity-based brand management approach incorporates the

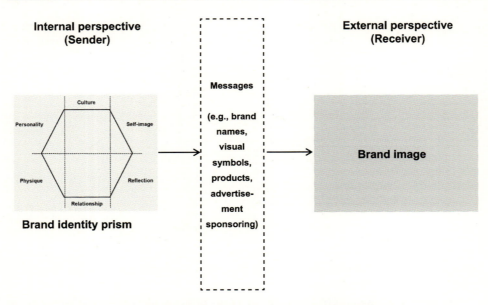

Fig. 2.5 A summary of the brand management approach by Kapferer (2012, p. 152, 158)

inside-out perspective (brand promise, brand behaviour) as well as the outside-in perspective (customer needs, customer experiences).

Hence the proposed identity-based brand management approach is the first to apply a modern understanding of brands, considering both the internal perspective (brand identity) and the external perspective (brand image), as well as the interaction between the internal and external target groups of a brand.

2.5   The Current Status of Identity Research

The concept of identity is used in numerous scientific fields. Before its specific meaning within the context of identity-based brand management will be examined in detail, first a general understanding of the origin and significance of the concept is to be established in the following.

Etymologically speaking, the concept of "identity" is derived from the Latin word "idem", meaning "the same". In socio-scientific research, this concept is used in very different ways depending on the purpose of the research and the contemplated subject matter—there is no generally accepted definition of the term (cf. Frey and Haußer 1987; Achterholt 1988; Conzen 1990; Gugutzer 2002). For instance, in sociology "identity" is often used to identify a bundle of typical roles of an individual. In psychology, the concept of identity stands for the self-concept of people (cf. Rosenberg 1979; Hogg et al. 2000), whilst moral theologians and philosophers define identity as a set of personal values and ethical principles that have been relatively stable over time. And finally, psychiatry uses identity for the integrity and efficiency of all organisational achievements of the nervous sy-stem (cf. Conzen 1990).

In colloquial language, the concepts of "identity" and "personality" are often used synonymously. However, identity is a more comprehensive construct. In psycho-analysis, the identity represents the totality of the personality traits that amalgamate into more than just the sum of their parts. Irrespective of the change and development of individual personality traits, they enable us to identify someone as "the same" and to recognise him or her as a being who remains the same over time (cf. Conzen 1990). Many fundamental insights of socio-scientific research regarding identity can be traced back to John Locke (cf. Thiel 2001). Subsequently, two approaches have emerged that have attracted particular attention: the **psychoanalytic approaches** according to Erikson (1950) and Marcia (1980), and the more **sociological and interactionist approaches** according to Mead (1934), Goffmann (1959) and Krappmann (1971). The identity of a brand is ultimately also based on the insights of socio-scientific identity research. Therefore, in the following, some key results of the social sciences will be introduced, and on this basis, the definition of brand identity will be derived.

2.5.1   Socio-Scientific Approaches to Identity Research

2.5.1.1   The Origin of Identity Research

John Locke (1632–1704) was the first to make a distinction between the "identity as man" and the "identity as a person". The "identity as man" refers solely to the existence of the physical body and must therefore be seen as a given. Only with the decay of his body would a dead man's identity cease to exist. The "identity as a person", however, is constituted by the existence of a thinking consciousness (cf. Welling 2003). According to Locke, the latter concept of identity requires a **self-referential consciousness** in order to determine the identity of one's own person by connecting past and present through reflection. Therefore, it is a subjective structure of identity, frequently also referred to as the so-called "self-identity" or "personal identity", which only develops in man through a process of self-reflective thinking. This means that people form their identity by processing their knowledge and their experiences of themselves in both the past and the present. This so-called **self-concept** unites the identity subject and object in a person (cf. Frey and Haußer 1987). With his theory John Locke was the founder of identity research. Even today, parts of his understanding can be found in modern science.

2.5.1.2   Psychoanalytic Approaches to Identity Research

The works by Erik Erikson constitute a significant contribution to identity research. They are based largely on Freudian psychoanalysis (cf. Abels 2009). In his model, the formation of a person's identity constitutes an **individual psychological development**

process. In his works Erikson proceeds from three fundamental assumptions (cf. Becker 2012; Lührmann 2006):

– Identity is the result of a psychosocial development process.
– From the interaction between psychological and social mechanisms arise crises, the management of which constitutes the foundation of identity development.
– The solutions to these crises are retained by the individual throughout their entire life's journey and indeed shape their entire life.

Therefore, Erikson defines identity as the perception of a person to be autonomous and holistic, in spite of all their experiences and the conflicts associated with them. Thus, the identity has its origin primarily in the crises of early stages of life. It is based on a person's capability of **internal, subjective synthesis** (cf. Lührmann 2006). As a result of this, **continuity** and **consistency** are two constitutive characteristics of identity according to Erikson.

The identity development process according to Erikson is called into question by newer research approaches, as in his understanding identity formation is a one-time process that is concluded at some stage. Against the background of modern society with its constant changes, the conclusiveness of the development nowadays lacks a foundation (cf. Keupp 1989). As a reaction to this change in the environment, the "**open identity process**" was developed within the context of psychoanalytic identity research, proposed in particular by the works of Marcia (1980). In contrast to the finite development process according to Erikson, the open identity process sees the development of an individual identity as a **lifelong development task**. Within the course of this open development, temporary identities are formed that are stable in the short term but have be stabilised and adjusted over the course of one's life due to the regular occurrence of crises. As a consequence, the consistency loses somewhat in importance compared to Erikson's understanding (cf. Keupp et al. 1999).

A fundamental criticism which applies to all approaches to identity formation from a psychoanalytic perspective concerns the fact that they consider identity merely from the perspective of the individual. Even though the identity is formed at the intersection between the individual and society, in the psychoanalytic understanding it is just the subjective perception of the person concerned (cf. Lührmann 2006).

2.5.1.3 Interactionist Approaches to Identity Research

In contrast, **communication and interaction processes** play a more important role during the formation of an identity within the context of interactionist approaches. Here the identity is formed more from the outside to the inside (cf. Keupp et al. 1999).

Following Mead (1973), a distinction has to be made between a person's "I" and "me". The "I" describes the individual characteristics of a person and thus is largely congruent with the psychoanalytic understanding of identity formation. However, in contrast to these approaches Mead assumes that the "I" cannot recognise itself; to do so, the "me" is required. This describes the image a person has of themselves through their interaction with others (cf. Joas 2000). This image is not always consistent. Instead, it consists of a multitude of different attributions by the various people a person interacts with (cf. Mead 1973). In most cases, the social perception and the self-perception of the same person are not congruent. The individual characteristics that are reflected in the "I" differ from the attributed roles that are ascribed to the "me". An identity is formed through the progressive adjustment of the self-perception and the social perception (cf. Keupp et al. 1999).

2.5.1.4   The Concept of Patchwork Identities

Due to the significant increase in the dynamics, complexity and insecurity in modern everyday life existing identity concepts have undergone further development. In this context the concept of "**patchwork identities**" according to Keupp et al. (1999) deserves particular mention.

In this approach, "patchwork" refers to both time and content. From a **temporal perspective**, the formation of an identity is not linear with a clear objective, as proposed by Erikson. Since the individual is continuously making new experiences, of the personal identity concept is constantly put into question. Therefore, the formation of an identity is an ongoing process, during which the individual has to combine new experiences with the existing identity concept. In this understanding, **continuity** becomes a temporal link with the goal of achieving a coherent overall concept that embraces the past, the present and the anticipated future.

The **content perspective**, on the other hand, refers to the necessity to do justice to different, constantly changing roles that an individual has to assume in society, e.g., the different roles in a person's professional life, within their family or circle of friends (cf. Becker 2012). According to these different roles, **partial identities** are formed which are matched to the respective role expectations (cf. Luhmann 1994). In the light of this, the integration of all partial identities into one single global identity is not always feasible. Nor may the partial identities be allowed to be completely separate, as otherwise the contradictions between them would result in the loss of authenticity of the individual (cf. Lührmann 2006).

Thus, the key achievement of identity formation consists of the coherent connection of the partial identities into a structure which Keupp et al. refer to as a **meta-identity**. At this higher level, the contradictions between the individual partial identities must be kept to a minimum in order to achieve **consistency** across all parts. To this end, we must identify where the partial identities overlap because this will constitute the **core of the identity** (cf. Keupp et al. 1999).

2.5.2   Socio-Scientific Identity Research and Brand Identity

According to the current understanding of socio-scientific identity research, two perspectives can be differentiated in the determination of identity. An identity is always formed by the interaction between the internal perspective, or **self-perception**, and the external perspective, or **social perception**. The social perception is characterised by role expectations—the expectations of others with regard to how a person should act within a certain role (e.g. as a colleague). These are referred to as an **image**. From the internal perspective, these role expectations are reflected in role perceptions, which are in turn reflected in partial identities. Thus, role perceptions are a part of the **identity**.

Furthermore, according to Keupp et al. (1999), we must distinguish **between individuals and groups of people** with respect to the reference object of the identity. Within the context of identity attribution, brands are to be understood as groups composed of the executives and the employees of the brand company. Table 2.2 summarises the perspectives and reference objects with regard to identity determination. The distinction between individuals and groups as reference objects of the attribution of identity is examined in detail in the following sections.

2.5.2.1 Constitutive Characteristics of Brand Identity

The identity of a person describes the existence of an image the individual has of themselves (cf. Conzen 1990). People use this self-image both to distance themselves from other people and as a guideline for their own behaviour. Within this context, we can also refer to an individual concept of one's own self (cf. Müller 1987).

This understanding focuses on the reciprocity of the internal and the external perspective. The external perspective manifests itself in the image (cf. Table 2.2), i.e. the individual is attributed an image by other persons in terms of a bundle of characteristics (cf. Frey and Haußer 1987). The personal identity is continuously compared with the perception by third parties, i.e. the image, and is adjusted if any discrepancies occur (cf. Weidenfeld 1983). Therefore, an identity can only be formed if at least two people establish a relationship (cf. Haußer 1995). The continuous interaction between the personal identity and the externally attributed image is therefore a constitutive characteristic of the identity and is used to develop it further (in terms of an open identity process). Irrespective of the definition of identity, four fundamental constitutive characteristics of the concept of identity can be derived from socio-scientific identity research (see Table 2.3):

Table 2.2 Perspectives and reference objects of identity determination

	Perspective of the verification of identity	
Reference object of the attribution of identity	Internal perspective (self-perception)	External perspective (social perception)
Individuals	Identity of a person	Image of a person
Group of people	group identity (identity of the group as perceived by its own members)	Group image (subjective image of a group attributed by non-members of the group)
Brands (executives and employees of a brand company)	Internal self-perception of the brand = brand identity	External public image of the brand = brand image

Source Based on Haußer (1995)

Table 2.3 Constitutive characteristics of the concept of identity

Constitutive characteristics	Individuals	Brands
Reciprocity	An identity is formed by establishing a relationship between a person and other people	The brand identity is formed by establishing a relationship with consumers and other reference groups
Continuity	Retention of essential characteristics over time for identifying the person. These characteristics describe the type and nature of the person. Accidental characteristics can change over time	Retention of the essential brand characteristics over time
Consistency	Consistent combination of personality traits (referring to a particular point in time)	Avoidance of contradictions in the brand appearance and in the behaviour of executives and employees of the brand. Ongoing adjustment of the essential and accidental characteristics
Individuality	Biologically and sociologically determined uniqueness of the individual	Uniqueness of fundamental identity characteristics compared to competing service offerings

Source Based on Meffert and Burmann (1996)

Reciprocity: An identity can only be formed by reciprocal interaction between people. This reciprocity of the identity is also referred to as the "paradigm of identity research" (cf. Frey and Haußer 1987). The situation is similar with respect to brands: the identity of a brand is formed and changes through the relationship with its consumers (and other reference groups) and the resulting interactions. From the perspective of brand management, long-lasting relationships between the brand and its consumers are particularly relevant. Only if the brand manages to establish reciprocal relationships which are stable over time with a multitude of individual consumers, can the brand identity develop and remain stable. Consequently, the resulting **brand–customer relationship** is a part of the identity.

Continuity characterises the retention of fundamental characteristics of a person or a group over a period of several years. This set of **essential characteristics** describes the essence of the identity object. If these essential characteristics are lost, the identity ceases to exist. In contrast to the essential characteristics, **accidental characteristics** of an identity object can change without the person or group losing their identity (cf. Böhm 1989). Therefore, continuity of the accidental characteristics is not required to establish a clear identity. However, accidental characteristics also exert an influence on the identity, as the degree to which the accidental characteristics fit with the essential ones shapes the clarity of the identity and, therefore, its relevance to behaviour. The essential identity characteristics of a person include, for example, the sex, date and place of birth, as well as certain physical features. A person can be identified as the same person during their entire life by means of their essential characteristics. In contrast, their professional position, the economic situation and the style of clothing are part of the accidental characteristics of a person, which can change over time without the individual losing their identity as a result.

In contrast to continuity, **consistency** does not refer to a period of time but to a point in time. It implies the avoidance of contradictions (cf. Wiedmann 1994). Only an internally and externally largely consistent combination of characteristics results in a clear identity. In other words, only an integrated, internal and external alignment of all characteristics and behaviours of a brand and its employees (external role expectations and internal role perceptions) can lead to a clear brand identity.

Individuality describes the uniqueness of an identity object. This uniqueness may be due to a single individual characteristic or to the individual combination of characteristics that are also present elsewhere. With regard to human beings the requirement of individuality or uniqueness is automatically fulfilled for biological reasons. In contrast, the identity of many modern brands is weak because they lack individuality in the perception of both the consumers and their own employees. In these cases we cannot really speak of brands, but rather of "labels" in terms of consistently branded products.

Within the context of developing a personal identity, the role expectations of the environment are of great importance. As individuals can rarely meet all the role expectations of both society and their personal environment, which will lead to role conflicts, they require a strong personal identity (self-identity), i.e. **a confident sense of themselves, so as not to be demoralised by these conflicts** (cf. Bonus 1994). The brand identity has the same function for the employees of a brand in the light of diverse and conflicting requirements of the brand from the market and social environment. Personal identity is characterised by a temporal consistency. A personality or identity change always takes place very slowly. The roots of the personal identity are anchored in the life history of the person (cf. Krappmann 1988), the roots of the identity of a brand in its origin.

A strong personal identity is a prerequisite for the reliability of a person. You can only trust people who have an identity. At this point the correlation between the construct of identity and the construct of trust becomes apparent: **trust requires identity** (cf. Luhmann 1973). Section 2.8 will explore this correlation in more detail. Identity generates clear expectations and is prepared to honour them. Competence as a part of the identity ensures the **capability**, whilst the other components of identity ensure the **motivation** to meet the expectations. Only a clearly recognisable brand identity results in the consumers trusting the capability and motivation of the brand.

In this context, trust does not only have a socio-scientific meaning; in fact, for providers and consumers, a tangible economic meaning also arises (cf. Ripperger 2003). From **a business perspective,** the existence of trust results in decreased transaction costs for the provider. Furthermore, the consumers' trust constitutes a **very important competitive advantage**, which is reflected in the relevant economic performance indicators of the provider (cf. Kenning 2003). With growing trust, the consumers perceive less risk of being disappointed by the provider and the offered services. This enables the consumers to save costs which would otherwise accrue due to the need to reduce their subjectively perceived risk (cf. Plötner 1995). This includes, for instance, costs for taking out insurance policies, information costs related to the search for alternatives and costs for setting up financial reserves to cover potential risks.

2.5.2.2   Groups as the Object of the Attribution of Identity

Groups of people constitute the second category of identity reference objects. The group identity can be used to describe the identity of social systems (e.g. cultures, associations, cities, regions and companies). Here, the **self-reflection of the group members** with respect to their existence as a group is constitutive. The group identity encompasses those characteristics of a group that remain constant, even if individual group members leave the group (cf. Werthmöller 1994). The group identity expresses itself in common values, convictions, characteristics and behaviours, which arise from shared experiences and insights. It distinguishes the group from other groups (cf. Schein 1985). A strong group identity becomes a part of the personal identity of its members, acting as a frame that holds the group together.

Companies and brands, as groups of people, also exhibit such a form of group identity. Hans Domizlaff stated as early as in the 1930s that every brand has its own "face" (cf. Domizlaff 1994), thus suggesting an analogy with the human identity, which arises from different essential characteristics that are constant over time, and is unique to every person. According to Domizlaff, the same should apply to brands.

Since within the socio-scientific understanding, identity is fundamentally regarded as the result of human interaction and reflection, the socio-scientific concept of identity cannot be transferred to "brands" if they are seen only as trademark rights or bundles of symbols (cf. Welling 2003). Therefore, the identity of a brand refers to the identity of the group of people who are behind the brand. Consequently, the collective of people carrying the brand has a **self-reflective identity, which distinguishes it from other collectives** of people (e.g. competitors) and from other individuals (e.g. customers). In this context, the collective of people is not necessarily congruent with the legal affiliation to a company. For instance, the brand identity can also be shared by the employees of an economically autonomous, exclusive retailer (cf. Maloney 2007). In the light of this, the **brand identity** can be defined as:

> "... those characteristics of a brand which sustainably define the character of the brand from the perspective of internal target groups." (Burmann et al. 2003, p. 16)

With respect to the perspective (cf. Table 2.2), a distinction can be made between the brand identity as the **self-perception** from the perspective of the internal target groups (e.g. owner, executives, employees) and the brand image as the **public image** of the brand from the perspective of the external target groups (e.g. customers, suppliers, consumer associations, conservation groups, authorities and residents). Therefore, the **brand identity is constituted** with regard to two aspects:

– A collective, self-referential process of becoming aware of one's own existence within a group and affiliation to this group among all people working for a brand. These are the internal target groups of brand management.
– The interaction with people and groups of people external to the brand and their perception of both the brand and the collective of people behind the brand.

Just as the personal identity and the identity of groups consist of various components, so the brand identity also arises from the interrelation of different components. However, just like the identity of a person, the brand identity is also perceived as a homogeneous entity. The manifestation and combination of the individual identity components of a brand must therefore produce a coherent "gestalt" that is consistent in itself and that ultimately differentiates itself from other service offerings in the relevant market (cf. Meffert and Burmann 1996). Identity components that do not match, complicate or prevent such a differentiation.

2.5.3 Economic Approaches of Identity Research

Socio-scientific identity research does not provide any evidence regarding the economic relevance of the construct of identity. However, the perspective of the **New Institutional Economics** (e.g. Erlei et al. 2007) helps substantiate the economic significance of identity (cf. Dörtelmann 1997) by relinquishing the restricted image of man as "homo oeconomicus", as suggested, in particular, by the work of Nobel Prize winner Douglass C. North. The introduction of **mental models** as the internal, subjective representation of the outside world and so-called path-dependent processes, i.e. the consideration of coincidences and states of imbalance (cf. North 1992), meant that even complex problems of economics could be brought closer to a solution (cf. Denzau and North 1994; Bonus 1995).

The New Institutional Economics defines an **institution** as "a system of values and standards that, in the event of a violation, has penalties attached to it" (cf. Bonus 1995). Institutions create **general conditions for human action**. Institutions are mental models of the individual (cf. Denzau and North 1994). Due to their temporal consistency, people use them for guidance. We distinguish between fundamental and secondary institutions (cf. Dietl 1993).

Fundamental institutions are, for instance, rooted in the history of a nation and change only very slowly. They cannot be changed by man directly. In contrast, secondary institutions can be consciously shaped. Secondary institutions are only "effective" if they are embedded in the system of values and standards of the funda-mental institutions. For instance, the population's sense of justice can be interpreted as a fundamental institution, whilst the specific laws and the administration of justice can be understood as a secondary institution. Laws and administrations of justice can only fulfil their purpose if they are in harmony with the population's sense of justice (cf. Bonus 1995).

An identity can also be interpreted as a system of values and standards with a high level of temporal consistency, serving as a framework for the behaviour of people. Like the institution, the identity is a subjective representation. In the light of this, the **group identity of all employees of a brand** can be understood **as a secondary institution**. A brand identity can only develop and exert influence on the behaviour of employees and consumers if it is embedded in the framework of values and standards of the surrounding society. This means that the regional or national culture in which the company or the brand organisation is established is a fundamental institution for the brand identity as defined by the New Institutional Economics.

Therefore, the identity concept is of major significance with respect to explaining and influencing economic circumstances. The brand identity changes only slowly; it can generally not be controlled in the short term and often it cannot be controlled directly in terms of a deterministic relationship. Furthermore, a clear brand identity can be established only if it has been embedded coherently in the identity of the company as a whole and is in harmony with it.

In addition to the New Institutional Economics, other fields of **business economics** have also addressed the construct of identity, in particular within the context of studies on corporate culture, corporate philosophy and corporate identity. The analysis of the respective publications shows that many authors largely equate the concept of culture with that of identity (cf. e.g. Deal and Kennedy 1982; Schein 1985; Heinen 1987; Bonus 1994). Accordingly, a strong corporate culture is primarily characterised by a strong group identity of all members of the company. Vice versa, the identity of a company can be "cultivated" and made visible through appropriate rituals and collectively practised values and standards (cf. Deal and Kennedy 1982; Schein 1985; Bonus 1994).

But even though the concepts of culture and identity are close in terms of their content, they cannot be equated. The majority of organisational and market researchers regards **corporate culture as a contextual factor** of the identity (cf. Hatch and Schulz 1997; Berggold 2000; Meffert 1994). Corporate culture encompasses the entirety of all common basic assumptions, values and standards which are shared by the members of a company and communicated to new members. It shapes the thinking, the perceptions, decisions and behaviours of the members of the company (cf. Schein 1992). Basic assumptions are mostly self-evident, often subconsciously held, long-term views of the environment, reality, the human being, actions and relationships. In corporate culture, values express a view of what is desirable in the long term. Standards describe a specific code of conduct which is accepted by all members of the company and linked to penalties in the event of a violation. Corporate cultures always have their origin in the past of the company, as they have formed over a long period of time. Over time, culture becomes increasingly independent and turns into an emergent phenomenon of group behaviour, which eludes the specific control by the management. Consequently, in contrast to brand identity, corporate culture does not constitute a management tool. The influence of corporate culture as a contextual factor of the brand identity refers primarily to the brand origin. In addition, the standards of the corporate culture exert an influence on the implementation of the brand identity in employee behaviour (cf. Sect. 4.1).

Corporate culture research provides preliminary answers to the question from which components the brand identity arises. According to their results, brand identity may be attributable to "objects that can be observed and experienced" by consumers and employees, such as characteristics of the production and the products, particular features of the language and communication used, specific behaviours of the employees and symbols that are typical of the brand (cf. Schein 1985).

Research on corporate identity shows that the corporate philosophy as the core of the corporate identi-ty can be distinguished from the company's behaviour, communication and formal appearance (cf. Birkigt et al. 1998; Meffert 1994). In addition, we can differentiate between the verbalised self-perception of the corporate identity (vision, corporate philosophy), the implemented self-perception (communication, appearance, behaviour) and the public image of the corporate identity (cf. Achterholt 1988).

2.6   Conceptual Design of Brand Identity

2.6.1   Brand Identity as an Internal Management Concept

A number of key requirements of the identity of a person and therefore, also of the identity of a brand, are known from the findings of socio-scientific identity research; they were introduced in Sect. 2.5. These requirements regarding the formation of an identity constitute the basis on which a strong identity can be distinguished from a weak one. According to Keupp et al. (1999), the key achievement of the formation of an identity is to consolidate all partial identities of a person into one meta-identity and, in doing so, to create a concise core of the identity as a common interface. Thus, the core of a strong identity manifests itself around a few specific characteristics of a person. In contrast, a weak identity is characterised by a lack of this reduction and the presence of numerous only supposedly specific characteristics. In addition, all interactionist approaches of identity research (cf. Sect. 2.5.1.3) refer to the fact that the formation of an identity is an ongoing process, which has to be continuously revised and adapted. Every adjustment of one's own identity entails certain risks. People who shy away from this risk and try to maintain their status quo, consequently prevent the adjustment of their own identity, even if this becomes necessary as a result of a crisis or new interactions. A strong identity, however, is characterised by the necessary readiness to assume these risks, combined with a sense of innovation and experimentation with respect to the personal development.

Further characteristics of strong or weak identities arise from the interaction of the self-perception and the social perception. A person can only preserve the individuality of their own identity if they do not fully adjust their self-perception to the social perception. As social perceptions are dependent on the associated role expectations, the complete adoption of all of these external values and visions would prevent the formation of a consistent core identity. One characteristic of a strong identity is therefore the shaping of one's own values. The same applies to the establishment of one's own vision of the future, as a strong focus on the changing values of the environment would inevitably result in inconsistencies. A high degree of self-confidence constitutes another characteristic of a strong identity since it prevents the compliant adoption of external influences. The last characteristic of a strong identity is closely linked to self-confidence. John Locke already emphasised the importance of a self-referential consciousness which connects experiences from the past with the present (cf. Frey and Hauser 1987). This concept is reflected in modern identity research within the context of consistency (cf. Keupp et al. 1999). Therefore, the consciousness of past achievements and accomplishments motivates someone with a strong identity to further develop it. In contrast, a weak identity is characterised by a lack of this consciousness.

The pairs of characteristics in Table 2.4 indicate that in people strong identities are formed through the clear accentuation of their specific features in conjunction with a consciousness of their skills and their own past. The same applies to brands, or rather to the identity of the group of people behind the brand.

Table 2.4 Characteristics of weak and strong identities in people and brands

Characteristics of a		Transfer to brand identities
Weak human identity	**Strong** human identity	
Many supposedly "specific" identity characteristics	Only a few distinguished identity characteristics	Brand promise and brand offer
Risk aversion, anxious maintenance of the status quo	Role conflicts are used actively to advance one's own identity into new areas (innovative spirit)	Personality
Adoption of values from other (external) identities	Shaping of one's own values	Values
Strong focus on the environment	Development of a clear vision	Vision
Low level of self-confidence	High level of self-confidence	Competences
Lack of consciousness of one's own achievements (capability)	Achievements and accomplishments of the past provide motivation for new projects	Origin

2.6.2   Dimensions of Brand Identity

Thus, on the basis of socio-scientific and psychological identity research, we can identify **six constitutive components** which allow a comprehensive description of the brand identity (cf. Fig. 2.6). The brand origin constitutes the basis of the brand identity. Without being rooted in its own origin, the brand lacks a reference point for self-reflection. The brand competences, which are based on the resources and organisational skills of a company, substantiate the brand's specific competitive advantage/s and safeguard it/them. At the same time, the clear formulation of the brand competences facilitates the necessary motivational effect for further identity negotiation, which is part of a strong identity. The type of the offered services determines how a brand becomes useful for the consumer. The design of the identity is managed in the long term alongside the competences and is motivated by the brand vision. The brand values purport what the brand and its representatives believe in. The brand personality defines the verbal and non-verbal communication style of the brand.

As Fig. 2.6 shows, the origin and the vision of a brand set the frame for the development of the remaining components. The importance of these two components, which point to the past and the future, has already become apparent in the theoretical analysis of the resource- and competence-based views in Sect. 1.2. In the light of identity

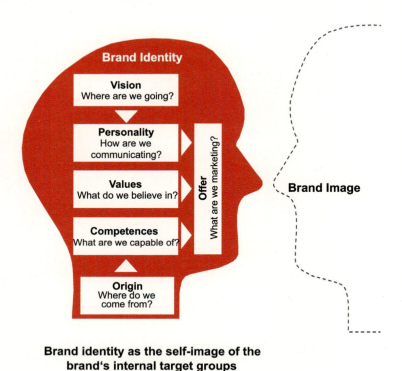

**Brand identity as the self-image of the
brand's internal target groups**

Fig. 2.6   Components of the brand identity as an internal management concept

research, these two components also constitute the basis for the ongoing development and adjustment of the brand identity.

2.6.2.1 Brand Origin

The origin of the brand forms the basis of the brand identity, answering the question: "Where do we come from?" The **brand origin** is of great relevance to brand management, as a brand is initially perceived and interpreted by the internal and external target groups within the context of its origin. "Knowing the roots of a person, place, or firm can help create interest and a bond. The same is true for a brand" (Aaker and Joachimsthaler 2000, p. 249). Thus, origin is a much-noticed phenomenon in psychoanalysis, New Institutional Economics and management theory according to the concept of **path-dependency**. "History matters" is the slogan that describes the process of past decisions shaping future decisions. As a result, the number of possible alternative paths of action is reduced over time, as people responsible become increasingly dependent on the decision paths of their origin (cf. Schreyögg et al. 2003; Burmann 2002).

The brand origin is closely connected with the history of a brand, but it must not be equated to or confused with the latter. While the brand origin singles out individual facets of the brand history and emphasises them in a particular manner, the brand history comprises all past events that are associated with this brand. Therefore, in contrast to the brand history, the brand origin is an identity component that can be shaped in the long term by brand management. In the best-case scenario it lends all further brand management activities a high degree of credibility and authenticity. Within this context, it can be regarded as a kind of repository of provided services or as the "accumulated performance history" (cf. Menninger and Robers 2006).

The brand origin is based on three different facets: the geographic origin, the company origin and the industry origin (cf. Becker 2012).

Studies in **country of origin research** examine the connection between the country of origin/manufacture of a product and the associated quality perception by the consumers (cf. Usunier 2006). The influence of the country of origin is closely connected to the competence structures which are attributed to a country or region (cf. Stolle 2013). For instance, Germany is traditionally attributed with a high level of competence with regard to engineering services. Consequently, the VW brand uses the German slogan "Das Auto." in its communication even at an international level, emphasising its German roots. A key problem of the country of origin research lies in the increasing globalisation of companies. In the course of international business operations, numerous companies separate the country of origin from the country of manufacture. In order to counteract this problem, in recent years extensions of the country of origin approach have emerged, such as the differentiation between the country of manufacture, the country of corporate ownership (the country in which the company has its legal headquarters), the country of design and the country of parts (the country in which the suppliers are located) (cf. Becker 2012). The attribution of a brand to a country can vary greatly between the different perspectives. To exemplify this, Fig. 2.7 shows the attribution of the "Swedish"

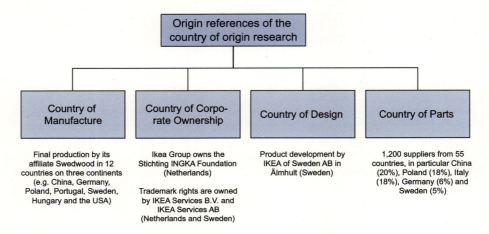

Fig. 2.7 References to the origin of the IKEA brand. (Source: Becker 2012, p. 52)

brand IKEA, which can only be defined as Swedish according to the country of design. In the light of this, the origin which has been actively designed and communicated by the brand as well as the brand's **origin** as **perceived** by the consumers gain in importance (cf. Thakor and Kohli 1996).

However, the identity-based brand origin does not refer to the geographic dimension of origin only. Based on the findings of **culture of brand origin research**, the cultural origin can also shape the identity of a brand significantly. As it is often very difficult for consumers to identify a specific country as a brand's country of origin due to the currently prevalent international set-up of company activities, they tend to fall back on "cultural cues" instead when identifying the origin of a brand. According to Lim and O'Cass, these "cultural cues" are significantly more available to consumers than information on the legally determined country of origin (cf. Lim and O'Cass 2001). For instance, the name of the vehicle brand Hyundai will already produce associations with an Asian origin, without the consumer knowing that it is a Korean brand. The beer brand Paulaner can be identified as a brand that has been shaped by the Bavarian culture, not just as a German beer. Both the geographic and cultural origins of a brand therefore encompass all influences which arise from the countries and regions of origin for the brand identity and which can strengthen them (cf. Charmasson 1988; Leclerc et al. 1994). However, all approaches introduced so far focus primarily on the perception of the origin by the consumer or external target groups. With respect to the understanding of identity-based brand management they therefore fall short.

Within the context of the identity-based brand management approach the **brand origin** describes that part of the brand identity which arises from the identification of the organisation managing the brand with an area (culture), an industry sector or an organisation (based on Becker 2012).

The **company origin** encompasses the attribution of a brand to an organisation or a company. In the case of a company with only one brand, this attribution is largely trivial. However, if a company manages several brands, these may be attributed to the corporate brand to varying degrees (cf. the discussion of brand architecture in Sect. 3.4). Consequently, brand management has significant creative leeway in the definition of the brand origin (cf. Becker 2012). In this context, further important determinants are the corporate culture, the company's founders and outstanding management leaders (cf. Burmann and Maloney 2004). In particular the company's founders and leaders can significantly shape the company's brand identity, as well as the identities of individual product brands. For instance, the founders of the Aldi Company, Theo and Karl Albrecht, have significantly shaped the corporate culture of the group, which is geared to frugality and efficiency. Similarly, Dr. Claus Hipp, the successor of the company's founder and its present CEO, vouches "with his name" for the organic cultivation of the ingredients and the product quality of the baby food brand Hipp. A company's origin can also be characterised by the product line of a brand. For example, Fig. 2.8 shows selected vehicle models of the automotive brands VW and Fiat. Individual classic vehicle models, which each have a distinct connection with the past of the brands, have in recent years been successfully relaunched with a modernised design.

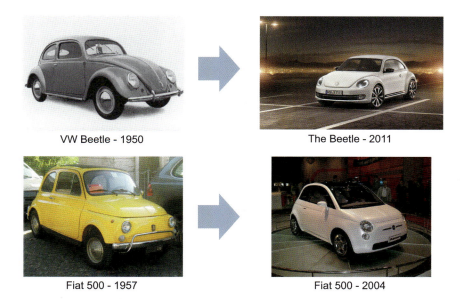

VW Beetle - 1950   The Beetle - 2011

Fiat 500 - 1957   Fiat 500 - 2004

Fig. 2.8 Model development of VW Beetle and Fiat 500. (Source: Volkswagen AG und Wikipeda)

Regarding the **industrial origin**, companies can often choose between various options (cf. Schäefer 2006). For instance, the Siemens Group is active in many industry sectors such as drive technology, automation, lighting, energy, building technologies, healthcare and communication networks. Which of these industry sectors is defined by the group as the origin is largely at the discretion of brand management (cf. Becker 2012). On the other hand, the perception of watches, handbags, sunglasses, perfumes and shoes of the Gucci brand is shaped by the company's origin in the clothing industry.

Brand management can change the perceived origin of a brand in the long term by emphasising individual facets of origin. Similarly, the brand origin can be expanded and enriched but also diluted through partnerships and mergers. Furthermore, outsourcing decisions or the relocation of important business units abroad can significantly affect the perception of the brand origin and, ultimately, the brand strength.

2.6.2.2 Brand Vision

The **brand vision** determines the brand's long-term development trend. A time scale of five to ten years should be set for this purpose. The brand vision should be an important source of motivation for the working and purchasing behaviour of all internal and external target groups. Ind (2003) speaks, in this context, of a so-called "ideology" that offers all employees a shared credo in which they believe and with which they can identify (cf. Ind 2003). The significance and purpose of the brand with respect to the realisation of the long-term business objectives should be presented by means of pictorial guidelines.

The concept of brand vision has to be differentiated from the concept of corporate philosophy which comprises the fundamental values of the company with its corporate assumptions and convictions (cf. Melewar and Karaosmanoglu 2005). The complexity of the corporate philosophy often is in conflict with the operationalisation of a brand identity. In contrast to the brand vision, **brand targets** are characterised by their more concrete nature as well as a more short-term focus.

The brand vision has a coordinating role over time and is intended to ensure that all the company's activities are in compliance with the brand targets. It should encompass both the market segments aimed for and the fundamental, differentiating factors in comparison to competitors. For that matter, the brand vision must express a viable, long-term notion in order to be able to activate internal motivational and identification forces (cf. Kapferer 1992). At the same time, a clearly formulated vision provides guidelines which help the employees of a brand to identify necessary competences that are essential to the fulfilment of the vision. However, if unrealistic ideas are included in the vision, it loses its motivational nature since these are not attainable by the employees, no matter how hard they work to achieve them. It is also problematic if senior management sets unrealistic targets or guidelines which contradict the brand vision or brand identity.

This problem of utopian ideas has, for example, been a problem on two occasions in the past for Mercedes-Benz AG. Edzard Reuter, appointed in 1987 as CEO of Mercedes-Benz AG, had a vision to transform the company from a purely vehicle manufacturing business into an integrated technology group. This led to numerous major acquisitions and majority stakes in companies such as AEG and the aviation and aerospace group Dornier. Within a few years, this deviation from the core of the brand identity resulted in considerable problems. In 1995, Reuter finally left the group. His successor, Jürgen Schrempp (CEO from 1995 to 2005), also pursued a new, utopian vision. Under his leadership, Mercedes-Benz was meant to develop into a global player in the automotive industry. To this end, Mercedes-Benz AG merged with the third largest American automotive manufacturer, Chrysler Corp, and acquired shares in numerous other automotive companies. However, the vision of becoming a "global player" discouraged the workforce, since it overextended the available resources and competences, and subsequently led to serious quality issues at Mercedes-Benz, as well as to the loss of its once superior position (cf. Tietz 2009).

2.6.2.3 Brand Competences

Besides the origin, brand identity is primarily based upon the competences of the institution managing the brand. They represent the specific, organisational abilities of a business for the market-driven identification, processing and combining of resources.

Competitiveness, i.e. dominance over competitors, is only possible if the brand provides at least equal, or rather superior, customer benefits. Persistently superior customer benefits are always based on the **core competences** of a brand, whereas the mere availability of competences is usually sufficient for simply sustaining one's market position (cf. Freiling 2001). From the perspective of identity-based brand management, the economic value of competences and core competences can be assessed by the **extent to which the customer is willing to pay for the customer benefits on offer**.

Based upon the findings of Blinda (2007), the necessary competences for brand management can be divided into three categories: refinement, market supply and meta competences (see Fig. 2.9).

Refinement competences encompass the brand information absorption competence and the strategic brand planning competence. Together they create a brand's potential for action with respect to organising the employees' motivation. The brand information absorption competence is of particular importance. It represents the ability to notice the relevant market information, for instance trends, and to respond adequately (cf. Stichnoth 2013). The task of strategic brand planning is to ensure a consistent focus of the value chain on fulfilling the brand promise. This also concerns the decisions on outsourcing and insourcing in all sections of the value chain. Furthermore, the future strategic development of the brand promise must be based on this competence (cf. Blinda 2007).

Market supply competences facilitate the design of goods and services. Based on the brand's evolution competence, the brand is adjusted to the changing environmental and competitive conditions over time. Here, the aim is to maintain a high differentiation potential of the brand vis-à-vis its competitors. The internal brand assertion competence includes all brand management measures that are geared towards the internal target groups. Within the context of identity-based brand management, this is also referred to as internal brand management (cf. Sect. 4.1). Finally, the operational brand implementation

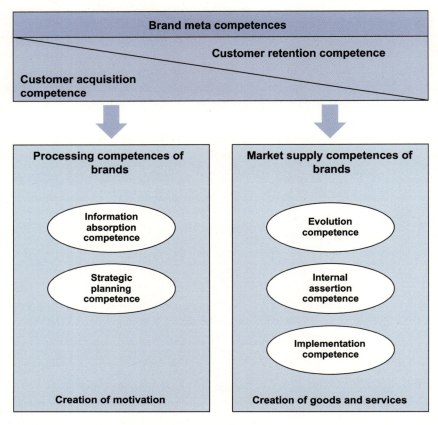

Fig. 2.9 Relevant competences according to the identity-based brand management approach. (Source: closely based on Blinda 2007, p. 322)

competence is used to safeguard the fit between brand identity, the range of products/services and brand communication (cf. Chap. 4).

In addition to refinement and market supply competences, two **meta competences** play a key role in identity-based brand management. With the customer acquisition competence and the customer retention competence, a company is able to acquire new customers and bind existing customers to the brand. When comparing these two meta competences, Blinda was able to prove that customer retention contributes more to success (cf. Blinda 2007). This substantiates the high degree of relevance and the intrinsic value of long-term brand-customer relations, which are the result of the consistent fulfillment of the brand promise vis-à-vis the consumers.

As all competences and core competences of a brand are based on a lead in knowledge, they are always temporary. Therefore, permanent investments in the renewal of competences and core competences are required in order to keep up a lead in knowledge and the associated competitive advantages of the brand. Similarly, continuous investments in the retention of human resources, which are responsible for the development of the competences and core competences of a brand, are required. Long-term successful brand management is therefore not possible without an identity-based development of all organisational structures and processes, of the human resources department, of leadership behaviour and incentive schemes. Identity-based brand management concerns, first and foremost, the management of employees and not the promotional decoration of facades!

2.6.2.4 Brand Values

Brand values represent the fundamental beliefs of the executives and employees behind the brand. They express important emotional components of the brand identity and take into account the expectations of the relevant target groups with respect to an ideal brand. Therefore, they express what the brand "believes in". Condensed in a few statements, brand values are, above all, intended to convey the non-functional benefits of the brand. In business practice we often find rather generic brand values which promise responsible dealings with employees and the environment or a high product quality. For instance, Robert Bosch GmbH, a large German industrial company producing, among many other things, household appliances and automotive parts, addresses responsibility, fairness and reliability in its values. The multinational company Henkel KG & Co. KGaA, active both in the consumer and the industrial sector, lists, inter alia, the value propositions "We put our customers at the centre of what we do", "We value, challenge and reward our people" and "We are committed to leadership in sustainability" on its website. General and hence interchangeable phrases such as these, however, do not contribute much to differentiating and strengthening a brand.

Additionally, brand values play an important part with respect to the authenticity of the brand (cf. Schallehn 2012). Therefore, they must actually be practised by all employees so they will become an integral part of the brand identity and genuinely charge the brand emotionally.

A suitable example of a brand with particularly distinctive brand values is "The Body Shop". The brand managers of "The Body Shop" have formulated five clear values for their brand and have strictly kept to them in recent years (cf. Fig. 2.10).

The positive public image that comes with the authentic representation of brand values is apparent from two very contrasting examples from the German drugstore market. In contrast to its former competitor, Schlecker, the drugstore chain dm consistently focuses on its brand values. Götz W. Werner, founder and member of the company's board of directors, summarises the basic claim as follows: "If there were no people, there would be no economy. Consequently, the economy exists for the people, not vice versa." Derived from this motto, dm focuses on the three key values of "live responsibly", "be humane" and "act in a sustainable manner". In contrast, Schlecker was repeatedly criticised in public for serious shortcomings in personnel management, since its brand man

THE BODY SHOP.

Against Animal Testing: Here at The Body Shop we've always been passionately against animal testing. We've never tested our products on animals. This means you can be sure that our products have not been tested on animals for cosmetic reasons.

Support Community Trade: We make our products with love and care. We source some of the finest raw ingredients from the four corners of the globe. We harness the skills of artisan farmers and add our expertise to create effective products that are wonderful to use. We have 25 Community Fair Trade suppliers and we will be featuring more and more of them on this map in the coming months.

Activate Self Esteem: We believe that true beauty comes from confidence, vitality and inner wellbeing. We strive to use imagery which doesn't play on women's insecurities, and to bring you products that enhance your natural beauty and express your unique personality.

Defend Human Rights: We have always campaigned on issues close to our heart, where we believe we can make a real difference. Since 1994 we've helped to raise funds and global awareness of domestic violence. Since 2004, over £4m[1] has been donated to local partners who fund the prevention, support and protection of abused women and children.

Protect The Planet: protecting the planet is even more important today than it was in 1976, when we first published our five core values. We're committed to reducing our impact on the environment by reducing the energy we consume and generating less waste. We take full responsibility for the way we run our business. We're using our global network to help change attitudes around the world. And we're building on positive efforts already being made by our suppliers, franchisees, colleagues and customers.

Fig. 2.10 The brand values of "The Body Shop". (Source: The Body Shop 2015)

agement was solely focused on cost optimisation instead of values. For instance, in 2009 Schlecker closed approximately 800 small outlets and opened so-called "XL" shops, which were often located in the immediate vicinity of the former shops. Instead of being able to continue working for Schlecker at the standard wage of EUR 12 per hour, the previous employees were offered contracts through a temporary employment agency at EUR 6.50 per hour. Any employees who did not agree to this were relocated to branches further away. In contrast to its competitors who had recorded constant growth in recent years, Schlecker generated a loss of EUR 200 million in 2011. As a result, the company was forced to file for insolvency in January 2012. Schlecker's lack of an identity-based brand management was also reflected by the past and current conduct of its founder and CEO, Anton Schlecker. He always remained invisible to his employees, entering the company headquarters via the underground car park and a private lift. Even following the insolvency, he neither made a statement nor did he address his staff (cf. Amann and Tietz 2012). The contrasting public image of the brand identities of dm and Schlecker is made clear in the evaluation of both companies on the rating portal dooyoo.de. Here, dm achieved a very good score, with five stars, in comparison to only three stars for Schlecker.

2.6.2.5 Brand Personality

Originally only used with respect to people, personality theory can also be applied to brands.

> Azoulay and Kapferer (2003, p. 151) define **brand personality** as "the set of human personality traits that are both applicable and relevant for brands". Personality traits are defined as "relatively enduring styles of thinking, feeling and acting".

This view of the **brand personality** is supported by Gilmore's (1919) "Theory of Animism" which argues that humans essentially tend to "anthropomorphise" inanimate objects by ascribing to them human attributes in order to facilitate interaction with these objects. From this perspective, brands also have "human" characteristics in terms of their own personality (cf. Aaker 1997; Fournier 1998; Huber et al. 2001; Hermann et al. 2005).

When creating a brand identity, the intended brand personality must also be defined. Within this context, we refer to the **target brand personality**. It describes which "human traits" internal and external target groups are supposed to associate with this brand. In order to achieve differentiating power and relevance for consumer behaviour, the brand personality must take the relevant competitors and the self-concept of the target groups into account (cf. Schade 2012). The target brand personality is expressed in the verbal and non-verbal communication style of a brand (cf. Schade 2012).

In order to define the target brand personality, it has to be operationalised and made measurable. As a rule, brand personality scales are used for this purpose. In recent years, numerous brand personality scales have been introduced both in theory and practice. These scales are based on findings of personality psychology. According to this approach, the human personality can be described using five dimensions, the so-called "Big Five" (cf. Cattell 1944; Eysenck and Eysenck 1987; Fisseni 1998; Goldberg 1990). The "Big Five" include the dimensions of "extraversion", "agreeableness", "conscientiousness", "neuroticism" and "openness to experience" (cf. McCrae and Costa 1997).

The application of this concept to brands was already attempted by Wells et al. in 1957 and in subsequent years by Plummer (1984) as well as Batra et al. (1993). However, none of these three approaches could be evidenced empirically. In 1997 Jennifer Aaker provided the most prominent, albeit heavily criticised, approach with the **Brand Personality Scale** (BPS) developed by her. Aaker identifies five dimensions of brand personality: "sincerity", "excitement", "competence", "sophistication" and "ruggedness".

The Brand Personality Scale has been examined many times in recent years with the aim to prove its universal validity; however, this has not been successful. Instead it became clear that different dimensions have to be chosen for different countries and product categories (cf. for instance Aaker et al. 2001; Ferrandi et al. 2000; Supphellen and Gronhaug 2003). Due to this problem, today numerous brand personality scales exist which are geared specifically towards individual countries or product categories (cf. Schade et al. 2014).

Such specific scales must meet four requirements:

– the scale may only contain personality traits,
– the scale must constitute a statistically reliable and valid measuring tool,
– all the selected traits must be suitable for describing the specific brand personalities (e.g. in a defined product category),
– it has to be possible to record differentiating traits.

For example, Schade et al. (2014) developed and validated a specific brand personality scale for professional sports clubs in Germany (Sports Club Brand Personality Scale, SCBPS). The scale consists of four dimensions (see Table 2.5).

These dimensions differ from those of existing generic scales like the BPS by Aaker (1997). On the item level, only a few traits appear in the BPS, too (cheerful, family-oriented, hard-working; Aaker 1997). These results confirm the need to develop specific brand personality scales.

Two dimensions of the SCBPS ("Extraversion" and "Conscientiousness") are related to the "Big Five" scale of human personality (cf. McCrae and Costa 1997). These dimensions enable sports clubs to establish emotional connections with external target groups. The dimension "rebelliousness" offers the opportunity to build a differentiating brand image for sportive underdogs (e.g., the football club FC St. Pauli or the baseball club Chicago Cubs).

Different researchers have developed further specific brand personality scales for various product categories (e.g. Herbst and Merz 2011 for B2B brands in Germany).

Table 2.5 Brand personality scale for professional sports clubs (SCBPS) in Germany

Brand personality dimensions	Extraversion	Rebelliousness	Open-mindedness	Conscientious-ness
Brand personality traits	Traditional	Rebellious	Open-minded	Hard-working
	Faithful	Bold	Tolerant	Fighting spirit
	Sociable	Alternative	Sophisticated	Diligent
	Family-oriented		Socially responsible	Tough
	Humorous			
	Cheerful			

Source Schade et al. (2014, p. 659)

2.6.2.6 Brand Offer

The specification of the fundamental type and nature of the offered products and services of a brand is based primarily on the brand competences. The fundamental nature of the **brand offer** determines in which way a brand becomes useful for the consumer. Just as a person, within the context of their personal identity, decides which role and function they would like to fulfil within society (e.g. in terms of the occupation they hold), a brand has to decide which functional benefit it is to provide to the consumer. The brand offer in terms of identity-based brand management must be clearly differentiated from the company's product policy.

This differentiation is clearly evident in the Dyson brand. The original product with which James Dyson founded his company in the 1980s was a revolutionary bagless vacuum cleaner. The nature of the brand offer at Dyson, however, is not the development of bagless vacuum cleaners; instead, James Dyson sees the offer of his brand as making existing products better. Thus, in addition to an entire series of bagless vacuum cleaners, the company also developed products in other categories, e.g., the Sea Truck which constitutes an efficient watercraft. Or the Ballbarrow, a wheelbarrow with a rubber ball instead of a wheel, which became the market leader in England within a mere three years (cf. Dyson 2012). Furthermore, the product range includes innovative hand dryers for restaurants and bladeless fans (see Fig. 2.11).

| First vacuum cleaner | Sea Truck | Ballbarrow |

| Current vacuum cleaner | Hand dryer | Fan |

Fig. 2.11   Selected products offered by the Dyson company. (Source: Dyson 2012)

In conclusion it can be said that statements regarding the importance of the six identity components introduced above for the actual development of the brand identity can only be made in individual cases and when taking the general conditions into account. With this in mind, Aaker and Joachimsthaler (2000) developed the following four questions which may help identify the identity components relevant in the individual case:

– Does it help differentiate the brand from its competitors?
The differentiation potential plays an important part in developing one's own identity. Identity components of strong practical relevance and differentiation potential should always be particularly emphasised.

– Does it resonate with the customer?
An identity component can only make a positive contribution to the image of a brand if it is judged as positive by the consumers. For instance, BMW's competence in building dynamic engines and vehicles manages to achieve this.

– Does it energize employees?
Every identity component should be able to motivate the brand's employees. When developing the brand identity, this must always be taken into account.

– Is it believable?
The last question concerns the credibility of the individual identity components and is reflected in the authenticity of a brand (cf. Sect. 2.9). Only an authentic brand is accepted by both the internal and external target groups.

The significance of the individual identity components ultimately also depends on the product category in question (services, investment goods, convenience products, specialty goods etc.). Furthermore, the structure of the target groups, the type of the key brand benefit, the brand identity of the key competitors and the structure of the company's brand portfolio also constitute essential determinants.

2.7   The Brand Image Concept

A **brand image** is based on all individually and subjectively perceived and decoded signals issued by that brand. In particular, it reflects the brand's ability to fulfil the consumers' or other stakeholders' needs.

A **brand image** is a multidimensional attitudinal construct (cf. Foscht and Swoboda 2011; Trommsdorff 2011) which represents the perceptions of the brand in the mind of external stakeholders.

In the following subsections we first define the meaning of the brand image in an identity-based brand management approach. Thereafter, we illustrate the process of **storing brand-related information**, which leads to a discussion of the creation of brand images from a neuroeconomics perspective. Neuroeconomics helps explain how consumer behaviour reflects neural relationships in the human brain (cf. Kenning 2014). In contrast to more traditional consumer behaviour concepts (cf. e.g. Kroeber-Riel et al. 2013), neuroeconomics combines findings from psychology, neuroscience and economics to explain the (mental) processes that ultimately lead to consumer behaviour (cf. Bielefeld 2012).

2.7.1 The Brand Image Concept in Identity-Based Brand Management

Brand awareness is a precondition for establishing a brand image among external target groups. It measures a person's ability to recall a brand symbol, such as a trademark, logo or some combination thereof (i.e. brand recall), or to recognise it when prompted with acoustic or visual aids (i.e. brand recognition), and then to assign it to a product category (cf. Aaker 1991). Because brand awareness is defined as a precondition for establishing brand images, it is not part of the brand image itself.

In the identity-based brand management approach, the brand image comprises two main components (see Fig. 2.12): subjectively perceived brand attributes and, on the basis of those attributes, functional and non-functional brand benefits for the individual

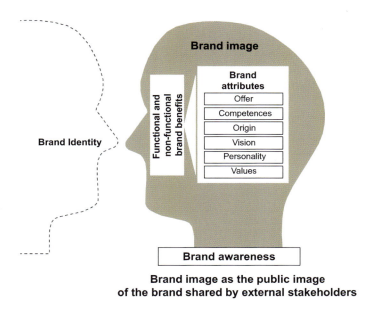

Fig. 2.12 Brand image components

consumer (cf. Vershofen 1940; Keller 1993). **Brand attributes** are characteristics that describe the brand; they represent an individual's knowledge of the brand. The degree to which a brand can satisfy the needs of a consumer depends on its brand attributes and represents the **brand benefit** (cf. Diller 1992; Perrey 1998).

The **functional brand benefit** perceived by consumers is primarily based on their knowledge of the brand's products, services and, especially, competences. In contrast, **non-functional brand benefits** derive primarily from the brand's personality, values or vision. Brand heritage can influence both functional (e.g., red wine from Bordeaux, IT products from Silicon Valley) and non-functional (e.g., a San Francisco-based brand represents a "Flower Power" lifestyle) benefits.

The **functional benefits** can be further divided into utilitarian and economic benefits (see **Fig.** 2.13). **Utilitarian benefits** are based on the physical and technical characteristics of the brand offering. For example, the utilitarian benefit of a BMW is that it provides transportation from one location to another, but it also includes the specific characteristics of the car, such as its driving dynamics. The **economic benefits** of a brand are based on the cost–benefit ratio and the financial consequences for the consumer as a result of using this brand. In the case of a car, this would include maintenance and fuel costs (cf. Stolle 2013).

Due to ever-shortening product life cycles (e.g. consumers replace their mobile phones every few months), it is almost impossible to establish a differentiating brand image based solely on functional brand benefits. Even technical innovations usually support only a short period of differentiation, so non-functional brand benefits become increasingly important for the creation of a sustainable and differentiating brand image. This element is especially relevant in saturated and mature markets (cf. Burmann et al. 2007).

Non-functional benefits emerge if a brand is able to offer an additional benefit (such as prestige) unrelated to its functional benefits (cf. Meffert et al. 2015). Non-functional brand benefits comprise social and individual benefits (see Fig. 2.13). Consumers perceive **social brand benefits** if the brand is able to satisfy their needs for esteem, group affiliation, and self-expression in a social context (cf. Stolle 2013). **Individual**

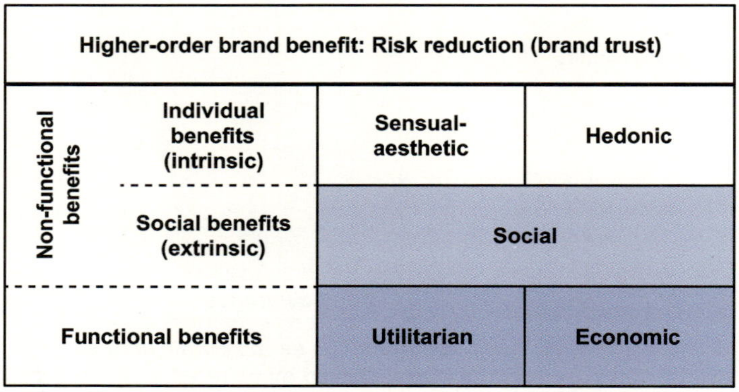

Fig. 2.13 Types and levels of brand benefits. (Source: based on Burmann and Stolle 2007, p. 15.)

intrinsic brand benefits encompass a **sensual/aesthetic brand benefit** and a **hedonic brand benefit**. The former addresses the need for beauty; in the automotive industry, for example, it might be achieved by the attractive external and internal design of a car. The latter fulfils the consumer's need for personal fulfilment, passion, pleasure, and cognitive and emotional stimulation (cf. Stolle 2013).

A higher-order brand benefit is a brand's ability to **reduce risk**, which can be a component of all five benefit dimensions. Consumers might perceive risk in the context of functional/utilitarian (e.g., vehicle safety), economic (financial risk) or social (not being accepted by a peer group) benefits. Risk also exists for sensual/aesthetic brand benefits (e.g., an evening gown ordered online does not look as good as expected) and hedonic benefits (e.g., reading a bestselling book fails to provide the expected mental stimulation). The greater the individually perceived risk, the more important **brand trust** becomes for buying behaviour. Brand trust is based on a consumer's conviction that the brand will fulfil its brand promise (cf. Hegner 2012).

In contrast to brand identity, a brand image cannot be influenced directly by brand management. It depends on dynamic interaction processes that take place while conveying the brand promise to external stakeholders. This interaction is influenced by the activities of the brand (activities of both the management and the employees), by consumers (e.g., online and offline recommendations, comments by opinion leaders), by the reactions of competitors and by environmental conditions.

Initially, the **brand promise** is an abstract construct which has been reduced to a small set of keywords. This reduced form of the brand promise cannot be transferred effectively to internal and external stakeholders because it usually allows for too much interpretation. Therefore, it is essential to convert the brand promise into specific **symbols** that are able to express the brand promise and to subsequently use these symbols to communicate the brand promise to the stakeholder or target groups.

> **Brand symbols** are sensory signs that refer to a brand and allow for identifying and communicating information about the brand. In this way, brand symbols convey the brand promise (cf. Müller 2012).

For the identity-based brand management approach, brand symbols encompass not only brand names and logos (primary symbols) but also any additional aspects that might communicate the brand's image and promise (secondary symbols). Secondary symbols might take the form of slogans (e.g., Nike's "Just do it"), fictional advertising characters (e.g., the Michelin Man), colours (e.g., the red of Coca-Cola) or events (e.g., Red Bull Air Races). The symbolic communication of the brand promise must be consistent across all brand touch points (i.e. all places where a consumer comes in contact with the brand).

According to communication science research, communicating the brand promise through symbols happens in the following way (cf. Müller 2012). The sender (brand holder) tries to transmit the brand promise to the receivers (external target groups) in order to influence their behaviour in favour of the brand. To achieve this influence, the sender converts the verbally defined brand promise into concrete, secondary symbols. For example, the German insurance company Provinzial translated its abstract brand promises of "reliability", "trust", "protection" and "lifelong partnership" into the symbol of a guardian angel. This secondary symbol is communicated through multiple channels (e.g., advertising posters, television spots). Ideally, the receivers perceive the advertisement and the primary symbol (i.e. the brand name Provinzial) together with the secondary symbol (guardian angel). Successful communication between the sender and the receivers requires that both sides share the perception of the meaning of the secondary symbol. If this meaning is mutually identical, the receivers can decode the secondary symbol as intended by the sender. Due to this decoding, the receivers (e.g., consumers) now associate the brand name with the attributes of "reliability", "trust", "protection" and "lifelong partnership". In this case, the brand has successfully managed to communicate its brand promise through the appropriate secondary symbol of the guardian angel.

A classic example of symbolic communication is the Marlboro brand (cf. Müller 2012). Marlboro's brand promise includes "freedom", "manhood" and "adventure". To communicate this promise, it has for many years used the theme of the American Wild West. In numerous films and novels, the Wild West theme has been strongly associated with the attributes of "freedom", "manhood" and "adventure." Marlboro's communication has focused especially on cowboys and their typical actions (e.g., using a lasso, sitting at a campfire). The brand further enhanced this effect by using an established acoustic Wild West symbol in television advertisements: the musical theme from the classic Western film *The Magnificent Seven*. Its slogan, "Come to Marlboro Country", also signals the idea of a separate "Marlboro world" to receivers. Thus, Marlboro has applied well-established symbols of the Wild West as secondary symbols to connect its primary symbol (the brand name Marlboro) with the desired attributes.

Thus, consistently communicating the brand promise to consumers through adequate secondary symbols across all brand touch points is one of the main challenges for brand management (cf. Müller 2012).

2.7.2 Associative Neural Brand Networks as the Product of Stimulus Processing in the Brain

According to the current state of brain research (cf. Roth 2003) we know that all sensory impressions, such as touch and smell, as well as mental images of brands are stored in the brain in the form of **neural networks**, i.e., interconnected nerve cells (cf. Bielefeld 2012). All facts, experiences, valuations, emotions etc. that are subjectively linked to a brand are stored in these neural networks.

The part of this neural network which can be articulated verbally by the consumer is referred to as an **associative network** (cf. Spitzer 2008). With regard to brands these associations include the benefits communicated by the brand and perceived by the consumer. In addition to these associations which are controlled by brand management, the consumer incorporates further brand-related information in their personal associative brand network. This may be, for instance, episodic memories, i.e. special occurrences or stories they have experienced with a brand in the past. In turn, these memories can be stored in the form of emotions, feelings and thoughts (cf. Bielefeld 2012). The distinction between **emotions** as a physiological state of excitation and **feelings** arises from the degree of consciousness with which the physiological conditions are experienced and articulated by a person. While emotions are experienced unconsciously, feelings are sensory patterns that already exist in the mind of a person as an image and that can therefore be articulated (cf. Bielefeld 2012, p. 200).

Figure 2.14 shows the schematic structure of a neural brand network in the brain of a consumer in the form of cross-linked subnetworks.

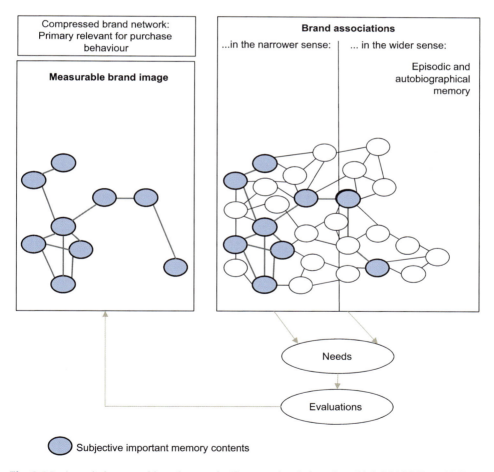

Fig. 2.14   Associative neural brand network. (Source: closely based on Bielefeld 2012, p. 175.)

The ovals in the networks in Fig. 2.14 symbolise specific content, which may be information or associations. Information refers to largely objective knowledge within the network with a direct reference to the brand (e.g., "Milka is a chocolate brand"). In contrast, associations constitute knowledge that has only an indirect and mostly personal relation to the brand and was not directly communicated by the brand (e.g., "my grandmother used to give me a bar of Milka for my birthday"). The lines between the ovals indicate connections between the individual pieces of information. The way they are linked in this network is dependent on the subjective perception of the individual consumer.

The memory contents connected with a certain brand (the ovals in Fig. 2.14) may have a close or a loose connection with the brand. Memory contents that are directly connected to the functional and symbolic brand promise made by the brand are called **semantic associations**. Semantic associations create connections that are typical for the brand and establish a specific context as well as a unique meaning of the brand (cf. Bielefeld 2012). They include all brand associations which the consumers have "learned" and stored in their brain as important from their subjective perspective (cf. Birbaumer and Schmidt 2006). The **subjective importance** of a piece of information (its reward value) is of pivotal significance for including this piece of information in the associative network, as only "important" information is relevant enough to be stored. Information regarding the visual, verbal or other sensory identification of the brand is also stored. On the one hand, the identification refers to the concrete design, such as the logo, jingle or slogan, whilst on the other hand it also refers to symbolic characteristics, such as, for example, the typical dune landscape in the marketing communication by the beer brand Jever. Thus, semantic associations directly represent the effect of the identity-based brand management in the mind of the consumer and are specifically influenced by the brand management as the sender of this information (cf. Bielefeld 2012).

Brand associations in the wider sense (see the right-hand side of Fig. 2.14) are all associations of a consumer which are connected to the brand, but which do not have their origin in the functional or symbolic promise communicated by the brand (e.g., a special memory in connection with using the brand). The origin of these associations lies in the experiences of the individual consumers, in their specific knowledge and emotions. The consumer is often not fully aware of these associations (cf. Koch 2008). Nonetheless, the connection of these associations in the wider sense with the conscious associations in the narrower sense takes a central position in the evaluation of a brand. Only this individual background allows the consumers to integrate their knowledge of a brand in their neural network structures and, at the same time, imbues the information with subjective meaning.

The significance of individual pieces of brand information within a network differs from consumer to consumer. The more important the associations are for a consumer, the easier and faster they can be recalled (cf. Bielefeld 2012; Recke 2011). Important information and connections are marked with bold lines in Fig. 2.14. The stronger the connection between two memory contents, the more dominant the activation of these associations in the consumer's memory (cf. Spitzer 2008). The grey ovals in Fig. 2.14

are pieces of information that are both important for the consumer and have a direct relation to the functional and symbolic brand value. Thus, they shape the brand image in the mind of an individual consumer in a specific way. Only this small part of the neural brand network is recalled by the consumer when making selection decisions, e.g. at the supermarket shelf (cf. Bielefeld 2012).

The conscious part of the neural brand network comprises two levels (see Fig. 2.15). The inner core of the conscious brand network consists, on the one hand, of the functional associations linked to the brand and, on the other hand, of the symbolic associations directly connected with them. Together they constitute the brand knowledge of the consumers which they can easily recall and articulate, for instance in surveys. Around the inner core we find individual biographical associations connected with a brand (area 2 in Fig. 2.15). This includes, for example, personal experiences and event-related motives for consumption. In contrast to the information in the inner oval, these items represent almost exclusively non-functional value associations that, due to the connection with personal experiences, are of great significance to the purchasing behaviour (cf. Bielefeld 2012).

Figure 2.15 illustrates this using the example of Milka chocolate. The smooth and softly melting chocolate offered by the Milka brand is advertised with the slogan "the tenderest temptation since chocolate was invented". The smooth and delicately melting texture of the chocolate first of all represents a functional value. This is stored in area (1), the inner core of the conscious brand network. The advertising slogan extends this functional value with an additional symbolic one, as it is emotionally charged with the term "temptation". This information is stored in area (2), although it is close to area (1),

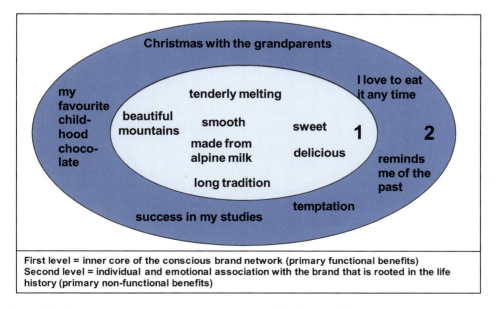

First level = inner core of the conscious brand network (primary functional benefits)
Second level = individual and emotional association with the brand that is rooted in the life history (primary non-functional benefits)

Fig. 2.15 Two levels of an associative network exemplified by the Milka brand. (Source: based on Bielefeld 2012, p. 157)

as there is still a clear reference to the formally communicated brand experience. If, in addition, the consumer associates a personal experience with the delicately melting quality of the chocolate, then the information moves deeper and deeper into the peripheral, individual and emotional area (2). What comes to mind here is, for instance, a childhood memory of cosy Christmas celebrations at Grandma's, where each child was given a bar of Milka chocolate as a present so Milka was their favourite childhood chocolate. Another personal experience might be a student "rewarding" herself with a bar of Milka after succeeding in an exam.

"Alpine milk" and "mountains" represent subjective brand knowledge and are directly linked to the communicated origin of the brand. This connection exists, irrespective of the fact that the Milk brand (which originates from Switzerland, where it was registered in 1901) has been a part of the Kraft Foods Group since 1990. Associations such as "tradition" and "ideal world" in turn reflect the consumer's subjective knowledge of the brand values and vision. Associations concerning the quality and texture of the products ("delicious", "smooth" and "sweet") are connected with the competences of the brand and the actual brand performance.

The subjective assessment of brand stimuli is based on prior information stored in the consumer's associative neural networks and takes into account the following two criteria: "Is it a new stimulus/object?" and "Is this stimulus important to me?" (cf. Roth 1997). The possible combinations of this valuation result in the matrix in Table 2.6.

Stimuli that are both unimportant and unknown (area 4 in Table 2.6) are not processed by the brain and are therefore not perceived consciously. The same applies to stimuli that are known but classified as unimportant. A stimulus that is both known and important (area 1) is processed by the brain with little conscious effort. Existing neural networks connected with this stimulus are activated and trigger a cognitive response to the object (cf. Roth and Menzel 1996). However, the low conscious effort of the consumer can have a detrimental effect: due to the minimal attention this process requires, new information, such as additional instructions on the packaging or information on a new product recipe, may not be considered by the consumer (cf. Bielefeld 2012). The greatest impact in terms of attention and therefore consciousness is caused by stimuli which are both important and new (area 2). Here, the importance and the novelty of a stimulus depend on what is already known to the individual consumer. In order to be recognised as both important and new, a connection with the existing associative neural networks

Table 2.6 Assessment of brand stimuli

	Known brand stimulus ("old")	Unknown brand stimulus ("new")
Important brand stimulus	(1)	(2)
Unimportant brand stimulus	(3)	(4)

closely based on Bielefeld (2012, p. 187)

must be possible. A strongly stimulating effect can therefore only emanate from a brand with which the consumer has already established such a network (cf. Bielefeld 2012).

If a stimulus is strong enough to receive further attention, a **comprehensive evaluation** is carried out on the basis of the information already stored in the memory. Here, a brand is mostly evaluated either in comparison to alternative offers ("Is brand A or brand B better?") or in comparison to not making a purchase ("Is this brand worth this much attention right now?"). A wealth of information which the consumer is only to some extent aware of is incorporated into this evaluation process. The more trivial the buying process, e.g. when purchasing coffee in the supermarket, the more the evaluation is determined by feelings such as pleasure or indulgence which are associated with the brand. The stored feelings are based directly on the communicated symbolic value associations of a brand with respect to need satisfaction (cf. Bielefeld 2012).

In summary it can be said that a brand's relevance to behaviour arises primarily from the consumer's perception and storage of symbolic value associations. The more detailed and in-depth this coding (achieved principally through episodic autobiographical memories), the more relevance to behaviour, and therefore strength, has the brand (cf. Bielefeld 2012).

2.7.3   Storage of Brand-Related Information in the Memory

According to neuroeconomics research, strong brands are distinguished from weak ones by more consolidated associative neural networks. This correlation can also be described as the consumer's familiarity with a brand. When buying a certain brand, brand familiarity gives the consumers the security of receiving the reward that is subjectively important to them (cf. Birbaumer and Schmidt 2006). The fulfilment of the expected reward or the absence of this reward is stored by the consumers in their reward memory. The rewards experienced in the past and stored in the memory create reward expectations which motivate to select this brand again (cf. Roth 2007). Figure 2.16 illustrates the process of storing and recalling information in and from associative neural networks, which accompanies the perception of brands.

The diagram shows the processing of brand stimuli in the memory systems according to their significance to people with respect to content and hierarchy. Information processing starts with the **perception of the brand stimuli**. First of all, these are pre-processed in the ultra-short-term memory. Here the stimulus disintegrates without being perceived consciously if it is noticed only very briefly (no longer than 50 ms) and if it is not in the focus of attention, if it is superimposed by stronger stimuli or classified as unimportant (cf. Roth 2003; Dehaene et al. 2006).

If, in contrast, the stimulus is sufficiently strong, the so-called priming takes place; here, the stimulus activates already existent memory contents, thus facilitating slightly easier processing. This way, **priming** allows a consumer to perceive the stimulus faster if it is presented repeatedly, for instance when searching for a brand which the consumer is only vaguely and fleetingly familiar with on a supermarket shelf (cf. Roth 2003).

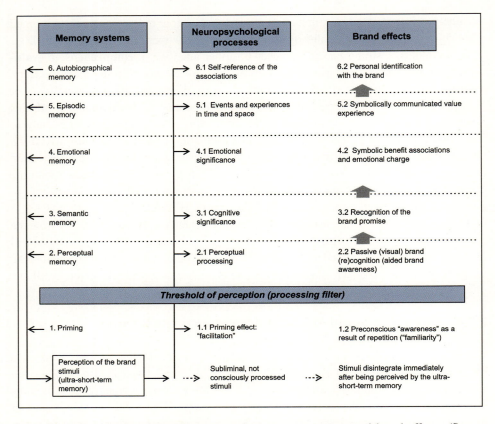

Fig. 2.16 Links Between information processing, memory systems and brand effects. (Source: closely based on Bielefeld 2012, p. 244)

If the stimulation effect of a brand increases further (see Fig. 2.16), i.e. the stimulus is noticed consciously, the actual **perceptual processing** of the stimulus ensues. The perceptual processing is initially restricted to simple perception without any activation of the entire brand network. The stimulus is compared with the information stored in the memory so that brand recognition, for instance by means of the typical packaging or logo, is made possible. In concrete terms, this effect is called aided brand awareness, as a brand presented (on the shelf) is recognised by the consumer (cf. Bielefeld 2012).

The **semantic memory** constitutes the next level of the processing procedure. At this level, the consumer perceives the name and the significance of the brand; this includes the brand, its products, characteristics, prices etc. This kind of information is initially only perceived as a brand promise in the semantic-cognitive sense, i.e. rationally. It does not yet include any associative connections with the information stored in the associative neural network. Therefore, at this level of processing **the understanding of the brand is purely rational** (cf. Bielefeld 2012; Roth 2003).

The emotional interpretation of the brand ensues at the next level of the stimulus processing and happens in the **emotional memory**. On this level, the semantically and symbolically communicated brand stimuli are valued and weighted by means of the emotions stored in the memory. This step is of vital significance to brand management, as the brand is emotionally charged through the connection of the brand stimuli with the stored emotions. The brand promise is transformed into emotional value associations, giving the brand a subjective reward value in the consumer's mind (cf. Bielefeld 2012).

If a brand is used repeatedly, these bits of information are connected to form behaviour patterns (courses of action) in the **episodic memory**. If the repeated use takes place on typical occasions, such as regular facial care using the same cosmetics brand, then this behavioural habit is also linked to the brand associations.

An even stronger emotional relevance develops if the use of a brand is imbued with autobiographical significance and is therefore stored in the **autobiographical memory**. In this way, the brand's symbolic value associations acquire an individual self-reference for the consumers, which results in their distinctive identification with the brand. This applies particularly to brands that are important to the consumers' personality structure, such as their pursuit of prestige, recognition and self-gratification (cf. Bielefeld 2012).

Therefore, from the brand's perspective, the perceptual and memory processes detailed in Fig. 2.16 can only proceed successfully if the brand stimulus exceeds the threshold of perception. To do so, the stimulus must already unconsciously be perceived as relevant by the consumer. **The greater a consumer's familiarity with a brand, the easier can the threshold of perception be overcome by means of the priming effect**. Conscious perception and a more in-depth stimulus processing will then ensue as described above. For this process to proceed as a whole, **once again the consumer's familiarity with the brand**, initially at the level of its physical appearance (e.g. uniform packaging and consistent logos), **is required**. Symbolic values, which are attributed to a brand by the consumer, only develop if the information broadcast by the brand is somehow linked with the highly subjective knowledge of the respective individual. This finding is of vital significance to brand management.

2.7.4   Neuroscientific Implications for Identity-Based Brand Management

First of all, it is of vital significance that brands are formed in the brain of the consumer by connecting the perception of brand stimuli with individual memory contents. Therefore, in most cases consumers do not perceive and experience brands the way the responsible brand management has intended. Unlike tangible objects which can be rendered in a specific and consistent form, brand perception develops on the basis of personal and highly subjective memory contents of the individual consumer. In order to ensure that the brand perception is, nonetheless, as homogeneous as possible, the conceptual design of a brand must be frequently reassessed with regard to the emotions and feelings which the brand is intended to communicate.

Here, the distinction between emotions and feelings is important. Even though both terms are frequently used synonymously in common parlance, in neuroscience they describe two different things. Emotions always precede feelings and trigger them. Generally, emotions are not directly connected with the object that triggers them; in fact, they are stereotypical processes. The **six universal emotions** are fear, happiness, sadness, anger, surprise and disgust (cf. Damasio 2000). People experience the emotions that an object triggers, e.g. happiness over a glass of cold beer of a certain brand on a warm summer evening, as a feeling; a direct neural link is then established between this feeling and the object. In the memory, the feeling is stored in connection with the object, here the glass of cold beer, and recalled at a later date if required. The emotion, however, is not recalled.

The stimulation effect that a brand has on the consumer is processed and stored in a hierarchical manner. In this process, the perceived stimuli are initially identified by means of design characteristics that are typical of the brand and, in a next step, connected with stored feelings. To ensure that a brand is noticed by the consumer, the stimuli connected with it have to be perceived as subjectively important on an unconscious level. This classification is already stored by the brain.

The various details of a brand, e.g. the brand logo, packaging, products, jingle, etc. are not perceived and stored as a whole by the consumer. Instead, the information is fragmented into small units, which are perceived and subsequently connected and stored in the form of associative neural brand networks. The more typical certain design characteristics are, both with respect to different products and over time, the more the brand network will be consolidated within the mind of the consumer. The more the network has been consolidated, the more relevant to behaviour and, thus, the stronger the brand. As a result, it will be able to prevail over other brands whose neural networks are not as strongly consolidated. The same applies vice versa if the brand design lacks stability and consistency. Frequent changes and inconsistent designs lead to an increase in the required neural subnetworks, as a separate network must be created for each design variant. This prevents the consolidation of a neural "core" network, thus weakening the representation of the brand in the consumer's brain (cf. Bielefeld 2012).

It is sensory information that allows consumers to attribute a certain stimulus to the respective brand. Sensory information enables them to absorb and understand the brand message. In the neural brand network, this information is connected with feelings as well as individual episodic memories. This connection facilitates the evaluation of the brand stimuli with respect to personal relevance and novelty. This evaluation decides whether a consumer pays attention to a brand stimulus and thus, ultimately, whether a brand will be purchased or remain unnoticed. In this context, emotions can be the same for different brands, such as the emotion of "happiness" about a cool beer on a warm summer day. In contrast, feelings may differ significantly between different brands (cf. Bielefeld 2012). For example, we can assume that the feelings connected with the "Nordic" brand Jever on the one hand and the "Bavarian" brand Paulaner on the other hand are very different. **The feelings triggered in the consumer by a certain brand constitute the core of**

the brand experience and are, as a differentiating factor, the key starting point for identity-based brand management.

The closer the benefit associations communicated by the brand are connected with the consumer's personality and need structures (autobiographical brand information), the stronger the identification and, consequently, the loyalty of the consumer to the brand. However, symbolic value associations can only be effective if they are of individual significance and relevance to the consumer (cf. Bielefeld 2012). This means that a brand can only entrench the intended symbolic value associations in a largely homogeneous part of the consumers with similar neural network contents. Therefore, from a neuroscientific perspective the selection of the value dimensions and their alignment with the relevant **consumer groups** in terms of **brand positioning** is also of central significance to brand management.

The entrenchment of the brand in a consumer's neural network can, from a neurological perspective, be understood as brand strength and therefore, a brand's relevance to behaviour. Brands that are strong in this sense have a wealth of synaptic connections in which the typical, concise sensory characteristics of a brand are linked to the emotionally tinted value associations of the consumer. Brand networks are reinforced by repeatedly new perceptions of both the brand and the behaviour associated with it. In the process, these networks store information on the consumer's own behaviour, for instance with respect to the purchase, use and occasions when the product would be used, as well as their experience, for instance experiences with or the endorsement of the product by a third party. In any similar situation the brand network consolidated in this way is activated and has a behaviour-controlling effect on the consumer (cf. Bielefeld 2012).

The above-mentioned findings of the neurosciences regarding brand management are of great value for a more in-depth understanding of consumer behaviour. While not radically new, these insights contribute to the consolidation, differentiation and confirmation of fundamental, well-known facts. Psychology examined the correlation between neural processes and behaviour as early as during the 1970s (cf. Birbaumer 1975). Even back then it was recognised that stimuli are perceived by matching their patterns with stored knowledge and that information is stored in neural cell structures (cf. Birbaumer 1975). The great significance of feelings for purchase decisions has also been well-known in marketing for more than 50 years; now it can be substantiated by neurobiological analyses.

The great popularity of neuroeconomics is mainly based on technical instruments which may be used to make processes in the brain visible. These imaging techniques, such as magnetic resonance tomography (MRT), can indicate which areas of the brain are activated by certain stimuli. However, the findings from these studies must be considered with extreme caution. On the one hand, this is due to the inadequate resolution of these imaging techniques and the high level of influence the user has on the imaging process (cf. Vul et al. 2009); on the other hand, it is due to the frequently incorrect and oversimplified interpretation of imaging analyses by self-appointed experts from industrial economics and, in particular, marketing (cf. Bielefeld 2012).

As Bielefeld (2012) shows by means of numerous examples, even neuroscience is unable to identify a "buying button" in the brain of the consumer. Within this context, the finding that people perceive the fronts of vehicles very much like human faces enjoys great popularity. According to supporters of this view, pleasant vehicle fronts are perceived more positively, leading to higher sales figures. This interpretation is based on the findings of imaging techniques that the same areas of the brain are activated when test subjects view photos of faces and of vehicle fronts. However, this does not actually prove an equal ranking (cf. Bielefeld 2012) and it it not possible to infer new design recommendations from these findings.

2.8   Brand Trust in Identity-Based Brand Management

2.8.1   Relevance of Brand Trust

An important requirement for the establishment of strong brands is the consumer's trust in the brand. Within this context, the German Brands Association ("Markenverband") examined the correlation between brand image/brand preference and the trust in a brand, its emotional closeness, its differentiating power and its technological progressiveness in 2009. Within the scope of the study, 5028 people were questioned online about a total of 357 brands. This study showed that trust has the strongest correlation to the brand image and also takes an eminent position with respect to brand preference (see Fig. 2.17).

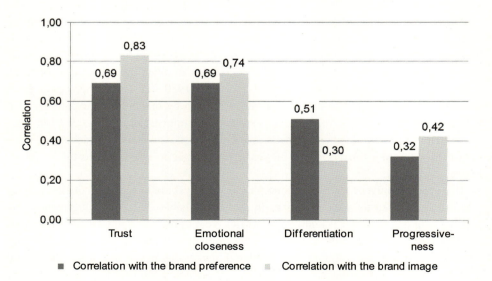

Fig. 2.17 Correlation results of the ethical brand monitor study. (Source: Brands and Values, Markenverband 2009)

Furthermore, the customers' trust in a brand also has a direct correlation to the brand value. For example, the results of the brand value study "BrandZ" by Millward Brown show a strong increase in the brand value with increasing trust of the consumers in the brand. For the BrandZ brand value study, approximately 150,000 people worldwide are questioned about more than 60,000 brands on an annual basis (cf. Millward Brown 2014).

Trust could also be identified as an important distinguishing feature. TNS Infratest (2009) showed in its study "Building Brands in Troubled Times", which was based on 1026 interviewees in Germany, that trust, for instance in the automotive sector, is an important driving force for brand differentiation. Although quality is to a high degree attributed to all automotive brands in Germany, it does not have the differentiating power of trust.

Within the scope of an international study, Hegner (2012) was also able to prove that brand trust has a very strong effect on the purchasing behaviour of consumers in Germany, South Africa and India (cf. Hegner 2012). In 2012, her study was presented with the Science Award of the German Brands Association (cf. press release of the Markenverband dated 06/06/2012).

Today the tremendous importance of trust for the success of a brand is no longer disputed in science (cf. Bruhn and Eichen 2007; Plötner 1995). In practice, this finding is also becoming increasingly accepted. This is not least due to the numerous cases of banks and financial service providers showing that, in the case of a severe loss of trust, companies first of all lose their legitimacy in society, then their profitability and ultimately they are threatened with insolvency. In the light of this understanding, it becomes obvious why the management of Pampers posted the following comments on Facebook within the context of a product recall in 2010: "TRUST: To those of us who work at Pampers, trust is more than a word. It's our mission. Parents trust us with their babies, and that is a responsibility that we take to heart. For nearly 50 years, we've worked with parents and babies to continually improve the way our diapers wrap babies in comfort and protect them as they grow. We're humbled by the trust parents place in us, and we work hard each day to earn and keep it."

This clear communication about trust within the context of the product recall shows another positive aspect of brand trust: If consumers put their trust in a brand, this acts as a protective shield against potential damage in case of future crises (cf. Edelmann 2011).

2.8.2 Components of Brand Trust

Brand trust may be defined as a consumer's willingness to become vulnerable vis-à-vis the brand. This willingness is based on the conviction that a brand has both the **capability** and the **willingness** to fulfil its brand promise (cf. Hegner 2012). Therefore, brand trust is only relevant if subjectively perceived risks exist, as only these risks make the consumer "vulnerable". The greater the subjectively perceived risks, the more important the brand trust as a determinant of buying behaviour.

Brands enjoy trust if they fulfil the promises they have made. By not disappointing their customers' trust today, they vindicate their future trust. Therefore, the establishment of trust starts even before the actual transactions between the brand and the consumer. The consistency and continuity of a brand's identity are necessary requirements for trust (cf. Meffert and Burmann 1996). Consistency as the basis of trust arises from the fit of the brand promise with the brand behaviour. Only if the consumer perceives both components as identical, does the brand appear reliable and, therefore, capable (cf. Blinda 2007). Continuity describes the temporal stability of the essential brand identity characteristics, which enables the consumer to compare the brand promise with the historic brand behaviour. Only if there is a high level of congruence, does the brand signal a dedicated willingness to comply with the brand promise in the longer term. Therefore both the perceived capability and motivation of a brand are required for consumers to put their trust in this brand (cf. Hegner 2012).

However, consumers do not just compare the brand promise and their brand experience. In total, brand trust is composed of **four dimensions** (cf. Hegner 2012; see Fig. 2.18), which can be categorised into two cognitive and two affective dimensions. The cognitive dimensions of trust include the **competence** attributed to a brand and its

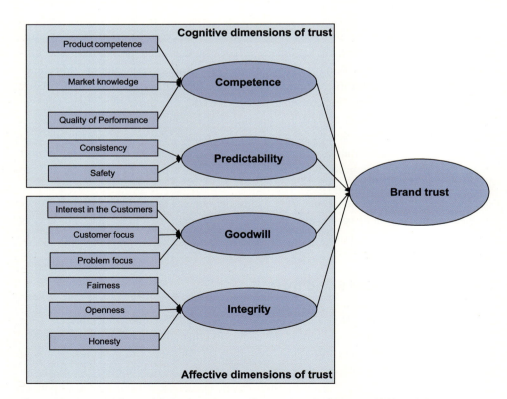

Fig. 2.18 A model for explaining brand trust. (Source: based on Hegner 2012, p. 117)

predictability, while the perceived **goodwill** and the **integrity** of a brand constitute the affective dimensions. Therefore, brand trust develops both cognitively and affectively. If trust could be evaluated on a purely cognitive basis, it would be a question of established knowledge, and in the case of a purely affective evaluation, "blind" faith would be a more fitting term (cf. Hegner 2012).

The **evaluation of the competence** of a brand reflects the consumer's confidence that the brand has all the necessary organisational capabilities to provide the promised brand benefit (e.g., Brodie et al. 2009). With respect to the effect of trust in a brand's perceived competence, Hegner was able to show that the latter comprises the three factors of **product competence**, **market knowledge** and **quality of performance** (cf. Hegner 2012). Product competence and quality of performance reflect the capability to deliver the brand promise. Market knowledge is a measure for the extent to which the consumers are under the impression that a company has all relevant market information. In order to increase the consumers' trust in the brand's perceived competence, the company must first of all determine which competences it has. For instance, Audi achieved a significant increase in trust by focusing its brand management on its technological competences. Due to frequent and well-received innovations, the technical capability of Audi had always been perceived as very high. This was additionally supported by communicating the claim "Vorsprung durch Technik" (*Advancement through technology*) (cf. Berger et al. 2007). But only at the beginning of the 21st century did the management of Audi realise that their technical expertise could also be used to develop ground-breaking design with a high-quality look and feel and to build quality (cf. Hegner 2012). Due to this realisation, Audi expanded its expertise from product competence to the fields of market knowledge and quality of performance.

The **predictability** of a brand reflects the extent of the perceived consistency in its behaviour (e.g., Einwiller 2003). According to Hegner, the perceived predictability is comprised of the components **consistency**, **continuity**, **fidelity to principles** and **safety** (cf. Hegner 2012). Consistency and continuity imply delivering the brand's promise at all times, and fidelity to principles requires the strict adherence to the core values of a brand. Safety as a component of predictability aims to give consumers the feeling that they can always rely on the high quality standards of the products. A brand that fulfils all aspects of predictability particularly well is Porsche (cf. Burmann and Schallehn 2010). For instance, Porsche communicates continuity through presenting the brand's history during which the brand promise was always reliably delivered (cf. Schallehn 2011). Furthermore, in the company museum in Zuffenhausen consumers are given the opportunity to directly experience the brand's continuity. To guarantee consistency, all subsidiaries in more than 100 countries are controlled centrally in order to ensure that consumers have an identical brand experience at all brand touch points worldwide (cf. Porsche 2011). The fidelity to principles is firmly rooted in the brand identity: "Porsche is a unique company with strong ideals. Our values and our philosophy permeate everything we do. We have a definite idea about who we are and how we approach things. This is how we manage to remain true to our principles and meet our own high standards." (Porsche 2011,

p. 5). Ultimately, the high quality standards at Porsche also guarantee for product safety (cf. Porsche 2011).

Goodwill is understood as the consumers' belief that, in addition to its own interests, the brand also considers the well-being of its customers in a reasonable manner (cf. Li et al. 2008). In concrete terms, the company's customer focus must have an externally perceivable significance and be in an appropriate balance to the pursuit of profit. The severe loss of trust suffered by many banks (cf. Bartz and Clausen 2015) is to be attributed to the complete loss of goodwill vis-à-vis these banks, whose behaviour is dominated by their managers' greedy pursuit of profit culminating in fraud perpetrated on the customer, which is why many banks are in court today.

According to Hegner (2012), a brand's goodwill can be operationalised by means of its **interest in the customers**, its **customer focus** and its **problem focus** (cf. Hegner 2012). Here, the interest in the customer reflects the perceived level of genuine interest of a brand in its customers and their problems. If this interest is translated into brand performance, then the brand operates with a customer focus. The problem focus of a brand becomes apparent in that problems occurring on the consumer's side are rectified as quickly as possible. In order to make the customer focus and the interest in the customer tangible for the consumer, the brand can, for example, include consumers in the innovation process (cf. Füller et al. 2009). This provides the company with an opportunity to enter into a dialogue with committed customers. The ensuing interaction with consumers can be used to demonstrate the company's capability and motivation. A case in point is BMW that launched the Internet portal "Customer Innovation Lab" which provides consumers with the opportunity to participate in the development of new ideas and concepts (cf. BMW Group 2003). The aspect of the problem focus requires that the brand management is able to identify and rectify any potential or current consumer problems early on. This can be achieved by establishing a comprehensive complaint management system (cf. Borth 2004). Today, social networks such as Facebook and Youtube provide additional information channels for companies. By consistently monitoring social media, information concerning consumer problems can be gathered quickly, and the sender of the information can often be addressed directly in order to offer quick troubleshooting.

Finally, **integrity** includes the consumers' subjective belief in the brand's exemplary dealings with the customers (e.g., Füller et al. 2008; Ipsos Mori 2009). According to Hegner (2012), the integrity of a brand can be subdivided into the aspects of **fairness**, **openness** and **honesty** (cf. Hegner 2012). Fairness demands that a brand does not take advantage of its consumers. Under openness we understand the exchange of all relevant information by the brand with its consumers. Honesty demands of a brand that it communicates only correct and true information. Essentially, integrity demands that a brand always carefully checks the truth of all statements in every direct and indirect communication with consumers (cf. Neumann 2007). Even minor deviations from the reality as perceived by the consumers can damage the integrity of a brand. Furthermore, integrity is particularly relevant in critical situations, e.g. in the case of product defects. The Canadian food chain Maple Leaf Foods was confronted with such a situation in 2008; one of their products had infected a number of consumers with listeriosis. As a result, 21 people died of the infection (cf. Charvet 2010). In this situation the CEO of the brand, Michael McCain, distinguished himself by behaving with great integrity. He immediately ensured that all Maple Leaf Foods products were recalled and that TV commercials paid for by Maple Leaf Foods informed the Canadian public of this danger. Furthermore, the CEO cooperated very closely with the health authorities and assumed responsibility in front of the media. Moreover, he campaigned avidly for increasing the safety regulations in this industry in order to prevent future infections. In spite of the devastating events in 2008, the consumers' trust in Maple Leaf Foods did not diminish. Both the respect and the loyalty of the customers could be retained (cf. Hegner 2012).

2.8.3 Implications for Identity-Based Brand Management

The great relevance of consumer trust to the success of a brand raises the question as to how brand management can establish trust. The fundamental basis for establishing trust is the consistent **fulfilment of the brand promise** at all brand touch points. Here, the top priority is to always meet the promised quality standards of a brand's products and services, as well as the clearly communicated brand image. This is also the result of a survey involving 10,653 consumers in Germany, carried out by GfK Verein (2012), a German market research think tank. The brand's understanding of consumer needs and its reputation play merely a secondary role when it comes to establishing trust (see Fig. 2.19).

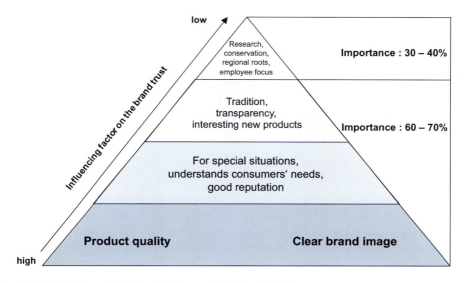

Fig. 2.19 The "Pyramid of Trust". (Source: GfK Verein 2012)

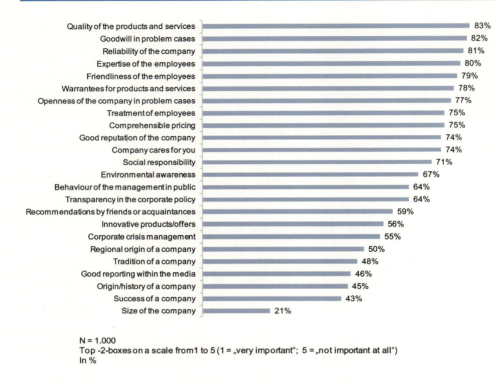

Quality of the products and services — 83%
Goodwill in problem cases — 82%
Reliability of the company — 81%
Expertise of the employees — 80%
Friendliness of the employees — 79%
Warrantees for products and services — 78%
Openness of the company in problem cases — 77%
Treatment of employees — 75%
Comprehensible pricing — 75%
Good reputation of the company — 74%
Company cares for you — 74%
Social responsibility — 71%
Environmental awareness — 67%
Behaviour of the management in public — 64%
Transparency in the corporate policy — 64%
Recommendations by friends or acquaintances — 59%
Innovative products/offers — 56%
Corporate crisis management — 55%
Regional origin of a company — 50%
Tradition of a company — 48%
Good reporting within the media — 46%
Origin/history of a company — 45%
Success of a company — 43%
Size of the company — 21%

N = 1.000
Top -2-boxes on a scale from 1 to 5 (1 = „very important"; 5 = „not important at all")
In %

Fig. 2.20 Determinants of brand trust. (Source: brand trust study 2014 , p. 16)

A representative study on brand trust carried out by Lebensmittel Zeitung (Germany's leading trade and business paper of the consumer goods sector) and Sasserath Munzinger (German brand consultancy) (2014) among 1000 people comes to a similar conclusion. In this study, it is again the quality of the products and services that is the key requirement for establishing trust, followed by the reliability of the brand, its goodwill when dealing with problems and the expertise of its employees (see Fig. 2.20).

In conclusion, this means that the brand identity is of great significance for establishing and retaining the consumers' trust. Only a strong brand identity is able to safeguard the brand promise, as it ensures both the quality of the service provision and a clear, reliable brand image.

2.9   Brand Authenticity in Identity-Based Brand Management

2.9.1   The Relevance of Brand Authenticity

In recent years, the authenticity of a brand has increasingly gained in importance as a lever for differentiation. This is due to the severe loss of trust as a result of the non-authentic behaviour of many brands, e.g. in the banking sector, the food industry and the energy sector. While a vague brand positioning leads to a reduced credibility of the brand promise, an authentic brand guarantees for the "genuineness" of the brand promise. Authentic brands use this to strengthen the trust placed in them. **Brand authenticity is therefore a determining factor that comes before trust**.

The high relevance of authenticity arises from an increasing need for authenticity on the part of the consumers (cf. Brown et al. 2003; Schallehn 2012). This need also results from the perceived homogeneity of product offers and the high number of "me-too" brands (cf. Luckner 2008). Furthermore, it has been proven that consumers increasingly reject questionable, non-authentic offers (cf. Gilmore and Pine II 2007).

2.9.2 The Object of Brand Authenticity

By definition, the **authenticity of a brand is the degree to which the brand behaviour is causally linked to brand identity** (cf. Schallehn 2012; Schallehn et al. 2014). This definition is based on the actions of a brand, i.e. of the employees behind this brand. In principle, these actions can arise from two different motives. On the one hand, they may be motivated by environmental stimuli. In this case, the brand would always attempt to respond promptly to new environmental conditions, for instance, by copying competitor brands. On the other hand, they may be motivated by the identity of the brand. In this case, the brand's actions are based on its self-image, its identity. If the identity of a brand always determines its actions and behaviours to a high degree, this brand can be called highly authentic.

From the perspective of the consumers, an objective evaluation of the motivation behind the actions of a brand and its employees is scarcely possible. Instead, consumers establish their subjective knowledge of a brand's identity based on their personal experiences. Therefore, the consumers' evaluation of authenticity depends on perceivable external indicators.

The model of brand authenticity developed and empirically tested by Schallehn (2012) identifies three dimensions through which consumers perceive the authenticity of brands (see Fig. 2.21): the consistency, continuity and individuality of a brand.

The **consistency** of a brand corresponds to the fit of the brand promise with the brand characteristics and behaviours as perceived by the consumer at all brand touch points. Consistent behaviour means that the brand fully delivers its promise without contradictions at all brand touch points at the current point in time. Therefore, consistency reflects the current perspective with regard to authenticity.

The second dimension is **continuity**. This corresponds to the perceived fit of the brand promise with the characteristics of the brand over a longer period of time. If a brand exhibits a high degree of continuity, its current brand promise can to a large extent be confirmed by the past behaviour of the brand (cf. Schallehn 2012).

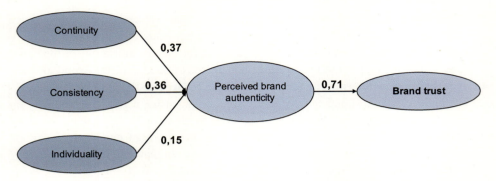

Fig. 2.21 Model explaining the perceived brand authenticity. (Source: Schallehn 2012, p. 168)

Individuality constitutes the third dimension of brand authenticity. The individuality of a brand is defined as the "perceived fit of the brand promise with those characteristics that make the brand unique and distinctive as compared to its competitors" (Schallehn 2012, p. 83). The consumer's perception of the individuality of a brand is based on its behaviour at all brand touch points.

2.9.3   Implications for Identity-Based Brand Management

Even though the perceived authenticity of a brand generally depends on the three dimensions of consistency, continuity and individuality, the analyses of Schallehn (2012) based on an online survey involving 510 test subjects showed that **individuality** has a weaker impact than the two other dimensions (see Fig. 2.21). With a path coefficient of merely 0.154, the uniqueness of a service offering takes an inferior position with respect to communicating authenticity, while the dimensions of continuity and consistency, with coefficients of 0.37 and 0.36, respectively, have a largely equal effect on the perceived brand authenticity.

This result may at first seem surprising. However, if we revisit the reasons for the increasing significance of brand authenticity, it becomes clear that consumers have a need for authentic brands, as previously unique services are nowadays quickly imitated. Given these dynamics, uniqueness is only short-lived and can no longer be a permanent basis for brand authenticity.

Therefore, the two dimensions of consistency and continuity have become more important for establishing and maintaining an authentic brand. As Schallehn (2012) was able to show, the product quality and the product range take a central position with respect to the perception of a brand's consistency.

A brand that constantly strives to maintain a high level of consistency is the German beer brand Oettinger. Oettinger's brand promise focuses on offering a high-quality beer at an affordable price (cf. Mehringer and Vossen 2010). Oettinger achieves consistency, and thus authenticity, primarily through its low price, the complete lack of print, radio and TV advertising and a strict focus on a small number of core products. The product design reinforces the self-image of the brand, with plain and therefore cheaper crown caps. In addition, the brand does without back labels, which are otherwise common in the beer market. With respect to distribution, the brand is only available via the retail trade and is not supplied to catering businesses. Dirk Kollmar, managing partner of Oettinger, summarises the brand's self-image as follows: "We are not cheap. Cheap are those who copy us. Oettinger is consistently good value for money. We strictly follow a no-frills strategy and put all our resources into quality" (Mehringer and Vossen 2010, p. 29). The high level of consistency is also reflected in the brand's success. Oettinger is Germany's top-selling beer brand (see Fig. 2.22).

Unlike consistency, the perceived **continuity** of a brand is based less on its current brand services and more on the maintenance of the brand services over a longer period

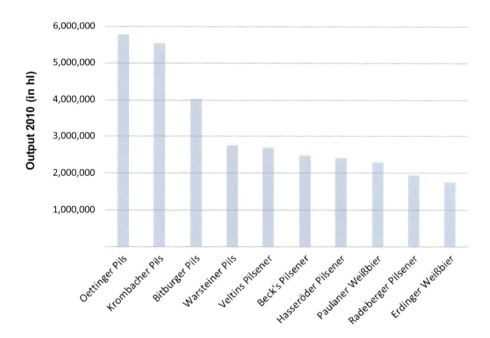

Fig. 2.22 The top 10 beer brands in Germany 2013. (Source: Inside 2014)

of time. Consequently, a positive impact on the perception of continuity through current products alone is scarcely possible. Yet in order to manage the perception of continuity, the brand can avail itself of certain self-presentation strategies, with the aim of influencing the interpretation of the communicated contents by emphasising specific facts ("framing") (cf. Raab et al. 2009). Essentially, the self-presentation is used to create a framework with which all other information can be connected so it is no longer interpreted independently (cf. Rhodewalt 1998). With respect to the perceived continuity, the brand origin lends itself as the basis for this framework. To this end, the brand promise can be framed in the context of the brand history and communicated accordingly (cf. Schallehn 2012). This context offers the consumer an authenticating interpretive framework (cf. Jones et al. 2005).

The positive effect of this approach was verified by a study of the Institut für Automobilwirtschaft (*Institute of the Automotive Industry*). This study showed that consumers who knew that Mercedes had been conducting systematic crash tests as far back as the 1950s rated the quality of the vehicles much higher than consumers who were not familiar with this fact (cf. Diez 2006). Sporting goods manufacturer Adidas also uses this strategy with their so-called "originals stores", which run under the motto "Once innovative, now classic, always authentic" and offer fashion lines that have a direct connection with the brand's past (cf. Hofer 2008). Consumers are able to use the communicative framework offered by these "originals stores" to link the history of the Adidas brand to their own sporting experiences and memories, such as the "Miracle of Bern" in 1954 when the German national team won the Football World Cup in Switzerland. It was an event in which Adi Dassler, the founder of Adidas, played a role as the equipment manager of the German national team.

In this context, **storytelling** has a particularly strong effect on the communication of brand authenticity (cf. Mangold 2008). To this end, emotionally charged stories about a brand are developed and disseminated. The aim of storytelling is to present the brand within the context of a meaningful story which appeals to the consumer and at the same time highlights the brand's assets. If consumers can link the story of a brand with their own experiences, the effect is further enhanced. If a brand story can be directly linked with the consumers' episodic, autobiographical memory, it will go straight into their neural network. The resulting link between the consumer's history and the history of the brand increases the subjective significance of a brand and thus consolidates the brand image. Under the motto "Content 2020", the Coca-Cola brand has placed storytelling at the centre of its communication strategy since 2011. As part of this initiative, Jonathan Mildenhall, Vice President Global Advertising Strategy and Creative Excellence, is asking consumers to describe their experiences with Coca-Cola in the form of stories. The contributions created this way are to be made accessible to the general public via social media.

In addition to storytelling, **mimicry marketing** also offers an opportunity to communicate authenticity, especially for young brands. The term "mimicry" has its origin in biology, where it describes the behaviour of some animal species that mimic other animals. For instance, while the hornet moth looks very similar to a hornet, it is, in contrast to the latter, completely harmless, as it is in fact a butterfly. Translated into marketing, mimicry means to adapt the look and behaviour of one's own brand to a given context (cf. Schallehn 2012). Especially suited for young brands is a cultural context which is relevant to the intended target group. The prevalence of this cultural context within the target group is an important selection criterion. Using the mimicry strategy, young brands can orchestrate and control their own authenticity from the start. For instance, the dairy brand Landliebe, which was launched as recently as the 1980s and which used the imagery of typical country life to establish its brand identity, has successfully utilised this strategy. The typical imagery is not only reflected in the traditionally designed packaging, but also in the brand lettering and name. However, if a brand identity is staged by means of mimicry, without actually having developed, this may also constitute a risk. So, Landliebe was faced with the allegation of using genetically modified feed (cf. Franzenburg 2007), which would have been in direct opposition to the staged cultural context of typical country life. Whilst mimicry can be used to quickly establish an identity, the long-term assurance of brand authenticity always requires permanent consistency between the brand promise and the brand behaviour (cf. Schallehn 2012).

2.10   The Process of Identity-Based Brand Management

The following process of identity-based brand management may be used to plan, coordinate and control all measures that pursue the establishment of strong brands with all relevant target groups. It is intended to facilitate the cross-functional and cross-company integration of all decisions and activities concerning the brand management.

The management process comprises the three sub-processes of strategic and operative brand management and brand controlling as depicted in Fig. 2.23. In this context, these three sub-processes must not be understood as a one-off exercise. Instead, the results of brand controlling provide important feedback for strategic brand management, thus enabling it to optimise strategic planning. This optimised strategy is in turn incorporated into operative management, leading to another controlling process at the end of which another feedback loop starts.

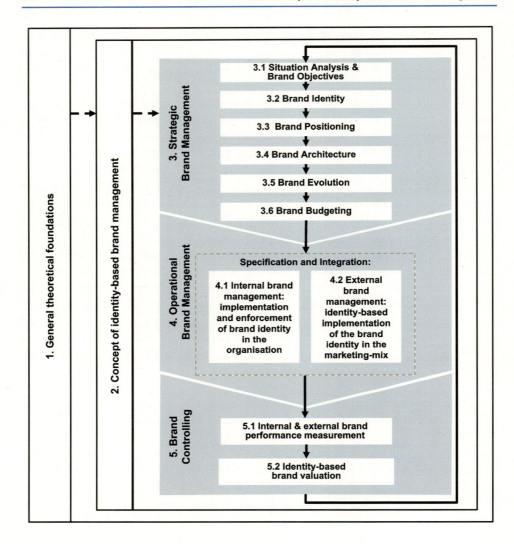

Fig. 2.23 Management process of identity-based brand management

Chapters 3–5 of this book are geared to these sub-processes of identity-based brand management. Thus, Chapter 3 deals in depth with strategic brand management. Chapter 4 is devoted to operative brand management. Finally, Chap. 5 discusses brand controlling.

References

Aaker, D. A. (1991). *Managing brand equity: Capitalizing on the value of a brand name*. New York: Freepress.

Aaker, D. A. (1996). *Building strong brands*. New York: Free Press.

Aaker, D. A. (2010). *Building strong brands*. London: Pocket Books.

Aaker, D. A., & Joachimsthaler, E. (2000). *Brand leadership*. New York: Freepress.

Aaker, D. A., & Keller, K. L. (1990). Consumer Evaluations of Brand Extensions. *Journal of Marketing, 54,* 27–41.

Aaker, J. (1997). Dimensions of brand personality. *Journal of Marketing Research, 34,* 347–356.

Aaker, J., Benet-Martinez, V., & Garolera, J. (2001). Consumptions symbols as carriers of culture: A study of Japanese and Spanish brand personality constructs. *Journal of Personality and Social Psychology, 81*(3), 492–508.

Abels, H. (2009). *Einführung in die Soziologie. Band 2: Die Individuen in der Gesellschaft*. Wiesbaden: Springer VS.

Achterholt, G. (1988). *Corporate Identity. In zehn Arbeitsschritten die eigene Identität finden*. Wiesbaden: Gabler.

Alewell, K. (1974). *Handwörterbuch der Absatzwirtschaft*. Stuttgart: Schäffer-Poeschel.

Amann, S., & Tietz, J. (2012). Endstation Schleckerland. *Der Spiegel, 26*.

Angehrn, O. (1969). *Handelsmarken und Herstellermarken im Wettbewerb*. Stuttgart: Poeschel.

Azoulay, A., & Kapferer, J.-N. (2003). Do brand personality scales really measure brand personality. *Journal of Brand Management, 11*(2), 143–155.

Bartz, T., & Clausen, S. (2015). Deutsche bank, Deutsches drama. *Manager Magazin, 2015*(1), 30.

Batra, R., Lehman, D. R., & Singh, D. (1993). The Brand personality component of brand goodwill: Some antecedents and consequences. In D. A. Aaker & A. L. Biel (Eds.), *Brand equity and advertising: Advertising's role in building strong brands* (pp. 83–96). Hillsdale: Psychology Press.

Becker, C. (2012). *Einfluss der räumlichen Markenherkunft auf das Markenimage: Kausalanalytische Untersuchung am Beispiel Indiens*. Wiesbaden: Springer Gabler.

Berekhoven, L. (1978). Zum Verständnis und Selbstverständnis des Markenwesens. In E. Dichtl (Ed.), *Markenartikel heute—marke, markt und marketing* (pp. 35–48). Wiesbaden: Gabler.

Berger, H., Willner, R.-G., & Einhorn, M. (2007). Kundenorientierte Produktentwicklung am Beispiel des Audi Q7. In S. Albers & A. Herrmann (Eds.), *Handbuch Produktmanagement* (pp. 969–980). Wiesbaden: Gabler.

Berggold, C. (2000). *Unternehmensidentität: Emergenz, Beobachtung und Identitätspolitik*. Berlin: VWF.

Bielefeld, K. W. (2012). *Consumer Neuroscience—Neurowissenschaftliche Grundlagen für den Markenerfolg*. Wiesbaden: Gabler.

Birbaumer, N. (1975). *Physiologische Psychologie*. Berlin: Springer.

Birbaumer, N., & Schmidt, R. F. (2006). *Lernen und Gedächtnis*. In R. F. Schmidt & H.-G. Schaible (Eds.), *Neuro- und Sinnesphysiologie* (pp. 420–423). Heidelberg: Springer.

Birkigt, K., Stadler, M. M., & Funck, H. J. (1998). *Corporate identity: Grundlagen, Funktionen, Fallbeispiele*. Landsberg am Lech: Moderne Industrie.

Blinda, L. (2007). *Markenführungskompetenzen eines identitätsbasierten Markenmanagements: Konzeptualisierung, Operationalisierung und Wirkungen*. Wiesbaden: Dt. Univ.-Verlag.

BMW Group. (2003). *Customer innovation lab*. http://www.bmwgroup.com/d/nav/index.html? http://www.bmwgroup.com/d/0_0_www_bmwgroup_com/forschung_entwicklung/science_club/veroeffentlichte_artikel/2003/news200318.html. Last visit: June 22, 2011.

Bonus, H. (1994). *Das Selbstverständnis moderner Genossenschaften*. Tübingen: Mohr Siebeck.

Bonus, H. (1995). *Europäische Identität aus ökonomischer Sicht.* Volkswirtschaftliche Diskussionsbeiträge des Instituts für Genossenschaftswesen der Westfälischen Wilhelms-Universität Münster, Beitrag Nr. 216. Münster.

Böhm, B. (1989). *Identität und Identifikation. Zur Persistenz physikalischer Gegenstände.* Frankfurt/M: Peter Lang.

Borth, B.-O. (2004). *Beschwerdezufriedenheit und Kundenloyalität im Dienstleistungsbereich - Kausalanalysen unter Berücksichtigung moderierender Effekte.* Wiesbaden: Dt. Univ.-Verlag.

Brandmeyer, K., & Schulz, R. (1989). Die Markenbilanz. *Marketing Journal, 22,* 360–363.

Brands & Values, Markenverband. (2009). *Ethical Brand Monitor.*

Brodie, R. J., Whittome, J., & Brush, G. J. (2009). Investigating the service brand: A customer value perspective. *Journal of Business Research, 62*(3), 345–355.

Brown, S., Kozinets, R. V., & Sherry, J. F., Jr. (2003). Teaching old brands new tricks: Retro branding and the revival of brand meaning. *Journal of Marketing, 67*(3), 19–33.

Bruhn, M., & Eichen, F. (2007). Marken-Konsumenten-Beziehungen: Bestandsaufnahme, kritische Würdigung und Forschungsfragen aus Sicht des Relationship Marketing. In A. Florack & E. Primosch (Eds.), *Psychologie der Markenführung* (pp. 221–256). Munich: Vahlen.

Burmann, C. (2002). *Strategische Flexibilität und Strategiewechsel als Determinanten des Unternehmenswertes (simultaneously habilitation thesis at the University of Münster).* Wiesbaden: Dt. Univ.-Verlag.

Burmann, C., Blinda, L., & Nitschke, A. (2003). *Konzeptionelle Grundlagen des identitätsbasierten Markenmanagements.* Working paper no. 1, chair of innovative brand management (LiM), University of Bremen.

Burmann, C., & Maloney, P. (2004). *Vertikale und horizontale Führung von Marken.* Working paper no. 9, chair of innovative brand management (LiM), University of Bremen.

Burmann, C., Meffert, H., & Feddersen, C. (2007). *Identitätsbasierte Markenführung.* In A. Florack, A. Scarabis, M. E. Primosch (Eds.), *Psychologie der Markenführung* (pp. 3–30). Munich: Vahlen.

Burmann, C., & Schallehn, M. (2010). *Konzeptualisierung von Markenauthentizität.* Working paper no. 44, chair of innovative brand management (LiM), University of Bremen.

Burmann, C., & Stolle, W. (2007). *Markenimage—Konzeptualisierung eines mehrdimensionalen Konstrukts.* Working paper no. 28, chair of innovative brand management (LiM), University of Bremen.

Cattell, R. B. (1944). Interpretation of the twelve primary personality factors. *Character and Personality, 13,* 55–91.

Charmasson, H. (1988). *The name is the game.* Homewood/Illinois: McGraw-Hill Inc.

Charvet, S. R. (2010). *Oh nein, schon wieder ein Kunde.* Paderborn: Junfermann.

Conzen, P. (1990). *E.H. Erikson und die Psychoanalyse. Systematische Gesamtdarstellung seiner theoretischen und klinischen Positionen.* Heidelberg: Asanger.

Damasio, A. R. (2000). *Ich fühle, also bin ich. Die Entschlüsselung des Bewusstseins.* Berlin: List.

Deal, T., Kennedy, A. (1982). Corporate cultures—the rites and rituals of corporate life. Bonn: Reading.

Dehaene, A. T., Changeaux, J.-P., Naccache, L., Sacker, J., Sergent, C. (2006). *Conscious, preconscious, and subliminal processing: a testable taxanomy.* In Trends in Cognitive Sciences, o.w.A., published from Elsevier sciencedirect.com.

Denzau, A. T., North, D. C. (1994). Shared mental models: Ideologies and institutions. *Kyklos 47,* 3–31 (cited from Bonus, H., *Europäische Identität aus ökonomischer Sicht,* Münster).

Dichtl, E. (1978). Grundidee, Entwicklungsepochen und heutige wirtschaftliche Bedeutung des Markenartikels. *Markenartikel Heute,* 17–33.

Dietl, H. (1993). *Institutionen und Zeit.* Tübingen: Mohr Siebeck.

Diez, W. (2006). Grundlegende Potentiale von Tradition im Markenmanagement. In N. O. Herbrand & S. Röhrig (Eds.), *Die Bedeutung der Tradition für die Markenkommunikation* (pp. 181–195). Stuttgart: Edition Neues Fachwissen.

Diller, H. (1992). Euro-key-account-management. *Marketing-ZFP, 1992,* 239–245.

Domizlaff, H. (1939). *Die Gewinnung des öffentlichen Vertrauens. Ein Lehrbuch der Markentechnik.* Hamburg: Hans Dulk.

Domizlaff, H. (1951). *Die Gewinnung des öffentlichen Vertrauens. Ein Lehrbuch der Markentechnik.* Hamburg: Hans Dulk.

Domizlaff, H. (1994). Grundgesetze der natürlichen Markenbildung. In M. Bruhn (Ed.), *Handbuch Markenartikel* (pp. 689–724). Stuttgart: Schäffer-Poeschel.

Dörtelmann, T. (1997). *Marke und Markenführung – Eine institutionstheoretische Analyse.* Bochum.

Dubber, D. (1969). *Die Bedeutung des Markenartikels im Prozess der industriellen Entwicklung.* Berlin: Duncker & Humblot.

Dyson. (2012). www.dyson.de. Last visit: July 25, 2012.

Edelmann, R. (2011). Edelman Trust Barometer. http://www.edelman.com/trust/2011. Last visit: May 04, 2011.

Einwiller, S. (2003). *Vertrauen durch Reputation im elektronischen Handel.* Wiesbaden: Dt. Univ.-Verlag.

Erikson, E. H. (1950). Wachstum und Krisen der gesunden Persönlichkeit. In E. H. Erikson (Ed.), *Identität und Lebenszyklus* (pp. 55–122). Frankfurt a.M.: Suhrkamp.

Erlei, M., Leschke, M., & Sauerland, D. (2007). *Neue Institutionenökonomik.* Stuttgart: Schäffer-Poeschel.

Esch, F.-R. (2003). *Strategie und Technik der Markenführung.* Munich: Vahlen.

Eysenck, H. J., & Eysenck, M. W. (1987). *Persönlichkeit und Individualität—Ein naturwissenschaftliches Paradigma.* Munich: Psychologie-Verlag-Union.

Ferrandi, J.-M., Valette-Florence, P., & Fine-Falcy, S. (2000). Aaker's brand personality scale in a french context—A replication and a preliminary test of its validity. *Developments in Marketing Science, 23,* 7–13.

Findeisen, F. (1925). *Der Marktanteil im Rahmen der Absatzökonomie der Betriebe.*

Fisseni, H.-J. (1998). *Persönlichkeitspsychologie. Auf der Suche nach einer Wissenschaft. Ein Theorieüberblick* (4th ed.). Göttingen: Verlag für Psychologie.

Foscht, T., & Swoboda, B. (2011). *Käuferverhalten: Grundlagen – Perspektiven – Anwendungen.* Wiesbaden: Gabler.

Fournier, S. M. (1998). Consumers and their brands: Developing relationship theory in consumer research. *Journal of Consumer Research, 24*(March), 343–373.

Franzen, O., Trommsdorff, V., & Riedel, V. (1994). Ansätze der Markenbewertung und Markenbilanz. In M. Bruhn (Ed.), *Handbuch Markenartikel* (pp. 1373–1402). Stuttgart: Schäffer-Poeschel.

Franzenburg, A. (2007). Landliebe bald ohne Gen-Milch. http://www.greenpeace.de/themen/gentechnik/landliebe_bald_ohne_gen_milch. Last visit: October 27, 2014.

Freiling, J. (2001). *Resource-based View und ökonomische Theorie – Grundlagen und Positionierung des Ressourcenansatzes.* Wiesbaden: Dt. Univ.-Verlag.

Frey, H. P., & Haußer, K. (1987). Entwicklungslinien sozialwissenschaftlicher Identitätsforschung. In H. P. Frey, K. Haußer (Eds.), *Identität. Entwicklungslinien psychologischer und soziologischer Forschung* (pp. 3–26). Stuttgart: Enke.

Füller, J., Matzler, K., & Hoppe, M. (2008). Brand community members as a source of innovation. *Journal of Product Innovation Management, 25*(6), 608–619.

Füller, J., Mühlbacher, H., & Bartl, M. (2009). Beziehungsmanagement durch virtuelle Kundenein-
bindung in den Innovationsprozess. In H. H. Hinterhuber & K. Matzler (Eds.), *Kundenorientierte Unternehmensführung* (pp. 197–221). Wiesbaden: Gabler.

GfK/Gesellschaft für Konsumforschung. (2012). GfK Consumer Index Total Grocery 01/2012.
http://www.gfkps.com/imperia/md/content/ps_de/consumerindex/ci_01_2012_od.pdf.   Last
visit: July 24, 2012.

Gilmore's, G. H. (1919). Animism, Boston.

Gilmore, J. H., & Pine, B. J., II. (2007). *Authenticity - what consumers really want*. Boston: Harvard Business School Press.

Goffmann, E. (1959). *The presentation of self in everyday life*. New York.

Goldack, G. (1948). *Der Markenartikel für Nahrungsmittel*. Nürnberg.

Goldberg, L. R. (1990). An alternative "Description of personality": The big-five factor structure.
Journal of Personality and Social Psychology, 59(6), 1216–1229.

Goodyear, M. (1994). Marke und Markenpolitik. *Planung und Analyse, 3,* 60–67.

Gugutzer, R. (2002). *Leib, Körper und Identität – Eine phänomenologisch-soziologische Untersuchung der personalen Identität*. Wiesbaden: Westdt. Verlag.

Haedrich, G., Tomczak, T., & Kaetzke, P. (2003). *Strategische Markenführung: Planung und Real-
isierung von Markenstrategien*. Bern: Haupt.

Hansen, P. (1970). Der Markenartikel - Analyse seiner Entwicklung und Stellung im Rahmen des
Markenwesens. *Betriebswirtschaftliche Schriften (BWS)*. Band 36.

Hartmann, V. (1966). *Markentechnik in der Konsumgüterindustrie*. Freiburg: Haufe.

Hatch, M. J., & Schulz, M. (1997). Relation between organizational culture, identity and image.
European Journal of Marketing, 31, 356–365.

Haußer, K. (1995). *Identitätspsychologie*. Berlin: Springer.

Heinen, E. (1987). *Unternehmenskultur*. Munich: Oldenbourg.

Hegner, S. (2012). *Die Relevanz des Vertrauens für das identitätsbasierte Management globaler
Marken - Ein interkultureller Vergleich zwischen Deutschland, Indien und Südafrika*. Wiesbaden: Springer Gabler.

Herbst, U., & Merz, M. A. (2011). The industrial brand personality scale: Building strong busi-
ness-to business brands. *Industrial Marketing Management, 40,* 1072–1081.

Hermann, A., Huber, F., & Braunstein, C. (2005). Gestaltung der Markenpersönlichkeit mittels der
"means-end"-Theorie. In F. R. Esch (Ed.), *Moderne Markenführung* (pp. 177–207). Wiesbaden:
Gabler.

Hofer, J. (2008). Adidas erweitert Netz eigener Läden. Handelsblatt, 6. March 2008, p. 14.

Hogg, M. K., Cox, A. J., & Keeling, K. (2000). The impact of self-monitoring on image congruence and product/brand evaluation. *European Journal of Marketing*, (5/6), 641–666.

Huber, F., Hermann, A., & Weis, M. (2001). Markenloyalität durch Markenpersönlichkeit – Ergebnisse einer empirischen Studie im Automobilsektor. *Marketing ZFP, 7,* 5–15.

Ind, N. (2003). Inside out: How employees build value. *Journal of Brand Management, 10*(6),
393–402.

Inside. (2014). *Inside-Marken-Hitliste 2013*. http://www.inside-getraenke.de/fileadmin/user_
upload/PDF/Hitliste2013.pdf. Last visit: April 22, 2015.

Ipsos Mori. (2009). *The flight to value*. http://www.ipsos-mori.com/Assets/Docs/The-flight-to-
value.pdf. Last visit: October 27, 2014.

Joas, H. (2000). *Praktische Intersubjektivität. Die Entwicklung des Werkes von G.H. Mead*.
Frankfurt/M: Suhrkamp.

Jones, C., Anand, N., & Alvarez, J. L. (2005). Manufactured authenticity and creative voice in cultural industries. *Journal of Management Studies, 42*(5), 893–899.

Kapferer, J. N. (1992). *Die Marke – Kapital des Unternehmens*. Landsberg/Lech: Verlag Moderne
Industrie.

Kapferer, J. N. (2012). *The new strategic brand management – advanced insights & strategic thinking.* London: Kogan Page.

Keller, C. (2015). *Identitätsbasierter Markenschutz – (Re-)Konzeptualisierung im Kontext der neuen Marken- und Produktpiraterie.* Wiesbaden: Springer Gabler.

Keller, K. L. (1993). Conceptualizing, measuring, and managing customer-based based brand equity. *Journal of Marketing, 57,* 1–22.

Keller, K. L. (2013). *Strategic brand management – building, measuring, and managing brand equity.* Essex: Pearson.

Kenning, P. (2003). *Customer trust management. Ein Beitrag zum Vertrauensmanagement im Lebensmitteleinzelhandel.* Wiesbaden: Dt. Univ.-Verlag.

Kenning, P. (2014). *Consumer neuroscience. Ein transdisziplinäres Lehrbuch.* Stuttgart: Kohlhammer.

Keupp, H. (1989). Auf der Suche nach der verlorenen Identität. In H. Keupp & H. Bilden (Eds.), *Verunsicherungen* (pp. 47–69). Göttingen: Verlag für Psychologie Hogrefe.

Keupp, H., Gmür, W., Höfer, R., Mitzscherlich, B., Kraus, W., & Straus, F. (1999). *Identitätskonstruktionen. Das Patchwork der Identitäten in der Spätmoderne.* Reinbek: Rowohlt-Taschenbuch-Verlag.

Koch, C. (2008). *Bewußtsein, ein neurobiologisches Rätsel.* Heidelberg: Spektrum Akademischer Verlag.

Krappmann, L. (1971). *Soziologische Dimensionen der Identität.* Stuttgart: Klett.

Krappmann, L. (1988). *Soziologische Dimensionen der Identität: Strukturelle Bedingungen für die Teilnahme an Interaktionsprozessen.* Stuttgart: Klett.

Kroeber-Riel, W. (1988). *Strategie und Technik der Werbung: Verhaltenswissenschaftliche Ansätze.* Stuttgart: Kohlhammer.

Kroeber-Riel, W., Weinberg, P., & Gröppel-Klein, A. (2013). *Konsumentenverhalten.* Munich: Vahlen.

Leclerc, F., Schmitt, B. H., & Dube, L. (1994). Foreign branding and its effects on product perceptions and attitudes. *Journal of Marketing Research, 32,* 263–270.

Leitherer, E. (1955). Die Entwicklung der modernen Markenformen. *Markenartikel, 17,* 539–566.

Leitherer, E. (2001). Geschichte der Markierung und des Markenwesens. In M. Bruhn (Ed.), *Die Marke – Symbolkraft eines Zeichensystems.* Bern/Stuttgart: Haupt.

Lewin, K. (1963). *Feldtheorien in den Sozialwissenschaften: Ausgewählte theoretische Schriften.* Bern.

Li, F., Zhou, N., Kashyap, R., & Yang, Z. (2008). Brand trust as a second-order factor. *International Journal of Market Research, 50,* 817–839.

Lim, K., & O'Cass, A. (2001). Consumer brand classifications: An assessment of culture-of-origin versus country-of-origin. *Journal of Product and Brand Management, 10*(2), 120–136.

Linxweiler, R. (2001). *BrandScoreCard: Ein neues Instrument erfolgreicher Markenführung.* Groß-Umstadt: Sehnert Verlag.

Luhmann, N. (1973). *Vertrauen – ein Mechanismus der Reduktion sozialer Komplexität,* 2. Aufl., Stuttgart.

Luhmann, N. (1994). *Copierte Existenz und Karriere. Zur Herstellung von Individualität.* In U. Beck & E. Beck-Gernsheim (Eds.), *Riskante Freiheiten. Individualisierung in modernen Gesellschaften.* Frankfurt/M.: Suhrkamp.

Lührmann, T. (2006). *Führung, Interaktion und Identität. Die neuere Identitätstheorie als Beitrag zur Fundierung einer Interaktionstheorie der Führung.* Wiesbaden: Dt. Univ.-Verlag.

Maloney, P. (2007). *Absatzmittlergerichtetes, identitätsbasiertes Markenmanagement: Eine Erweiterung des innengerichteten, identitätsbasierten Markenmanagements unter besonderer Berücksichtigung von Premiummarken.* Wiesbaden: Dt. Univ.-Verlag.

Mangold, M. (2008). *Markenmanagement durch Storytelling, Arbeitspapier zur Schriftenreihe Schwerpunkt Marketing*. München: FGM Verlag.

Marcia, J. E. (1980). Identity in adolescence. In J. Adleson (Ed.), *Handbook of adolescent psychology* (pp. 159–187). New York: Wiley.

Markenverband. (2012). http://www.markenverband.de/presse/archiv2012/pmwissenschaftspreism-v2012foe.

McCrae, R. R., & Costa, P. T. (1997). Personality trait structure as a human universal. *American Psychologist, 52,* 509–516.

Mead, G. H. (1934). *Mind, self, and society*. Chicago: University of Chicago Press.

Mead, G. H. (1973). Geist, Identität und Gesellschaft. Aus der Sicht des Sozialbehaviorismus. Frankfurt/M.: Suhrkamp.

Meffert, H. (1974). Interpretation und Aussagewert des Produktlebenszyklus-Konzeptes. In P. Hammann, W. Kroeber-Riel, C. W. Meyer (Eds.), *Neuere Ansätze der Marketingtheorie*, Festschrift zum 80. Geburtstag von Otto Schutenhaus (pp. 85–134). Berlin.

Meffert, H. (1979). *Der Markenartikel und seine Bedeutung für den Verbraucher. Ergebnisse einer empirischen Untersuchung*. Hamburg: Gruner + Jahr.

Meffert, H. (1988). *Strategische Unternehmensführung und Marketing*. Wiesbaden: Gabler.

Meffert, H. (1994). Entscheidungsorientierter Ansatz der Markenpolitik. In M. Bruhn (Ed.), *Handbuch Markenartikel, Anforderungen an die Markenpolitik aus Sicht von Wissenschaft und Praxis* (pp. 173–197). Stuttgart: Schäffer-Poeschel.

Meffert, H., & Bruhn, M. (1984). *Markenstrategien im Wettbewerb*. Wiesbaden: Gabler.

Meffert, H., & Bruhn, M. (2012). *Dienstleistungsmarketing*. Wiesbaden: Springer Gabler.

Meffert, H., & Burmann, C. (1991). Konsumentenzufriedenheit als Determinante der Marken- und Händlerloyalität. *Marketing Zeitschrift für Forschung und Praxis, 13,* 249–258.

Meffert, H., & Burmann, C. (1996). Identitätsorientierte Markenführung—Grundlagen für das Management von Markenportfolios. In H. Meffert, H. Wagner, K. Backhaus (Eds.), *Arbeitspapier Nr. 100 der Wissenschaftlichen Gesellschaft für Marketing und Unternehmensführung e.V.* Münster.

Meffert, H., Burmann, C., & Kirchgeorg, M. (2015). *Marketing: Grundlagen marktorientierter Unternehmensführung*. Wiesbaden: Springer Gabler.

Mehringer, M., & Vossen, M. (2010). Der Druck kommt von oben. *Lebensmittelzeitung, 34,* 29–30.

Melewar, T. C., & Karaosmanoglu, E. (2005). Seven dimensions of corporate identity. A categorisation from the practitioners' perspectives. *European Journal of Marketing, 40,* 846–869.

Mellerowicz, K. (1963). *Markenartikel. Die ökonomischen Gesetze ihrer Preisbildung und Preisbindung*. München: Beck.

Menninger, J., & Robers, D. (2006). *Markenwert—Paradigmenwechsel im Marketing? Die Bedeutung der Tradition für die Markenkommunikation*. Stuttgart: Edition Neues Fachwissen.

Millward Brown. (2014). *BrandZ Top 100 Most valuable global brands*. http://www.millwardbrown.com/brandz/2014/Top100/Docs/2014_BrandZ_Top100_Chart.pdf. Last visit: 06. October 2014.

Murphy, J. M. (1987). *Brand Strategy*. Cambridge: Director Books.

Müller, W. R. (1987). Identität und Führung. In A. Kieser, G. Reber, & R. Wunderer (Eds.), *Handwörterbuch der Führung*. Stuttgart: Schäffer-Poeschel.

Müller, A. (2012). *Symbole als Instrumente der Markenführung - Eine kommunikations- und wirtschaftswissenschaftliche Analyse unter besonderer Berücksichtigung von Stadtmarken*. Wiesbaden: Springer Gabler.

Neumann, M. M. (2007). *Konsumentenvertrauen. Messungen, Determinanten und Konsequenzen*. Wiesbaden: Deutscher Universitätsverlag.

North, D. C. (1992). *Institutionen, institutioneller Wandel und Wirtschaftsleistung*. Tübingen: Mohr.

Perrey, J. (1998). *Nutzenorientierte Marktsegmentierung. Ein integrativer Ansatz zum Zielgruppenmarketing im Verkehrsdienstleistungsbereich.* Wiesbaden: Gabler.

Plötner, O. (1995). *Das Vertrauen des Kunden. Relevanz, Aufbau und Steuerung auf industriellen Märkten.* Wiesbaden: Gabler.

Plummer, J. T. (1984). How Personality Makes a Difference. *Journal of Advertising Research, 24*(6), 27–31.

Porsche. (2011). URL: http://www.porsche.com/germany/aboutporsche/overview/principleporsche. Last visit: July 25, 2012.

Raab, G., Gernsheimer, O., & Schindler, M. (2009). *Neuromarketing.* Wiesbaden: Gabler.

Recke, T. (2011). *Die Bestimmung der Repositionierungsintensität von Marken, Ein entscheidungsunterstützendes Modell auf Basis von semantischen Netzen.* Wiesbaden: Gabler.

Rhodewalt, F. (1998). Self-presentation and the phenomenal self. The "carryover effect" revisited. In J. M. Darley, J. Cooper, E. E. Jones (Eds.), *Attribution and social interaction: The legacy of Edward E. Jones* (pp. 373–421). Washington: American Psychological Association.

Ripperger, T. (2003). *Ökonomik des Vertrauens - Analyse eines Organisationsprinzips.* Tübingen: Mohr.

Rosenberg, M. (1979). *Conceiving the self.* New York: Basic Books.

Roth, G., & Menzel, R. (1996). Verhaltensbiologische und neuronale Grundlagen des Lernens und des Gedächtnisses. In G. Roth & W. Prinz (Eds.), *Kopf-Arbeit, Gehirnfunktionen und kognitive Leistungen* (pp. 239–277). Heidelberg: Spektrum Akademischer Verlag.

Roth, G. (1997). *Das Gehirn und seine Wirklichkeit.* Frankfurt: Suhrkamp.

Roth, G. (2003). *Fühlen, Denken, Handeln, Wie das Gehirn unser Verhalten steuert.* Frankfurt: Suhrkamp.

Roth, G. (2007). *Persönlichkeit, Entscheidung und Verhalten.* Stuttgart: Klett-Cotta.

Sasserath Munzinger, Gesellschaft für umsetzungsorientierte Markenberatung. (2014). *Markenvertrauen 2013.*

Schade, M. (2012). *Identitätsbasierte Markenführung professioneller Sportvereine – Eine empirische Untersuchung zur Ermittlung verhaltensrelevanter Markennutzen und der Relevanz der Markenpersönlichkeit.* Wiesbaden: Gabler.

Schade, M., Piehler, R., & Burmann, C. (2014). Sport club brand personality scale (SCBPS): A new brand personality scale for sport clubs. *Journal of Brand Management, 21*(7/8), 650–663.

Schaefer, K. (2006). *Branchenimages als Determinanten der Markenprofilierung.* Wiesbaden: Gabler.

Schallehn, M. (2012). *Marken-Authentizität - Konstrukt, Determinanten und Wirkungen aus Sicht der identitätsbasierten Markenführung.* Wiesbaden: Springer Gabler.

Schallehn, M., Burmann, C., & Riley, N. (2014). Brand authenticity: Model development and empirical testing. *Journal of Product & Brand Management, 23*(3), 192–199.

Schein, E. H. (1985). *Organizational culture and leadership.* San Francisco: Jossey-Bass Publishers.

Schein, E. H. (1992). *Organizational Culture and Leadership.* San Francisco: Jossey-Bass Publishers.

Schenk, H.-O. (1994). Handels- und Gattungsmarken. In M. Bruhn (Ed.), *Handelsmarken.* Stuttgart: Schäffer-Poeschel.

Schreyögg, G., Sydow, J.,& Koch, J. (2003). *Organisatorische Pfade – Von der Pfadabhängigkeit zur Pfadkreation.* In G. Schreyögg & J. Sydow (Eds.), *Strategische Prozesse und Pfade* (p. 261). Wiesbaden: Gabler.

Simon, H. (1994). *Management-Lernen und Strategie.* Stuttgart: Schäffer-Poeschel.

Spitzer, M. (2008). *Geist im Netz, Modelle für Lernen, Denken und Handeln.* Heidelberg: Spektrum.

Steiner, S. (2007). *Category Management Zur Konfliktregelung in Hersteller-Handels-Beziehungen*. Wiesbaden: Dt. Univ.-Verlag.

Steffenhagen, H. (2008). *Marketing – Eine Einführung*. Stuttgart: Kohlhammer.

Stichnoth, F. (2013). "State of the Art" der Marktorientierung – Konzeptionalisierung, Determinanten und Wirkungen, Wiesbaden.

Stolle, W. (2013). *Globale Markenführung in heterogenen Märkten - Empirische Analyse eines moderierten Markenimagemodells für die Marken der Automobilindustrie in Brasilien, China, Deutschland, Russland und den USA*. Wiesbaden: Gabler.

Supphellen, M., & Gronhaug, K. (2003). Building foreign brand personalities in Russia: The moderating effect of consumer ethnocentrism. *International Journal of Advertising, 22*(2), 203–226.

Tietz, I. (2009). *Krisenmanagement zur Sicherung und zum Ausbau der Markenstärke – Eine Analyse der Automobilindustrie*. Berlin: Lit Verlag.

Thakor, M. V., & Kohli, C. S. (1996). Brand origin: Conceptualization and review. *The Journal of Consumer Marketing, 13*(3), 27–42.

Thiel, U. (2001). Personen und persönliche Identität in der Philosophie des 17. und 18. Jahrhunderts. In D. Stuma (Ed.), *Person: Philosophiegeschichte – Theoretische Philosophie – Praktische Philosophie* (pp. 79–101). Paderborn: Mentis.

Trommsdorff, V. (1992). Multivariate Imageforschung und strategische Marketingplanung. In A. Hermanns & V. Flegel (Eds.), *Handbuch des Electronic Marketing* (pp. 321–338). München: Beck.

Trommsdorff, V. (2011). *Konsumentenverhalten*. Stuttgart: Kohlhammer.

Usunier, J.-C. (2006). Relevance in business research: the case of country-of-origin research in marketing. *European Management Review, 3,* 60–73.

Vershofen, W. (1940). *Handbuch der Verbrauchsforschung*. Berlin: Heymann.

Vul, E., Harris, C., Winkielmann, P., & Pashler, H. (2009). Puzzlingly high correlations in fMRI studies of emotion, personality, and social cognition. *Perspectives on Psychological Science, 4*(3), 274–290.

Weidenfeld, W. (1983). Die Identität der Deutschen - Fragen, Positionen, Perspektiven. In W. Weidenfeld (Ed.), *Die Identität der Deutschen. Schriftenreihe der Bundeszentrale für politische Bildung Band 200* (pp. 13–49). Bonn: Bundeszentrale für politische Bildung.

Wells, W. D., Andruiuli, F. J., Goi, F. J., & Stuart, S. (1957). An adjective check list for the study of "product personality". *Journal of Applied Psychology, 41*(5), 317–319.

Werthmöller, E. (1994). Räumliche Identität als Aufgabenfeld des Städte- und Regionenmarketing. In H. Meffert (Ed.), *Schriften zu Marketing und Management Band 24*. Frankfurt/M.

Wiedmann, K. P. (1994). Markenpolitik und corporate identity. In M. Bruhn (Ed.), *Handbuch Markenartikel Band 2* (pp. 1033–1054). Stuttgart: Gabler.

Welling, M. (2003). Bausteine einer integrierten image- und identitätsorientierten Markenführung als Beitrag zur Markentheorie. *Schriften zum Marketing 47*. Bochum: Ruhr Universität Bochum.

Welling, M. (2006). *Ökonomik der Marke: Ein Beitrag zum Theoriepluralismus in der Markenforschung*. Wiesbaden: Gabler.

Strategic Brand Management

3

Contents

3.1   Situational Analysis 93
    3.1.1   Objectives of Internal Brand Management............................. 93
    3.1.2   Objectives of External Brand Management 102
3.2   Brand Identity 106
3.3   Brand Positioning.. 106
    3.3.1   Classifying and Demarcating Brand Positioning 106
    3.3.2   The Positioning Process in Identity-Based Brand Management 109
    3.3.3   Brand Repositioning as a Special Form of Positioning 113
    3.3.4   Analysing Brand Positioning by Means of Positioning Models 115
    3.3.5   Choosing Appropriate Positioning Strategies......................... 117
    3.3.6   Multi-sensual Brand Positioning 119
3.4   Brand Architecture.. 122
    3.4.1   Definition 122
    3.4.2   The Process of Brand Architecture Design 124
3.5   Brand Evolution.. 140
    3.5.1   Definition and Overview 140
    3.5.2   Brand Dynamisation.. 140
    3.5.3   Brand Restructuring 149
3.6   Brand Budgeting 162
    3.6.1   The Purpose of Brand Budgeting.................................... 162
    3.6.2   The Budgeting Process.. 163
References... 165

Structure and Learning Objectives of This Chapter

This third chapter will focus on strategic brand management within the framework of identity-based brand management. Accordingly, the following questions will be answered:

© Springer Fachmedien Wiesbaden GmbH 2017
C. Burmann et al., *Identity-Based Brand Management*,
DOI 10.1007/978-3-658-13561-4_3

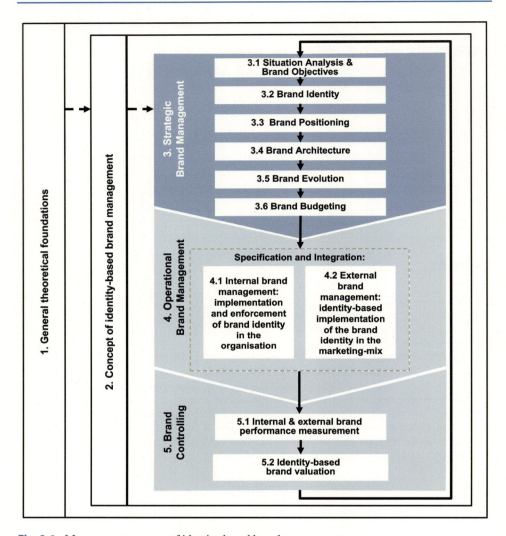

Fig. 3.1 Management process of identity-based brand management

- What are the functions of strategic brand management?
- What should be taken into account at each individual step of the strategic brand management process?
- How do the internal and external perspectives of identity-based brand management come together in strategic brand management?
- What are the current challenges facing strategic brand management in in its various areas?

To this end, all the steps of strategic brand management in the process of identity-based brand management (see Fig. 3.1) will be presented in turn, and connections will be explained and illustrated through examples.

3.1 Situational Analysis

The starting point of the identity-based brand management process is a sound analysis of the current situation of one's own brand(s). The contents and process of a **situation analysis** are based on a marketing situation analysis (for more detailed information, cf. Meffert et al. 2015).

Establishing the needs of the target groups and the actual positioning of one's own brand in comparison to competitors is of great significance within the external situation analysis. Furthermore, all relevant **brand touch points** should be identified, in order to investigate to what extent the individual touch points are contributing to the brand experience. In addition to an external situation analysis, an internal situation analysis should also be conducted.

A situation analysis enables us to deduce **brand objectives**. They should be operational, i.e., precisely formulated with regard to content, scope, time reference and segment relationship so as to be suitable for managing brand employees and to be monitored later on with regard to target attainment (cf. Meffert et al. 2015). An operational brand objective for the US market could be, for instance, a 5% increase (scope) in brand awareness (content) within two years (time reference) in the target group of 30–59 year old men (segment). Brand objectives are identified by a 1–5 year time frame and can be divided into economic and pre-economic (behaviour-related and psychographic) target categories. With regard to **economic brand objectives**, which are closely linked to corporate objectives, the key issues comprise measurable results in key aspects of the brand, such as **brand equity**, **customer equity** or the brand's acquisition costs and customer retention costs. The behaviour-related and psychographic brand objectives have to be defined for the employees (internal brand management) as well as for the actual and potential customers (external brand management).

3.1.1 Objectives of Internal Brand Management

Only a few years ago, the topic of **internal brand management** (or internal branding) played merely a minor role in business practice. Brand management was considered the exclusive responsibility of the marketing department and, above all, communication. Other functional areas did not have anything to do with the brand. This was confirmed by a survey among the top 100 companies in Germany in 2005 (see Fig. 3.2).

Nowadays, internal brand management is perceived differently. Due to the fact that functional benefits are becoming increasingly interchangeable, the employees themselves have become a competitive advantage. The main goal of internal brand management is to ensure that employee behaviour is compliant with the brand in order to fulfil the brand promise at each and every brand touch point (see Fig. 3.3).

The consumer perceives the brand as credible and trustworthy only if the communicated brand promise corresponds to the actual behaviour of all brand employees

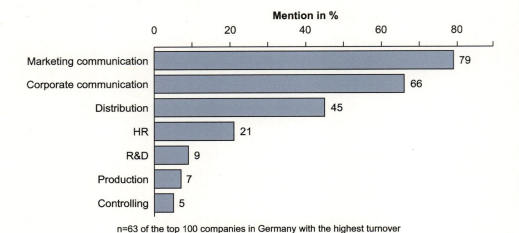

Fig. 3.2 Brand influence on working and functional processes in companies. (Source: Henrion Ludlow Schmidt 2005, p. 18)

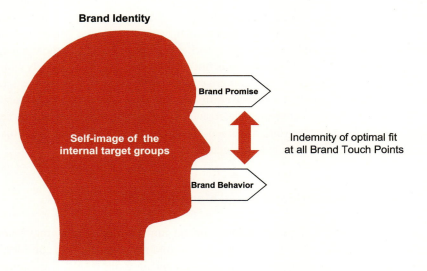

Fig. 3.3 The purpose of internal brand management

(cf. Schallehn et al. 2014). This applies not only to employees within the marketing department, but to every single one of the brand's employees. By way of example, the German insurance company LVM illustrates the diverse brand touch points that can be used to convey the brand promise (see Fig. 3.4).

The importance of a close correlation between the brand promise and the actual brand behaviour with regard to all brand touch points becomes particularly clear in the case of

Fig. 3.4 Selected brand touch points used by LVM insurance

a misfit between brand promise and brand behaviour, usually resulting in lasting damage to the brand's image. A prominent example of this is the corporate mission statement of Deutsche Bahn AG (German Railways), which claims the following employee behaviour (cf. Deutsche Bahn 2012):

– **Customer focus**: "Wir setzen für jeden einzelnen unserer Kunden alles in Bewegung, damit er seine eigenen Ziele einfach, zuverlässig und sicher erreicht." (We do everything we can for every single one of our customers so that they will reach their destination easily, reliably and safely.)

– **Social responsibility**: "Wir engagieren uns aus Überzeugung für eine soziale Gesellschaft […]." (We are firmly committed to a social society […].)

However, numerous incidents have shown that the behaviour of railway employees is often diametrically opposed to these claims. Media attention particularly focused on an incident in which a 16 year old girl who did not have a ticket was expelled from a regional train in the middle of winter, with temperatures below zero, and had to wait for several hours in front of a train station that was already closed (cf. Süddeutsche Zeitung 2010). In addition, an increasing number of cancellations and delays (only 79.1% of all long-distance passenger trains were on time in 2013, and this figure decreased to 73.9% in 2014; cf. Deutsche Bahn 2014), due to insufficient investment in the maintenance of trains, rail networks and train stations, shapes the public image of Deutsche Bahn AG, contradicting the communicated mission statement (cf. Welt 2011).

The significance of internal brand management today is demonstrated not only by this kind of mismanagement, but also by the increasing number of publications (cf. Joachimsthaler 2002; Ind 2003; Burmann and Zeplin 2004; Maloney 2007; Piehler 2011; Vallaster and de Chernatony 2005; Brexendorf and Tomczak 2005; Esch 2008; Krause 2013).

In order to develop a strong brand, it is necessary to establish an institutionalised internal brand management. In the following sections, the behaviour-related (brand citizenship behaviour) and psychographic objectives (brand understanding and brand commitment) of internal brand management will be presented in detail.

3.1.1.1 Brand Citizenship Behaviour

> **Brand citizenship behaviour** (BCB) is defined as all employee behaviours that are consistent with the brand identity and brand promise and in sum strengthen the brand (Piehler et al. 2015, p. 54).

The central role of BCB is due to the fact that the brand identity is ultimately only "brought to life" through the employees' decisions and actions. This is particularly true in service-intensive industries, but not limited to employees who come into direct contact with the customers. Gummesson (1987) coined the term "part-time marketer" for employees outside of the marketing and distribution sectors in order to stress that they, too, have a major indirect influence on the consumers' experiences due to the fact that they are responsible for the quality of the products and services.

BCB includes the dimensions of "**brand compliance**", "**brand endorsement**" and "**brand development**". Accepting the formal rules and directives with regard to the brand (**brand compliance**) is the first and most basic manifestation of brand citizenship behaviour. **Brand endorsement** refers to the employees' conscious engagement on behalf of the brand including, above all, the recommendation of one's "own" brand, as well as defending it against threats. **Brand development** represents the most advanced form of brand citizenship behaviour and may come in two shapes. First, this comprises the proactive actions of the employees that influence the further development of the brand and its identity. But it also includes the employees' efforts to further develop their individual brand-related knowledge, skills, and aptitudes.

"Living the brand" is fundamentally relevant for all the employees of a branded company. However, in practice, it depends on the hierarchical level and the employees' functional area. Burkhardt et al. (2008) showed that employees in management, and particularly in top management, perceive a noticeably stronger influence of the brand identity on their day-to-day behaviour than the average employees do. This indicates how poorly many brands are managed for if a company does not comprehensively involve all employees in the management of the brand, discrepancies between the brand promise and the actual brand behaviour at the different brand touch points will result.

3.1.1.2 Brand Understanding

> **Brand understanding** is defined as "the employees' comprehension of brand-related information" (Piehler et al. 2015, p. 55).

We distinguish between four different facets of brand understanding. The first one is the understanding of the **relevance of the brand** for the survival and long-term success of the company. This is not yet a matter of a particular brand's specific significance, but rather of a fundamental understanding of the connections between a brand, the brand image, the target group's buying behaviour and the success of the company.

Thus, in the brand academy of the BMW Group employees are first of all trained in the significance of brands with regard to consumer behaviour in general. It is only in subsequent training sessions that BMW's own brand identity, i.e. "innovation", "dynamism" and "aesthetic design", as well as the brand promise, "sheer driving pleasure", are conveyed (cf. Burmann and Kranz 2008).

The second facet of brand understanding is the awareness of the **relevance of one's own behaviour** for the brand and its success (cf. Piehler et al. 2015). The role that his/her behaviour plays in the brand's success must be clear to every employee (cf. Kimpakorn and Tocquer 2009). Understanding the relevance of one's own behaviour strongly contributes to motivating an employee to behave in a brand-compliant manner. Empirical evidence has proven that employees of successful brands are very much aware of their contribution to the brand's success (cf. de Chernatony and Cottam 2006).

Detailed knowledge about the brand constitutes the third facet of brand understanding. This includes knowledge regarding the brand objectives, the brand identity and the brand promise. A study by the consultancy firm Gallup shows that fewer than half of

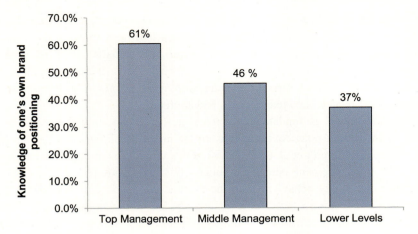

Fig. 3.5 Knowledge about the brand positioning at different hierarchical levels. (Source: McEwen 2007)

all employees are aware of the promise of their company's brand and, moreover, that this knowledge clearly decreases down the hierarchy (see Fig. 3.5). Of course, this deficit on the part of a company's lower level employees is of particular interest since at these levels, the employees are often in direct contact with the customers and are thus directly responsible for fulfilling the brand promise through their behaviour.

Without sufficient knowledge about the brand it is virtually impossible to convey **an understanding of brand-compliant behaviour** to employees. This is the fourth and most relevant facet of brand knowledge. For the company's management, the challenge is to translate the brand promise, which is often abstract, into practical action for the employees. Claims such as "Wir lieben Lebensmittel" (We love food) by the German retailer EDEKA offer much room for interpretation in terms of how this "love" should be reflected in daily employee behaviour. It could manifest in continuously monitoring expiry dates, in a special attention to hygienic conditions or in providing competent advice, e.g. at the fish or cheese counters. If concrete examples of employee behaviour are demonstrated in advertising, then care must be taken to ensure that this behaviour will also be experienced by the customers in reality. In light of this, creating excessively high expectations, such as employees being able to accurately estimate the weight of sausages down to the last gram, is problematic.

3.1.1.3 Brand Commitment

Brand commitment is defined as the "employee's emotional attachment to the brand" (Piehler et al. 2015, p. 55).

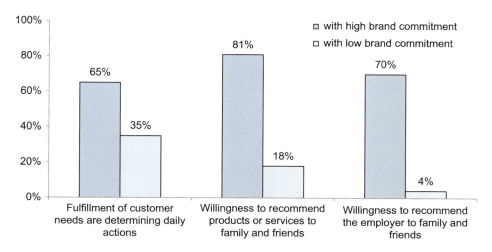

Fig. 3.6 Behavioural differences between employees with high versus low brand commitment. (Source: closely based on Gallup 2009, p. 82)

The high practical relevance of an employee's emotional connection to the brand has been repeatedly proven. It has been shown, for example, that employees who have a high level of brand commitment have half as many days off per year than employees with a low level of brand commitment (cf. Gallup 2009; Nink 2009). Employees also differ significantly with regard to their customer focus and brand recommendation behaviour depending on whether they feel a connection to the brand or not (see Fig. 3.6). This has been proven by a study on 500 employees aged 18 and above conducted in 2009 by the consultancy firm Gallup in Germany (cf. Gallup 2009).

Companies frequently use "job satisfaction" or "satisfaction with the employer" instead of "brand commitment" as the target variable. According to scientific studies, however, BCB is only to a limited extent influenced by satisfaction (cf. Piehler 2011). Therefore, companies should focus on brand commitment as an internal brand management objective.

Brand commitment comprises two dimensions: the employees' identification with the brand and their internalisation of the brand. **Identification** refers to the sense of belonging to the internal group (management and employees of the brand) and the sense of being inextricably linked to the fate of this group. It is based on the interpretation of a brand identity as a group identity. The more pronounced the employees' identification is, the more strongly they consider the organisation's successes as their own (cf. Mael and Ashforth 1992). A strong identification promotes a dedication to the brand due to feeling a personal obligation towards colleagues and superiors. This component is related to "job satisfaction" and "satisfaction with the employer".

The **internalisation** of the brand identity describes the employees' perceived match between their personal identity (self-concept) and the brand identity (cf. Piehler 2011).

Due to the process of internalisation, a complete or partial adoption of the brand identity in the employees' own self-concept occurs. Self-concept is here defined as the entirety of an individual's thoughts and feelings with regard to oneself (cf. Rosenberg 1979), including their characteristics, skills and values (cf. Leonard et al. 1999). Individuals strive for self-congruence and therefore behave in a manner consistent with their self-concept. Internalisation is a result of organisational socialisation, if a strong compatibility between the employee's personal identity and the brand identity has not already existed before the individual joined the organisation. The socialisation process comprises both the informal transmission of brand identity through colleagues and formal communication.

The brand commitment of any individual results from both of these dimensions (see Fig. 3.7). In field "0", there has been no internationalisation: the personal identity is at odds with the brand identity. In this case there can be only a weak brand commitment, even with a high degree of identification. In field "1" (indifference), internalisation is relatively weak. If, at the same time, a high degree of identification with colleagues exists, then some degree of brand commitment will appear in the form of "blind loyalty". However, "blind loyalty" can disappear quickly if the object of identification, e.g. the CEO, the employee's line manager or the team, changes. This could be observed when the charismatic founder of the low-cost airline easyJet, Stelios Haji-Ioannou, resigned from

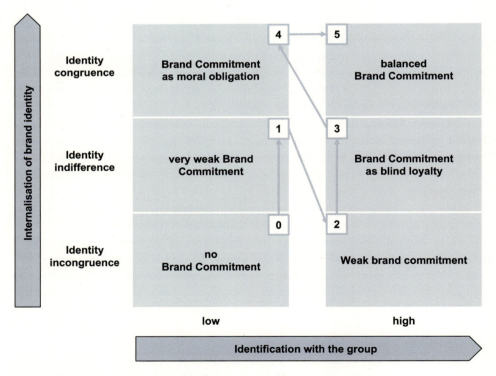

Fig. 3.7 Dimensions of brand commitment. (Source: Zeplin 2006, p. 93)

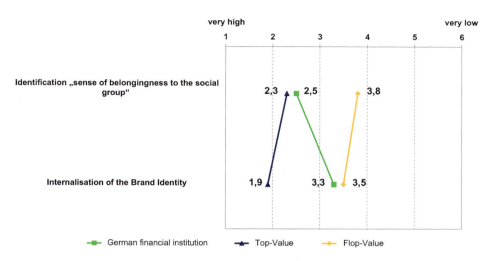

Fig. 3.8 Brand Commitment of Employees at a German Financial Institution

the board of management (cf. Schmidt 2003). With a lower identification, but a strong internalisation, a strong brand commitment emerges in terms of a "moral obligation". The most stable form of brand commitment is "balanced" and based on a strong internalisation of, as well as an intensive identification with, the brand (cf. Zeplin 2006).

In 2014 the University of Bremen conducted an empirical study examining the brand commitment of the employees of a German financial institution. For this purpose, the dimensions of identification and internalisation were tested. In total, 357 employees from all departments and hierarchies were surveyed. The results of this analysis, presented in Fig. 3.8, show a high level of identification and only a low level of internalisation. Consequently, brand commitment is only at a medium level because it is mainly based on identification. In order to increase brand commitment, a clear brand identity needs to be defined and communicated to the employees. This is supported by a comparison with other companies listed in a database available at the Chair of Innovative Brand Management at the University of Bremen, which analyses the identification and internalisation of employees from companies in different industries (insurance, fast-food restaurants, logistics, etc.). In Fig. 3.8, the results of the surveyed German financial institution are compared with the TOP and FLOP values from these other companies. This analysis shows that it is necessary to measure brand commitment by using both dimensions of commitment.

3.1.1.4 Internal Brand Management in Multi-brand Companies

Nowadays companies mostly use multiple brands at the same and/or at different hierarchy levels (cf. Sect. 3.4.2.1). Thus, a marketing employee of the product brand Phaeton, for example, needs to behave in a manner which is compliant with this product brand as well as the corporate brand VW. Some employees may even work in parallel for multiple product brands (e.g. VW Golf, VW Passat and VW Phaeton). In both scenarios, the employee has to handle role conflicts because each of these different brands has its own brand identity. The more the brand identities differ, the higher the risk of role conflicts. Companies with multiple brands face the challenge of how to reduce these role conflicts. Thus, for each employee it has to be defined which brand his/her behaviour (BCB) should be focused on. For example, for logistic staff it would be suitable to focus the BCB on the corporate brand, in order to develop a common infrastructure for the different product brands. In contrast, the BCB of the employees of the design department should be focused on the product brand in order to be able to develop differentiated identities (cf. Jentschke 2015).

Brand commitment is of high relevance for focusing the BCB of the employees on the correct brand. Employees of a multi-brand company are in contact with different brands. Consequently, they show multiple brand commitments, commonly of varying degrees (cf. Jentschke 2015). Generally it can be said that the commitment towards product brands is higher than towards the corporate brand. This phenomenon can be explained by the "nested groups" theory (cf. Lawler 1992). According to this theory, different social groups are nested within each other (e.g., inhabitants of a city and inhabitants of a country). The sense of belonging to subordinate social groups (e.g. inhabitants of a city) is in most cases higher than that of belonging to social groups at a superordinate level (e.g. inhabitants of a country). This finding can be transferred to multi-brand companies. Employees usually show a higher identification with the subordinate product brand in comparison to the corporate brand. Furthermore, product brands are more concrete than corporate brands. Hence, the commitment towards subordinate product brands is mostly higher than that towards corporate brands.

In some cases it may be desirable to focus the BCB of particular employees on a brand that attracts only a low commitment. By using different tools of operational internal brand management such as internal brand communication, brand-oriented HR management or brand-oriented leadership behaviour (see Sect. 4.1), commitment towards the respective brand can be strengthened.

3.1.2 Objectives of External Brand Management

The external as well as internal strength of a brand is measured by means of its relevance for actual behaviour. External **behaviour-related brand objectives** are, for example, the **purchase** or **recommendation** of a brand. A strong brand has a high **acquisition rate** (with regard to new customers) and a high level of **brand loyalty** (repurchase rate).

These behaviour-related brand objectives are determined by **psychographic brand objectives**, e.g. **purchase and recommendation intention**, **customer satisfaction** (cf. Skala-Gast 2012), **brand trust** (cf. Hegner 2012) and **brand awareness. Brand attachment** is a very important psychographic brand objective (cf. Kleine-Kalmer 2016).

The term "attachment" stems from psychology and describes emotional connections between two people (cf. Bowlby 1979). The construct of attachment has been further explored in the context of objects such as places, buildings or brands (cf. Thomson et al. 2005). A high level of attachment to a brand predicts loyalty, even if the expectations towards the brand are sometimes not fulfilled (cf. Kleine-Kalmer 2016). In an empirical study regarding brands from different product categories (including Apple and Nike), Park et al. (2010) showed that the actual purchase and repurchase as well as **share of wallet** (the percentage of expenses a consumer spends on a certain brand in a specific product category) is strongly influenced by brand attachment.

Due to the high level of behavioural relevance and prediction quality, brand attachment is the main psychographic external brand objective in the identity-based brand management approach. While there are different conceptualisation models and definitions of brand attachment (cf. Kleine-Kalmer 2016), the concept and definition by Park et al. (2010) is the most prevalent. These authors define **brand attachment** as follows:

> "The strength of the bond connecting the brand with the self. [...] Two critical factors reflect the conceptual properties of brand attachment: brand–self connection and brand prominence" (Park et al. 2010, p. 2).

Brand-self connection describes the consumer's perception regarding the meaning of a brand in relation to the self-concept. Park et al. (2010) distinguish two kinds of brand–self connections: one rests upon the self-identity and the other has an instrumental basis. Connections based on the self-identity arise because the brand stands for what the consumer believes in. For example, if individuals wear clothes from a brand that produces outdoor clothing, they want to express their sportiness as well as their natural and adventurous lifestyle (cf. Kleine-Kalmer 2016). An instrumental basis is given when the connection to the brand helps the consumer to pursue personal targets. Referring to the example of an outdoor clothing brand, the waterproof rain jacket and extra durable hiking shoes may support the individual while climbing a difficult mountain and thus fulfilling a personal dream.

The second dimension of brand attachment is **brand prominence**. Brand prominence indicates how easily the brand name is recalled by the consumer. While the brand–self connection is the central element of the construct, brand prominence helps to specify how strong the connection really is (cf. Park et al. 2010). If the brand is not easily accessible in the consumer's memory, the brand-self connection may be strong, but the overall attachment is weak.

The impact of brand attachment on the willingness to accept **location-based advertising** (LBA) was analysed in an empirical study conducted in Germany in 2014. LBA is targeted advertising by an identified sponsor (e.g., a restaurant or a supermarket) that is specific to the location of the consumer and that is delivered to a mobile device. The

Brands using LBA as communication instrument	Coca Cola	Deutsche Telekom	EDEKA	McDonald's	Media Markt	Nestlé	REWE	Starbucks
sample size	156	155	157	156	154	157	156	159
path coefficient Brand Attachment on intention to use LBA	0.475	0.518	0.376	0.381	0.365	0.427	0.403	0.575
t-value	6.264	6.195	4.105	5.37	4.574	7.266	5.951	9.018

LBA providers	Bild.de	Couplies	Facebook	Gettings	Google	O2		
sample size	216	189	222	185	225	213		
path coefficient Brand Attachment on intention to use LBA	0.351	0.163	0.336	0.407	0.245	0.349		
t-value	4.908	1.983	4.405	4.987	3.689	4.429		

Fig. 3.9 Empirical results concerning the willingness to accept location-based advertising. (Source: Warwitz 2016)

increasing diffusion rate of GPS-enabled smart phones and the possibility to collect and handle a huge amount of data in real time (so called big data), now allow marketing managers to use LBA (cf. Warwitz 2016). Figure 3.9 presents sample sizes, path coefficients and t-values of the empirical study mentioned above. In this study six LBA providers and eight brands using LBA as a communication tool were analysed (cf. Warwitz 2016).

The results show that the relation between brand attachment and the willingness to accept LBA is positive and highly significant. Consequently, it can be stated that the willingness to accept LBA depends on the consumer's attachment to the LBA provider and to the brand using LBA as a communication tool.

The most relevant **objectives** of internal and external brand management are summarised in Fig. 3.10. Brand understanding and brand commitment determine brand citizenship behaviour. Brand attachment influences behaviour-related external brand management objectives (e.g., purchase and repurchase behaviour). The behaviour of internal and external target groups towards the brand determines the economic brand objectives as the final evaluation of the success of a brand.

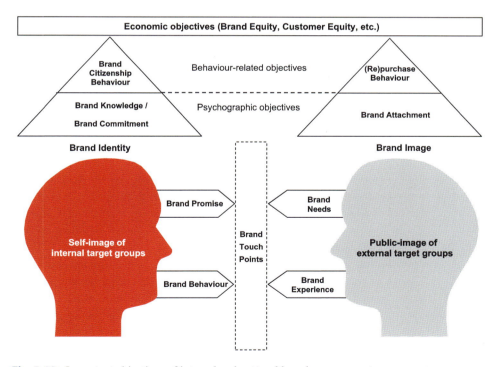

Fig. 3.10 Important objectives of internal and external brand management

3.2   Brand Identity

Developing a brand identity for all individual brands is of primary importance within
strategic brand management since the brand identity forms the substance of every brand.
The development of a target brand identity is based on a situation analysis as well as the
defined brand objectives and forms the basis for further process steps. For detailed information on brand identity see Sect. 2.6.

3.3   Brand Positioning

3.3.1   Classifying and Demarcating Brand Positioning

Today, the task of brand positioning (cf. Fig. 3.11) is made more difficult by the high,
and ever increasing, interchangeability of brands (cf. Sect. 1.1). This growing approximation of brand offerings is described in scholarly debate by the **homogenisation
hypothesis**. This refers to the fact that brands are increasingly perceived as interchangeable with regard to their functional benefits (cf. Hansen et al. 2001; Bruhn 2005; Bohmann 2011). Homogenisation is, in essence, a consequence of maturing markets. As the
markets are aging, the number of brands competing with each other increases, technological know-how is strongly diffused, and the same distribution channels will be used
by the brands (for more information on market life cycles cf. Meffert et al. 2015).

Product reviews by the British website www.which.co.uk or the German consumer
organisation Stiftung Warentest provide exemplary proof of this functional quality
alignment. An analysis of the 483 tests conducted by Stiftung Warentest of over 1300
products between 2007 and 2012 revealed that around 45% were rated as "good".
Thus, a successful differentiation on the basis of functional characteristics is becoming
extremely difficult.

The continuing homogenisation is, however, not only caused by the technological
approximation of products as part of the maturing markets; this development is also reinforced by means of **similar advertising messages** in many saturated markets (cf. Calloway
2003). In view of this, professional positioning has become the most important success
factor in brand management today.

The term **positioning** was defined by Ries and Trout in 1972: "Positioning starts with
a product. A piece of merchandise, a service, an institution, or even a person. Perhaps
yourself. But positioning is not what you do to a product. Positioning is what you do to
the mind of the prospect. That is, you position the product in the mind of the prospect"
(Ries and Trout 2001, p. 2). This general understanding of positioning has subsequently
been transferred and adapted to the brand context (cf. Trommsdorff 1975). Nowadays,
both in theory and in practice, positioning has assumed a vital importance for the success of a brand (cf. Blankson and Kalafatis 2007; Blankson et al. 2008), a notion which
Aaker and Shansby (1982) already stressed at the beginning of the 1980s (cf. Aaker and

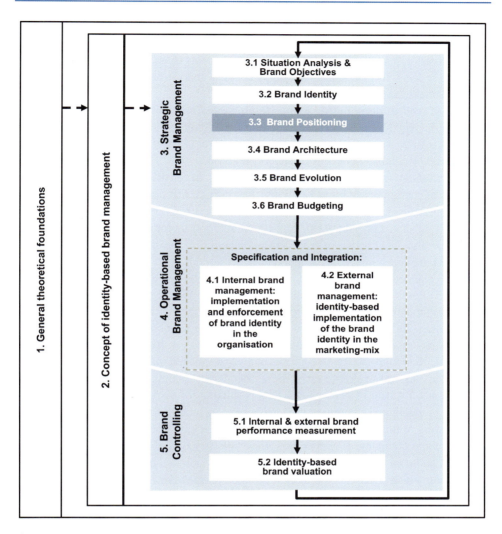

Fig. 3.11   Brand positioning in the process of identity-based brand management

Shansby 1982). Likewise, Keller et al. (2008) underlined the high relevance of brand positioning, placing it firmly in the centre of all marketing strategies (cf. Keller et al. 2008). At the same time, in practice it often turns out that **problems within brand management can be traced back to deficits in brand positioning**. Frequently, companies are not able to clearly define the positioning of their brand(s) and the brand promise, which itself is central to positioning.

The aim of positioning is to develop, among the consumers, unique images and associations with the brand which are relevant to buying behaviour (in B2C and B2B markets). The most important parameters for the success of positioning are the image of the brand and the consumers' brand attachment (cf. Sect. 3.1.2).

Despite brand positioning having a recognised high relevance for brand management, there is no generally valid definition of this term. Therefore, Feddersen (2010) systematised the predominant definitions identifying three forms of understanding the term positioning: a reduced form of understanding, a classical market-oriented understanding, and a holistic understanding.

The **reduced understanding of positioning** goes back to old publications and was mainly propagated by practitioners (cf. Alpert and Gatty 1969; Trout 1969). Here, positioning is restricted to a **means of communication** for altering the way in which a brand is perceived by a consumer (cf. Ries and Trout 2001).

The **classical market-oriented understanding of positioning** emerges from the construct of market orientation. Kohli and Jaworski (1990) define market orientation as the "organization-wide generation, dissemination, and responsiveness to market intelligence" (Kohli and Jaworski 1990, p. 2 f.). In addition to consumer orientation, market orientation also includes an orientation to competition. The market-based view (MBV) constitutes the conceptual basis of market orientation (cf. Sect. 1.2.1).

In the classical market-oriented view, the term positioning can be traced back to Michael E. Porter, who defines positioning as follows: "Strategic positioning attempts to achieve sustainable competitive advantage by preserving what is distinctive about a company" (Porter 2006, p. 6). This view is often found in textbooks on strategic marketing and is characterised by a focus on the image of a brand (cf. Ries and Trout 2001; Kotler et al. 2007; Romaniuk 2001). In contrast to this instrumental understanding of brand positioning, the classical market-oriented view extends positioning to include every object in the consumer's sphere of perception which is suitable for marketing (a product, a brand, services, an individual, a company etc.) and also to include all four marketing instruments.

According to this understanding, positioning is the basis for the overall market development of the company. However, this view fails to explicitly consider the company's resources and competences. So, in a next step, this leads to a **holistic understanding of positioning** which combines the market-oriented perspective and the resource and competence-oriented perspective (cf. Tomczak and Roosdorp 1996; Feddersen 2010).

In modern research on positioning, it is understood that only a **synthesis of the market-oriented and the resource and competence-oriented perspectives** enables competitive advantages to be established and guaranteed in the long run. On the other hand, unique resources and competences can only lead to competitive advantages if they are implemented in appropriate brand performances (cf. Kuß et al. 2009). Put into the context of identity-based brand management, this leads to the following definition:

> "**Brand positioning** is the planning, implementation, control, and continued development of a position which conforms to the brand identity within the relevant target groups' perception, is geared to the consumers' wishes, is differentiated from its competitors, and can be achieved by the company's own resources and competences" (Feddersen 2010, p. 29).

3.3.2 The Positioning Process in Identity-Based Brand Management

In identity-based brand management the market-based side of positioning is represented by the brand image and the consumer needs with respect to the brand (outside-in-perspective). The consumers' **brand needs** are characterised by their wishes, ideals and previous experience with regard to the brand and its competitors. In addition to analysing consumer preference structures, analysing the resources and competences (inside-out-perspective) is an equally important element of identity-based positioning, for without it, the **brand promise** cannot be fulfilled. The brand promise is created by consolidating the six components of identity into functional and/or non-functional customer benefits.

With regard to the target group, the brand promise must be **understandable, relevant to buying behaviour, credible** and **superior to** competitor brands in order to effect a brand purchase. In this context, the various identity components have a varying influence on the functional and non-functional brand benefits. Brand performance primarily determines the functional elements of the brand promise, whereas brand personality, brand value and brand vision determine the non-functional components. Brand origin and brand competences, on the other hand, shape both the functional and non-functional elements of the brand promise.

As a part of the positioning process, a decision has to be made whether a brand should be positioned either by emphasising several benefits or by highlighting a single core benefit (cf. Ries and Trout 2001; Meffert et al. 2015). Likewise, as brand positioning develops, a balance between **a reactive and an active positioning** must be ensured. A reactive positioning is geared primarily to the articulated wishes of the consumers. An active positioning, on the other hand, aims at addressing latent needs and aspires to fulfill desires which are hitherto unknown to the consumer and yet are pertinent to their purchasing decision (cf. Burmann et al. 2007).

The **credibility of a brand promise** greatly influences the success of positioning. Credibility is based on the brand's authenticity and therefore depends on the consistency, continuity, and individuality of the brand (cf. Sect. 2.9).

In order to ensure the sustained success of brand positioning, the brand promise must be fulfilled through actual **brand behaviour**. In practice, there often are great discrepancies leading to the failure of the target brand positioning. In many cases, this is due to the fact that brand management is limited to logo design and classic advertising, while the internal aspects of brand management are neglected. It is the task of internal brand management to ensure that the employees' behaviour honours the brand promise at each and every one of the consumer's brand touch points. **Brand experience** is a reflection of brand behaviour. It is the result of the multi-sensual perception and processing of all the signals which are conveyed by the brand to the consumer (see Fig. 3.12).

Following the amalgamation of the six components of brand identity to a target identity and its consolidation and translation into a brand promise, this brand promise must be adequately communicated to the target groups. This is achieved not only via the

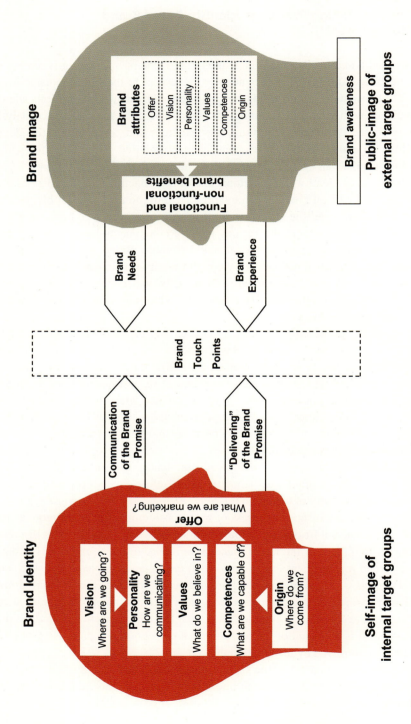

Fig. 3.12 Positioning within the context of identity-based brand management

known instruments of communication policy, but it also **comprises the entire marketing mix as well as the employees' brand behaviour at all brand touch points** (see Fig. 3.13).

The four steps of **development, consolidation, translation** into the language of the target group, and **communication** represent the management process of brand positioning (see Fig. 3.14). The result of this process is a concrete brand positioning in the mind of the consumer, and thus a concrete brand image.

In addition to these activities aimed at the consumer's perception, **internal brand management** must internally generate the conditions for the implementation of the brand promise. Thus, the positive differentiation of the brand with respect to its competitors also is important for the employees' identification with the brand and their motivation. Likewise, the way in which the organisational structures and processes are arranged

Fig. 3.13 Selected brand touch points of the brand "Lufthansa"

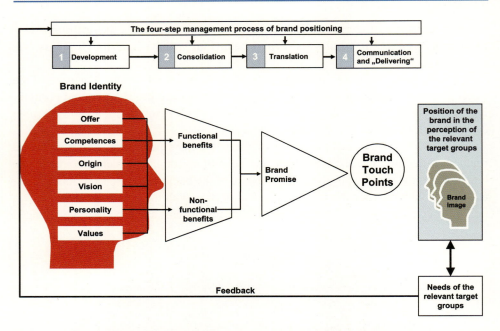

Fig. 3.14 The management process of identity-based brand positioning. (Source: based on Recke 2011, p. 45)

is of considerable importance for the brand identity and the brand promise. The organisational structures and processes should support brand-conformant employee behaviour. If the brand promise, for example, includes customer enquiries being promptly processed, then the organisational structures and processes must enable this promise to be fulfilled and must therefore be aimed at ensuring a short reaction time.

A typical case in point is the German internet provider "1&1". Since 2009, 1&1 has promised outstanding customer service. To reinforce this promise 1&1 promoted the then head of customer satisfaction, Marcell D'Avis, who appeared in numerous TV spots, obtained his own blog, and consequently became, for the customers, the face of 1&1 customer service. But 1&1 did not carry out the customer service in the promised manner; the first blog entry by Marcell D'Avis on December 25, 2009 already generated 751, for the most part critical, comments, which went unanswered. It became clearer and clearer to the customers that it had been an empty promise since even e-mails sent to Marcell D'Avis directly just ended up in the e-mails intended for customer service and remained unanswered. As a consequence, the company and Marcell D'Avis were confronted with the customers' hostility, which was expressed in synchronised YouTube clips and even by publishing Marcell D'Avis' obituary. This induced 1&1 to remove Marcell D'Avis from his position as head of customer satisfaction and from the company's corporate communication (cf. König 2010).

Another example where the structure does not support the brand promise are the low-priced long-haul flights that "Lufthansa" is offering since 2015 under the brand

Fig. 3.15   Aircraft designs of Germanwings and Eurowings in comparison

"Eurowings". In the communication the affiliation of Eurowings is pointed out, and is also underlined by the fact that Eurowings uses the same shade of colour as "Germanwings", another brand that belongs to the Lufthansa Group (see Fig. 3.15). At the same time, the entire operations of Eurowings is outsourced to the airline SunExpress. SunExpress also operates aircrafts of the Turkish low-cost airline "Anadolu Jet" and part of the fleet of "Turkish Airlines". The Eurowings flights are sometimes even carried out with aircraft of the Brazilian Airline "Gol" (cf. Röben 2015), and maintenance and repair as well as the training of the cabin crews are done by third parties. Thus, contrary to the impression given by the communication, low-priced long-haul flights for the brand Eurowings have no connection with Lufthansa at all.

3.3.3   Brand Repositioning as a Special Form of Positioning

Once a brand positioning has been achieved, it can usually not just be statically maintained over time. External market conditions, e.g. new competitors or changes in consumer preferences, can make modifications of brand positioning necessary. In our definition of brand positioning above, the phrase "continued development" indicates that brand positioning has a dynamic component, which results in a process of constant revision and adaptation. **Brand repositioning** describes this process of adaptation (cf. Feddersen 2010). Positioning can thus be divided into two different phases. The first phase comprises the **establishing of a position**. The second, dynamic phase is identified as maintaining or changing this position (cf. Roosdorp 1998). The **repositioning** of a brand is part of this second phase of positioning.

The term repositioning, much like the term positioning, does not have a standard definition in the literature. First of all, repositioning has to be differentiated from the terms "variation" and "relaunch". A product variation may be defined as "an alteration in the bundle of features through which a product which is already on offer has been determined thus far" (cf. Brockhoff 1999). Nommensen differentiates variation from repositioning, pointing out that variations solely refer to objective characteristics, whilst repositioning involves subjective judgments on the part of the consumer (cf. Nommensen 1990).

A further related term is "**brand re-launch**". Meffert et al. (2015) define the term re-launch as a form of product variation: "a product modification, also termed a product re-launch, refers to the comprehensive alteration of one or several properties of a product which has already been introduced on the market" (Meffert et al. 2015, p. 447). The authors differentiate the term from product maintenance in which only small changes are carried out in order to continually improve the products introduced on the market. Repositioning refers to the subjective perceptions of the consumer, whereas the terms variation, re-launch und maintenance refer to the design of objective technical attributes from the perspective of the manufacturer. Thus, the terms re-launch, variation, and maintenance are associated with the operative rather than strategic level of brand management.

A further term associated with brand positioning is **re-branding**. Re-branding is often used synonymously with the term re-naming and focuses on changing the brand name and other formal brand characteristics (cf. Muzellec and Lambkin 2006). Prominent recent examples include Andersen Consulting and Philip Morris Corp. which have renamed themselves Accenture and Altria, respectively. Muzellec and Lambkin (2006) define re-branding as "[…] the creation of a new name, term, symbol, design or combination of them for an established brand with the intention of developing a differentiated (new) position in the mind of stakeholders and competitors" (Muzellec and Lambkin 2006, p. 803). In view of this, brand repositioning within identity-based brand management is defined as follows:

> **Brand repositioning** describes the addition, elimination, or modification of functional and/or non-functional benefit features of a brand which has already been introduced on the market, with the intention of altering the benefit associations of relevant target groups (cf. Feddersen 2010, p. 33).

3.3.4   Analysing Brand Positioning by Means of Positioning Models

An analysis of the current situation in the relevant market forms the basis of brand positioning and brand repositioning. In this context, both the consumer preferences and the
position of competitors should be taken into account. Positioning models reflect the positions of brands from the consumer's perspective and can be understood as a simplified
representation of the memory structures on the part of the consumers (cf. Esch 2008).
Based on multivariate methods of analysis, so-called cognitive spaces are created and
depicted on the basis of their intrinsic distances. It is important to register and analyse
all relevant framework conditions, not only the known consumer needs, but also latent
needs. This enables future positioning opportunities to be identified early on (cf. Mühlbacher et al. 1996; Tomczak and Roosdorp 1996). Since only two- or three-dimensional
representations of the determined spaces are possible, it is necessary to restrict the positioning model to the most important attributes. The dimensions of such a positioning
model represent the relevant functional and/or symbolic benefit dimensions from the
consumer's point of view. Both the actual position of a brand and its target position after
repositioning are depicted in such a model, the distance between the two points indicating the repositioning intensity (see Fig. 3.16).

Recke (2011) defines repositioning intensity as follows:

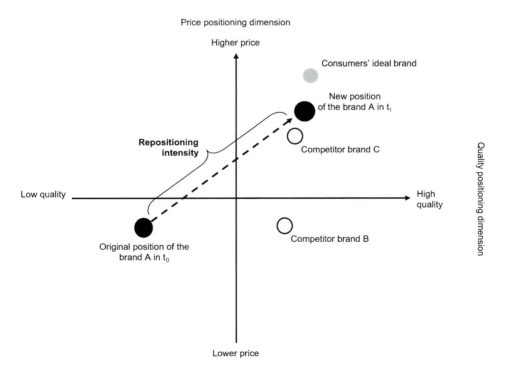

Fig. 3.16 Repositioning intensity as derived from a positioning model. (Source: Burmann and Recke
2009)

"**Repositioning intensity** indicates the extent to which relevant consumers perceive the brand position to have changed with regard to its functional and/or nonfunctional benefit dimensions when comparing two distinct points in time." (Recke 2011, p. 62)

A variety of different methods are available for analysing brand positioning. These include multidimensional scaling (MDS), conjoint analysis, factor analysis, and discriminant analysis (cf. Backhaus et al. 2016).

3.3.4.1 Brand Positioning Based on Multidimensional Scaling (MDS)

Multidimensional scaling represents one of the most important statistical methods for analysing brand positioning. The aim of MDS is to present brands in a space with as few dimensions as possible, in which the relative position of the brands reflects their similarity or dissimilarity. Besides, preference data can also be analysed (cf. Backhaus et al. 2016), leading to ideal brands which are presented in the analysis as ideal vectors or ideal points (cf. Feddersen 2010).

In the analysis of brand positioning, MDS has different advantages and disadvantages. The main advantages are that the dimensions of the perceptual spaces are based on the judgements and preferences of the consumer with respect to a brand, and that the consumers' actual perception of a brand and the "ideal brand" can be presented simultaneously and in one space. The lower the distance between the actual position of the brand and the ideal point is, the greater is the probability of brand choice.

A considerable disadvantage of MDS is the fact that the dimensions of the perceptual spaces do not take into account their relevance with regard to purchasing behaviour. Thus, a brand can indeed lie close to the consumers' ideal point on one dimension, but may still be ignored by the consumers since the dimension in question is irrelevant to buying behaviour. Furthermore, at least 7–8 brands have to be included in the analysis in order to be able to span perceptual spaces of two to three dimensions. This can lead to problems if the evoked set (the brands which are on offer) includes fewer brands. It should also be taken into account that all the subjectively relevant brands have to be included since it leads to a distortion of the results if one of them is lacking.

On the whole, MDS is very well suited to the analysis of established markets with a large number of brands, for which the attributes relevant for buying behaviour are known. However, the usefulness of MDS for determining concrete measures is limited because it does not link the perceptual dimensions with specific performance characteristics (cf. Backhaus et al. 2016; Kullmann 2006)

3.3.4.2 Brand Positioning on the Basis of Conjoint Analysis

Conjoint analysis has been used for brand positioning since the 1980s. Its primary objective is to determine the relevance different benefit dimensions have for the overall

Table 3.1 Evaluation of the two most important methods for positioning analysis

Method	Approach	Advantages	Disadvantages	Most common uses
Multidimensional scaling	Based on distances; the more similar the investigated brands are, the closer they will be within the perceptual space	The resulting dimensions are based on the consumers' assessments or preferences	The relevance of the dimensions is not taken into account	Depicting perceptual spaces in established markets
		The results do not depend on the attributes in question	At least 7–8 brands are required to open up a perceptual space	As a starting point for market segmentation
		The consumers' ideal point(s) and the brands can be presented in one perceptual space	No possibility of presenting USPs	Presenting the likelihood of brand choice
Conjoint analysis	Generates detailed benefit values and direct trade-offs	All parameters can be directly manipulated	Poor representation of non-functional brand dimensions	Brand design
	Allows an individual analysis of each consumer as well as an aggregated analysis based on segments	Links prices and non-price brand attributes		Conception of new products
	Allows to determine the relative importance of individual benefit dimensions	High degree of flexibility		Market segmentation
				Product line design
				Simulation models
				Optimisation model

Based on Feddersen (2010, p. 120)

benefit of a brand and, thus, the buying decision. Whilst in the case of MDS real brands are assessed, conjoint analysis mostly focusses on the evaluation of fictitious brands, i.e. of possible combinations of benefits. The analysis assumes an accumulation of the overall benefit and is mainly applied in the positioning of new products (cf. Feddersen 2010). However, it is also suited to identifying and monitoring consumer preferences regarding brand characteristics and can thus be used for brand controlling (cf. Fischer 2001). Based on conjoint methodology, it is also possible to perform consumer segmentations, to make pricing decisions, and to determine the relevance of individual positioning dimensions.

The main advantage of conjoint analysis is the possibility of flexibly processing the results since the variables can be easily manipulated by the management, and the analysis links prices with non-price features. The disadvantages include the fact that attributes have to be determined in advance, and that it is difficult to integrate symbolic brand benefits. Yet exactly these benefits are of considerable importance for brand choice today. Also, the number of attributes that can be examined is restricted. In the case of older methods, a maximum of 7 variables, each with 3 attributes, can be dealt with; in the case of newer approaches, 30 attributes can be used (cf. Feddersen 2010).

In short, conjoint analysis is very well suited to measuring product and brand preferences. Consequently, it constitutes the most frequently employed method for preference measurements.

Table 3.1 summarises and evaluates these two different methods of positioning analysis:

3.3.5   Choosing Appropriate Positioning Strategies

After ascertaining the actual positioning, the target positioning should be determined. This depends significantly on the chosen positioning strategy. Promising positioning strategies can be identified by determining a brand's ideal position and the existing offers of the competitors. In principle, two basic options are available. In the case of a **points-of-difference** (PoD) strategy, attempts are made to position the brand as far away as possible from its competitors. In the case of a **points-of-parity** (PoP) strategy, the aim is to imitate a competitor (cf. Keller 2003). If the competitor is imitated in all benefit dimensions, it becomes a **me-too strategy**. Both strategies are often combined. Competitors are imitated with regard to some brand benefit components, whereas with others, the aim is to differentiate them. Imitating competitors in the case of individual benefit components can, for example, serve to eliminate the competitor's points of difference. Furthermore, a brand can be positioned by highlighting several benefit components or simply the core benefit. A particular type of positioning is based on a distinctive benefit offer, the **unique selling proposition (USP)** (cf. Reeves 1960; Ries and Trout 2001, p. 19 f.). In this case, emphasis is placed exclusively on a brand's unique benefits.

3.3.6 Multi-sensual Brand Positioning

By and large, most markets are nowadays saturated. In these markets with relatively homogenous products, functional features are often unsuitable for differentiation. Instead, an emotional orientation is regarded as key to success in these markets (cf. Freundt 2006). An emotionally oriented positioning also benefits from the trend towards experience-oriented consumption. Additional factors which reinforce the importance of emotional positioning include a collective shift in values and the information overload of the consumer. This change in values has been evident in society since the middle of the 20th century and is reflected in a shift from a culture of obligation to a culture of self-realisation, in which aims such as hedonism and individuality are more and more prominent. This is reinforced by an increase in the consumers' leisure time. Along with this change in values, safeguarding one's existence as the primary goal of consumption has become less important. Consumption nowadays increasingly serves to express one's personal identity and lifestyle (cf. Springer 2008; Müller 2012). The demand for individual experiences has significantly increased. Due to today's information overload it is much harder to convey brand messages through classic means of communication (cf. Burmann et al. 2010). **Information overload** describes the proportion of information which is individually apprehended out of all the information available to that individual. As a result, the relevance of visual communication increases because it avoids the problem of cognitively overloading the consumer and it is particularly suitable for conveying emotional experiences (cf. Kroeber-Riel et al. 2013).

Neurobiological findings also confirm the importance of emotions and feelings. The emotions linked to a brand are stored in the mind of the consumer together with the brand attributes. When a consumer subsequently comes into contact with the brand again, not only the brand attributes but also the emotions and feelings which are associated with it will be recalled. In this way, the consumer can assess the subjective "reward value" of a brand prior to purchasing it.

On this occasion, the rewards system is activated in the brain. The areas of the brain associated with this rewards system are directly connected to the sense organs. A brand's sensory stimuli are able to trigger a cumulative effect. Thus, a multi-sensual brand experience can be more easily linked to emotions, meaning that just thinking about a brand will activate the rewards system and this "colours" the perception and the corresponding expectations of the sense organs, both positively and negatively. This is increasingly relevant to brand management since the customers often evaluate the brands not via cognitive assessment, but rather via the feelings associated with the brand. The term 'feelings' covers emotions (physiological states of excitement) which can be experienced and expressed verbally. Since no great quantities of new information have to be processed, information overload canthus be avoided (cf. Bielefeld 2012). Therefore, emotions and feelings, by means of their significance for non-functional brand benefits, have a considerable influence on the success of brand positioning.

An important success factor in multi-sensual brand positioning is the authenticity of the brand promise (cf. Sect. 2.9). Since the brand promise stems from the consolidation of the six components of identity, the communicated positioning has to be reconciled with the consumers' perception of the brand identity. Only if this is the case is the brand positioning perceived as **authentic**. Due to the consumers' increased desire for authenticity this success factor has gained particular importance.

Multi-sensual brand experiences are intended to satisfy the consumer by enabling **unique brand experiences**. This is based on a modern understanding of communication, which extends far beyond the one-way brand communication of the past and is oriented on two-way dialogue communication. Via personal and often emotional interactions with the consumers individual customer wishes will gain greater recognition and trends can be identified. In this context, social media nowadays offer companies more possibilities than ever before.

Proof of the increasing significance of multi-sensual brand management is the growing number of "**brand lands**", as well as the multi-sensual design of numerous brand touch-points. Brand lands are characterised by personal, direct, two-way communication. They can be defined as permanent, stationary, three-dimensional, real places which are operated by companies in order to enable the brands to be multi-sensually experienced by internal and external target groups (cf. Springer 2008). The "World of BMW" in Munich is a case in point here. It aims at sustainably emotionalising the brand in order to differentiate it from its competitors. A requirement for this is the existence of a clear brand identity, since multi-sensual experiences can otherwise be copied quite easily and do not have a sustainable differentiation potential. The most important component for the multi-sensual design of a brand promise is brand personality (cf. Schade 2012) since this is closely linked to the affective evaluation of the brand. Strategic brand positioning has to determine which senses are suited to the mediation of a specific brand personality and which aspects of the brand personality should be multi-sensually mediated. These strategic guidelines can then be implemented via measures of operative brand management (cf. Müller 2012). In accordance with the process of identity-based brand management, brand-controlling has to measure the customer's perception of multi-sensual stimuli, ascertain whether it matches the objectives, and, if necessary, make adaptations. Figure 3.17 indicates the necessary steps for the multi-sensual design of the brand promise.

The process of multi-sensual design can be illustrated using the brand Starbucks as an example. The first step consists in determining the senses which are responsible for conveying the brand promise. In this example, sight and smell are selected. Step two consists of translating the brand promise into a multi-sensual form. In order to do so, it is necessary to determine what should be conveyed (e.g. the brand origin), where it should take place (e.g. in the Starbucks stores) and how it should be conveyed (e.g. through the interior design). In the third step, this objective has to be implemented via the specific configuration of on-site stimuli. Starbucks implements this by means of a brand design called "Heritage". Old wood, concrete, or ceramic tiles with signs of wear and tear are used together with seating partially made of metal as well as club chairs, factory-inspired

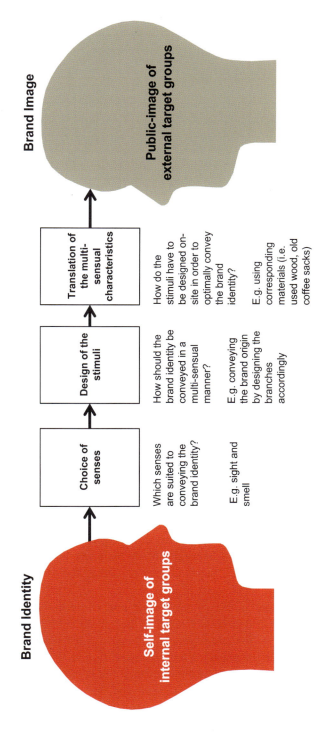

Fig. 3.17 The multi-sensual design process of the brand promise using Starbucks as an example. (Source: based on Müller 2012, p. 71)

lighting, large shared tables and wooden blinds. All this is meant to reflect the atmosphere of the turn to the 20th century and to act as a reminder of the company's origin as a trading house on Pike Place Market in Seattle (cf. Starbucks 2012). The sense of smell is addressed not only by preparing the fresh coffee but also by means of old sacks of coffee hanging on the walls.

In principle, multi-sensual brand experiences should address as many senses as possible to garner greater attention, recognition and stronger differentiation, which, in turn, will lead to an increase in the recall effect and in the emotionality of the experience (cf. Müller 2012).

3.4   Brand Architecture

If a company owns several brands, the identity-based management of these brands has to be coordinated within the framework of a brand architecture (see Fig. 3.18; cf. Kanitz 2013 for more details).

3.4.1   Definition

The term **brand architecture**' is extremely complex and often used synonymously with the terms 'brand hierarchy' (cf. Keller 2003), 'brand structure' (cf. Laforet and Saunders 1994, 2005, 2007), 'brand system' (cf. Aaker 1996) and 'brand strategy' or 'branding strategy' (cf., inter alia, Kapferer 2008; Keller 2003; Kotler 2003; Laforet and Saunders 1999; Rao et al. 2004). In the following, we will define some of the most important terms and concepts.

The term **brand portfolio** refers to the all the brands (cf. Meffert and Burmann 1996) which a company is entitled to use as the brand proprietor or due to contractual agreements (license, alliance) with the brand proprietor (cf. Aaker and Joachimsthaler 2000). This also includes the brands which are jointly set up and administered with other companies.

The term **brand hierarchy** refers to the allocation of the portfolio's brands to the organisational levels of a company. Important brand hierarchy levels include the company level, the business area level, the product group level, the product level and the product version level.

Brand architecture design comprises **the formal and content-related structure of the brand portfolio**. The formal structure refers to the definition of the hierarchical levels of the brand architecture, the allocation of the brands to the individual hierarchical levels, and the way in which the brands in a company portfolio are marked. The content-related structure refers to the linking of the individual brand with products or services, with market segments, geographical market areas, and the corresponding brand identity. Brand architecture design is based on the **brand architecture strategy**, a global,

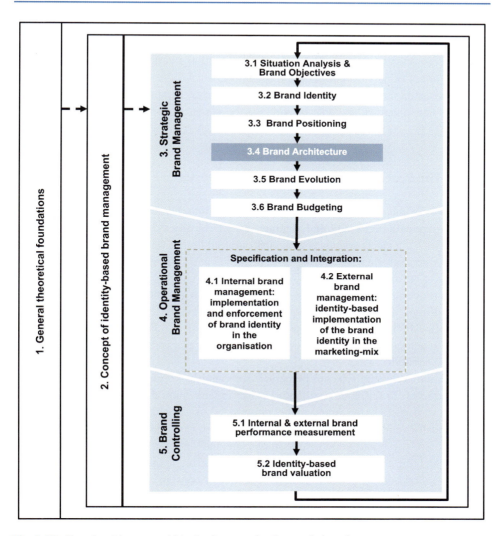

Fig. 3.18 Brand architecture within the framework of strategic brand management

long-term performance plan for the management of the entire brand portfolio. Brand architecture design aims to create internal synergies and to make optimum use of the demand potential in the markets in which the company operates (cf. Aaker 2004; Burmann and Meffert 2005). In order to achieve these objectives, the brand architecture has to be coordinated in a coherent manner so that the identity of the company brand and the identities of the other brands blend well.

Brand architecture as **subjectively perceived** by the consumers can differ from the brand architecture implemented by the company. The perceived brand architecture is crucial because it determines the consumers' behaviour and therefore the extent to which the company's objectives can be achieved. Besides visible components (e.g. brand logos, product packaging, the employees' clothing), subjectively perceived brand architecture is also determined by non-visible components (brand associations). If a company uses a purely product-oriented brand strategy, the consumer will be unable to see the connection between the brands. If, however, a combination of company and product brands is used, the consumer will be able to perceive the connections between different product brands.

3.4.2   The Process of Brand Architecture Design

An analysis of the various approaches to designing brand architecture indicates that it is useful to **separate hierarchy and strategy**. Hierarchically systematising the brand portfolio allows for a clear, organised presentation of all brands belonging to a company. On this basis, the strategic options have to be identified and systematically evaluated in order to be able to set up a strategic, goal-orientated brand architecture design (see Fig. 3.19).

In the process, a clear distinction between **the strategic perspective of brand architecture design** and **the detailed, implementation-related perspective** is of major importance. The latter deals with the implementation of the chosen brand architecture at all brand touch points, translating it into specific strategies and measures for every brand within the portfolio.

The brand architecture has to be periodically analysed with regard to its internal and external effects. To this end, **results and achievements should be regularly monitored**, which in turn enables the brand architecture to be systematically adapted on the basis of empirically verifiable target attainment. In this context, it is necessary to examine the acceptance of the brand architecture among the staff and the managers, as well as the way in which the consumer perceives and assesses the brand architecture.

In the following, the process of brand architecture design, as illustrated in Fig. 3.19, will be discussed in detail.

3.4.2.1   Structuring Brand Portfolios

The identity-based process of setting up a brand architecture is based on Aaker (1996). Aaker's approach allows a very detailed structuring of the brand portfolio, taking the following **hierarchical levels** into account: the corporate level, the business unit level

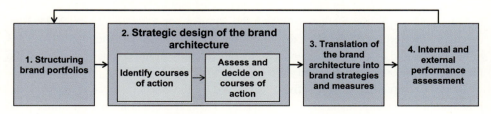

Fig. 3.19   The Identity-based process of brand architecture design. (Source: Burmann and Kanitz 2010, p. 39)

(often synonymous with a certain product range), the product level, and the level of certain product features (see Fig. 3.20). Modelled after ingredient branding, brands on the product feature level refer to commodities (e.g. raw materials, input materials, product parts) which represent a branded product from the perspective of the respective target groups (cf. Freter and Baumgarth 2005). These may be elements of product brands or by-products which may be managed as independent brands (cf. Aaker 1996).

3.4.2.2 Strategic Brand Architecture Design

The systematic approach to designing a brand architecture is based on three dimensions, as detailed in Fig. 3.21.

(a) The Vertical Dimension of Brand Architecture

The **vertical dimension** is based on the "brand relationship spectrum" proposed by Aaker and Joachimsthaler (2000). A **branded house architecture**, often referred to as "corporate branding" or "umbrella branding", represents one end of the scale. The hierarchically superior umbrella brand dominates the market presence, and the influence of any inferior brands—if they exist at all—is reduced to a minimum (cf. Aaker and Joachimsthaler 2000). In the branded house structure, all products and services of a

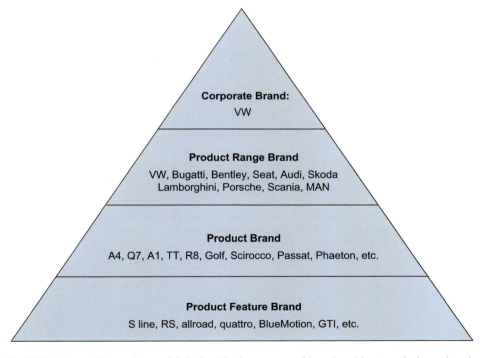

Fig. 3.20 A brand hierarchy model derived in the process of brand architecture design using the example of the Volkswagen Group

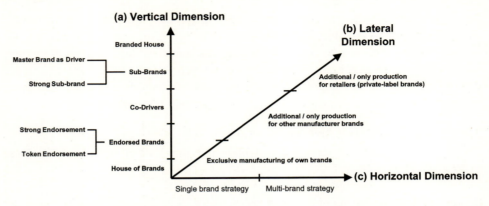

Fig. 3.21 Strategic dimensions of brand architecture design. (Source: Burmann and Kanitz 2010, p. 41)

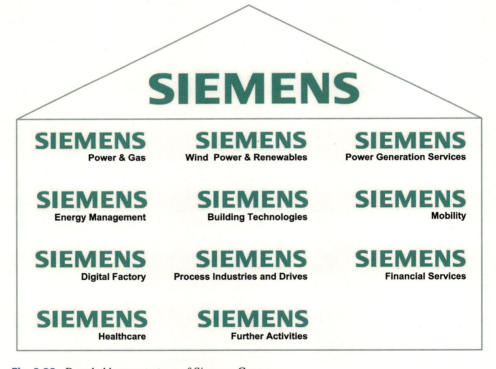

Fig. 3.22 Branded house strategy of Siemens Germany

company are marketed under a single umbrella brand. A good example of this strategy is offered by Siemens (see Fig. 3.22).

The other end of the vertical dimension is represented by a **house of brands**, in which every product brand shapes its own market presence (cf. Aaker and Joachimsthaler 2000).

Procter & Gamble uses this strategy for its brands, which include Pampers, Oral-B, Ariel and Head & Shoulders (see Fig. 3.23).

Several hybrid forms also exist between these two extremes. A **sub-brand archi-tecture** features a dominant, umbrella brand, which provides the main driving force in purchasing decisions, whilst hierarchically subordinate brands also have more than just purely descriptive roles (cf. Aaker 2004). If heterogeneous market segments require brands to appear differently in certain segments, but a strong image transfer effect from the umbrella brand can also be beneficial, a sub-brand architecture should be employed.

In an **endorsed brand** architecture, the subordinate brands dominate the hierar-chically superior brand; in this case the umbrella brand has a purely supporting role. The product brand is the main driving force in purchasing decisions (cf. Aaker 2004). The architecture of endorsed brands and sub-brands also can be divided further (see Fig. 3.21). For example, a weak, token endorsement makes only a symbolic reference to the hierarchically superior brand (e.g. Ristorante by Dr. Oetker), whereas strong endorse-ments (e.g. Persil by Henkel) offer comprehensive support from the hierarchically supe-rior brand.

With the **master brand as driver** option (e.g. Kinder: Kinder Surprise, Kinder Choc-olate, Kinder Joy), the focus is on the superior brand, whatever its hierarchical level, complemented by a descriptive addition. If the sub-brand is very strong (e.g. Channel No. 5), this strong product brand is combined with a dominant, hierarchically superior umbrella brand. This option differs from the master brand as driver approach in that the subordinate brand has a stronger presence; yet, unlike the sub-brand as a co-driver archi-tecture, (e.g. Gillette Venus), the hierarchically superior and subordinate brands do not appear equal, but the focus remains on the superior brand (cf. Aaker 2004). Figure 3.24 illustrates the different options of the vertical dimension of brand architecture using selected examples.

Depending on the various courses of action along this vertical dimension, **suitable evaluation criteria** have to be identified (see Fig. 3.25). In accordance with identity-based brand management, we can distinguish between the internal and external perspec-tives, which produce **internal and external evaluation criteria**. One of the internal

Fig. 3.23   House of brands strategy as used by Procter & Gamble (2015)

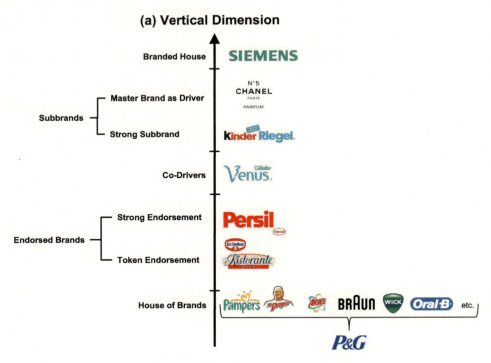

Fig. 3.24 The vertical dimension of brand architecture with various examples

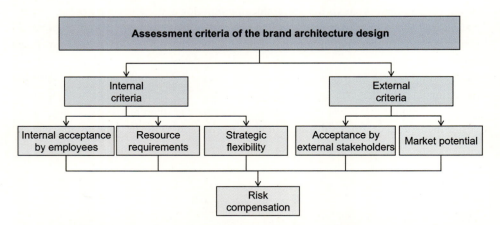

Fig. 3.25 Evaluation criteria for assessing courses of action in an identity-based brand architecture design

criteria is the employees' **internal acceptance** of the brand, which is particularly crucial to the successful implementation of a brand architecture. In the case of brands with a limited brand commitment, the employees might not behave in accordance with the brand's values. If such a commitment is lacking, the employees cannot be expected to exhibit brand citizenship behaviour, which in turn will weaken the brand.

For example, the brand Seat is part of the VW Group. In recent decades, Seat has continuously incurred losses. In recent years, the brand has attempted to distance itself from other VW Group brands through the claim of "auto emoción", emphasising a Spanish spirit and passion in its brand promise. In terms of product policy, though, this differentiation is lost due to the considerable similarity between Seat models and models of other VW Group brands. Similarly, the brand promise is inadequately implemented internally. In 2010 James Muir, the CEO of Seat at that time, noted that if a company wanted to purchase Seat, VW would have to give this buyer money to take it (cf. Krogh 2010). Muir also criticised Seat's brand image. Such negative statements from top management indicate low brand commitment throughout the company management, which is likely to have a detrimental impact on the employees' brand commitment. An English CEO who questions the economic viability of the company and does not believe in the Spanish spirit and passion supposedly exemplified by the brand serves to destroy the brand from within.

Another internal criterion pertains to **resource requirements**, which include market investments, potential synergy effects, implementation time and coordination needs (cf. Burmann and Spickschen 2004). Using a brand in different market segments can result in synergy effects due to image transfers and the potential for greater brand awareness. For example, SCA leverages synergies across the toilet paper and handkerchief markets by consistently using the brand Tempo. If a company maintains several brands that act independently in similar markets, it incurs higher costs due to redundant marketing measures. For example, the brands Zewa, Danke and Tempo in the German market all belong to the SCA Company and compete in the toilet paper sector. Regarding different architectural approaches, greater complexity in the brand portfolio will generally lead to higher costs and lower synergies, while simultaneously increasing the possibility of exploiting the full demand potential.

A final internal criterion is **strategic flexibility**, which describes the ability of a company to replicate operational processes and organisational skills for several brands on the one hand and, on the other hand, to comprehensively reconfigure its resources and competencies. This latter effort aims to acquire new organisational skills (cf. Burmann 2002). Regarding the brand architecture design, strategic flexibility describes the ability of a company to successfully adapt to changes in external conditions, such as new competitors in the market. If a company is active in several business areas that change at different speeds, a branded house architecture will make it impossible to adapt flexibly. In contrast, a house of brands architecture requires less consideration of brands in other business areas, due to the high degree of independence of each brand. Strategic flexibility is therefore greater.

For example, Procter & Gamble has two brands with a very masculine positioning, Old Spice and Meister Proper (Germany)/Mr. Clean (USA). Yet it also owns the brands Always, Ariel and Wella, which clearly target female consumers. If these products were marketed under a shared umbrella brand, P&G would face a considerable risk of diluting the brand image, due to the distinct positioning approaches and target groups.

While the first two criteria mentioned above can be determined individually for every relationship between brands on different hierarchical levels, **strategic flexibility** pertains to the overall brand portfolio. This overall portfolio flexibility depends on the company's capacity for replication and reconfiguration. Reconfiguration is operational-ised in the form of the employees' ability and willingness to learn and to implement new strategies, as well as the company's strategic competence. The capacity for replication is determined by of the quality of knowledge codification and knowledge transfer (cf. Burmann 2002). Furthermore, strategic flexibility depends heavily on the managers' flex-ibility, which should be manifested in a high level of emotional stability, openness and willingness to take risks (cf. Nadkarni and Herrmann 2010). Ultimately, it is preferable to use a variety of single independent brands if the company has a high level of strategic flexibility. If the company instead exhibits a low level of strategic flexibility, a branded house architecture should be favoured.

In addition to the internal criteria, two essential external criteria exist. The first cri-terion involves **external stakeholder acceptance**, which comprises consumers, alli-ance and cooperation partners, and shareholders (cf. Burmann and Spickschen 2004). To ensure external stakeholders' acceptance, brand managers might seek synergy effects by using existing brands, through sub-branding, co-driver or endorsed brand strategies. However, if any threat of a negative image transfer looms, an independent brand within a house of brands is preferable.

The phasing out of the toilet paper brand Charmin offers a compelling example that highlights the need for brand owners to pay appropriate attention to external stake-holders. The licence for this successful brand was sold to the Swedish Group SCA in 2007, together with several other brands, such as Tempo. In 2009, the German branch of SCA announced it would be phasing out Charmin, as part of a change in its brand architecture. Zewa Soft was introduced as an umbrella brand for all Zewa toilet paper products. Thereafter, all products were marketed under the brand "Zewa Soft samtstark". After a transitional period, the well-known Charmin bear disappeared from the packag-ing and marketing communications. In a blog on Charmin's website, consumers could write encouraging words for the bear, in light of his "move". Instead, though, the brand received 54 pages of criticism from disappointed consumers. In 2012, Zewa sought to establish a tiger—which has been affiliated with and been a part of the brand personality of Zewa Soft since 2010—as a replacement for the bear, even holding a fun competi-tion to have consumers name it (cf. Zewa 2012). In 2009, Charmin and Zewa together accounted for 8.5% of the market share, of which Charmin claimed 3.5%. Today, SCA's brands Zewa and Tempo achieve an estimated market share of only 7.5%, with the newly introduced brand Tempo being responsible for only 1.5% (cf. Günther 2012).

As this example illustrates, brand owners need to determine how well the targeted buyers have already accepted their brands. Brands at different hierarchical levels may have different impacts on consumers' purchasing behaviour. While the empirical research on the behavioural relevance of single brands is quite advanced, the exploration of multiple brands at different hierarchical levels is less well developed.

Kanitz (2013) has started to address this research gap by studying the behavioural relevance of corporate brands and their associated product brands for German consumers across multiple industries. This empirical study, which involved data collected from eight sectors (fast moving consumer goods, electronics, automotive, pharmaceutical, banking, hotel, sports and holiday destinations), produced three main findings:

– Both the corporate brand image and the product brand image have significant positive impacts on consumers' purchasing behaviour. Across all industries, product brands have greater behavioural relevance than corporate brands (see Fig. 3.26).
– The perceived width of the range of products and services offered by a corporate brand has a significant impact on the purchase of corporate and product brands. The wider the perceived range of products and services, the stronger the behavioural relevance of the product brand and the weaker the behavioural relevance of the corporate brand. With a wide range of services, it is difficult to consider the variety of services available as they relate to the positioning of the corporate brand (cf. Kanitz 2013). With an overly complex or generic positioning, the corporate brand loses its behavioural relevance. The relative behavioural relevance of brands, however, increases because their specific benefits can be conveyed in a credible and targeted way. Therefore, with a broad range of services, a house of brands or endorsed brands are likely to be advisable.

Kanitz (2013) also provides industry-specific analyses (see Fig. 3.27), in which he shows that in the food (FMCG) and pharmaceutical industries, product brands have very high behavioural relevance because the perceived range of products and services of each corporate brand is very wide. For example, in the fast moving consumer goods market,

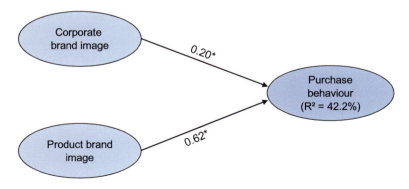

*significance level< 0.01

Fig. 3.26 The effects of corporate brand image and product brand image on purchase behaviour. (Source: Kanitz 2013, p. 180)

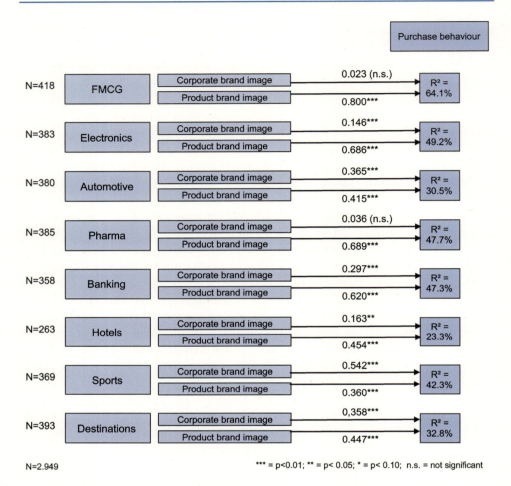

Fig. 3.27 Relevance of corporate and product brands to purchase behaviour in different industries. (Source: Kanitz 2013, p. 189)

Danone Actimel designs all its communication around the product brand; the Danone logo merely appears on the product packaging. This focus on the product brand is evident even on the independent product brand websites, www.actimel.de and www.teamactimel.de, the latter of which appeals specifically to children and their parents (cf. Kanitz 2013). Yet, a different picture emerges in the automotive industry, where a co-driver strategy makes more sense (cf. Kanitz 2013). Thus, for the Mercedes-Benz C-class the company uses its corporate and product brands on an equal footing. In this instance, Kanitz could find impacts of both brands on customers' purchasing behaviour, though the behavioural relevance of the C-class product brand is slightly greater, corresponding to the relatively wide product portfolio maintained by Mercedes. In general, and in most industries, the corporate and the product brands both affect purchase behaviour. Therefore, in many cases it is advisable to adopt a sub-brand strategy, such as the co-driver strategy or endorsed brand strategy.

Another external criterion relates to **market potential**, which includes both the actual and potential market exploitation of the core market, as well as any cross-selling potential. In this context it is important to decide whether a single or a multi-brand strategy promises better market exploitation, according to the existing coordination costs and potential for cannibalisation. The higher the brand independence within the brand portfolio, the higher will be the degree of market potential utilisation. At the same time, resource requirements will also increase; therefore it is necessary to determine the optimal ratio of market potential utilisation and resource requirements.

The **balancing of risks** represents a criterion of particular importance. Markovitz's (1952, 1959) portfolio theory is useful here since it regards companies as portfolios of strategic business units or brands, so risk can be distributed across several brands. In the case of a failed product development a company with a branded house architecture will likely suffer from negative image transfers because cognitive and emotional processes lead to the transfer of associations and ideas between two or more brands in the consumers' minds (cf. Meffert and Heinemann 1990). This risk can be limited by a house of brands architecture because the individual brands are independent. Consider the example of Kraft Foods and the brand Onko. In 2010, Kraft changed the recipe for Onko coffee by adding maltodextrin and caramel as flavour substitutes and reducing the amount of more expensive roasted coffee in the product. Onko coffee thus became a coffee blend (cf. Hesseling 2010), but the shift was not clearly communicated, prompting criticism from consumer watchdogs. Due to Kraft's house of brands architecture, though, the company was able to avoid tarnishing the images of its other brands with this product controversy.

(b) The Horizontal Dimension of Brand Architecture

The **horizontal brand architecture dimension** refers to the **number of brands offered by a company in each market segment**. It indicates whether a selected market segment is addressed by only one brand or by several competing brands. In the case of a **single brand strategy**, each brand is geared towards a specific market segment, such as the brand Viagra by Pfizer. In the case of a **multi-brand strategy**, at least two brands of the same company serve an identical market segment. The car brands VW, Audi, Seat and Skoda, all of which belong to the VW Group, are good examples of this strategy. A multi-brand strategy can be advantageous when dealing with larger, heterogeneous market segments. Financial strength is required to establish multiple brands, as is comprehensive know-how of brand management to achieve credible differentiation. Furthermore, multi-brand approaches incur substantial risks of **cannibalisation** if the brands are not very clear cut (cf. Koers 2001; Meffert and Koers 2005). Table 3.2 offers an overview of the most important opportunities and risks associated with single-brand and multi-brand strategies.

Table 3.2 Opportunities, risks and requirements of single-brand and multi-brand strategies

Type of strategy	**Single-brand strategy** Management of a single brand per market segment	**Multi-brand strategy** Parallel management of at least two brands per market segment
Opportunities	Targets individual customer segments	Better market exploitation
	Specific brand differentiation through optimal coordination of need profiles	Allows brand switching (without switching to a competitor)
	allows to establish an unmistakable product image	Higher barriers to market entry for rival brands, due to wider shelf space coverage
	Little risk of negative spill-over effects onto other brands	
	Lower coordination costs	One brand with an aggressive price positioning can protect the other brands from price wars
Risks	Brand costs have to be attributed to a single product line	Cannibalisation through a mutual substitution of market shares
	Insufficient amortisation of the costs spent in the case of a short lifespan of an individual brand	Suboptimal use of financial and human resources
	In the case of a successful brand the name may become generic, thus leading to a loss of differentiation	
	No support for the product brand from adjacent brands	
Central requirements	A worthwhile market segment	Sufficient financial strength and management know-how
		Credible brand differentiation

(c) The Lateral Dimension of Brand Architecture

The **lateral dimension of brand architecture** design determines whether a company produces only its own brands or, additionally or exclusively, products for some other company/ies. In the latter case, a company can produce brands for direct competitors or **private-label brands** for retailers. Due to the increasing market share of large retailer groups, manufacturing of private-label products is becoming increasingly important. In Germany, the market share of private-label food products has increased notably (see Fig. 3.28), often through the displacement of medium-priced brands. For producers, the risk of cannibalising their own brands thus increases if they produce private-label brands (cf. Burmann and Kiefel 2012).

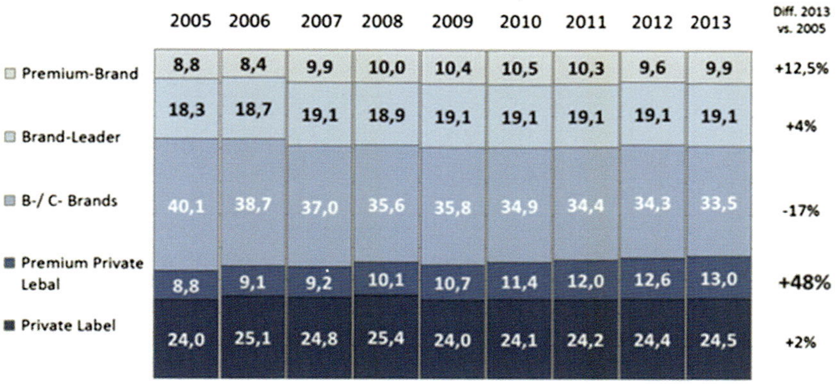

	2005	2006	2007	2008	2009	2010	2011	2012	2013	Diff. 2013 vs. 2005
☐ Premium-Brand	8,8	8,4	9,9	10,0	10,4	10,5	10,3	9,6	9,9	+12,5%
☐ Brand-Leader	18,3	18,7	19,1	18,9	19,1	19,1	19,1	19,1	19,1	+4%
▨ B-/ C- Brands	40,1	38,7	37,0	35,6	35,8	34,9	34,4	34,3	33,5	-17%
▪ Premium Private Lebal	8,8	9,1	9,2	10,1	10,7	11,4	12,0	12,6	13,0	+48%
▪ Private Label	24,0	25,1	24,8	25,4	24,0	24,1	24,2	24,4	24,5	+2%

Fig. 3.28 Market shares of manufacturer and private label brands in the German fast moving consumer goods market. (Source: GfK 2012; Adlwarth 2014)

> **Private label brands** are those brand names which are used by a trading company, such as a retailer, to identify selected products which are distributed exclusively in its own sales outlets (cf. Ahlert and Berentzen 2010; IfH Cologne 2006).

Many trading companies, as part of their trademark strategy, design their own products or imitate successful brands. Accordingly, various producers either focus exclusively on producing private label products (e.g. Handelsmarken GmbH in Offenburg) or they dedicate their spare capacities to them (e.g. the German confectionery Coppenrath & Wiese). Attractive margins and the increasing interchangeability of the images of retailer brands are fuelling the growth of private labels (cf. Batten and Company 2014).

> A **retailer brand** is legally owned by a trading company and used by that company to identify its **retail outlets** (cf. Gröppel-Klein 2005; Morschett 2012).

Thus it is becoming increasingly important to establishing a profile for a trading company in the retail sector. Since private labels can be obtained only in the retail outlets of the specific trading company, dealers are in a position to differentiate themselves from other enterprises. Margins often are higher for private labels than for manufacturer brands, because the manufacturer does not accrue any R&D, sales or marketing expenses. Especially in product ranges where manufacturer brands cannot offer the desired price level or where high margins can be achieved, private labels are a popular option for retailers.

According to the criteria in Fig. 3.29 various types of private labels can be distinguished. Thus the strategic question is: which private label, at what price level, with what

Criteria	Characteristics
Competence width	Single-Brand / Group-of-goods-Brand / Range-Brand
Price level	Premium-Brand / Imitation-Brand / Low-Budget-Brand
Competence depth	regional / national / international
Brand-Name	Company-Name / Fantasy-Name
Range significance	Core-Brand / Additive Brand

Fig. 3.29 Criteria for distinguishing private labels. (Source: based on Bruhn 2012, p. 552)

geographic scope, and what kind of name should a retailer use, and which role should private labels play across the entire range?

Competence width refers to the spectrum of, and the necessary fit between, the individual products offered under a common brand name. Single brands such as Ratskrone or Tandil (by the German retailer Aldi) offer the advantage of a clear brand positioning, simultaneously reducing the risk of image transfer effects to other brands (cf. Meffert and Heinemann 1990; Hanf and Wettstein 2008). The disadvantage of single brands is their high resource requirements. Product group brands offer a defined range of goods under a common brand name (cf. Bruhn 2012), such as the private labels Dulano (belonging to the discounter Lidl) and Wilhelm Brandenburg (REWE Group) which offer sausages and meat products. Finally, a label that offers products from a variety of product groups or even over the entire range of a retailer, is called a product line brand (cf. Hanf and Wettstein 2008). Range brands face the particular challenge of having to create a differentiated brand image. Ultimately, the image of the retailer will be transferred to all or many of the assorted goods. Thus, range brands are usually equivalent to private label brands.

Regarding the **price level**, the seller has to determine the levels of quality and price that should be established. Premium private labels provide high quality, an active market presence and a positioning in the upper price segment (cf. Bruhn 2012). With an imitation brand strategy, the private label offers quality comparable to that of a manufacturer brand but at a lower price. Such brands are sometimes called "me-too" brands (cf. Berentzen 2010), and their packaging often mirrors that of the imitated brand, in an effort to create some degree of confusion. To emphasise the aspect of affordability, the placement at the point of sale usually is right next to the imitated brands (cf. Kumar and Steenkamp 2007). Retailers also frequently offer low budget brands in everyday product categories, which offer a very simple design, minimum quality and a much lower price than competitor brands (cf. Berentzen 2010). The labels Gut&Günstig by EDEKA or TiP by real are examples of such low budget brands in Germany.

Depth of competence determines whether the private label will be offered at the regional, national or international level. Recently, retailers have increasingly focused on regional labels, such as "Unsere Heimat – echt und gut" (Our home—genuine and good) launched by EDEKA in 2006. It offers regional products and is limited to a geographical sales area in the southwest of Germany. For private labels such as Rewe regional or EDEKA regional, the situation is different. These labels highlight the regional origin of the products offered, but the labels themselves are available throughout Germany and thus constitute national brands.

The depth of competence also influences brand name selection. If the name of the private label is the same as the retailer's, an image transfer across the two entities is possible (cf. Bruhn 2012). If a fictitious name is chosen, such an image transfer is more difficult. Finally, a private label can be an additional or marginal brand or play a central role in the overall brand portfolio. Thus, the label MinuLakt by Aldi Süd is an additional brand which only includes lactose-free milk, yogurt and whipping cream. In contrast, if a private label serves as a core brand, it maintains a broad and deep product portfolio, such as the private label "ja!" by the German retailer Rewe (see Fig. 3.30).

Trade Company / Criteria	Rewe	EDEKA	ALDI Süd
Competence width			
Single-Brand	▪ Wilhelm Brandenburg	▪ Booster Energy Drink	▪ Tandil
Group-of-goods-Brand	▪ Rewe Beste Wahl	▪ Bauerngut	▪ Choceur
Range-Brand		▪ EDEKA	▪ One World
Price level			
Premium-Brand	▪ Rewe Feine Welt	▪ EDEKA Selection	▪ Gourmet
Brand for Imitations	▪ Rewe Beste Wahl	▪ EDEKA	▪ Alpenmark
Low-Budget-Brand	▪ ja!	▪ Gut & Günstig	
Competence depth			
regional		▪ Unsere Heimat*	
national	▪ clever (Österreich)	▪ EDEKA regional	
international	▪ ja!		▪ alio
Brand-Name			
Company Name	▪ Rewe Feine Welt	▪ EDEKA	
Fantasy-Name	▪ Vivesse	▪ Booster	▪ Moser Roth
Range significance			
Core-Brand	▪ ja!	▪ EDEKA	▪ Cucina
Additive Brand	▪ Rewe regional	▪ EDEKA Espania	▪ MinuLakt

Fig. 3.30 Categorisation of private labels offered by the German retailers Rewe, EDEKA and Aldi Süd

Because of the growth of private labels in Germany, manufacturer brands are often confronted with situations in which retailers that were formerly only their distribution partners are now among their strongest competitors. The resulting power of the retail sector leads to an improved negotiating position, which puts the profit margins of brand manufacturers under strong pressure (cf. Burmann and Kiefel 2012). Several strategies are available to brand managers to respond to this development.

Originally, manufacturer brands have a clear advantage over private labels. As Fig. 3.31 shows, a manufacturer brand usually focuses on a particular product area: thus, Schöfferhofer specialises in beer and mixed beverages based on beer. In this very narrow product portfolio, it can build a very strong and clear brand image. In contrast, the private label TiP by real is not limited to any specific product area but offers a wide range of products from nearly every commodity group. Therefore, TiP can only build a very diffuse brand image, with limited opportunities to develop an autonomous brand identity. Private labels therefore cannot usually claim the same level of innovation competence as national manufacturer brands. However, the competitive position of manufacturer brands may deteriorate if private labels are increasingly positioned as single brands or product group brands and if manufacturer brands lose their innovation advantages (cf. Indrest 2013).

This scenario is quite realistic, as demonstrated by the German discounter Lidl. The companies Bonback (bakery), Solent (chocolate) and MEG (beverages) all produce private labels exclusively for this discounter. Their next step thus would be to develop their own innovations. As these private labels develop and grow, manufacturer brands have to engage in increased innovation activities and ensure consistent, identity-based brand management to defend themselves against the private labels.

Other strategies that manufacturer brands might adopt (see Fig. 3.32) include building a direct relationship with the consumers, establishing an online or direct sales channel

Fig. 3.31 Examples of different competence ranges

Strategy	Description
Innovation	Continuous investment in new products and new product features
Customer Relationship	Generating Relationship between Producer and Customer
Online- and Direct-Sales	Sales thru company owned Brand- or Online-Shops
Communication-Pull	Generating of demand thru direct sales activities without retailers

Fig. 3.32 Alternative strategies for manufacturer brands

and generating a pull effect through communication activities so as to be admitted into the discounters' product range (cf. Szeliga 1996).

The objectives of these strategies are to expand market access and intensify the direct contact with buyers. The latter goal is particularly important because manufacturers often show a clear deficit in their link to end users. With their extensive customer data, generated by loyalty programmes or discount cards, retailers can predict the needs and the behaviour of consumers more quickly and more precisely. To address this problem, manufacturers might develop their own brand-specific brick and online shops. Through direct and online sales, manufacturer brands can collect and leverage their own customer data. With exclusive points of sale, a manufacturer can offer a unique brand experience to consumers, which traditional retail stores cannot imitate. A particular and popular variant of such direct distribution is the use of pop-up stores (cf. Baumgarth and Kastner 2012).

Pop-up stores are designed to be installed in a particular location for a short period of time; they usually sell only the products of a specific brand.

Pop-up stores can generate substantial media interest and a quick rush of visitors, something which might enable the brand to attract new target groups (cf. Duncan 2008). One example of a brand that uses pop-up stores is Ritter Sport (see Fig. 3.33).

Finally, manufacturer brands may try to leverage demand by a direct and out of the ordinary approach to the consumer (pull communication). In the best-case scenario, retailers will have to stock the brand in their product range because their clients demand it (cf. Meffert et al. 2015). For example, before 2009, the energy drink Monster was not available in traditional retail stores. Through sponsorships in the fields of motorsport, motocross and monster truck rallies, the company increased the demand for its brand by the consumers. As a result, the energy drink is now widely available in food retail stores in Germany, resulting in a 39.0% market share by 2013 (cf. o.V 2013).

Fig. 3.33 Ritter sport pop-up store. (Source: www.ritter-sport.de)

Additionally, conflicts with retailers should be avoided, since, in extreme cases, they can even lead to temporary or permanent delisting. For example, in early 2014 the German discounter Lidl delisted all Coca-Cola products after failed price negotiations and focused instead on the distribution of its private label (cf. o.V 2014). Although Coca-Cola later returned to the shelf, this example illustrates the possible consequences of conflicts between manufacturer brands and retailers—even for brands as renowned as Coca-Cola.

3.5 Brand Evolution

3.5.1 Definition and Overview

While the brand management decisions discussed so far considered **a specific point in time**, **brand evolution** adopts a **long-term perspective**, dealing with decisions over time. This is necessary because brands must be developed further over time due to changing market and business conditions (see Fig. 3.34).

In contrast to brand architecture, which refers to all brands within a portfolio, brand evolution must be individually planned and implemented for each brand. Brand evolution planning is influenced by the brand vision, which is anchored in each brand's identity and is an integral part of the brand strategy. There are two courses of action for brand evolution: communicative and/or distributive brand dynamisation (cf. Sect. 3.5.2) and brand restructuring, which is primarily concerned with a brand's product range (cf. Sect. 3.5.3).

3.5.2 Brand Dynamisation

Brands need to be enabled to adapt to new developments and changes by making them more dynamic. The relevance of this ability to adapt has increased substantially in recent

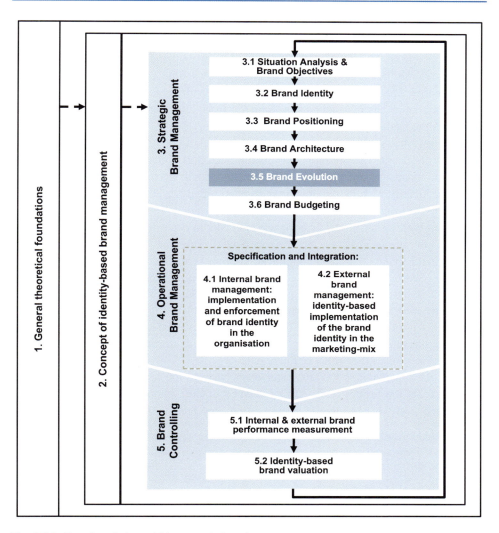

Fig. 3.34 Brand evolution within strategic brand management

years due to increasingly shorter product life cycles, growing international competition, as well as changes in the communication landscape.

Brand dynamisation can be sub-divided into three manifestations:

– dynamisation by ensuring topicality,
– dynamisation by changing the identity,
– dynamisation by addressing new target groups (rejuvenation).

One of the preconditions for successful dynamisation is a clear brand identity which should not be radically changed to ensure authenticity. Here a distinction must be made between **essential identity traits** (the brand core) and **accidental traits**. A brand's essential identity traits should neither be changed over time, nor be eliminated from the brand identity. The more essential traits a brand's identity comprises, the sooner individual essential traits can be adapted over time (cf. Boch 2012). In contrast, accidental traits can be adapted, added, or removed any time.

The basis for such an adaptation of accidental traits is a situation analysis (cf. Sect. 3.1) and a brand positioning analysis (cf. Sect. 3.3). Changes to brand identity must not be too extensive since otherwise the consumer will no longer be able to reconcile the brand identity with its previous brand image (cf. Boch 2012). The right fit between new and old information is crucial for brand dynamisation. The model proposed by Ernst Ulrich von Weizsäcker in 1974 can be used in order to determine the best fit. Changes to brand identity are recorded on the horizontal axis, whilst the vertical axis represents the changes in the market, i.e. the communication impact (see Fig. 3.35).

As von Weizsäcker states, successful dynamisation can only succeed if a sufficient number of important identifying features remain unchanged. This "medium" mix of old, reinforcing information (which confirms expectations) and new characteristics ensures maximum communication impact. Both too many new features ("insufficient fit") and too little innovation ("overdone fit") must be avoided. Attracting attention by way of some surprises raises the profile of the brand.

Since the brand image has a weaker connection to the accidental traits than to the essential traits the former ones may be deemed of little importance for brand continuity. Consequently, it can also be assumed that they are of limited relevance for brand

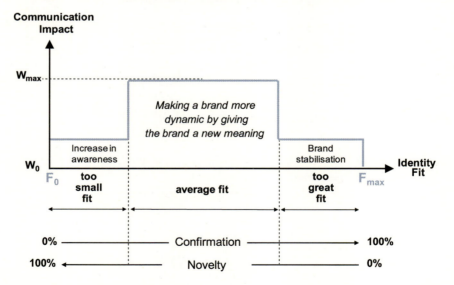

Fig. 3.35 Determining the fit between known and new identity traits. (Source: von Weizsäcker 1974; Nitschke 2006)

preference. The more continuously the essential traits of a brand have been managed in the past, the lower the margin for change because they have a strong influence on brand choice. The higher the influence of essential traits, the smaller the influence of accidental traits on purchasing decisions. Thus, the margin for change increases in the case of these traits, and, consequently, the extent to which these accidental features can be made more dynamic depends on the continuity of the essential traits (cf. Boch 2012).

3.5.2.1 Dynamisation by Ensuring Topicality

Dynamisation by ensuring topicality comprises the measures which are continuously implemented in brand management with the aim of being perceived as modern and up-to-date. This is based on the brand's close relationship with its target group, which makes it possible to recognise trends. For example, Adidas has for decades managed to recognise trends early on. The company's particular multi-channel distribution with sales outlets managed by "trendy retailers" is an important aspect in this respect (see Fig. 3.36).

By recognising trends at an early stage, Adidas is able to act as a trendsetter and keep the desirability of its brand at a high level (cf. Adidas Group 2012). This is achieved by around twenty "trendy retailers" worldwide, which are closely linked with the trendsetting target groups and are themselves opinion leaders.

These "trendy retailers" (see Fig. 3.37 for an example) which act as a link between the trend target groups and the company, ensure the authenticity of new marketing activities since they are perceived as the sole interaction partner for the customers, while Adidas keeps in the background. New product ideas are implemented in very small, limited editions and are distributed via these "trendy retailers" and their special stores (brick-and-mortar and online). If Adidas receives positive feedback on these limited editions,

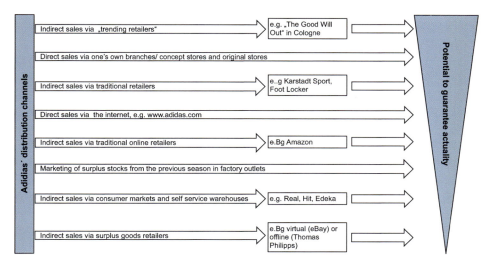

Fig. 3.36 Distribution channels of the brand Adidas and their contribution to ensuring topicality

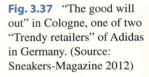

Fig. 3.37 "The good will out" in Cologne, one of two "Trendy retailers" of Adidas in Germany. (Source: Sneakers-Magazine 2012)

these sometimes quite unusual products are adapted for a wider target group and subsequently sold in large quantities via the other distribution channels.

Thanks to the internet, new possibilities for brand management have emerged which make it possible to recognise current consumer needs early on. The brand Starbucks, for example, implements this ongoing analysis via its platform "My Starbucks Idea" (see Fig. 3.38). Here, consumers have the opportunity to present their own ideas in the fields of "product", "experience", and "society". These ideas can be rated by other platform users thus giving clues as to the relevance of these ideas. By constantly registering consumer needs and implementing their ideas, Starbucks succeeds in continually optimising the brand experience and orienting it to the wishes of the consumers.

3.5.2.2 Dynamisation by Changing the Identity

A dynamisation by changing the identity becomes necessary whenever a brand's external environment changes, primarily due to changing consumer needs, which renders the previous brand benefit irrelevant or makes it necessary to add a new brand benefit to the brand promise. Dynamisation by changing the identity is thus based on a repositioning of the brand (cf. Sect. 3.3.3). Again, the optimal mix between reinforcing and new brand information is critical to the success of such adaptations (see Fig. 3.35).

Two well-known examples of dynamisation by changing the identity can be found in the fast food industry. In recent years, McDonald's has added a new brand benefit by introducing healthier products and a corresponding communication. This repositioning was based on the consumers' increased health awareness as well as the ensuing criticism of fast food in general and McDonald's in particular. In connection with this new positioning, various aspects, such as store design, underwent an overhaul, and in Europe the company colour of red was replaced by green. Furthermore, the new benefit was

Fig. 3.38   How starbucks ensures topicality. (Source: http://mystarbucksidea.force.com/)

emphasised within brand communication by using Heidi Klum as a celebrity endorser (see Fig. 3.39).

The brand Burger King took the opposite route by eliminating the identity trait "typically American" which it had been using for a long time. However, this trait was dropped after it was discovered by market research that it was irrelevant for the consumers' buying behaviour. The aim was to focus on benefits which are relevant for the consumers in order to strengthen the clarity of the brand image.

Co-branding is another form of dynamisation by changing the identity. As opposed to adding benefits, an offer within a co-branding strategy is defined by two or more brands in conjunction (cf. Aaker and Joachimsthaler 2000). Co-branding is (cf. Baumgarth 2003):

– a combination of at least two brands
– which cooperate in the eyes of the consumer
– in order to create a common bundle of offerings
– while they are, from the consumer's point of view, independent both before and after the co-branding cooperation.

Co-branding has recently become more important since many manufacturers expect it to improve the brand's image as well as broaden the brand competence. Co-branding's special challenge is the difficulty of having to combine at least two independent brand identities without this leading to conflicts between them.

Well-known examples of **horizontal co-branding** (where companies cooperate at the same stage of the value chain) include, among others, McDonald's and Cornetto with the ice cream varieties McFlurry Cornetto Chocolate, McFlurry Cornetto Royal Amarena,

New logo

until 2006   2012

Change of the company colour, illustrated using branch's facades

Change in the brand communication

Fig. 3.39 Dynamic brand management by adding benefits as exemplified by McDonald's

and McFlurry Cornetto Red Berry, or Häagen-Dazs and Baileys with the special ice cream edition Häagen-Dazs Baileys.

A special form of co-branding is the creation of a new (additional) brand identity (a so-called mega-brand), which restricts the freedom of action for the individual brands (cf. Rao and Ruekert 1994; Blackett and Boad 1999). A typical example is Star Alliance,

Fig. 3.40 Various examples of co-branding: McFlurry and Cornetto, Häagen-Dazs and Baileys, and star alliance

an alliance of several air transport service providers (Lufthansa and others), in which the brands involved continue to exist as independent brands, even after the cooperation agreement (cf. Netzer 1999) (Fig. 3.40).

In **vertical co-branding**, the cooperation involves the upstream and downstream stages of the value chain, as, for example, in the collaboration of IBM with the chip manufacturer Intel. This form of co-branding is also termed **ingredient branding**.

The success of co-branding is determined by two essential factors (cf. Baumgarth 2004; Kumar 2005):

– **Complementarity of the brand identities**—the identities of the cooperating brands must complement each other to a large extent. Added value is created both for the consumer and for the brand employees only if the cooperating brands bring complementary identities, and especially complementary competences, to the co-brand (cf. Park et al. 1996). Thus, a high fit or high uniformity between the cooperating brands is not desirable.
– **Fit of the target groups**—without a partial overlap of the target groups the brand image of the cooperation partner is not or only marginally relevant for the behaviour of the company's own customers.

The possibility of a mutual transfer of brand image and brand trust is the main opportunity or **advantage** of co-branding. Moreover, by means of co-branding, additional sales potentials and price premiums can be exploited and new markets may be reached which would be difficult to access for the individual brands due to high entry barriers. This is exemplified by the co-branding of Philips and Nivea in the case of the NIVEA FOR MEN shaver. While Philips provided the shaver, Nivea marketed the corresponding conditioner.

However, co-branding is also associated with **disadvantages**. While the possibility of a positive image transfer exists, there is also a danger of adverse effects on the brands involved. Furthermore, combining the brands increases the danger of confusing the customers and employees since this may erode positionings which were once self-evident. Also, the joint presence requires a close coordination between the parties concerned with regard to their brand-related activities (coordination costs) and restricts the scope for brand positioning.

3.5.2.3 Dynamisation by Rejuvenation

Whereas the brand's target group remains mostly unchanged in the case of the first two forms of brand dynamisation, rejuvenation aims at addressing a new and younger target group. This can help to achieve various objectives, for example in connection with **employer branding**, or it can be an integral part of brand repositioning, as exemplified by the brand "Old Spice". After the brand had been registering declining turnover for years and was associated with a very old target group, the brand management decided to neglect the old target group and to reposition the brand by revising the products and focussing brand communication on a young target group. After several TV commercials addressing a young target group, the brand succeeded in devising the most successful viral campaign to date worldwide with the commercial "The Man Your Man Could Smell Like". A campaign is described as viral if at first only a small number of individuals exchange views on the campaign and this then spreads "explosively" through various media, after having reached a "critical mass" (cf. Gladwell 2001), often via social media. By means of this campaign and the corresponding videos, Old Spice reached 175 million consumers (cf. Visible Measures 2012). Even the first commercial attracted a great deal of attention. In the next step, "The Man Your Man Could Smell Like" responded to questions posed via Twitter by prominent celebrities, bloggers, and consumers, with personalised videos on YouTube. As a result, the viral distribution of the commercial rose sharply. In the space of three days, Old Spice generated more than 180 video responses on YouTube, became fully involved in direct interactions with the consumers, and created a permanent brand experience with these personalised video responses. Within the first 24 h the commercial had been viewed by 6.7 million people; after 36 h this figure had risen to 23 million (cf. Wiancko 2010). However, such a radical measure in brand management is only advisable if the old target group has become so small that its loss poses a low risk. It is often the last step before a brand is wiped out.

Another area in which rejuvenation is relevant for brands is **employer branding** since attracting young employees is important for all brands and will strongly increase in significance in the future. Employer branding deals with the transfer of identity-based brand management principles to human resource management. The aim is to be successful in the competition for qualified employees by creating a strong employer brand (cf. Sponheuer 2010; Böttger 2012). The term 'employer brand' can be defined as follows:

> "An **employer brand** [...] is a bundle of benefits with specific employer-related features which ensures that in the long term this bundle of benefits can be differentiated from other bundles of benefits which fulfil the same basic needs from the perspective of the relevant, employer-specific target group" (Böttger 2012, p. 27).

Usually, an employer brand has to address all age groups; thus, too strong a rejuvenation of an employer brand is often criticised as not being authentic. The optimal balance between rejuvenation and a high fit with the brand identity (which is aimed at all employees) is critical for success.

3.5.3   Brand Restructuring

Restructuring represents the second strategy of brand evolution. A distinction can here be made between brand consolidation and brand expansion (see Fig. 3.41).

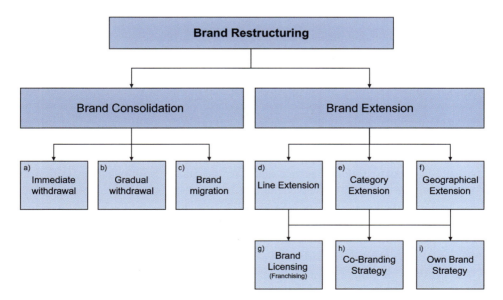

Fig. 3.41   Various options of brand restructuring

3.5.3.1 Brand Consolidation

Companies increasingly face the problem of stagnant and dwindling markets. As a consequence, companies are more and more frequently scaling down their brand portfolio. With these brand consolidation strategies, company resources are removed from individual brands in order to use them for other purposes. A brand consolidation strategy should be used if the resources which are tied to a company's brand can be used more efficiently for other activities, thus improving the company's long-term competitive position.

The **over-complexity of many brand portfolios** often results from mergers and acquisitions (M&A) and frequently hinders a company's expansion (cf. Sachs 2002). Since the mid-1990s, many companies have therefore consolidated their brand portfolios. Unilever, for example, has followed a brand portfolio consolidation strategy entitled "Path to Growth", which was intended to reduce the portfolio from 1600 brands in 2000 to 400 brands by the end of 2004. One reason for this decision was that more than 1000 of the 1600 brands accounted for only 8% of Unilever's total turnover. The elimination of the brands entailed a loss of 25,000 jobs (10% of the total number of employees) and the closure of numerous product plants. Ultimately, however, the "Path to Growth" strategy fell short of its objectives. Although Unilever saved around 4 billion euros between 1999 and 2004, both the market share and turnover and profit decreased.

Reasons for the "consolidation trend" can be assigned to four areas:

– **Market saturation**: In western countries many industry sectors exhibit market saturation tendencies. As a result, companies are finding it more and more difficult to expand their market share. This results in an increase in competitive pressure and expenditure for brand management, which can no longer be sustained by weak brands. Moreover, due to the large number of brands positioning becomes more and more difficult. Without differentiated positioning, brands will lose market share in the long run, thus increasing the need for brand consolidation.
– **Profitability pressure**: Due to increasing competitive pressure, shorter product life cycles, and the growing demands of global capital markets, the profitability pressure on a company's brand portfolio is constantly increasing. Empirical research has revealed that companies with a focussed brand portfolio are growing more strongly than companies which have a variety of similar brands (cf. Sachs 2002).
– **Popularity of private labels**: Due to the increasing concentration in the retail industry and the popularisation of private labels on the side of the suppliers as well as the consumers the so-called 'B' and 'C' brands of branded goods companies are becoming less important (cf. Burmann and Kiefel 2012). Often, only the strong 'A' brands of a branded goods manufacturer remain in the retailers' range. These are then supplemented by private labels of lower quality levels. This development intensifies the pressure on branded goods manufacturers.
– **The pressure of globalisation**: In some areas, increasing globalisation is leading to an alignment of lifestyles. This opens up additional opportunities for globally oriented brands. The implementation of a global brand strategy, however, places high demands

on a company's resources (cf. Meffert et al. 2010). Similarly, defending established market positions vis-à-vis new global brands which have penetrated the market is becoming ever more costly. Both effects of globalisation increase the necessity of brand consolidation.

For a brand consolidation strategy, three options are available: immediate withdrawal, gradual withdrawal, or employing a migration strategy (cf. Bieling 2005; Varadarajan et al. 2006; Mao et al. 2009; Haas 2010).

(a) **Immediate Withdrawal**

In the case of immediate withdrawal, the brand is removed from the market as quickly as possible. This strategy should be chosen if a brand's cash flow is strongly negative, and, more importantly, has a negative impact on the company's brand image. The chemical and pharmaceutical company Bayer, for example, had to remove its product brand Lipobay from the market when several deaths were reported as a result of having taken this medication. In some cases it is possible to sell the brand to third parties. Usually, considerable **barriers** must be overcome which can make an immediate withdrawal difficult or inadvisable. Often, only low revenues can be gained from selling the brand's assets. Furthermore, high costs may be incurred through the dissolution of the strategic business unit supervising the brand. Sometimes there will be negative spill-over effects onto a company's other brands, which has an overall negative impact on the company as a whole. Thus the implementation of brand consolidation can adversely affect the motivation of the entire workforce if, for instance, the reasons for the consolidation are inadequately communicated to the internal and external stakeholders. On the other hand, eliminating brands can free up resources which can then be used in the long term to support other brands (cf. Varadarajan et al. 2006).

(b) **Gradual Withdrawal**

In the case of gradual withdrawal, the number of loyal customers and the potential cost savings are still large enough to ensure a sufficient return on assets in the short to medium-term. To this end, specific disinvestments are made. Normally, this begins with a cutback in the brand's communication budget and a reduction in sales-supporting measures. Moreover, the number and types of products under the brand are often reduced, as well as the level of customer service provided. In a final step, product quality can be lowered (e.g. by switching to substandard ingredients) and price increases can be enforced. All of these measures lower the costs of brand management. With this strategy, the brand lives off its substance, which slowly deteriorates. It is only kept on the market for as long as it generates positive cash-flows, without investing anything further.

A similar approach is represented by a focussing strategy, when a brand's product range is significantly reduced. Normally this is accompanied by a withdrawal from specific market sectors. Due to a more strongly focussed product range, complexity costs can be reduced, and the brand image can be strengthened (cf. Bliss 2000).

The brand Nivea by Beiersdorf AG, for example, has gone through a focussing strategy (cf. Brandtner 2011).

Focussing strategies can be necessary, for example, if a brand has been expanded too much, by line or by category extensions, or if it has been damaged by an inadequate consistency of services. A focussing strategy can help eliminate the expansion products which do not really match the brand identity. This strengthens the clarity and conciseness of the brand image. Additionally, considerable savings may be realized with respect to direct, and especially overhead, costs. These savings can then be used to improve the quality and features of the remaining products, and to increase the brand's profitability (itself useful for future investments in the brand) (cf. Bliss 2000). In its aims, the focussing strategy resembles brand dynamisation by changing identity (cf. Sect. 3.5.2.2).

(c) **Brand Migration**

In the case of a **migration strategy**, a brand's offer remains mostly unchanged on the market, but the trademarks used so far are replaced by another label. Thus, this is also known as a substitution strategy (cf. Burmann and Blinda 2004). Migration often coincides with the sale of parts of a company in order to free up assets. It is also used within an internationalisation strategy in order to replace national brands with international ones. Thus, the American company Mars Inc. substituted the brand name 'Raider', which was only used in Germany, with the internationally employed label 'Twix' (for a chocolate bar).

The following conditions should be fulfilled for a successful migration strategy (cf. Sachs 2002):

– The consumers must be willing to accept the offers of the original brand under another brand name, or to see these offers as better fulfilled. Customer loyalty towards the original brand should therefore be primarily based on functional rather than non-functional benefits since the functional benefits remain mostly untouched by a migration strategy.
– The external target groups' associations with regard to the new brand must match the image of the old brand (external perspective).
– Cost savings made from the standardisation of the brand management as a result of a migration strategy must over-compensate the profit margin loss owing to customer migration.
– The internal target groups have to be convinced of the necessity of the migration (internal perspective). This should be primarily assured through an open top-down communication of the necessity or the strategic motives for the brand migration.

Examples of brand migration include the migration of Texaco to DEA and a few years later to Shell, the migration of the brand PriceWaterhouseCoopers Consulting to IBM Business Consulting Services, the migration of KKB to Citibank and then to Targobank, the migration of BfG Bank to SEB and later on to Santander Bank, or the migration of the brand BASF to EMTEC (in the market for date- and sound-recording media).

In principle, brand migration can occur gradually or on an ad hoc basis. In the case of a **successive migration**, the brand trademarks are gradually substituted by the new trademarks over a period of several months or even years (cf. Backhaus and Bieling 2005; Bieling 2005). As a result, the old and the new brands appear in parallel for some time, which often causes a great deal of confusion and uncertainty on the part of the customers and employees. This is especially pronounced in the case of migrations due to mergers and acquisitions because there often is a fundamental uncertainty with regard to the new brand owner's strategic objectives. The advantage of this form of brand migration is the high degree of continuity since employees and customers can slowly adjust to the change of trademark. Moreover, the necessary investments for brand migration can be extended over a longer period of time and thus more easily financed. An example of the implementation of this approach is the migration of the brand D2-Mannesmann to Vodafone (see Fig. 3.42).

In the case of an **ad hoc migration**, the trademarks of the brand to be substituted are immediately replaced with the new label without any parallel appearance of the old and new trademarks. This form of implementation is preferable if the substituting brand has a different positioning than the replacing brand. Furthermore, this form of brand migration should be chosen if the aim is to achieve a clear break with the old brand's past and origin. This was the intention, for example, in the migration of the brand Arthur Andersen to Accenture, which was meant to signal a radical rethinking and the end of the consulting firm's scandalous past (see Fig. 3.42). The main disadvantages of this option lie in the destruction of the substituted brand's equity and the substantial investments necessary within a very short period of time.

In general, a migration strategy should only be used if a stronger brand emerges in the long run. This is not always the case, as Procter & Gamble's attempt to migrate the German brand 'Fairy Ultra' to the internationally used brand 'Dawn' illustrates (cf. Esch 2012). Fairy Ultra had become well-known due to its TV and print campaign which focussed on a cleaning competition between the two neighbouring Spanish villages "Villarriba" and "Villabajo". Within its internationalisation strategy, Procter & Gamble substituted the brand Fairy Ultra in an ad hoc migration. The new brand name and the label

Fig. 3.42 Brand migration as exemplified by the brands D2-Mannesmann/Vodafone and Arthur Andersen/Accenture

design for Dawn were only supplemented by a brief reference to Fairy Ultra. The migration fell short of expectations, however, and, after a considerable loss of market shares, Procter & Gamble re-introduced the brand Fairy Ultra.

In the case of a brand migration, it should also be ensured that the rights of the substituted brand remain protected for as long as possible in order to keep them from being accessed by competitors. Wal-Mart, for example, secured the rights for the brand White Cloud following the merger of the toilet paper brands White Cloud and Charmin by Procter & Gamble and successfully sold several nappy products under this brand name. As a result, Wal-Mart was able to draw both psychographic and economic benefits from White Cloud's existing brand image, with adverse effects for Procter & Gamble (cf. Keller 2003).

3.5.3.2 Brand Extension

Brand extension strategies refer to the expansive restructuring of brands (see Fig. 3.41). These business activities aim to transfer the positive image of an existing brand to new products. The new products may belong to a category already covered by the firm's portfolio, to related categories or to completely new categories. A brand extension attempts to provide cognitive support to consumers when making a brand choice and to stimulate them emotionally. The main advantage of brand extensions is their potential to quickly build brand awareness and positive images in a cost-efficient way.

Brand extensions mostly involve new products. According to a U.S.-based study, brand extension strategies (as compared to completely new product launches) in fast moving consumer goods (FMCG) markets increased from 40% to approximately 90% between 1977 and 1991 (cf. Rangaswamy et al. 1993). The popularity of this strategy also incurred increased academic interest in the topic (cf. Zatloukal 2002; Völckner 2003). Brand extension strategies affect the brand architecture, which means that managing the resulting interdependencies represents a challenging task for brand management (cf. Kanitz 2013).

The term **brand extension** is not clearly defined; it tends to be used interchangeably with terms such as brand transfer or brand stretching.

> The terms **brand extension**, **brand transfer** and **brand stretching** refer to a common principle, namely that the identity of an established brand serves to transfer positive elements of the brand image to a new product and/or service, within the framework of a common brand concept (cf. Völckner 2004).

Empirically, there are four determinants of successful brand extensions (cf. Sattler et al. 2003; Völckner 2003): the **fit** between the new product and the core brand, the **marketing support** for the extension, the **retailers' acceptance** of the new product (which

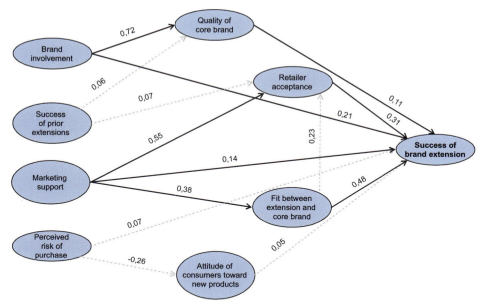

In an empirical analysis (n = 2,426 respondents), 66 transfer products from 49 product categories by 22 core brands were analysed.

Fig. 3.43 Success Factors of brand extensions. (Source: closely based on Völckner 2004, p. 76)

strongly depends on marketing support) and the **consumers' involvement** in the core brand (see Fig. 3.43). Additional success factors, including the breadth of the offered product range, quality perceptions of the core brand, the success of prior extensions and the consumers' attitude towards new products, appear less relevant (cf. Sattler 2001; Sattler et al. 2003; Völckner 2003).

The coefficients next to the arrows in Fig. 3.43 represent the relative strength of the effect, which varies between −1 and +1. Solid lines indicate the most important influences. Thus, marketing support has a strong, clear, positive effect on retailer acceptance, which, in turn, exerts a strong influence on brand extension success. The fit between the extension and the core brand is second most important factor and also strongly influenced by marketing support.

The positioning of an extension should reflect the identity of the core brand. For the **dynamic success of a brand extension** over time, three key aspects are relevant:

1. Management needs to provide internal and external target groups with **sufficient time** to become familiar with the extension of the core brand. This requires patience and financial resources.
2. Individual extensions should be launched **step by step** to support the learning processes of the target groups.

3. The core elements of the brand identity should remain the same for all extensions over time (cf. Boch 2012).

A positive example of an extension that allowed for sufficient time, using a step-by-step implementation process, is represented by the brand Nivea. Its management invested several years to extend the brand into different cream-based products, before extending further into different personal care categories. Thereby, the core of Nivea's identity (i.e. affordable care) was transferred successfully to the new products. When the brand management later tried to extend the brand into cosmetic categories, though, it over-stretched and weakened the core brand. Therefore, this extension (Nivea Beauté) was eliminated in 2011.

At a more detailed level, brand extension strategies can be subdivided into line extensions, category extensions and geographical extensions (see Fig. 3.41). Geographical extensions will be discussed in Chap. 7. **Line extensions** refer to the extension of a brand into **the same or closely related product categories**. **Category extensions** imply the extension of a brand into **new, unrelated product categories**. Thus, when the automotive brand Porsche extended into the sport utility vehicle (SUV) segment with the Porsche Cayenne, it was a line extension. In contrast, Porsche's extensions into fashion accessories or built-in kitchens represent a category extension (see Fig. 3.44).

(d) Line Extension

Line extensions increase the number of products and services offered by a brand within a product category already covered by the brand. Approximately 80–90% of all new product launches are line extensions (cf. Keller et al. 2008). Their main advantage lies

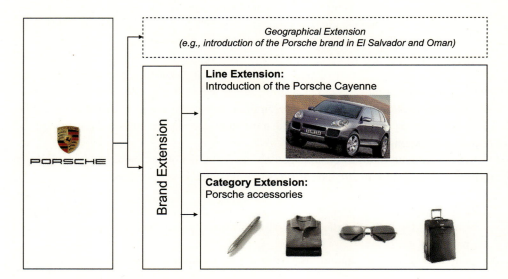

Fig. 3.44 Brand expansion as exemplified by Porsche

in the ease and cost efficiency of building awareness and an attractive image for the new product (cf. Völckner and Sattler 2006). Such an extension can be realised in three ways.

First, a **classical line extension** adds new offers that are similar to existing offerings on a technical and/or functional level. These extensions are launched in market segments close to those in which the core brand is already established, as exemplified by the extension of Nivea Creme to Nivea Milk. Similarly, Milka used this approach to extend its chocolate bar brand to different chocolate products (Milka Tender, I love Milka, Crispello and M-Joy).

Second, brands can be extended into new price/quality segments through **trading-up** or **trading-down** strategies. The brand Boss used both strategies in the fashion industry: It implemented a high-priced label Boss Black (trading up) but also introduced the Hugo label to target younger consumers with less disposable income (trading down) (see Fig. 3.45).

Trading-up strategies are especially challenging for mass market brands that traditionally target mainstream consumers. As discussed in Sect. 2.6.2, brand-related associations are stored in neural networks and brand extensions add new associations to these networks. A consumer's cognitive system attempts to integrate these new associations into an existing neural pattern. If the extension differs only slightly from the core brand, the neural filter systems suppress the new stimuli and reinforce the existing brand perception

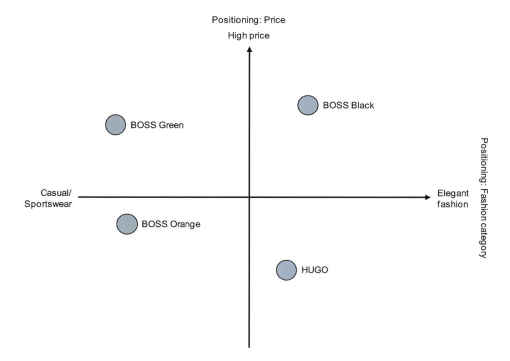

Fig. 3.45 Positioning of the brands of hugo boss AG. (Source: Hugo Boss AG 2012)

(cf. Bielefeld 2014). This phenomenon can be illustrated effectively using the example of the brand extension Milka Amavel.

In 2007–2008, Milka launched the brand extension Amavel, a premium chocolate bar filled with mousse, as a trading-up extension. In contrast to the standard Milka chocolate bar, which retails for EUR 0.79 for 100 g, Amavel sold for EUR 1.99 for a 160 g bar. However, the packaging design for Amavel strongly reflected the core brand's design, with the same colour, font and the Milka cow. The product name, "Amavel Mousse au Chocolat", also resonated with the name of the core brand offer, "Dessert au Chocolat". As a result, the stimuli associated with Amavel simply were not able to generate a new neural network of associations. Consumers perceived Amavel as just a more expensive Milka product, not as a premium chocolate. In response to the initially unsuccessful product launch, brand management tried to optimise the Amavel design in several waves in 2009, 2011 and 2012. Yet, due to its strong position as a market leader in the mainstream chocolate segment, Milka was unable to integrate the premium product into its portfolio. Ultimately, the company ceased the production of Amavel in Germany (cf. Bielefeld 2014).

On the other hand, if the differences between the core brand and the extensions are too large, the stimuli will create new, unrelated neural networks. These different and unrelated neural networks for the same brand hinder the development of a strong and unique brand image (cf. Bielefeld 2014). Accordingly, mainstream brands seeking to trade up are facing a dilemma: if the differences between the extension and the core brand are too small, consumers will not perceive the extension as a premium offer. If the differences are too large, the brand image of the core brand may be eroded. In any case, whether using trading-up or trading-down strategies, the brand management always has to make sure that the extension achieves a high degree of fit with the identity of the core brand.

Another kind of line extension involves a forward or backward extension along the value chain (**forward integration** or **backward integration**). Examples of forward integration strategies include the extension of the high-end audio brand Bang & Olufson (B&O) into the retail market, by implementing its own B&O stores, or the extension of the tour operator TUI into the travel agency market by implementing TUI ReiseCenter (TUI-branded travel agencies). And the German pharmaceutical company Merck used a backward integration strategy when it acquired its supplier Beijing Skywing Technology.

(e) **Category Extension**

Category extensions seek to move a brand into **new markets** that have **no technical or functional connection** to the brand's core market (therefore also termed **brand transfer**). Camel used this strategy to extend its product range beyond tobacco and into the male fashion and watch markets, using the Camel Active brand. Today, Camel Active generates a significant proportion of the company's sales. In 2012, Camel Active covered several fashion segments: shirts, trousers, jackets and coats, blazers, jeans, pullovers and knits, shoes, and accessories. Another successful category extension example comes from Apple, which has extended its brand to consumer electronics (iPod 2002, Apple TV 2007), mobile phones (iPhone 2007), and interactive watches (Apple Watch 2015).

Again, the key requirement for a successful category extension is the fit between the core brand and the extension (cf. Zatloukal 2002). Since there is no technical or functional connection, brand management has to emphasise object-based or symbolic/emotional associations (cf. Hätty 1989; Meffert and Heinemann 1990). A sports car thus tends to be associated with speed, quality and a high price (object-based associations) or with luxury and eroticism (symbolic/emotional associations). Any extensions beyond the automotive industry thus should leverage some of those associations. The importance of such connections becomes evident through two unsuccessful extensions: in the early 1980s, Levis tried to extend its brand to the suit market. The lack of connections between a jeans brand and the suit market made the extension ultimately fail (cf. Aaker 1990). Likewise, in 1999 Cosmopolitan failed to extend its brand to the yoghurt market because consumers did not find enough connections between a lifestyle magazine brand and the food category.

To create these necessary connections, a brand may also refer to identical usage situations, special worlds of experience or lifestyles. Thus, Michelin tyres and the Michelin Guide both refer to "driving a car"; Marlboro cigarettes and Marlboro fashion share the image of freedom and masculinity.

Using an established brand and its goodwill (i.e. the brand's positive image elements) offers great **potential** for a brand transfer. Lower market entry barriers reduce the risk of failure and facilitate entry into new market segments. Thus, for example, the U.S.-based confectionery company Mars Inc. was able to extend its product range from traditional chocolate bars to ice cream bars in the late 1990s. As a result, the company acquired new target groups and an additional strategic business sector.

Besides the image transfer to the extension product, there may also be a **backward transfer**, from the extension to the core brand, which may enhance or harm the core brand's image. Thus, Mövenpick Holding was able to strengthen its traditional restaurant and hotel business by extending the brand successfully to the markets for ice cream, coffee and sauces. Some additional benefits of brand extensions include generally lower costs for building a brand and the potential to reduce or circumvent advertising restrictions (e.g. for alcohol or tobacco).

Yet category extensions also carry inherent **risks**. If the transfer product(s) and the core brand are positioned too differently or aim at highly disparate target groups, the brand identity can be **eroded**. As a consequence, consumers may lose their trust in the brand (cf. Loken and Roedder 1993). It is also harmful for the brand as a whole if too many transfers take place in quick succession. For example, at some point in its long history, the Gucci brand offered more than 14,000 different products simultaneously. The extension into new market segments, often using licensing agreements, resulted in an enormous and costly coordination effort. In addition, the quality levels and marketing concepts across the different segments differed greatly. Ultimately, these differences led to a significant loss of brand trust among consumers. To reduce these risks, brand managers must carefully analyse the transfer potential of their brands, as well as the compatibility of the transfer product and the core brand (cf. Hätty 1989; Zatloukal 2002).

(g, h) Brand Licensing, and Co-branding

Line extensions, category extensions and geographical extensions may be implemented as licensing, franchising, co-branding or own brand strategies (see Fig. 3.41). If a company has identified extension potential for one of its brands, it needs to determine if it possesses sufficient resources and competencies to be able to implement the extension on its own (**own brand strategy**). If these internal resources and competencies are not sufficient, the company can consider licensing, franchising or co-branding strategies. Co-branding has already been discussed in Sect. 3.5.2.2.

With a **licensing or franchising strategy**, the brand owner grants a third party the right to use the brand name (cf. Binder 2005) in exchange for resources and competencies provided by the licensee or franchisee. In response to restricted financial and human resources, as well as management trends to focus on core competencies and core business sectors, licensing and franchising strategies have gained substantial appeal lately. Brand owners benefit from various **advantages** of these strategies (see Fig. 3.46).

Increased market presence facilitates **increased brand awareness.** Especially fashion brands like Calvin Klein, Joop or Boss rely on licensing agreements to increase awareness of their brands. A brand's product range is highly relevant to the consumers' evaluation of the brand, so a brand can benefit from licensing agreements that increase the number of products and services on offer. By using the licensee's resources and competencies, the brand can also enhance its image among consumers without needing to invest in costly processes to build new competencies. Thus, the sports fashion products of the sporting brand Head are produced by licensees, while Head focuses all its resources on its core competencies in the tennis racket and ski segments. And Camel and Marlboro have strengthened their images as being adventurous and free by licensing their brands to fashion producers in the outdoor segment.

1.	Increase brand loyalty
2.	Increase brand awareness
3.	Quickly build up product offerings under the brand name
4.	Strengthen the brand image
5.	Use additional distribution channels
6.	Earn licensing fees
7.	Increase communication pressure by usingthe licensing partner's budget

Fig. 3.46 Advantages of brand licensing for the brand owner. (Source: based on Binder 2005, p. 529 ff.)

Since extending the product range through licensing will increase the usage and contact frequency of a brand, it should also enhance brand awareness and consumer satisfaction, which in turn will positively affect brand loyalty over time (cf. Weinberg and Diehl 2001). In particular, FMCG brands can exploit licensing agreements to extend their brands into slower moving product categories and thereby enhance brand loyalty. Beck's beer, for example, has merchandised branded towels, ashtrays and t-shirts using a licensing strategy.

The brand owner also benefits from **licensing fees**, and most licensing agreements involve only minor costs for the brand owner. For brands such as Mövenpick, Jil Sander, Boss or Adidas, licensing fees account for a significant proportion of revenues. Licensing fees typically amount to 3–12.5% of the licensee's sales (cf. Binder 2005).

Moreover, brand licenses increase **legal brand protection** (see Chap. 6). Usually, a brand is legally protected only in market segments in which products are offered. A license agreement that involves additional market segments thus extends this legal protection.

The use of license or franchise contracts can also add new distribution channels. These channels increase the number of brand touch points without requiring any additional investment. This benefit is especially relevant in the case of franchise agreements.

Franchise agreements are distribution licenses between the owner of a brand (**franchisor**) and one or more distribution partners (**franchisees**). The franchisee pays a fee to be allowed to offer products and services under the franchisor's brand name (cf. Duong Dinh et al. 2010). Franchise agreements are common in the fast food industry (McDonald's, Burger King); other examples are hair dressers (Essanelle) or tanning shops (Sunpoint). A franchise fee usually consists of an entry free upon conclusion of the contract plus a percentage of the revenues earned.

Franchise agreements provide brand owners with extensive control over their brands. In particular, the franchisor retains the right to closely monitor the franchisee whose autonomy is strictly limited. In addition to financial revenues, franchise agreements therefore offer the benefits of strong control of the brand image by the brand owner. The brand's appearance remains highly standardised and consistent. Finally, the brand owner does not need to invest in outlets, which increases expansion capacity and growth speed.

Despite these advantages of licensing strategies, there are also **risks** for brand owners, mostly associated with the potential loss of a **consistent brand identity**. If a partner is chosen that strongly differs in its corporate culture or brand management principles, the resulting tensions can harm the brand. Moreover, licensees usually obtain the right to develop and produce products on their own. If these offerings do not fit with the brand identity or are positioned differently, the brand may be weakened over time. This risk increases with the amount of autonomy the licensee is given. Partner selection, supervision and coordination thus are crucial determinants of the success of expansion strategies via licensing and franchising.

3.6   Brand Budgeting

3.6.1   The Purpose of Brand Budgeting

Brand budgeting represents the final stage in the strategic brand management process (see Fig. 3.47). Particularly in the case of several brands, this is both an important and a complex step. Budgeting constitutes the last step in the process of strategic brand management. Its task is to assign budgets to the individual brands, taking the brand objectives

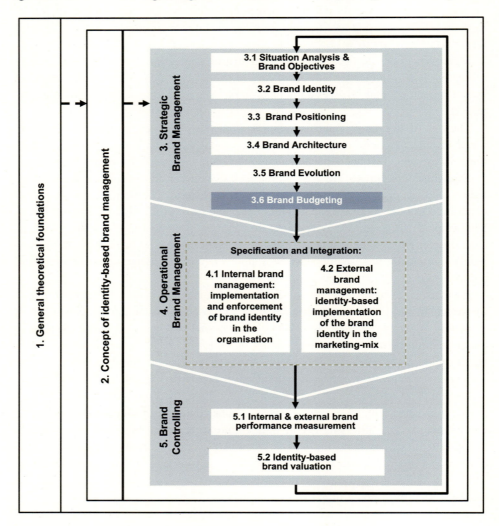

Fig. 3.47   Brand budgeting within identity-based brand management

into account (cf. Heemann 2008). It thus assumes an **important control and coordination task**. Welge and Al-Laham (2012) describe budgeting as "the central instrument which is used to implement plans in specific measures" (Welge and Al-Laham 2012, p. 596). Budgeting consequently enables strategic plans to be transferred into concrete, operative brand management measures.

The crucial importance of budgeting is also illustrated by the fact that formal budgeting systems are used in 99% of all European companies (cf. Kennedy and Dudgale 1999). Nevertheless, brand budgeting is often dominated by political motives rather than by the brands' strategic objectives and opportunities (cf. Greiner 2004). Actually, budgeting should be oriented to the situation analysis and the brand objectives. However, this is often not the case. Instead, inadequate financial provisions are made for the brand, which leads to a failure of the strategy so brand objectives are not achieved (cf. Kaplan and Norton 2000). Consequently, brand budgeting has to deal with the allocation of funds for the individual brands. Detailed individual brand budgets, e.g. for external brand communication, will then be determined in the course of operative brand management.

> **Identity-based brand budgeting** can be defined as "those specific processing and meta competences […] which in the long term enable an organisation to align the entire budgeting process to the brand's core, to specify the strategic positioning objectives of a brand to break these down into individual sub-targets, and to provide the financial means which the decision-making units need to achieve the positioning objectives derived from the brand identity" (Heemann 2008, p. 249 f.).

In order to minimise political influences, brand budgeting has to be based on an objective budgeting model. In order to achieve such objectivity, it is necessary to develop consensual directives on the budgeting process within the company. Also, the employees have to be familiar with the brand positioning and all aspects which are relevant to the brand. Equally important is the establishment of relevant performance indicators and manageable operational objectives which are based on the brand objectives. This applies to internal as well as external brand management. Only in this way can brand controlling evaluate the brands against the agreed targets, and corrections can be made during future brand budgeting.

3.6.2   The Budgeting Process

First of all, a situation analysis helps to analyse the actual state of brand budgeting. Central questions are: How high is the available marketing budget? How is the budget currently allocated? How has it been used up to now (cf. Meurer and Rügge 2012)? Once this information has been collected, the "investive marketing budget" has to be determined by subtracting the budgets for general measures such as market research or corporate PR from the total budget. The remaining budget can then be allocated to the individual brands in the further course of brand budgeting.

The situation analysis must primarily determine the strengths of the brands relative to each other. If a brand greatly contributes to the economic success of the company, it will receive a higher budget than a weaker brand. In order to prevent younger or smaller brands with a high development potential from being unfairly restricted, the growth opportunities of the individual brands in relation to market growth must also be taken into account.

In this context, a distinction is often made between a "safety budget" (that stabilises the actual business) and a "growth budget". The safety budget is based on the previous contribution to the economic success of the company. The growth budget, on the other hand, is geared towards the relative growth prognoses of the brand in relation to the development of the respective market or market segment. A brand with a high probability of above-average growth therefore will receive a higher growth budget than brands with a lower growth probability.

Achievement of the targets defined by the brand objectives and by brand budgeting, with the corresponding allocated funds, has to be verified in order to be able to make the necessary adjustments in the next budgeting cycle.

Because the distribution of the marketing budget was highly complex and difficult to understand, TUI was forced to revise their budget in 2008. Since then, marketing budgets are allocated according to the brands' contribution to added value. The aim here was a "budgeting which was oriented to the contribution of a brand or sub-brand to the company's economic results. In concrete terms this means the higher the return of a marketing initiative—measured in EBITA—the more budget [will be made available to a brand]" (TUI Marketing Director Michael Lambertz in Hermes 2009, p. 33). After establishing joint performance indicators and operational objectives, an actual analysis of the budget was carried out. As a result, the investment budget was calculated for the brands airtours, 1–2-Fly, TUI Schöne Ferien, TUI Weltentdecker and TUI Premium. Afterwards, the objectives were defined as a basis for the budgeting model, primarily EBITA, brand presentation and personal customer contact. Based on these targets, it was possible to ascertain the contribution of the individual brands. The inclusion of growth opportunities, which were recorded within the growth budget, was crucial here. Since the development of a budgeting logic and the assessment of growth opportunities were carried out with the help of the employees, it was possible to achieve a high internal commitment to the new brand budgeting process (cf. Hermes 2009).

References

Aaker, D. A. (1990). Brand extensions: The good, the bad, and the ugly. *Sloan Management Review, 47–56.*

Aaker, D. A. (1996). Misconceptions about brands. *The Journal of Brand Management, 3*(4), 212–214.

Aaker, D. A. (2004). *Brand portfolio strategy. Creating relevance, differentiation, energy, leverage, and clarity.* New York.

Aaker, D. A., & Joachimsthaler, E. (2000). *Brand leadership.* New York, USA: Free Press.

Aaker, D. A., & Shansby, J. G. (1982). Positioning your product. *Business Horizons May–June,* 56–62.

Adidas Group. (2012). Adidas Group Website. www.adidas-group.com. Zugegriffen: 24. Juli 2012.

Adlwarth, W. (2014). No-Names drängen stärker in die „Feine Welt". In Lebensmittelzeitung.net 16.05.2014. http://www.lebensmittelzeitung.net/business/themen/maerkte-marken/protected/handelsmarken-_130_15510.html. Zugegriffen: 27. Oktober 2014.

Ahlert, D., & Berentzen, J. (2010). Solution Selling für Handelsmarken im deutschen Einzelhandel. *Transolve-Projektbericht 7.*

Alpert, L., & Gatty, R. (1969). Product positioning by behavioural life-styles. *Journal of Marketing, 33*(2), 65–69.

Backhaus, K., & Bieling. M. (2005). Markenmigration. In F.-R. Esch (Hrsg.), *Moderne Markenführung - Grundlagen. Innovative Ansätze. Praktische Umsetzungen, S. 883–901.* Wiesbaden: Gabler.

Backhaus, K., Erichson, B., Plinke, W., & Weiber, R. (2016). *Multivariate Analysemethoden – eine anwendungsorientierte Einführung.* Berlin: Springer.

Batten & Company. (2014). Markenstärke Retail Brands 2014 - Die Klarheit der Markenimages deutscher Retail Brands nimmt drastisch ab. http://www.batten-company.com/presse/marketing-news/studie-markenstaerke-retail-brands-2014.html. Zugegriffen: 05. Mai 2015.

Baumgarth, C. (2003). *Wirkungen des co-brandings.* Wiesbaden: Dt. Univ.-Verlag.

Baumgarth, C. (2004). *Markenpolitik: Markenwirkungen, Markenführung, Markenforschung.* Wiesbaden: Gabler.

Baumgarth, C., & Kastner, O. L. (2012). *Pop-up-Stores im Modebereich: Erfolgsfaktoren einer vergänglichen Form der Kundeninspiration.* Arbeitspapier Nr. 69, Hochschule für Wirtschaft und Recht Berlin.

Berentzen, J. (2010). *Handelsmarkenmanagement: Solution selling in vertikalen Wertschöpfungsnetzwerken.* Wiesbaden: Gabler.

Bielefeld, K. W. (2012). *Consumer Neuroscience – Neurowissenschaftliche Grundlagen für den Markenerfolg.* Wiesbaden: Gabler.

Bielefeld, K. W. (2014). *Markenführung ist Kopfarbeit: Neurowissenschaftliche Grundlagen für den Markenerfolg – neue Erkenntnisse für die Marketingwissenschaft?* Arbeitspapier des Lehrstuhls für innovatives Markenmanagement (LiM) der Universität Bremen.

Bieling, M. (2005). *Internationalisierung von Marken - Eine Analyse aus konzeptioneller und empirischer Perspektive.* Hamburg: Kovač.

Binder, C. U. (2005). Lizenzierung von Marken. In F.-R. Esch (Hrsg.), *Moderne Markenführung - Grundlagen. Innovative Ansätze. Praktische Umsetzungen,* S. 523–548. Wiesbaden: Gabler.

Blackett, T., & Boad, B. (1999). *Co-branding.* Houndmills.

Blankson, C., & Kalafatis, S. P. (2007). Congruence between positioning and brand advertising. *Journal of Advertising Research, 3,* 79–94.

Blankson, C., Kalafatis, S. P., Cheng, J. M., & Hadjicharalambous, C. (2008). Impact of positioning strategies on corporate performance. *Journal of Advertising Research, 48*(1), 106–122.

Bliss, C. (2000). *Management von Komplexität.* Wiesbaden: Gabler.

Boch, S. (2012). *Die Nutzbarkeit der neuroökonomischen Forschung für die identitätsbasierte Markenführung – Eine Untersuchung mit Fokus auf den Repositionierungsspielraum von FMCG-Marken.* Wiesbaden.

Bohmann, T. (2011). *Nachhaltige Markendifferenzierung von Commodties - Besonderheiten und Ansatzpunkte im Rahmen der identitätsbasierten Markenführung.* Wiesbaden.

Böttger, E. (2012). *Employer Branding - Verhaltenstheoretische Analysen als Grundlage für die identitätsorientierte Führung von Arbeitgebermarken.* Wiesbaden: Gabler.

Bowlby, J. (1979). *The making and breaking of affectional bonds.* London.

Brandtner, M. (2011). Einladung zum Markenfrühjahrsputz. *Absatzwirtschaft – Marken 2011,* 30–33.

Brexendorf, T. O., & Tomczak, T. (2005). Interne Markenführung. In *Führungspraxis: motivieren, kooperieren, führen.* Düsseldorf.

Brockhoff, K. (1999). *Produktpolitik.* Stuttgart: Lucius & Lucius.

Bruhn, M. (2005). *Unternehmens- und Marketingkommunikation.* München: Vahlen.

Bruhn, M. (2012). Handelsmarken – Erscheinungsformen, Potentiale und strategische Stoßrichtungen. In J. Zentes et al. (Eds.), *Handbuch Handel* (pp. 453–563). Wiesbaden: Springer Gabler.

Burkhardt, A., Gündling, U., & Wexers, S. (2008). Status der internen Markenführung bei in Deutschland tätigen Corporate Brands: Ergebnisse einer empirischen Studie. *TAIKN Strategische Markenberatung.*

Burmann, C. (2002). *Strategische Flexibilität und Strategiewechsel als Determinanten des Unternehmenswertes* (zugl. Habilitationsschrift Universität Münster). Wiesbaden: Dt. Univ.-Verlag.

Burmann, C., & Blinda, L. (2004). Identitätsbasiertes Markenmanagement. In B. Wirtz & O. Göttgens (Eds.), *Integriertes Marken- und Kundenwertmanagement.* Wiesbaden: Gabler.

Burmann, C., Eilers, D., & Hemmann, F. (2010). Bedeutung der brand experience für die Markenführung im Internet. Arbeitspapier Nr. 46 des Lehrstuhls für innovatives Markenmanagement (LiM),

Burmann, C., & Kanitz, C. (2010). *Gestaltung der Markenarchitektur – Stand der Forschung und Entwicklung eines Managementprozesses.* Arbeitspapier Nr. 45 des Lehrstuhls für innovatives Markenmanagement (LiM) der Universität Bremen.

Burmann, C., & Kiefel, N. (2012). *Online-Handel und digitales Marketing – eine strategische Option für die Markenhersteller zur Verringerung der Verhandlungsmacht des Einzelhandels.* Arbeitspapier Nr. 51 des Lehrstuhls für innovatives Markenmanagement (LiM) der Universität Bremen.

Burmann, C., & Kranz, M. (2008). *Die Markenidentität zum Leben erwecken.* Interner Markenaufbau durch Mitarbeiterqualifikation: Universität Bremen.

Burmann, C., & Meffert, H. (2005). Theoretisches Grundkonzept der identitätsbasierten Markenführung. In H. Meffert, C. Burmann, & M. Koers (Eds.), *Markenmanagement - Identitätsorientierte Markenführung und praktische Umsetzung* (pp. 37–72). Wiesbaden: Gabler.

Burmann, C., Meffert, H., & Feddersen, C. (2007). Identitätsbasierte Markenführung. In A. Florack, M. Scarabis, & E. Primosch (Eds.), *Psychologie der Markenführung* (pp. 3–30). München: Vahlen.

Burmann, C., & Recke, T. (2009). Das Diktat der Markenführung: Gestaltung der Repositionierungsintensität als Herausforderungen an die Markenführung. In H. Hannemann & F. Keuper (Hrsg.), Das Diktat der Markenführung - 11 Thesen zur nachhaltigen Markenführung und -implementierung mit einem umfassenden Fallbeispiel der Loewe AG. Wiesbaden.

Burmann, C., & Spickschen, J. (2004). *Die Relevanz der Corporate Brand in der Markenarchitekturgestaltung internationaler Finanzdienstleister.* Arbeitspapier Nr. 8 des Lehrstuhls für innovatives Markenmanagement (LiM), Burmann, C. (Hrsg.), Universität Bremen.

Burmann, C., & Zeplin, S. (2004). *Innengerichtetes identitätsbasiertes Markenmanagement - State-of-the-Art und Forschungsbedarf.* Lehrstuhl für innovatives Markenmanagement, Arbeitspapier Nr. 7. Universität Bremen.

Calloway, J. (2003). *Becoming a category of one—How extraordinary companies transcend commodity and defy comparsion.* Weinheim: Wiley.

de Chernatony, L., & Cottam, S. (2006). Internal brand factors driving successful financial services brands. *European Journal of Marketing, 40*(5/6), 611–633.

Deutsche Bahn. (2012). Unternehmensleitbild. http://www.deutschebahn.com/file/2192512/data/konzernleitbild.pdf. Zugegriffen: 27. Oktober 2014.

Deutsche Bahn. (2014). Pünktlichkeitsentwicklung 2014. http://www.bahn.de/p/view/buchung/auskunft/puenktlichkeit_personenverkehr.shtml. Zugegriffen: 02. Januar 2015.

Duncan, E. (2008). Here today, gone tomorrow. *In the Black, 78*(8), 48–51.

Duong Dinh, H. V., Gehrmann, K., & Ahlert, D. (2010). Franchising – Ein Überblick. In H. V. Duong Dinh, K. Gehrmann, D. Ahlert (Hrsg.), *Handbuch Franchising und Cooperation – das Management kooperativer Unternehmensnetzwerke* (S. 29–58), Frankfurt: Dt. Fachverlag.

Esch, F.-R. (2008). Markenidentität als Basis für Brand Behavior. In T. Tomczak, F.-R. Esch, J. Kernstock, & A. Herrmann (Eds.), *Behavioral Branding* (pp. 35–46). Wiesbaden: Gabler.

Esch, F.-R. (2012). *Strategie und Technik der Markenführung.* München: Vahlen.

Feddersen, C. (2010). *Repositionierung von Marken - Ein agentenbasiertes Simulationsmodell zur Prognose der Wirkungen von Repositionierungsstrategien.* Wiesbaden: Gabler.

Fischer, J. (2001). Individualisierte Präferenzanalyse: Entwicklung und empirische Prüfung einer vollkommen individualisierten Conjpint-Analyse, 1- Aufl., Wiesbaden.

Freter, H., & Baumgarth, C. (2005). Ingredient Branding – Begriff und theoretische Begründung. In F.-R. Esch (Ed.), *Moderne Markenführung* (pp. 455–482). Wiesbaden: Gabler.

Freundt, T. C. (2006). *Verhaltensrelevanz emotionaler Markenimages – eine interindustrielle Analyse auf empirischer Grundlage.* Wiesbaden: Dt. Univ.-Verlag.

Gallup. (2009). Engagement Index Deutschland 2008. http://sas-origin.onstreammedia.com/origin/gallupinc/Gallup_Audio/090127_CD_Engagement_2008_v2.mp3. Zugegriffen: 28. Mai 2010.

GfK, Gesellschaft für Konsumforschung. (2012). GfK consumer index total Grocery 01/2012. http://www.gfkps.com/imperia/md/content/ps_de/consumerindex/ci_01_2012_od.pdf. Zugegriffen: 24. Juli 2012.

Gladwell, M. (2001). *The Tipping Point - How Little Things Can Make a Big Difference.* New York.

Greiner, O. (2004). *Strategiegerechte Budgetierung – Anforderungen und Gestaltungsmöglichkeiten der Budgetierung im Rahmen der Strategierealisierung.* München: Vahlen.

Gröppel-Klein, A. (2005). Entwicklung, Bedeutung und Positionierung von Handelsmarken. In F.-R. Esch (Ed.), *Moderne Markenführung* (pp. 1113–1137). Wiesbaden: Gabler.

Gummesson, E. (1987). The new marketing—Developing long-term interactive relationships. *Long Range Planning, 20*(4), 10–20.

Günther, H. (2012). Markendehnung Tempo Toilettenpapier: Ein Griff ins Klo? http://www.marketing-boerse.de/Fachartikel/details/1207-Markendehnung-Tempo-Toilettenpapier-Ein-Griff-ins-Klo/34779. Zugegriffen: 27. Oktober 2014.

Haas, S. (2010). *Markenportfoliobereinigungen - Entwicklung eines Planungsprozesses zur Strategieformulierung.* Wiesbaden: Gabler.

Hanf, J. H., & Wettstein, N. (2008). Bio-Handelsmarken als strategisches Instrument zur Positionierung und Imagebildung eines Lebensmittelhändlers - Chancen und Risiken. *Journal für Verbraucherschutz und Lebensmittelsicherheit, 4*(1), 15–22.

Hansen, U., Hennig-Thurau, T., & Schrader, U. (2001). *Produktpolitik* (3rd ed.). Stuttgart: Schäffer-Poeschel.

Hätty, H. (1989). *Der Markentransfer*. Heidelberg: Physica-Verlag.

Heemann, J. (2008). *Markenbudgetierung*. Wiesbaden: Gabler.

Hegner, S. (2012). *Die Relevanz des Vertrauens für das identitätsbasierte Management globaler Marken - Ein interkultureller Vergleich zwischen Deutschland, Indien und Südafrika*. Wiesbaden: Springer Gabler.

Henrion Ludlow Schmidt (2005). Markenmanagement 2005. http://markenlexikon.com/d_texte/hls_studie_markenmanagement_2005.pdf. last visit: 13. November 2008.

Hermes, V. (2009). *Die TUI revolutioniert ihre Budgetplanung*. Absatzwirtschaft, *01*(2009), 32–35.

Hesseling, C. (2010). Gestreckter Kaffee – Wie Röstereien tricksen. http://www.blogmaxe.de/2010/10/20/gestreckter-kaffe-wie-roestereien-tricksen. last visit: 27. Oktober 2014.

Hugo Boss, A. G. (2012). Hugo Boss Markenübersicht. http://group.hugoboss.com/de/brand_profiles.htm. last visit: 24. Juli 2012.

IfH. (2006). Institut für Handelsforschung an der Universität zu Köln, Katalog E – Definition zu Distribution und Handel. Köln.

Ind, N. (2003). Inside out: How employees build value. *Journal of Brand Management, 10*(6), 393–402.

Indrest, R. (2013). Implications of buyer power and private labels on vertical competition and innovation. http://www.markenverband.de/publikationen/studien/Vertical%20Competition%20and%20Innovation%20Report%20-%20Roman%20Inderst.pdf. Zugegriffen: 05. Mai 2015.

Jentschke, M. (2015). *Innengerichtete Markenführung in Unternehmen mit mehreren Marken – Wirkungen und Determinanten multipler Brand Commitments*, bislang unveröffentlichte Dissertation.

Joachimsthaler, E. (2002). Mitarbeiter - Die vergessene Zielgruppe für Markenerfolge. *Absatzwirtschaft, 4*(11), 28–34.

Kanitz, C. (2013). Gestaltung komplexer Markenarchitekturen - Eine empirische Untersuchung zur Ermittlung der Verhaltensrelevanz von Marken unterschiedlicher Hierarchieebenen. Wiesbaden: Springer Gabler.

Kapferer, J.-N. (2008). *Strategic brand management: Creating and sustaining brand equity long term*. London.

Kaplan, R., & Norton, D. P. (2000). *The strategy-focused organization*. Boston: Harvard Business School Press.

Keller, K. L. (2003). *Strategic brand management. Building, measuring and managing brand equity*. New Jersey: Upper Saddle River.

Keller, K. L., Apéria, T., & Georgson, M. (2008). *Strategic brand management—A European perspective*. Harlow: Prentice Hall.

Kennedy, A., & Dudgale, D. (1999). Getting the most from budgeting. *Management Accounting, 79*, 22–24.

Kimpakorn, N., & Tocquer, G. (2009). Employees' commitment to brands in the service sector: Luxury hotel chains in Thailand. *Journal of Brand Management, 16*(8), 532–544.

Kleine-Kalmer, B. (2016). *Managing brand page attachment—An empirical study on Facebook User's attachment to brand pages*. (bislang unveröffentlichte Dissertation).

Koers, M. (2001). *Steuerung von Markenportfolios: ein Beitrag zum Mehrmarkencontrolling am Beispiel der Automobilwirtschaft*. Frankfurt am Main: Lang.

Kohli, A. K., & Jaworski, B. (1990). Market orientation: The construct, reserach propositions and managerial implications. *Journal of Marketing, 54*, 1–18.

König, V. (2010). *Markenmanagement im Call Center: Eine empirische Analyse zur Konzep- tionalisierung, Operationalisierung und Wirkung von Maßnahmen zum Aufbau von Brand Commitment in Call Centern*. Wiesbaden.

Kotler, P. (2003). *Marketing management*. New Jersey: Upper Saddle River.

Kotler, P., Keller, K. L., & Bliemel, F. (2007). *Marketing-management*. Pearson Studium: Strategien für wertschaffendes Handeln. München u. a.

Krause, J. (2013). *Identitätsbasierte Markenführung im Investitionsgüterbereich - Management und Wirkungen von Marke-Kunde-Beziehungen*. Wiesbaden: Springer Gabler.

Kroeber-Riel, W., Weinberg, P., & Gröppel-Klein, A. (2013). *Konsumentenverhalten*. München: Vahlen.

Krogh, H. (2010). Seat-Chef Muir spricht Klartext über Probleme der spanischen VW-Marke. http://www.automobilwoche.de/article/20100513/NACHRICHTEN/100519972/seat-chef-muir-spricht-klartext-uber-probleme-der-spanischen-vw-marke#.VE4sxfl5PHQ. Zugegriffen: 27. Oktober 2014.

Kullmann, M. (2006). *Strategisches Mehrmarkencontrolling - Ein Beitrag zur integrierten und dynamischen Koordination von Markenportfolios*. Wiesbaden: Dt. Univ.-Verlag.

Kumar, P. (2005). The impact of cobranding on customer evaluation of brand counterextensions. *Journal of Marketing, 69*(3), 1–18.

Kumar, N., & Steenkamp, J.-B. (2007). *Private label strategy—How to meet the store brand challange*. Boston: Harvard Business School Press.

Kuß, A., Tomczak, T., & Reinecke, S. (2009). *Marketingplanung - Einführung in die marktorientierte Unternehmens- und Geschäftsfeldplanung*. Wiesbaden: Gabler.

Laforet, S., & Saunders, J. (1994). Managing brand portfolios: How the leaders do it. *Journal of Advertising Research, 34*(5), 64–76.

Laforet, S., & Saunders, J. (1999). Managing brand portfolios: Why leaders do what they do. *Journal of Advertising Research, 39*(1), 51–66.

Laforet, S., & Saunders, J. (2005). Managing brand portfolios: How strategies have changed. *Journal of Advertising Research, 45*(3), 314.

Laforet, S., & Saunders, J. (2007). How brand portfolios have changed: A study of grocery suppliers brands from 1994 to 2004. *Journal of Marketing Management, 23*(1/2), 39–58.

Lawler, E. J. (1992). Affective attachment to nested groups: A choice-process theory. *American Sociological Review, 57*(3), 327–339.

Leonard, N. H., Beauvais, L. L., & Scholl, R. W. (1999). Work motivation: The incorporation of self-concept-based processes. *Human Relation, 52*(8), 969–998.

Loken, B., & Roedder, J. D. (1993). Diluting brand beliefs: When do brand extensions have a negative impact? *Journal of Marketing, 57*, 71-84.s.

Mael, F. A., & Ashforth, B. E. (1992). Alumni and their alma mater: A partial test of the reformulated model of organizational identification. *Journal of Organizational Behavior, (13/2)*, 103–123.

Maloney, P. (2007). *Absatzmittlergerichtetes, identitätsbasiertes Markenmanagement: Eine Erweiterung des innengerichteten, identitätsbasierten Markenmanagements unter besonderer Berücksichtigung von Premiummarken*. Wiesbaden: Gabler.

Mao, H., Luo, X., & Jain, S. P. (2009). Consumer responses to brand elimination: An attributional perspective. *Journal of Consumer Psychology, 19*(3), 280–289.

Markowitz, H. M. (1952). Portfolio selection. *Journal of Finance, 7 Mar*, 77–91.

Markowitz, H. M. (1959). *Portfolio selection: Efficient diversification of investments*. New York: Yale University Press.

McEwen, W. J. (2007). Don't neglect your brand ambassadors. *Gallup Management Journal Online, 8*.

Meffert, H., & Burmann, C. (1996). Identitätsorientierte Markenführung – Grundlagen für das Management von Markenportfolios. In H. Meffert, H. Wagner & K. Backhaus (Hrsg.), *Arbeitspapier Nr. 100 der Wissenschaftlichen Gesellschaft für Marketing und Unternehmensführung e.V.*. Münster.

Meffert, H., Burmann, C., & Becker, C. (2010). *Internationales marketing-management: Ein marktorientierter Ansatz*. Stuttgart.

Meffert, H., Burmann, C., & Kirchgeorg, M. (2015). *Marketing: Grundlagen marktorientierter Unternehmensführung*. Wiesbaden: Springer Gabler.

Meffert, H., & Heinemann, G. (1990). Operationalisierung des Imagetransfers. *Marketing, Zeitschrift für Forschung und Praxis, 1,* 5–10.

Meffert, H., & Koers, M. (2005). Markenkannibalisierung in Markenportfolios. In H. Meffert, C. Burmann, & M. Koers (Eds.), *Markenmanagement* (pp. 297–318). Wiesbaden: Gabler.

Meurer, J., & Rügge, M. (2012). Kafka für Marketers. *Absatzwirtschaft, 7*(2012), 30–34.

Morschett, D. (2012). Retail Branding – Strategischer Rahmen für das Handelsmarketing. In J. Zentes, B. Swoboda, D. Morschett, & H. Schramm-Klein (Eds.), *Handbuch Handel* (pp. 441–4616). Wiesbaden: Gabler.

Mühlbacher, H., Dreher, A., & Gabriel-Ritter, A. (1996). Strategische Positionierung- Grundpfeiler des Marketings in komplexen und dynamischen Umwelten. *Die Betriebswirtschaft, 56*(1), 203–220.

Müller, J. (2012). *Multisensuale Gestaltung der Ladenatmosphäre zur Profilierung von Store Brands – Ein theoriegeleitetes, experimentelles Design zum Shopperverhalten*. Wiesbaden: Springer Gabler.

Muzellec, L., & Lambkin, M. (2006). Corporate rebranding: Destroying, transferring or creating brand equity? *European Journal of Marketing, 40*(7/8), 803–824.

Nadkarni, S., & Herrmann, P. (2010). CEO personality, strategic flexibility, and firm performance: the case of the Indian business process outsourcing industry. *Academy of Management Journal, 53*(5), 1050–1073.

Netzer, F. (1999). *Strategische Allianzen im Luftverkehr: nachfrageorientierte Problemfelder ihrer Gestaltung*. Frankfurt am Main u.a.: Lang.

Nink, M. (2009). *Ungenutztes Potenzial. Die Bank, 4,* 78–83.

Nitschke, A. (2006). *Event-Marken-Fit und Kommunikationswirkung – Eine Längsschnittsbetrachtung am Beispiel der Sponsoren der FIFA-Fußballweltmeisterschaft 2006*. Wiesbaden: Gabler.

Nommensen, J. N. (1990). Die Prägnanz von Markenbildern: Prüfung der Kommunikationsstrategie bei Produktrepositionierung, Heidelberg.

o.V. (2013). Mächtige Allianz will Red Bull die Flügel stutzen. http://www.welt.de/wirtschaft/article131344085/Maechtige-Allianz-will-Red-Bull-die-Fluegel-stutzen.html. Zugegriffen: 05. Mai 2015.

o.V. (2014). Lidl listet wieder Coca-Cola, in: https://www.derhandel.de/news/unternehmen/pages/Lebensmitteldiscounter-Lidl-listet-wieder-Coca-Cola-10329.html. Zugegriffen: 05. Mai 2015.

Park, C., Jun, S. Y., & Shocker, A. D. (1996). Composite branding alliances. *Journal of Marketing Research, 33*(4), 453–466.

Park, C. W., MacInnis, D. J., Priester, J., Eisingerich, A. B., & Iacobucci, D. (2010). Brand attachment and brand attitude strength: Conceptual and empirical differentiation of two critical brand equity drivers. *Journal of Marketing, 74*(6), 1–17.

Piehler, R. (2011). *Interne Markenführung – Theoretisches Konzept und fallstudenbasierte Evidenz*. Wiesbaden: Gabler.

Piehler, R., Hanisch, S., & Burmann, C. (2015). Internal branding—Relevance, management, and challenges. *Marketing Review St. Gallen, 32*(1), 52–60.

Porter, M. (2006). Leader as strategist—Gain and sustain a unique position. *Leaderhsip excellence, 23*(6), 6.

Procter&Gamble. (2015). Marken. www.pg.com/de_DE/produkte/index.shtml. Last visit: 08. Mai 2015.

Rangaswamy, A., Burke, R., & Oliva, T. (1993). Brand equity and the extendibility of brand names. *International Journal of Research in Marketing, 10,* 61–75.

Rao, V. R., Agarwal, M. K., & Dahlhoff, D. (2004). How is manifest branding strategy related to the intangible value of a corporation? *Journal of Marketing, 68*(4), 126–140.

Rao, A. R., & Ruekert, R. W. (1994). Brand alliances as signals of product quality. *Sloan Management Review, 36*(1), S. 87–97.

Recke, T. (2011). *Die Bestimmung der Repositionierungsintensität von Marken*. Ein entscheidungsunterstützendes Modell auf Basis von semantischen Netzen, Wiesbaden: Gabler.

Reeves, R. (1960). *Reality in advertising*. New York.

Ries, A., & Trout, J. (2001). *Positioning: the battle for your mind, 20th anniversary edition*. New York.

Röben, P. (2015). Hoffnungsträger SunExpress – Lufthansa setzt Ferienflieger auf Langstrecke ein. In *Weser Kurier* v. 20.02.2015, S. 2.

Romaniuk, J. (2001). Brand Positioning in financial services: A longitudinal test to find the best brand position. *Journal of Financial Services Marketing, Jg., 6*(2), 111–121.

Roosdorp, A. (1998). *Positionierungspflege: Phänomen*. St. Gallen: Herausforderungen und Konzept.

Rosenberg, M. (1979). *Conceiving the self*. New York.

Sachs, A. (2002). *Portfolio-management bei Unilever. Marketingjournal, 2,* 8–17.

Sattler, H. (2001). *Markenpolitik*. Stuttgart: Kohlhammer.

Sattler, H., Völckner, F., & Zatloukal, G. (2003). *Erfolgsfaktoren von Markentransfers. Marketing ZFP, 25*(3), 147–168.

Schade, M. (2012). *Identitätsbasierte Markenführung professioneller Sportvereine – Eine empirische Untersuchung zur Ermittlung verhaltensrelevanter Markennutzen und der Relevanz der Markenpersönlichkeit*. Wiesbaden: Gabler.

Schallehn, M., Burmann, C., & Riley, N. (2014). Brand authenticity: Model development and empirical testing. *Journal of Product & Brand Management, 23*(3), 192–199.

Schmitt, B. (2003). *Customer experience management—A revolutionary approach to connecting with your customers*. Weinheim.

Skala-Gast, D. (2012). *Zusammenhang zwischen Kundenzufriedenheit und Kundenloyalität: Eine empirische Analyse am Beispiel der deutschen Automobilindustrie*. Wiesbaden: Springer Gabler.

Sneakers-Magazine. (2012). http://sneakers-magazine.com/wp-content/uploads/2012/02/tgwo.jpg. Zugegriffen: 24. Juli 2012.

Sponheuer, B. (2010). *Employer Branding als Bestandteil einer ganzheitlichen Markenführung*. Wiesbaden: Gabler.

Springer, C. (2008). *Multisensuale Markenführung - Eine verhaltenswissenschaftliche Analyse unter besonderer Berücksichtigung von Brand Lands in der Automobilwirtschaft*. Wiesbaden: Gabler.

Starbucks. (2012). *Starbucks store design*. http://www.starbucks.com/coffeehouse/store-design. Zugegriffen: 24. Juli 2012.

Süddeutsche Zeitung. (2010). Deutsche Bahn - Schaffnerin wirft Mädchen bei Eiseskälte aus Zug. http://www.sueddeutsche.de/panorama/deutsche-bahn-schaffnerin-wirft-maedchen-bei-eiseskaelte-aus-zug-1.62316. Zugegriffen: 24. Juli 2012.

Szeliga, M. (1996). *Push und Pull in der Markenpolitik: ein Beitrag zur modellgestützten Marketingplanung am Beispiel des Reifenmarktes*. Frankfurt: Peter Lang.

Thomson, M., MacInnis, D., & Park, C. W. (2005). The ties that bind: Measuring the strength of consumers' emotional attachments to brands. *Journal of Consumer Psychology, 15*(1), 77–91.

Tomczak, T., & Roosdorp, A. (1996). Positionierung - Neue Herausforderungen verlangen neue Ansätze. In T. Tomczak, T. Rudolph & A. Roosdorp (Hrsg.), Positionierung Kernentscheidung des Marketing. St. Gallen.

Trommsdorff, V. (1975). *Die Messung von Produktimages für das Marketing: Grundlagen und Operationalisierung*. Köln: Heymanns.

Trout, J. (1969). "Positioning" is a game people play in today's me-too market place. *Industrial Marketing, 54*(6), 51–55.

Vallaster, C., & de Chernatony, L. (2005). Internationalisation of services brands: The role of leadership during the internal brand building process. *Journal of Marketing Management, 21*(1/2), 181–203.

Varadarajan, R., DeFanti, M. P., & Busch, P. S. (2006). Brand portfolio, corporate image, and reputation: Managing brand deletions. *Journal of the Academy of Marketing Science, 34*(2), 195–205.

Visible Measures. (2012). www.visiblemeasures.com. Zugegriffen: 24. Juli 2012.

Völckner, F. (2003). *Neuprodukterfolg bei kurzlebigen Konsumgütern: Eine empirische Analyse der Erfolgsfaktoren von Markentransfers*. Wiesbaden: Dt. Univ.-Verlag.

Völckner, F. (2004). Fünf Faktoren entscheiden über den Erfolg von Markentransfers. *Absatzwirtschaft*, 74-79.

Völckner, F., & Sattler, H. (2006). Drivers of brand extension success. *Journal of Marketing, 70*(2), 18–34.

von Weizsäcker, E. (1974). Erstmaligkeit und Bestätigung als Komponente der pragmatischen Information. In E. von Weizsäcker (Hrsg.), *Offene Systeme I. Beiträge zur Zeitstruktur von Information, Entropie und Evolution*, S. 82–113. Stuttgart: Klett-Cotta.

Warwitz, C. (2016). *Location-based Advertising*. bislang unveröffentlichte Dissertation.

Weinberg, P., & Diehl, S. (2001). Aufbau und Sicherung von Markenbindung unter schwierigen Konkurrenz- und Distributionsbedingungen. In R. Köhler, W. Majer & H. Wiezorek, H. (Hrsg.), *Erfolgsfaktor Marke - Neue Strategien des Markenmanagements*, S. 26–35. München: Vahlen.

Welge, M. K., & Al-Laham, A. (2012). *Strategisches Management: Grundlagen – Prozess – Implementierung*. Wiesbaden: Springer Gabler.

Welt. (2011). Erneut Zugausfälle wegen überlasteter Werkstätten. http://www.welt.de/vermischtes/article11943732/Erneut-Zugausfaelle-wegen-ueberlasteter-Werkstaetten.html. Zugegriffen 24. Juli 2012.

Wiancko, R. (2010). And the „Oldspice Maneuver" is created, blows the doors off of advertising. http://ryanwiancko.com/2010/07/15/and-the-oldspice-maneuver-is-created-blows-the-doors-off-of-advertising. Zugegriffen: 24. Juli 2012.

Zatloukal, G. (2002). *Erfolgsfaktoren von Markentransfers*. Wiesbaden: Dt. Univ.-Verlag.

Zeplin, S. (2006). *Innengerichtetes, identitätsbasiertes Markenmanagement*. Wiesbaden: Gabler.

Zewa. (2012). http://www.zewa.de/toilettenpapier. Zugegriffen: 24. Juli 2012.

Operational Brand Management

4

Contents

4.1 Operational Internal Brand Management. 175
    4.1.1 Moderators of the Relationships with Brand Citizenship Behaviour. 175
    4.1.2 Instruments to Influence Brand Understanding and Brand Commitment 177
4.2 Operational External Brand Management 189
    4.2.1 Brand Offering Policy 190
    4.2.2 Brand Price Policy 191
    4.2.3 Brand Distribution Policy. 191
    4.2.4 Brand Communication Policy 194
4.3 Identity-Based Brand Management in the Digital Context 195
    4.3.1 Challenges for Brand Management by Digitalization 195
    4.3.2 Instruments of Online Communication 198
    4.3.3 Special Position of Social Media in Identity-Based Brand Management 200
References. 225

This fourth chapter focuses on the operative implementation of brand management with respect to the brand's internal and external target groups. Based on strategic planning, internal operational brand management deals with conveying brand identity to the brand's internal target group. The following question should be answered here.

What brand management tools achieve the objectives of internal brand management?

Furthermore, external operational brand management focuses on the brand's external target groups. The aim here is to communicate the brand promise via the brand touch points to external target groups. The key questions here address the development of product, price, distribution, and communication policies.

© Springer Fachmedien Wiesbaden GmbH 2017
C. Burmann et al., *Identity-Based Brand Management,*
DOI 10.1007/978-3-658-13561-4_4

Due to the ever increasing influence of digitalization, this fourth chapter will focus on online communication and social media. Questions of key interest here include the following.

What online communication instruments are available to communicate the brand promise to external target groups?

What significance does social media have for external brand management? How can social media be used by brand managers in order to influence the brand's external target groups? (Fig. 4.1).

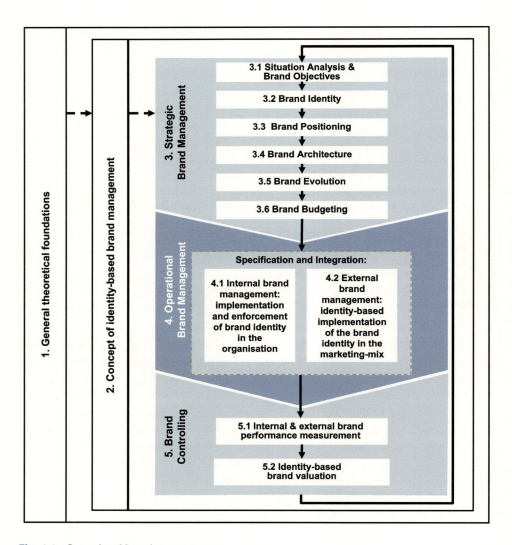

Fig. 4.1   Operational brand management

4.1   Operational Internal Brand Management

The relevance and outcomes of internal brand management are explained in detail in Sect. 3.1.1. Affecting the three outcomes **brand understanding**, **brand commitment**, and **brand citizenship behaviour** represents the core of internal operational brand management. Using a large employee survey from a German tourism company, Piehler (2011) was able to empirically validate that brand understanding and brand commitment positively influence brand citizenship behaviour with path coefficients of 0.37 and 0.40, respectively. In addition, with a highly significant path coefficient of 0.26, he also empirically validated that brand understanding has a positive effect on brand commitment (see Fig. 4.2). Similar results can be found in the study of Piehler et al. (2015) who conducted an employee survey in a German service company in the banking sector and in the Australian study of Xiong et al. (2013). The effect of brand understanding and brand commitment on brand citizenship behaviour is moderated by structure and process fit as well as by resource and competence fit (cf. Zeplin 2006; Piehler 2011).

4.1.1   Moderators of the Relationships with Brand Citizenship Behaviour

4.1.1.1 Structure and Process Fit

Developing brand citizenship behaviour amongst a brand's employees is based directly on their brand understanding and brand commitment. This causal effect is, however,

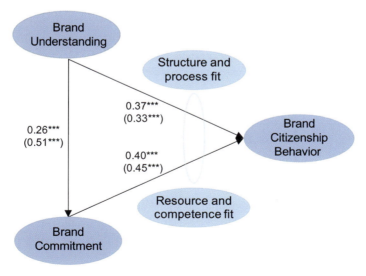

*= p < 0.1; ** = p < 0.05; *** = p < 0.01; n. s. = not significant

Fig. 4.2 Relationship between internal brand management outcomes. (Source: Adapted from Piehler 2011, p. 543; Piehler et al. 2015, p. 55)

influenced by the structures and processes which enable an employee within the organisation to put brand citizenship behaviour into practice.

The **structure fit** describes the extent to which the organisational structure of a company is suited to supporting the employees in implementing the brand identity. If the organisational structure encourages the employees to behave in a brand-consistent manner, then, at the same time, the significance of the brand and the employees' own behaviour is additionally made clear. If a brand stands, for example, for "service from a single source", then the organisational structure must also allow the employees to have access to all aspects of the brand products and services in terms of the customers. However, if the internal organisation is arranged in such a way that the individual products and services are looked after by separate departments, then it is practically impossible for the individual employees to implement the brand promise in their own behaviour towards the customers. If a tele-communication brand offers landline connections, internet access, and mobile access as integrated telecommunication services, then the organizational units which offer the services should not be managed separately. In addition, the brand promise "speed of service" cannot be delivered by a highly complex organizational structure with many hierarchical levels. Finally, an internationally decentralized organizational structure of a tourism company with a high degree of freedom regarding quality specifications in different countries contradicts the brand promise of worldwide identical quality standards.

The **process fit** describes the extent to which the organisational processes, and particularly the product- and service-related processes, support the employees in implementing the brand identity (cf. Piehler 2011). If, for instance, part of the brand promise consists of dealing with the customers problems in a quick and non-bureaucratic manner, then an employee in the call-centre, to whom the customer reports their problem, must already be able to initiate the respective measures to solve the problem without first having to consult with his superiors. A best practice example is the German bank Bremische Volksbank, which promises the customer to answer requests for credits within one day. In order to fulfil this brand promise, the bank revised the credit handling processes.

4.1.1.2 Resource and Competence Fit

Resource fit and **competence fit** deal with the skills and work equipment of the individual employees (cf. Zeplin 2006). In addition to understanding of the relevance and knowledge of the content of the brand identity, the employees also need the necessary competences in order to implement this brand understanding. For employees with direct customer contact this refers, for example, to social and linguistic skills. If the vision of a bank, for example, consists of being a financial services company operating worldwide, then the customer advisors in the local branches must also be able to speak at least one foreign language, in addition to the national language, in order to assist international customers on-site.

In order for the employees to be able to transform the existing brand commitment into brand citizenship behaviour, resources, such as financial, technological or human resources, are also necessary in addition to the aforementioned competences (cf. Zeplin 2006). The demand for adequate resources in order to implement the brand identity in the employees' behaviour is often opposed to rationalisation measures in which, from a purely financial point of view, for example, direct contact between the employees responsible and the consumer is replaced by the introduction of central call-centres. A practical example for a low resource fit would be a bank with a brand promise of discretion but with employees working in an open-plan office. This evaluation would also be true for a producer of construction equipment or airplanes with a brand promise of 48 h repair service for the products but with inadequate or missing tools and replacement parts for employees in order to repair the products quickly on-site.

4.1.2 Instruments to Influence Brand Understanding and Brand Commitment

Building, maintaining, and developing brand understanding and brand commitment as antecedents of brand citizenship behaviour is the aim of operational internal brand management. In order to accomplish this task, several instruments are available for management. In literature, the following managerial tools of internal branding have gained attention: (1) design of the brand identity, (2) continuity and consistency of brand management, (3) internal brand communication, (4) external brand communication, (5) brand-oriented human resource management, and (6) brand-oriented leadership (cf. Burmann and Zeplin 2005; Schmidt and Kilian 2012; Batt 2013; Burmann and Piehler 2013).

For several of these instruments Piehler (2011) was able to empirically validate a positive direct effect on brand understanding and brand commitment. His study of 790 participants revealed significant effects of the design of brand identity, the continuity and consistency of brand management, and internal and external brand communication. Further managerial tools which were not part of his empirical analysis are brand-oriented human resource management and brand-oriented leadership. These instruments were already investigated by Zeplin (2006) regarding their effect on brand commitment. In her study, 1783 employees from 14 different brands in six industries were surveyed. Therefore, they are integrated in the holistic model of internal brand management (see Fig. 4.3).

4.1.2.1 Design of Brand Identity

Differentiation, operationalisation, and culture fit belong to this category of instruments. **Differentiation** involves recognising the specific features and behaviour of one's own brand in comparison with competitor brands, as well as distinguishing it from competitors, by means of the employees. A high degree of interchangeability of one's own brand and its identity prevents the employees from being able to recognise the brand's relevance to success. Furthermore, the perceived uniqueness of one's own brand makes it

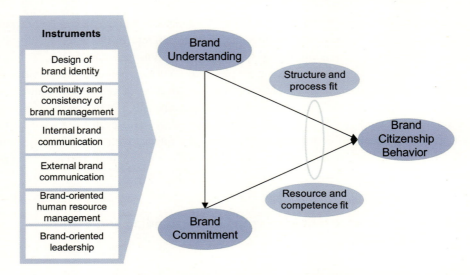

Fig. 4.3 Managerial tools of internal brand management. (Source: Adapted from Piehler 2011, p. 543; Zeplin 2006, p. 233)

easier for the employees to collectively identify with it. However, if employees cannot distinguish their own brand from competitor brands, then an identification with the brand is made more difficult since they themselves do not positively benefit from being part of this group in terms of increasing their sense of self-worth. If, however, the brand is experienced by the employees as something unique and positive, then a match between their own identity and the brand identity leads to a personal valorisation (cf. Piehler 2011).

The **operationalisation of brand identity** describes the degree with which the initially abstract brand identity is put into concrete terms with regards to the employees' daily behaviour. However, simply conveying the brand identity through brochures summarising the brand's identity on a highly abstract level is not enough to make it clear to employees what is expected of them in accordance with this identity. Sportiness as an attribute of the brand identity of a car brand does not initially give one of the research and development engineers of the brand an indication of how he can implement this aspect of identity in his daily behaviour. A concrete operationalisation of sportiness for the engineer might, however, consist of developing engines with high revolutions per minute, high torque, and a specific sound. Likewise, for the engineer the attribute of elegance when linked to a brand's identity could be operationalised by using particularly high-quality interior materials. For a sales representative of the same brand, on the other hand, elegance can be concretely implemented in his clothes and manner of speaking when in contact with the customer. Operationalisation leads to a better knowledge and understanding, of the brand and its identity. At the same time, this promotes the perceived relevance of the brand and the employee can more easily recognise that his own behaviour has an influence on the consumer's perception of the brand (cf. Piehler 2011).

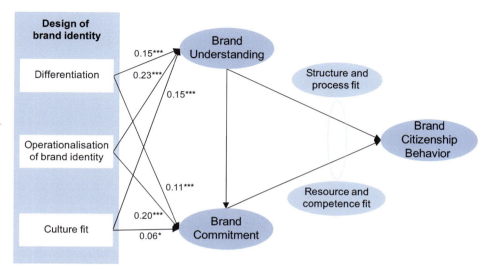

* = p < 0.1; ** = p < 0.05; *** = p < 0.01; n. s. = not significant

Fig. 4.4 Empirical results for design of brand identity as instrument of internal brand management. (Source: Adapted from Piehler 2011, p. 543)

Culture fit denotes a considerable conformity between the brand identity and the corporate culture, and requires the brand values to be in accordance with the values practiced within the company. An internalisation of the brand values is unlikely if they differ from the deep-seated values of corporate culture. In such a situation the employees are confronted with a conflict of roles (cf. Piehler 2011).

The empirical analysis for all the instruments regarding design of brand identity revealed a positive effect on brand understanding and brand commitment (see Fig. 4.4).

4.1.2.2 Continuity and Consistency of Brand Management

Continuity and consistency have already been presented in Chap. 2 as constituent components of brand identity. Both aspects also have a particular relevance with regards to the objectives of internal brand management. Knowledge of brand identity and its relevance can only then be formed amongst the employees if the brand identity does not change on an annual basis or even on a shorter basis.

Building up brand knowledge and brand commitment amongst the employees constitutes a learning process which makes **continuity** over time necessary. Frequent changes in the brand identity and the brand management adversely affect the formation of the employees' sense of group identity. However, this forms the basis for constructing the social identity of the employees during which the brand identity becomes part of the self-concept. A low continuity prevents a coherent self-concept. As a result, employees are unable to identify with the brand. Moreover, a lack of continuity also has a negative effect on the internalisation of the brand since in this situation the perceived congruency be-tween personal identity and brand identity is made more difficult (cf. Piehler 2011).

In addition to continuity, the **consistency** of brand management and brand identity is also an important antecedent of brand understanding and brand commitment. Inconsistencies between the brand identity components make it difficult to get to know a brand, to understanding its relevance, and to implement brand-consistent behaviour. Consistent behaviour ensures that identical stimuli are repeated in order to anchor brand-related information in a particularly firm manner in the minds of the employees. With regards to brand commitment, it becomes more difficult to assume group traits during brand identification if a lack of consistency is predominant and, as a result, this is opposed to the preservation of self-consistency amongst the employees (cf. Piehler 2011).

Empirically, Piehler (2011) only identified continuity of brand management as antecedent of brand commitment. However, only consistency of external brand management (e.g., advertising) was investigated in his study. Therefore, also considering internal consistency of brand management, a causal relationship between consistency and internal brand management outcomes can still be hypothesized (see Fig. 4.5).

4.1.2.3   Internal Brand Communication

Internal brand communication includes all activities related to conveying the brand-related messages between the employees of an organisation on different hierarchical levels (cf. Piehler 2011). Developing brand understanding amongst the employees,

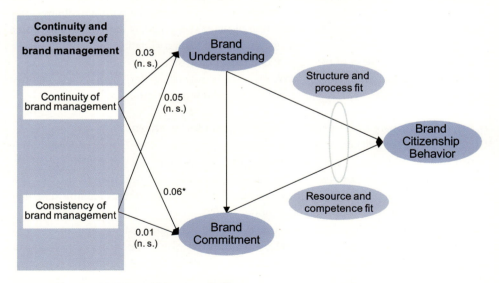

* = p < 0.1; ** = p < 0.05; *** = p < 0.01; n. s. = not significant

Fig. 4.5 Empirical results for continuity and consistency as instruments of internal brand management. (Source: Adapted from Piehler 2011, p. 543)

creating awareness of the relevance of the brand and communicating the brand identity to the brand management's internal target groups are key objectives of internal brand communication (cf. Burmann and Zeplin 2005; de Chernatony et al. 2006; Punjaisri et al. 2009; Hartmann 2010; Brexendorf et al. 2012; Esch et al. 2012; Burmann and Piehler 2013; Piehler et al. 2015). To this end, it is necessary to communicate the brand identity in a comprehensible and, if possible, vivid manner (cf. Maloney 2007).

Brand communication can basically occur in three different ways. In addition to central communication, cascade communication and lateral communication measures are available to management. All three forms of communication differ with regards to the ways in which the information is passed on (see Fig. 4.6).

In the case of **central communication**, information is solely sent from a central sender to the recipients of the information. On an organisational level, this is often conducted by a central communication department within a company. The transmission of information occurs mostly via written materials, such as, for example, an e-mail newsletter or employee magazines. Due to the one-sided and central dispatch of information, it is for the most part not possible to check whether the employees have received the contents of the communication. This way of transmitting information is therefore also referred to as the push principle, in which a reply on the part of the receiver is not envisaged (cf. Zeplin 2006). A further disadvantage of central communication is that information cannot be adapted to the individual needs of the addressees (cf. Larkin and Larkin 1996). Since a company's employees differ, generally speaking, in terms of their brand understanding and brand commitment, this form of communication does not offer the possibility of rectifying individual deficits amongst the employees. The use of central communication is therefore not restricted to the transmission of information of overriding importance which is relevant to all employees, such as, for example, a change of personnel in the top management.

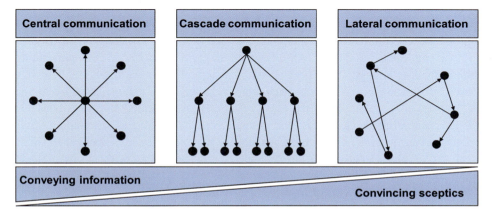

Fig. 4.6 Forms of internal brand communication. (Source: Zeplin 2006, p. 116)

As an alternative to central communication in accordance with the push principle, this can also be organised according to the pull principle. To this end, a centrally available pool of information is created, from which each employee can retrieve the specific information which he/she requires (cf. Bruhn 2015). On an organisational level, this can be solved, for example, via an intranet within the company.

Likewise, events are assigned to central communication. In this case, centrally organised information events are offered on particular topics. In contrast to communication according to the push or pull principle, events also pave the way for an interactive communication between the parties concerned. As a result, the information imparted and the persuasive effect of communication increase. At the same time, events are often not very efficient since the group of addressees is considerably smaller (cf. Zeplin 2006).

The second basic form of internal brand communication is **cascade communication**. On this occasion, information gradually extends from higher hierarchical levels to lower levels. In this way, the transmission of information can also be limited to parts of a company hierarchy (cf. Zeplin 2006). Meetings are a frequently used form of organisation within cascade communication. The managing director of a company, for example, can thus hold a meeting with the directors of the company's business divisions when starting to convey the information. They, in turn, call meetings with their respective heads of department in which only the information which is relevant for the corresponding business division is passed on. In the next step, the heads of department relay the information to the team leaders under their supervision. Personally passing on information via one's superior lends cascade communication a greater degree of credibility and means that it is appreciated more (cf. Zeplin 2006).

The third form of internal brand communication is **lateral communication**, which describes the informal passing on of information between the employees, regardless of hierarchical levels or organisational units (cf. Laux and Liermann 2005). Due to its informal and personal character, lateral communication has the greatest power of persuasion of all the aforementioned forms of communication. However, since it is often spontaneous and uncontrolled, it is simultaneously the least suited to a pure transmission of information. Thus, on occasion it is possible that information might be falsified, added or omitted. Lateral communication therefore constantly requires a high degree of trust vis-à-vis the employees (cf. Zeplin 2006). Even if a targeted use of lateral communication is often difficult to arrange, it has been shown that storytelling in particular can be used to convey information with regards to brand-consistent behaviour and the brand's relevance (cf. Wentzel et al. 2012). Thus, the effect of an employee's brand-consistent behaviour and its positive effect customers, for example, can be relayed as storytelling within reports on their personal experiences. Employees who have already experienced similar situations are able to perceive a direct connection to themselves without any problems and to adopt the behaviour recounted in the future.

Especially the positive effect of the usage frequency of central and cascade communication on brand understanding was empirically validated (see Fig. 4.7). A direct effect of usage frequency of the forms of internal communication on brand commitment was

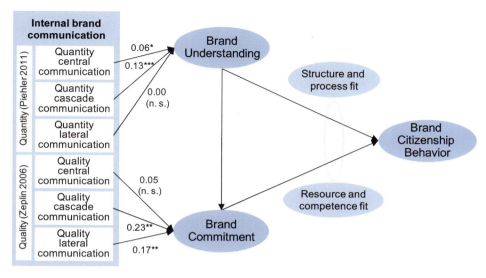

*= p < 0.1; ** = p < 0.05; *** = p < 0.01; n.s. = not significant

Fig. 4.7 Empirical results for internal brand communication as instrument of internal brand management. (Source: Adapted from Zeplin 2006, p. 215; Piehler 2011, p. 543)

not empirically validated in the study of Piehler (2011). One reason might be that not the quantity but the quality of communication is relevant for brand commitment. Based on a more quality-related operationalisation of internal brand communication, Zeplin (2006) was able to empirically validate an effect of cascade and lateral communication on brand commitment. These results support the hypothesis that for brand commitment not the quantity but the quality is important. To summarize, the effect of cascade communication and the influence of information transfer from supervisors seems to be quite important. For both outcomes cascade communication has the highest effect among forms of internal brand communication.

4.1.2.4 External Brand Communication

External brand communication includes all activities linked to the design of brand-related messages between an organisation and its external target groups (cf. Piehler 2011). Even if external brand communication is primarily directed at external target groups, it is nevertheless perceived by a company's employees. Here, it is necessary to keep in mind television advertising of the brand, for example. Since the addressees of this communication are first and foremost not one's own employees, and it primarily serves advertising purposes, the danger exists of creating inconsistencies between internal and external brand communication when developing this advertising. Inconsistencies lead to uncertainties amongst the employees and directly impede the development of brand understanding. The effect of external brand communication on the employee's brand commitment also behaves in similar vein. A lack of integration between internal and external brand communication leads to confusion and a resulting role conflict of employees. In this regard, it is particularly important that advertising slogans about a brand's employees are congruent with the internally communicated and desired means of behaviour.

Therefore, external brand communication should also be considered as instrument of internal brand management (cf. Burmann and Zeplin 2005; de Chernatony et al. 2006; Henkel 2008; Henkel et al. 2009, 2012; Piehler 2011; Brexendorf et al. 2012; Burmann and Piehler 2013; Piehler et al. 2015).

Practice examples of the effect of external brand communication on employees are Deutsche Telekom with the "Paul Potts" TV advertising and TUI Germany with the "Joachim Löw" TV advertising. In both companies the TV spots which were aimed at external target groups had positive effects on employees as there was positive feedback from employees. Another good example of considering employees as target groups of external brand communication is FedEX. With the "I am FedEX" campaign, the company uses stories of employees to communicate brand identity and brand promise of FedEX to external target groups (cf. FedEX 2014).

An effect of external brand communication is hypothesised for brand understanding and brand commitment of employees. Positive employee reactions to external brand communication occur when the external brand communication (1) is aligned with internal brand communication, (2) does not make exaggerated promises about products and services employees will not be able to fulfil, and (3) does not portray employees, values, and culture that does not match actual employees, values, and culture (George and Berry 1981; Gilly and Wolfinbarger 1998).

Zeplin (2006) confirmed a positive effect of external communication on brand commitment of employees (see Fig. 4.8). Especially in relation the effect of internal brand communication, the effect of external brand communication is outstanding. Therefore, managers should consider employees as additional relevant target group of advertising. Because the integration with internal brand communication is important for brand understanding, external brand communication should be checked regarding its congruence with internal brand communication. Finally, Piehler (2011) was empirically able to show the effect of the congruence of the communicated culture with the actual culture on brand understanding and brand commitment (see Fig. 4.8). Therefore, managers should also check the fit with actual values and culture of the organization in external brand communication.

4.1.2.5 Brand-Oriented Human Resource Management

The aim of **brand-oriented human resource management** is a brand-related personnel socialisation. This refers to the process of conveying and learning brand-related knowledge, skills, convictions, norms, and values which enable the employees to behave as "brand citizens". It includes brand-oriented personnel recruitment, selection, introduction and development, remuneration and incentive systems, staff appraisals and

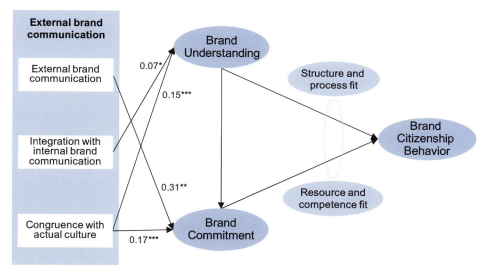

* = p < 0.1; ** = p < 0.05; *** = p < 0.01; n. s. = not significant

Fig. 4.8 Empirical results for external brand communication as instrument of internal brand management. (Source: Adapted from Zeplin 2006, p. 215; Piehler 2011, p. 543)

promotions, as well as staff redundancy (cf. Piehler 2011; Burmann and Piehler 2013; Piehler et al. 2015).

The individual instruments can be differentiated according to whether it is a matter of recruiting new employees (pre-entry phase), introducing them to the organisation (entry phase), or their further socialisation (metamorphosis phase). In the **pre-entry phase**, personnel recruitment and selection in particular provide the brand-oriented human resource management with starting points. Brand-related information, e.g. the brand's values and objectives and the employee's importance to achieving these brand objectives, should already be specifically communicated when recruiting new staff. The positive and, above all, realistic image conveyed in this way of one's own brand identity facilitates the recruitment of suitable potential employees (cf. Wittke-Kothe 2001). A brand-oriented personnel selection should ensure that those employees who fit with the brand identity particularly well should be chosen from the pool of potential, available employees. At the same time, this level of recruitment can also be used in order to convey knowledge of the brand via job interviews or assessment centres (cf. Piehler 2011).

The **entry phase** refers to the period of time during which successfully recruited new employees join the company. At this moment, the new employees are confronted by their colleagues who pressure them to adapt. At the same time, their own ideas and expectations are faced with the reality within the company. In this phase, the brand-oriented human resource management's task is to introduce personnel to the company in a brand-oriented manner. On the one hand, this can be facilitated through suitable initial training courses and events. On the other hand, it is possible to accelerate the mediation and internalisation of the brand's content via the conscious use of socialisation tactics. In order to achieve this, new employees can, for example, be specifically appointed to teams in which they are in close contact with experienced colleagues who have a high level of brand commitment and brand knowledge (cf. Piehler 2011).

In the last phase, the so-called **metamorphosis phase**, brand-oriented HR management is no longer limited to the recruitment of new employees, but includes the brand-oriented management of all the employees. In this phase, it is therefore possible to speak of a brand-oriented development of human resources. Instruments available primarily include developing remuneration and incentive systems, staff appraisals and promotions, and ultimately even staff redundancy. All of these instruments should be specifically used in order to achieve the brand's objectives and to reward brand-consistent behaviour. In this way, appraisals and bonus payments, for example, can be linked to achieving brand objectives. With the help of brand-oriented criteria for promotion, those employees who have firmly internalised the brand are more likely to rise through the company ranks. When laying off staff, however, a brand can specifically part with those employees who hardly match the brand identity (cf. Piehler 2011; Zeplin 2006).

The empirical study of Zeplin (2006) shows that there are positive effects with brand commitment in all three phases of socialisation (see Fig. 4.9). Especially personnel recruitment activities of the pre-entry phase affect brand commitment of employees. Therefore, managers should have a focus on a fit between potential employees and the brand identity already during personnel marketing and personnel selection. This is

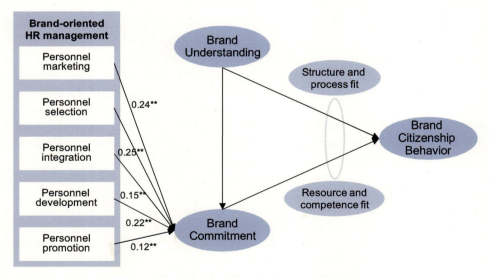

* = p < 0.1; ** = p < 0.05; *** = p < 0.01; n.s. = not significant

Fig. 4.9 Empirical results for brand-oriented human resource management as instrument of internal brand management. (Source: Adapted from Zeplin 2006, p. 215)

particularly important as a low fit with brand identity cannot be compensated by other human resource management activities and other instruments of internal branding. Therefore, already during personnel selection the basis for a high level of brand commitment is established.

4.1.2.6 Brand-Oriented Leadership

Brand-oriented leadership has a very high relevance to success because it adopts the constitutive feature of reciprocity and uses it to internally convey brand identity. It is vital that executives put the brand identity into practice in the form of brand citizenship behaviour (cf. Piehler 2011; Burmann and Piehler 2013; Piehler et al. 2015). Communication and learning theories (cf. Watzlawick et al. 2007; Bandura 1977) have demonstrated that humans learn attitudes and behaviour particularly through observing the behaviour of others. Since the managers in a company are particularly important due to their prominent position, they act as role models for the other employees. This function as role model is not limited to start-ups with their close relationship between founders and employees but is also valid for established companies. In this context, the behaviour of the top management is of particular importance. The downside of the top management's major role is that a few ill-considered words or actions, for example on the part of the CEO, can cause long-term damage to the brand image and the employees' self-image. An example here is the chief executive of Seat, James Muir, who stated the following in 2010: "If one would want to get rid of Seat, one would have to give the other party money to take it." (Krogh 2010).

Another danger is that the brand identity can become so dependent on the personality of the CEO that it becomes insubstantial and meaningless following a change in CEO. This was the case, for example, for easyJet following the departure of its charismatic founder, Stelios Haji-Ionnou. For this reason, then, it is crucial that the CEO supports the brand identity and not vice versa. A CEO exuding charisma and inner strength can support the brand identity if he/she is prepared and willing to subordinate his personality to the brand identity (Pälike 2000). Josef Hattig, former CEO of the Brewery Beck & Co. formulates this as follows: "Is the brand the boss or is the boss the brand? [...] The consumer interacts with the brand, not with the company and so the answer is: the brand is the boss!" (Zeplin 2006). The good example set by the company's management is conveyed to each executive via the individual hierarchical levels of a company. Through their behaviour, executives can strengthen the prominence and acceptance of the brand identity (cf. Vallaster and de Chernatony 2005).

In addition to managers' function as role models, it can be assumed that certain types of management behaviour lead to a higher level of brand commitment than others. Managerial behaviour, which is the most effective in generating a high level of brand commitment from the point of view of identity-based brand management, is best described by Burns' (1978) and Bass' (1985) transformational leadership theory. **Transformational leadership** describes a form of managerial behaviour through which the value systems and ambitions of the individual employees are influenced in such a way that they place their own interests behind the brand objectives (Yukl 1989). As a result, transformational leadership builds on the skills of the senior managers to communicate the brand identity and authentically integrate it into their daily actions, as well as to get the employees to see themselves as being responsible for the brand (cf. Morhart et al. 2009). Empirical studies enabled Bass (1985) to identify four factors which are characteristic of transformational leaders, namely charisma, inspirational motivation, intellectual stimulation and individualised consideration. Charismatic leaders demonstrate a vision and see the bigger picture; they inspire pride amongst their employees and earn their trust and respect. Inspirational motivation is revealed in the fact that leaders communicate high expectations, use suitable symbols in order to focus their efforts and easily communicate important objectives (cf. Müller 2012). They are then intellectually stimulating if they nurture intelligence, rationality and careful problem-solving. They give individualised consideration to their employees by treating each and every one individually, coaching them and giving them personal advice. All four factors can be learned in executive training days and through coaching (Bass 1990; Gardner and Avolio 1998; Nerdinger and von Rosenstiel 1999).

Zeplin (2006) empirically validated an outstanding positive effect of brand-oriented leadership on brand commitment. Living the brand identity by managers and transformational leadership have a strong effect on brand commitment of employees (see Fig. 4.10). Brand-consistent behaviour of managers is one of the most powerful success instruments of internal brand management (cf. Zeplin 2006). This result is in line with Piehler (2011) who identified cascade communication as the most effective form of communication

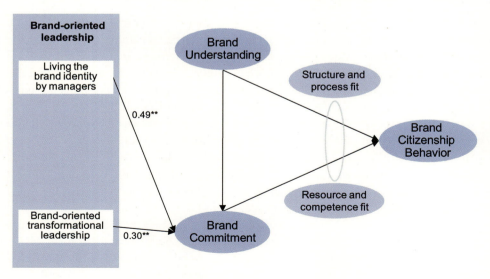

* = p < 0.1; ** = p < 0.05; *** = p < 0.01; n. s. = not significant

Fig. 4.10 Empirical results for brand-oriented leadership as instrument of internal brand management. (Source: Adapted from Zeplin 2006, p. 215)

regarding internal brand management outcomes, thus reinforcing the important role of leadership behaviour.

4.2 Operational External Brand Management

The external implementation of brand strategy involves translating the brand promise into the four classical instruments of the marketing mix. Its embodiment must be coordinated in form and content, as well as temporally. Of primary importance is the

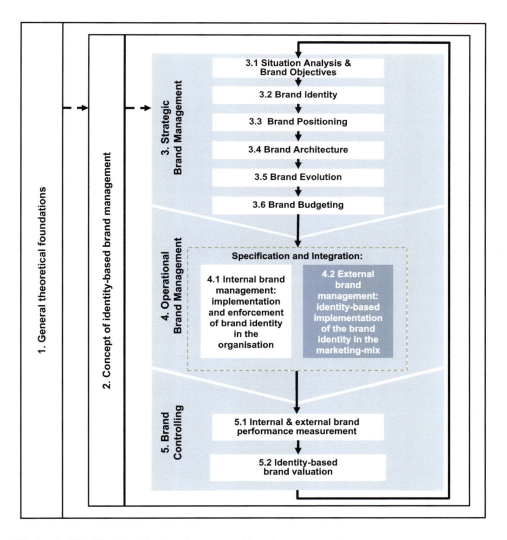

Fig. 4.11 Classification of external operational brand management

translation of the **brand promise** into concrete product policy decisions, including establishing an accepted price policy for the brand promise and range of offers. The distribution policy ensures that brand performance remains available to consumers; that is, distribution channels need to be selected and controlled in accordance with the brand promise. Through brand communication, the brand promise also gets transmitted to consumers. As Fig. 4.11 shows, this classification of the implementation of brand strategy involves a process of managing identity-based brand management. The quality of the implementation of brand strategy depends on the brand identity and internal brand management (cf. Sect. 4.1). If a brand organization suffers less clarity about its own self-image and the concrete, internal allocation of roles, when it transmits the brand promise, it is likely to create just a vague, interchangeable brand image in its external management—which ultimately increases the probability of the brand's failure.

4.2.1   Brand Offering Policy

The **product and program policy** defines decisions about the brand's embodiment. In this context, the term "**product**" refers to any bundle of technical-functional features that can generate consumer benefits (cf. Meffert et al. 2015). In turn, the terms "product" and "brand" are closely linked, because both are defined on the basis of the benefits they offer. Whereas products or services rely solely on utilitarian benefits though, brands are more broadly defined, such that they also include economic, social, sensual-aesthetic, and hedonic benefits.

Purchase behaviour depends on the entire offered bundle of benefits (brand), not just utilitarian benefits (product). The long-standing focus in marketing and brand management on utilitarian benefits corresponded with the prevalent idea of consumers as "homo economicus." The abandonment of this idea, together with the recognition that people act much less rationally than anticipated, has increased the importance of brand management. For example, even as more objective, rational information about various offers becomes available to consumers, through the Internet, brands seemingly have greater effects on their purchase behaviours, because consumers cannot process the vast amounts of data at their fingertips and also are driven by emotions.

The "**program**" of a brand refers to the totality of all relevant efforts it offers consumers to encourage their purchase. A product and program policy, according to identity-based brand management, aims to customize these efforts to each consumer's needs and thus help ensure the economic existence of the brand in the long run. In this case, the brand-leading institution requires some innovative capabilities (Hauschildt and Salomo 2011; Sammerl 2006). Because new product introductions often fail, firms must implement a systematic, competency-based innovation process, whether it is based on consumer needs ("market-pull"), initiated by technical inventions ("technology-push"), or some combination thereof.

4.2.2   Brand Price Policy

A brand's **pricing policy** should include all agreements about brand performance payments, possible discounts, and additional delivery, payment, or credit terms and conditions, as well as methods for enforcing the price on the market. These instruments should be developed in relation to brand managers' objectives. Pricing policy measures are effective, in that price changes exert direct influences on buying behaviour. Their short-term variability means that a price adaptation often leads to an immediate reaction by consumers. However, companies often face challenges associated with changing the direction of the price adjustments; price reductions, in particular, are difficult to take back.

Determining a pricing strategy is an important component of a pricing policy. A high price strategy for a luxury brand, for example, encompasses the need for the brand offers, distribution channels, and marketing communication to satisfy demands for luxury (cf. Burmann et al. 2012). Figure 4.12 provides an overview of some different pricing strategy options (cf. Meffert et al. 2015).

4.2.3   Brand Distribution Policy

The brand distribution policy includes all decisions and actions related to the distribution of material or immaterial services, from the manufacturer to the end consumer. Its objectives derive from the primary brand objectives. Achieving these objectives requires effective management of distribution channels, including selection and contract factors. The selection concept pertains to the **vertical and horizontal structure** of the brand's distribution channel. The contract concept specifies the extent of the contractual relationship between intermediaries. Operational implementation and control of the distribution

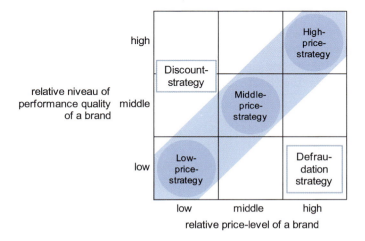

Fig. 4.12   Price related strategic options

channel system involves the tasks of stimulating the concept, supply chain management (SCM), and efficient consumer response management (ECR). Stimulation includes
recruiting intermediaries and creating emotional bonds with them. With SCM, the brand
must analyse the overall supply chain and find ways to increase its effectiveness and efficiency. Finally, ECR refers to specific cooperation efforts between manufacturers and
retailers, such that they commit to work together to satisfy consumers' needs at all times,
in the best way possible (cf. Meffert et al. 2015).

Distribution channels can be classified as physical or virtual. Physical distribution is
more traditional, including distribution through catalogue orders, telephone, television,
or brick-and-mortar stores. Sales of products and services that take place in a virtual
channel instead entail electronic commerce (e-commerce). In addition to its sales function, e-commerce may have communicative functions (e.g., increase brand awareness
and brand preferences).

Electronic distribution channels might be operated by retailers (e.g., Amazon) or by
manufacturer brands (e.g. Adidas), similar to physical distribution channels. However,
unlikely most physical distribution channels, an electronic distribution channel offers
permanent availability, 24 h a day, from virtually any location. It also has the distinct
ability to enrich the product range with value-added services. Decoupling the physical
presence of products from traditional shops allows e-commerce to offer a far greater
product range, with information and services individually adapted to the needs of the
target group. Furthermore, not all products need to be kept in inventory, because orders
can be passed on to manufacturers after customers place them. The resulting reduction in
inventory storage costs, combined with the general reduction in personnel needs, means
that e-commerce offers considerable cost savings, which can go to increase the seller's
margin or be passed on to consumers as price reductions.

The key challenge for e-commerce, from a brand management perspective, is the lack
of personal and physical contact between the brand and its consumers. Most contact is
virtual, which limits the transmission of emotional brand experiences (cf. Burmann et al.
2014). In this regard, combining e-commerce and social media might help generate more
positive brand experiences online (cf. Sect. 4.3).

The successful implementation of an e-commerce solution stems from several factors,
including (cf. Heinemann 2014).

1. Shop Attraction
Successful e-commerce strategies create substantial attraction and a differentiated brand
promise. Brand positioning is crucial to success. Consumers can easily conduct comparisons among many competing offers, especially in online environments. Therefore, a
unique, highly emotional brand experience becomes even more important.

2. Social Targeting
This factor refers to the importance of social media for e-commerce. Traditional media
address target groups as a whole; online users can be segmented more accurately into

various subgroups, using social targeting. Digital advertising can be addressed specifically to match the interests, behaviours, and personal circumstances of individual consumers. Such capacities help minimize wasteful coverage. Targeting also can reflect the users' technical equipment (e.g., operating system), socio-demographic data, or prior search and browsing behaviours (cf. Burmann et al. 2014).

3. Service and Search Solutions

Because it often cannot provide truly personal customer services at the point of sale, e-commerce must offer the best, most self-explanatory service, in the form of the technical design of the website. This demand requires a clear configuration of the user interface and well-structured search capabilities.

4. Customization and Personalization

Modern Internet technologies make it possible to identify each individual customer in an online store. These opportunities should be leveraged to personalize communication with the customer and provide individually compiled content. Ideally, such tactics can lead to an emotional bond between consumers and manufacturers.

5. Supply Chain Excellence

The success of an e-commerce platform depends on the proper functioning of the informational and physical operating procedures that get triggered by an online purchase. Enterprise resource planning is important here. The objective is the fast, reliable, cost-effective delivery of accurate, ordered goods to consumers.

6. Security Standards and Reputation

Processing Internet transactions is inherently accompanied by safety and privacy concerns among customers (cf. Burmann et al. 2014). Recurring data thefts and abuses of customer data have created substantial uncertainty. Higher safety standards, and sufficient communication about them, are therefore critical. Emphasizing these standards during all contacts with consumers can help the brand build a more positive, long-term reputation as a trusted provider, which should strengthen the brand and its image.

High safety standards are especially necessary for brands that engage in location-based advertising, because their advertising reflects the location of each consumer's smartphone (Sect. 3.1.2). People's willingness to use location-based advertising is lower when their privacy concerns are higher, as well as when they perceive a greater risk of a possible invasion of their privacy (cf. Warwitz 2015).

7. Supplement and Support Channel Strategy

Internet users can no longer be assigned to a specific medium or channel for their product searches, price comparisons, and the actual purchase. The Internet has matured into a central component of media strategies. But in multi-screening practices, people use multiple devices sequentially or simultaneously, so all relevant media have to be considered together. Consumers often sit at home watching television, with their laptop, smartphone, or tablet in close reach, so that they can access the Internet as necessary. The use of traditional media such as televised advertising thus is still important, because it can promote online shops and websites that consumers can access directly. Networked communication across different types of media reaches consumers, through cross-channel communication on various channels, and it avoids limiting their own flexible communication behaviour.

8. Sourcing Concept and Strategic Alliances
Outsourcing to external companies is widely used in online trading, yet it increasingly is being replaced by insourcing. When outsourced processes return to an internal environment, the brand gains more control over the various channels. For example, online merchants might enter a virtual partnership to ensure they are noticed by more potential customers; it would be difficult for them to achieve such a visible presence on their own. Typical partners include portals and virtual shopping malls (e.g. eBay).

Brand distribution rarely happens over only a single channel. If two or more channels are combined, it constitutes **multi-channel-distribution** (cf. Heinemann 2014; Schögel 2012; Schramm-Klein 2006). Yet this term is a little blurry, because a sale across multiple physical channels might also be described as multi-channel-distribution. In the absence of a virtual channel, the combination of several channels constitutes "traditional" multi-channel-distribution (cf. Heinemann 2014). Whatever its type, multi-channel-distribution seeks the seamless integration of all distribution channels, to offer additional benefits to consumers (cf. Meffert et al. 2015). In particular, it enables them to buy what they want, at any time and from anywhere. Despite the importance of multi-channel-distribution, this temporary value cannot replace a competitive, differentiating brand promise (positioning), which is more relevant to purchase behaviour. The constant, ubiquitous availability of a brand in various distribution channels alone does not mean that targeted customers will consider this brand in their purchase decision, just as construction of additional roads does not automatically create additional traffic. The concrete benefit of a road that leads to a desired location is the decisive element, just as is the brand's ability to meet key needs.

4.2.4   Brand Communication Policy

Marketing communication generally describes sending encrypted information, designed to have an effect on the receiver. Planning and controlling the entirety of a brand's communication measures is challenging in the modern media landscape. Technological developments and the substantial number of resulting new media create a high degree of complexity related to the choice of suitable communication instruments. Moreover, consumers face an abundance of information, which often extends beyond their capacity (information overload). Therefore, creating awareness of communication messages is of increasing importance today, and professionally planning and controlling all means of communication is critical.

Fig. 4.13 The decision making process: communication policy. (Source: based on Meffert et al. 2015, p. 569)

The communication process in Fig. 4.13 provides some guidance. To start, the company's communication goals derive from the company's and the brand's primary objectives. To meet these objectives, it needs a long-term communication strategy, which defines the use of communication instruments first and foremost. The communication budget then is determined and distributed on the basis of the goals set, through an adequate, suitable budgeting process (cf. Sect. 3.6.2). The communication message should be designed in line with the brand's identity and strategy (cf. Meffert et al. 2015).

A **multi-channel-approach** also appears in brand communication, though we need to distinguish it from the distributive concept. Multiple communication channels use various instruments in parallel, to interact with target groups. Cross-media is another term that applies in this context, to refer to the different media forms being used. The design of a media strategy thus relies strongly on the integration (in content, form, and timing) of the various measures, because consumers often engage in parallel uses of various media. Each brand must ensure that its communication is being perceived as consistent by customers (cf. Meffert et al. 2015).

4.3   Identity-Based Brand Management in the Digital Context

4.3.1   Challenges for Brand Management by Digitalization

In 2014, 79% of the German population used the Internet at least occasionally, and 58% went online daily. The amount of time that Germans spend on the Internet also has increased, up to 111 min per day (240 min spent watching television and 192 min spent listening to radio; (cf. ARD-ZDF-online study 2014) as Table 4.1 details. The increase

Table 4.1 Average usage of television, radio, and internet, 2000–4000, minutes per day

	2000	2003	2006	2007	2008	2009	2010	2011	2012	2013	2014
Usage television	203	221	235	225	225	228	244	229	242	242	240
Usage radio	205	195	186	185	186	182	187	192	191	191	192
Usage internet	17	45	48	54	58	70	77	80	83	108	111

ARD-ZDF-online-study (2014)

in Internet usage can be traced back largely to the growth of the mobile Internet, which has been accomplished through both technical developments and the rise in competition among Internet providers, resulting in lower prices for customers (cf. Büllingen 2010).

Also in 2014, 57% of German Internet users relied on their smartphones and 28% employed tablets to achieve mobile Internet access. The time spent on the Internet among users who access it through mobile devices is 195 min, compared with 108 min for those who do not use mobile access routes. Especially among "digital natives," or the so-called always on generation (i.e., those 14–29 years of age in 2014), the steady rise in Internet usage (248 min in 2014) reflects primarily the expanded uses of smartphones (cf. ARD-ZDF online study 2014).

As a result of this rapid growth, the importance of online communication for brand management has increased significantly. In addition, many new brand touchpoints and communication channels are enabled by the Internet (cf. Seidel 2014).

> **Online communication** refers to all communication activities between companies and consumers, as well as among consumers themselves, that affect the achievement of marketing and corporate objectives and are handled through an internet protocol (IP) (Meffert et al. 2015, p. 633).

The difference between online and traditional communication pertains mainly to the novelty of the technologies used and the conditions for their use (cf. Kollmann 2013). The internet, which offers globally standardized communication protocols, is a medium, though it is not comparable with newspaper, radio, or television media. Rather, it encompasses a bunch of different applications (cf. Beck 2010) that can be distinguished by several factors. In particular, they vary in their temporal dynamics (synchronous or asynchronous), initiation (push or pull communication), and the focal transmitters and receivers of the messages (e.g., 1 to 1; 1 to n; n to n) (cf. Pleil and Zerfaß 2014). To support planning, organizing, implementing, and controlling communication activities, online media mostly uses a combination of **instruments** (e.g., music, text, audio, video) to market digitalized and non-digitalized products and services (cf. Kreutzer 2014). The opportunities for message recipients to provide **feedback directly and immediately** is a central characteristic of online communication, resulting in interaction possibilities between the brand as the sender and consumers as recipients of a message, or vice versa. The communication structure in online environments tends to be heterarchical: The sender and recipient change within these media, as might the respective instruments they use. In chronological and geographical terms, online communication is **globally available** and has a high temporal relevance, because communication occurs in real time.

Hyper-mediality is another distinguishing factor. It refers to the principle of arranging various communication media (text, sound, film). For example, users of Siemens' website, seeking information about the company's sustainability, have several routes they can follow to find this information. Users with a high affinity for numbers and figures can read about the companies' target variables for sustainability in concise tables. In short abstracts, other readers can review the fundamentals. For those who prefer audio-visual messages, an integrated video featuring the chief sustainability officer describes the importance of sustainable actions and their implementation.

Digitalization thus has a huge impact in the development and management of brands (cf. Heun 2014). To keep the brand promise and act in accordance with the brand identity, even in digital areas, is a central requirement for online communication and the distribution of services over the internet (cf. Michelis 2014; Rowley 2004). Yet brands seem to fail consistently in this challenge.

We note three other pertinent challenges (cf. Totz and Werg 2014) that hitherto have been mostly neglected by brands in their brand management in digital contexts:

- Brands do not pay enough attention to digital interaction. But this interaction must take place between a brand and its consumers, and among consumers themselves, to ensure brand management on the brand's terms.
- An exaggerated insistence on consistency in form and content design is an obstacle to successful brand management in digital contexts. It is not enough to care about the consistent use of logos and typography in online communication tools. Much more important are interactions and coordinated communication as part of management processes, which must be internally and externally consistent.
- The networking of various functional areas and control of necessary processes also are critical. Fast, appropriate responses are essential in the context of digitalization, but they are impossible without an appropriate infrastructure. In practice, specialists must take the role of facilitators, familiar with both the brand and the digital contact points (cf. Totz and Werg 2014).

As private households began leveraging their access to the internet, companies started to send messages quickly to a vast mass of people. Initially, there was little effort to target promotional activities (cf. Tiago and Veríssimo 2014). But further technological advances have enabled modern companies to customize their messages for specific target groups and communicate with them individually. Key developments include technology that can detect people's geo-locations or behaviour in the form of surfing, information gathering, and purchasing, together with socio-demographic variables and preferences.

Another digitalization challenge stems from the restricted bandwidth for communication through online media. Despite technology advances, especially those manifested by mobile devices, communicating over the internet is limited to textual and audio-visual messages (cf. Michelis 2014). Multi-sensual experiences cannot be achieved; users can only be addressed through two senses (vision and hearing). As the on-going, intensive efforts reveal, finding ways to appeal to the remaining senses (feel, smell, taste) digitally will take time. However, multi-sensory experiences in the digital field offer vast potential for brand management efforts. The combination of physical and digital worlds (e.g., QR codes, augmented reality applications) represents an excellent option for creating brand experiences for consumers (cf. Munzinger and Wenhart 2012).

Finally, online communication trends have a short half-life, unlike those in other fields. Within a few years, cutting-edge findings become current practices. Instruments and applications also grow increasingly comprehensive and complex, and with increasing complexity, the number of tools expands too (cf. Lammenett 2012).

4.3.2   Instruments of Online Communication

Online communication involves millions of Internet users and different tactics. The **homepage** of a brand is a focal point for consumers and other stakeholders, such as job seekers who wish to apply online. Constructing a brand website thus is a central responsibility of a well-managed brand (cf. Kreutzer 2014). Users visiting the homepage should receive a subjective benefit, from both the content and the functional design and scheme of the website. The brand also can use this homepage to identify its other activities on the Internet, such as its blog, a brand community, or profiles on various social networks (cf. Kreutzer 2014).

Internet users also encounter various **online promotions**. For example, some companies place online advertising on the corporate websites of other, independent enterprises (cf. Lammenett 2012). **Web banners** remain the most widely used online advertising formats, with usage rates of 97%. These banners can be found on most websites. However, they rarely provide discernible benefits to users, who accordingly tend to ignore them. Companies therefore must take the next step: Online shops can personalize the banners shown to each visitor, by accessing their previous behaviour in terms of information gathering and shopping. Users then see banners that feature products similar to those they already purchased or that might complement a previously acquired item (cf. Bleier and Eisenbeiß 2015).

Similarly, **search engine advertising** involves search results paid for by companies that are displayed to users as links when they conduct topic-relevant searches. For many consumers, search engines, such as Google, are the first place to visit before they make a purchase decision. Prior to purchase, consumers search on the internet for information about products and brands, even if they plan to complete the purchase in a physical store. It seems obvious to search for products on search engines, because doing so immediately displays all providers of this product (websites, online stores) and links to information, such as price comparison platforms. Accordingly, 45.9% of consumers are introduced to new online shops first through search engines, which implies that search engine advertising, as a form of initial communication, is indispensable (cf. Lammenett 2012). Search advertising differs from **search engine optimization (SEO)**, which aims to place the brand's own website as high as possible in the results of relevant search requests, by aligning the attributes of the company's website with the algorithm used by the search engine. This method ensures that the brand homepage will gain exposure; most information seekers consider just the first few search hits relevant (cf. Kaiser 2009). In turn, it produces up to a four-fold increase in traffic on the website.

Emails and newsletters often serve to send product and company information to customers. In turn, sending **emails** is the most common use of the internet. Messages can be transferred relatively inexpensively and personalized to appeal to individual persons or groups with similar interests, and they can appear either in plain text form or supplemented by digital content (e.g., graphics, images, music). Because the scope of information dissemination is limited though, companies may try to bypass this limit by relegating information to websites.

Furthermore, a long-standing distinction separated Internet usage at home or work from usage on the go. When the costs of mobile transmission were high, consumers only requested information actively, and they decided when and for how long to maintain this mobile access. However, with the expansion of mobile networks, lowered costs, and increased mobile uses of the internet, consumers can go online at any time. Emails are no longer accessed only actively, at home, from the stationary computer. This shift has extended and modified the contact points between consumers and online advertising. Emails including "junk mails" show up directly on mobile devices, facilitated by push-notifications—like SMS, messages through online services like Whatsapp, or alerts about activities in their social networks. In this sense, they take up an equivalent amount of consumers' attention.

When planning the insertion and design of online communications about a brand, different types of user involvement need to be taken into account (cf. Pattloch and Rumler 2013). When an Internet user actively searches for information, it is **pull communication**. Users also can be distinguished into **actively seeking users** who search for information about a brand or company through its corporate website or search engines, and **actively accepting users**, who encounter banners or sponsored links while surfing and click on them to link to the website or online shop. **Actively reading users** instead are addressed by pop-up banners or emails and newsletters, as part of a **push communication** campaign (cf. Kreutzer 2014).

In addition to these instruments of online communication, communication using **social media** is gaining in importance for brands. With online communication, the relationship of the brand with its customer is ostensible, but newer instruments, as part of social media, take the interactions among consumers into account too. Modern online communication thus is based on a **network-oriented interaction model.**

4.3.3 Special Position of Social Media in Identity-Based Brand Management

Social media have resulted from the development of the Internet from "Web 1.0" to "Web 2.0." Few people could create content in web 1.0, so consumers used the Internet mainly to entertain themselves with music, videos, or news that offered distinct information. Technical developments around 2004 then granted users increased opportunities to engage actively with others, share opinions and ideas, and create content on their own. We thus adopt an existing definition of Web 2.0.

> **Web 2.0** describes the new behaviour of internet users. The previous one-dimensional communication on the internet from manufacturer to consumer has dissolved, users now produce content on their own and get in direct dialogue with their environment, companies, and brands (cf. Bender 2011).

Since its first use by Tim O'Reilly, the term Web 2.0 often has been used indiscriminately, to refer to almost anything associated with innovation on the Internet. Despite the many interpretations of this term, without any single, generally accepted definition, some consensus maintains that Web 2.0 describes technical characteristics that invoke changes in the Internet users' behaviour.

"Social media" is a collective term to refer to various technical platforms on the Internet, on which content can be distributed not only by brands but also by consumers. Social media facilitate new user behaviours, so they constitute part of the Web 2.0 (cf. Arnold 2010).

> **Social media** include bundles of internet-based applications, grounded in developed user behaviour in Web 2.0 and support the exchange of content created by brands and users (brand-generated content, user-generated content) (cf. Burmann et al. 2012).

Classic marketing theory long regarded the buyer as a passive recipient of services offered by brands. This out-dated view also assumed that only the company could generate value for the brand through its activities (cf. Deshpandé 1983). Customer relationship management shifted the focus of brand management, toward the construction of brand–customer interactions. With spreading social media, the relationships between buyers and brands grow deeper, supplemented by relationships among consumers. Interactions in networks thus have become a topic for brand management (cf. Tomczak et al. 2006). Communication about the brand thus takes place outside the brand's control or sphere of influence. In turn, consumers can contribute substantially to the value of the brand, through word of mouth, participation in brand communities, or suggestions for improvement (cf. Bijmolt et al. 2010). This form of commitment is observable and can be shaped by the potentially vast number of demanders (see Fig. 4.14).

But who are these buyers and users of social media? Marc Prensky offers a classification, distinguishing between so-called digital natives and digital immigrants, and argues that the digital age has led to a lasting change. According to Prensky, people who have grown up with the internet (**digital natives**) differ notably from those who had to find entertainment, exchange views with others, or look for information without the Internet medium (**digital immigrants**) (cf. Prensky 2001). These arguments sparked considerable discussion about the impacts of the internet on these divided populations. Communication works differently for young people who do not know a world without the internet. They are unique in their thinking, learning, and actions, especially compared with those who witnessed the development of the Internet in recent decades: from a slow access service, usually limited to a few hours per week, to today's nearly constant and everywhere availability (cf. Jandura and Kranowski 2015). The **social media index** in Fig. 4.15 depicts the sum of used media and usage intensity for social media among nearly 2000 German respondents. Digital natives (ages 16–24 and 25–34 years) exhibit high values for 2013, when the values for digital immigrants were significantly lower. In comparison with the previous year, the index numbers are constantly rising among the young, but they even have declined among older consumers (cf. vor dem Esche and Hennig-Thurau 2014).

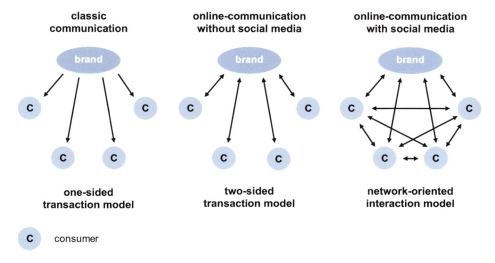

Fig. 4.14 Forms of interaction in brand management. (Source: based on Tomczak et al. 2006, p. 526)

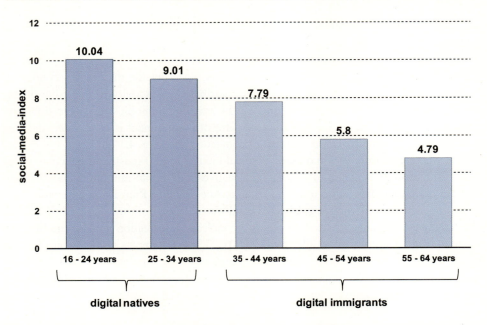

Fig. 4.15 User intensity of social media by age group. (Source: Jandura and Krankowski 2015, p. 64)

If a brand uses social media actively, it is necessarily represented by its **employees**. The contents provided by the staff constitute **brand-generated content (BGC)**, which usually reflects some degree of creative effort, though they are generated in a professional brand environment (cf. Wunsch-Vincent and Vickery 2007). This BGC consists of two categories: with performance-related attributes (e.g., technical product characteristics) or with non–performance-related attributes (e.g., sponsorship of a brand) (cf. Eilers 2014).

Because social media integrate users in all brand management activities, the focus shifts away from the content designed by the company (BGC) and toward the content generated by users themselves, that is, to **user-generated content (UGC)**. The term "users" in this context is limited to people who are not employed by the brand's leading institution. This group includes current and potential customers of the brand, as well as other external audiences. The contents they provide are very heterogeneous and distributed as text, pictures, graphics, images, music, audio, and video over multiple platforms, such as blogs, wikis, communities, microblogging services (e.g., Twitter), and social networks (e.g., Facebook, Google+).

A subset of UGC is **brand-related UGC**, or the voluntary creation and publication of personal, brand-related content on the internet by current and potential buyers of the brand (cf. Burmann and Arnhold 2008). Brand-related UGC can affect brand images and have repercussions for brand identity—which is why professional handling of brand-related

UGC is so critical (cf. Arnhold 2010). The process of managing brand-related UGC is called user-generated branding (UGB), defined as follows.

> **User-generated branding** is the strategic and operational management of brand-related UGC to achieve brand objectives.

Although UGB is not a management approach on its own, it can be integrated effectively into the proposed identity-based brand management approach (cf. Burmann et al. 2012). In particular, UGB can be divided into **non-sponsored** and **sponsored UGB**. Naturally formed, brand-related UGC is the non-sponsored form, because it includes all content generated and shared by users, independent of the brand. In contrast, sponsored UGB describes the management of purposefully created or stimulated brand-related UGC, as it emerges from the professional environment of a brand.

This distinction is especially relevant for companies that need to motivate consumers to create brand-related UGC on their own. The motivation of consumers who generate non-sponsored, brand-related UGC tends to be intrinsic, because their content generation happens without incentives from the brand. These users seek to meet their needs for creativity and self-expression, so they can be characterized as self-proclaimed brand activists with a strong emotional relationship with the brand. This relationship might be based on either positive or negative attitudes toward the brand. Companies have no control over the origin, substance, or statements of non-sponsored UGC, so their main tasks are to generate new content on their own, while also monitoring all non-sponsored UGC.

Unlike the creators of non-sponsored, brand-related UGC, users who create sponsored, brand-related UGC are motivated primarily by the pursuit of fame or recognition from other users and the brand. Without incentives, these users would not create content. The content they provide, similar to non-sponsored UGC, is not fully controllable (cf. Arnhold 2010).

Some users on the internet are characterized by particularly high interaction activity. They post substantial brand-related UGC, have many contacts, and are consulted by users to provide their opinions. These **opinion leaders** (cf. Wallace et al. 2014) have an important role in brand contexts. Content that refers to brands appears more credible to users when it is created by other consumers than if a brand uses classical modes of communication (cf. Arnhold 2010). In their function as experts, opinion leaders enjoy special respect and trust among Internet communities.

Eilers (2014) finds that UGC exerts a stronger effect on brand image when the brands are not very complex in their technical characteristics, so they require little explanation. This trend likely reflects the credibility of UGC: Whereas anyone can judge the taste of food, the assessment of an automobile engine requires certain skills and expertise (cf. Eilers 2014).

All brands, regardless of their industry or specific properties, suffer greater punishments due to their failure to comply with the brand promise or their unethical behaviour since start of the digitalization trend. A recent example demonstrates this claim. The environmental organization Greenpeace launched a campaign against the toy manufacturer Lego in 2014, calling for it to end its cooperation with the oil producer Shell in an effort to protect the Arctic from drilling. For centuries, Lego has produced its bricks and figures using oil supplied by Shell, and it continued to do so following Shell's announcement that it would drill for oil in the delicate Arctic, thus likely destroying the habitat of many endangered animals. The environmentalist group produced a shocking animated video, in which Lego animals and people drowned in a flood of oil. This video spread rapidly on the Internet and social media, where observers noted that Lego's commitment to sustainability and the polluting practices of the oil company it cooperated with were contrary. Ultimately, the toy manufacturer announced it would not renew its relationship with Shell (cf. Spiegel Online 2014).

4.3.3.1 Instruments of Social Media

Social media are complex, with a vast variety of channels and instruments. New options appear constantly, and others come to an end when users desert them, preferring other, more appealing social alternatives. For example, the German social networks StudiVZ and SchülerVZ were designed especially for students and pupils, but the increasing success of Facebook and its ability to network internationally made these German networks redundant, such that they ultimately ceased operations.

For both individuals and brands, virtually all actions undertaken on the Internet are stored permanently. An original comment, video, or photo might be deleted, but it may have been shared several times since its release and published elsewhere, without the knowledge of the author. Technology supports the quick and accurate duplication of data, with an almost unlimited range. With the assistance of search engines, these data also can be found from different sources, even long after the initial release (cf. Schmidt 2013).

The importance of social media and social networks for brand management also has increased. Social networks such as Facebook have enjoyed a steady rise in the number of users, and this growth is forecasted to continue in the years to come. Facebook is predicted to have 2.55 billion users worldwide in 2017 (cf. eMarketer 2013). To use these social media in an expedient way to support identity-based brand management, the brands need to know and understand the different platforms and their properties. Categorizing and characterizing these instruments is difficult though, due to the dynamic, fast pace of constant change. Tuten and Solomon (2014) define four social media zones (see Fig. 4.16) for classifying different platforms on the Internet. Some types are difficult to assign clearly to just one zone, because they contain features of several zones. For example, Facebook appears in different zones because of its acquisition of Instagram and Whatsapp and its strong efforts to help brands advertise on its various platforms.

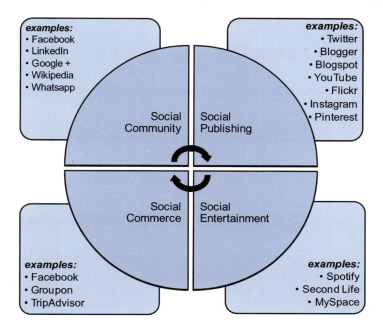

Fig. 4.16 Four zones of social media proposed by Tuten and Solomon (2014, p. 4)

Social Community

The first zone includes the most representative instruments of social media, namely, those focused on **relationships**. Users with same interests and abilities come together and share their experiences, photos, and videos. In these channels, user interactions are promoted, but brands also can communicate with current and potential consumers and thus build relationships with them. This category includes social networks, online communities, forums, chats, and wikis (cf. Tuten and Solomon 2014, p. 5).

Social networks (e.g., Facebook, LinkedIn, Google+) satisfy the need for communication; they have no direct equivalent in classical communication. The primary motives include exchanges with like-minded users or socializing. The social component thus is especially significant (cf. Burmann et al. 2010). Social networks facilitate this component, without the real presence of any people. However, extensive interactions also create difficulties in verifying content, and they also might threaten the privacy of members of these social networks. For example, users often must grant app operators or brands access to their data; they also share the rights to private photos with operators of the networks, simply by uploading them.

The most widely used social network is **Facebook**, founded in February 2004. It has more than 1.39 billion monthly users, of whom 890 million are active every day. The number of users accessing the platform on mobile devices is steadily increasing: 1.19 billion people use their smartphones or tablets, and 560 million use their mobile device exclusively to access Facebook (cf. Facebook 2015).

This site offers users many opportunities to network and interact with friends by uploading and sharing content. In addition, Facebook allows brands a means to create a Facebook page or develop an app (e.g., games, contests). In this context, apps refer to application programs used primarily with Internet-enabled smartphones. To connect with a brand, users can rely on the "Like" function, such that they can simply click a button to express that they like a brand and would like to receive more information about it. Users see the published information about the brand in their newsfeed. For example, the football clubs FC Barcelona and Real Madrid each have more than 800 million Facebook fans, whose newsfeeds get updated with information about matches and videos.

In addition, Facebook helps brands interact directly with customers on their Facebook page and gives them a chance to share media (both users and brand), such as with the Facebook Connect Login Function on users' own websites. Dell's Facebook page is a prime example: Next to detailed product information, users can find ways to interact with the brand and other consumers. Complete service requests are possible too. Direct interactions with the brand and innovative services clearly increase Dell's functionality and highlight the benefits of its Facebook presence.

Viral videos require special notice in this context. They offer a chance to convey messages without being perceived as direct advertising, and they can spread throughout social networks at high speed. Emotions are a key factor for ensuring a high redistribution rate; that is, users share videos not because of the advertised product but to provide entertaining content to other members of their social media networks (cf. Stenger 2012). To have positive effects for the brand, a virtual video should integrate the underlying advertising message in an emotional spot. For example, when LG wanted to promote its monitors with IPS displays, which offer high colour accuracy and thus very realistic images, it shot a video in an elevator equipped with hidden cameras and speakers. Monitors were added to the elevator floor, so they looked like a real floor. After a short ride, guests were surprised to hear cracking noises, right before the virtual floorboards loosened and "fell" downward. The reactions of the terrified elevator riders make up the viral video, which underlined how realistic the monitor's images appeared. LG thus has been able to amuse viewers in such a way that they wanted others to experience the surprise as well: The video has been seen more than 22 million times and shared nearly 600,000 times on Facebook, along with countless blogs and television channels. The promotional value reached several million euros (cf. LG 2012). At the same time, the brand was able to communicate the product benefit of the realistic display, such that after the spread of the video, the brand increased its market share in the Netherlands to 20%.

Online communities are groups of people on the internet who share the same interests. In addition to the idea of community, the focus is the exchange of information and experiences with like-minded others (cf. Schau et al. 2009). Online communities are usually accessible only to members and encourage high identification among supporters (cf. Stichnoth 2008). Membership allows expanded access to information and community-specific interactions (e.g., chats, forums), which in turn create a strong sense of community and social identity (cf. von Loewenfeld 2006). Both free and paid online communities are available. Many form on the basis of **gaming communities**, in which users share their experiences with certain computer games and provide tips for overcoming in-game barriers. But online communities have spread across multiple genres, such as travel, sports, dating, and **brand-related communities** (cf. Iltgen and Künzler 2008). These latter are characterized by close relationships of members with a particular brand (cf. Tomczak et al. 2006). They give companies opportunities to interact with their target audience and thereby potentially integrate customers into their business processes.

Online communities thus are effective instruments for influencing consumer behaviour, regardless of whether the websites are owned by the company or independent. Positive information shared by community members exerts a strong effect on purchasing behaviour, sometimes as much as negative information does (cf. Adjei et al. 2010). Related findings apply to both experienced and novice consumers, who have less in-depth contact with the brand. Therefore, community measures should address wider audiences than just brand fans (cf. Algesheimer et al. 2010).

Often **forums** are integrated into online communities. Unlike blogs, which belong to the second, social publishing zone, individual expressions are not in the foreground of the forums. Instead, the thematic exchange of information among interested parties is central, offering direct and personal communication with target groups that affects the opinion-formation process. Prior to the development of social media, forums were the only interactive form of online communication (cf. Iltgen and Künzler 2008).

Wiki websites (e.g., **Wikipedia**) are primarily used to gather information; they are comparable in some ways to print media or television. Large amounts of information, good clarity, actuality, and time-independent availability are some of their advantages. However, the quality of contributions fluctuates and can be very poor, so Wikipedia is generally best used as a starting point for further research (cf. Stanoesvka-Slabeva 2008). That is, because users have free access to create and modify wiki content, monitoring information accuracy is difficult. Companies therefore must check relevant entries continuously to confirm their correctness. Because anyone can create content in a wiki, the risk of false or incomplete information is high.

Social Publishing

Although primarily intended for users to present themselves to an audience, the social publishing zone also allows them to exchange information with others. With such instruments, users and brands can publish various kinds of content, whether created by the distributor or originally produced for other purposes but shared to reflect the interest of the user. Offline content such as newspaper articles or promotional posters can appear on the Internet when users take pictures and share them online. The publishing content thus might include opinions or attitudes of various topics, information, advice, guidance, and the presentation of projects such as photography or handmade items. Blog entries, press releases, newsletters, videos, photos, podcasts, and webinars are some of the forms used to publish content. Exemplary channels include photo and video communities, blogs and microblogging services, and news sites (cf. Tuten and Solomon 2014).

Blogs are similar to columns published in newspapers and magazines, in which individual authors communicate their experiences, perhaps with travel, products, or brands, and express their opinions, giving readers an opportunity to react. With their own blogs or by participating in other blogs, companies also can influence perceptions of their brand, such as by advertising their products in banners or providing bloggers with free products to test, in the hope of positive feedback. Potential consumers often appreciate the opinions of other users when they face a purchase decision, so they gather information before making their choice, through blogs or product comparison sites. A brand can participate in blogs either openly or covertly, using a foreign identity. Participation with a clear identity and transparent connection to the brand is always preferable, because a concealed identity inherently creates the danger that the connection will leaks out and inflict serious damage on brand credibility.

Microblogging services work similarly to blogs and allow users to publish short messages, which can be read from a connected network (cf. Burmann et al. 2010). The difference is that these messages are limited to a specific number of characters. Messages can also be shared or commented on in the network, and users can send messages directly to one another, which offers more privacy. Their main advantage is their ability to forward information fast and wide. The best known representative is Twitter.

Twitter allows users to publish messages with a maximum length of 140 characters. Approximately 290 million users create approximately 500 million of these tweets per day (cf. Twitter 2014). Users can follow other users, which makes them a follower; the number of followers is often taken as evidence of the impact of each Twitter user. The number of retweets (i.e., forwarding tweets by another user) and the composition of the group of followers (e.g., celebrities, other influential people) represent additional indicators of a user's influence (cf. O'Reilly et al. 2013). Direct interaction between users is possible with private messages or answering a tweet by adding the user name's, which begins with "@" (@username). When a tweet is shared, it is called a retweet and gets labelled "RT." The hash sign (#), or **hashtag**, mark groups, messages, or special events. All entries with the same hashtag are linked by Twitter, so searching for tweets about certain events is easier, and users can proclaim their approval or rejection to a recent incident.

In 2013, hashtags helped consumers respond to an announcement by Guido Barilla, head of the eponymous Italian pasta company, that Barilla advertisements would never feature a homosexual family, because the company only supports "traditional" family structures, with the wife and mother central. He added that if homosexuals were not satisfied, they could buy from competitors. The resulting boycott used the #boycottbarilla, which many customers used to publish images of Barilla products in trash cans or critiques such as "206 types of pasta—but never heard of diversity." The company head later apologized and attempted to explain that his statement did not reflect his own or his company's attitudes toward homosexuals or same-sex marriage. Instead, he claimed that he only wanted to point out that he is part of a traditional family business, which should be communicated in its advertising. But his apology was not perceived as sincere by the internet community. Barilla's competitors responded quickly: Bertolli, Althea, and Buitoni published images and statements such as "In the house of Buitoni there is room for everyone," following the broadcast of the interview with Guido Barilla, to demonstrate their more open minded attitudes.

Companies also can use Twitter for brand management, leveraging the important advantage of the high speed with which messages spread. However, brands need clear objectives and target groups, just as they would on any other communication channel. For example, the U.S. clothing company Bonobos uses Twitter mainly for immediate communication with customers, such as short-term special offers, to achieve a high level of attention and urgency among consumers that should help increase sales.

In addition to relationship building, many companies use Twitter as a service channel. The Deutsche Bahn AG (German Railway Company) and Deutsche Telekom AG (German Telecommunication Company) both offer customers and potential customers access to customer service representatives on Twitter who can handle their requests directly and quickly, enabling them to clarify specific questions about products or make complaints.

Photo and video communities such as Pinterest, Instagram, or YouTube represent a special form of data-based communities, used primarily for entertainment. Usage behaviour on video communities tends to be similar to that for television, in that they are strongly oriented toward satisfying needs for amusement. However, this usage is more active than watching television. Users can design their entertainment actively according to the videos they choose to watch, then integrate certain videos into their personal communication (e.g., as attachments in e-mails).

However, these communities struggle with copyright restrictions. Many videos (music videos, TV shows, film clips) have been uploaded without the permission of the copyright holder, so their sharing in various video communities or through links in social networks is not legal. Furthermore, there are concerns about individual rights and privacy; many private videos are published in video communities without the permission of all persons appearing in them.

On **YouTube**, the largest video community in the world, more than 100 million hours of video material is watched by 1 billion individual users daily, half of that on mobile devices. Every minute, 300 h videos are uploaded. About half of all users visit the platform at least once a week and recommend videos to their friends and family regularly (cf. YouTube 2015). These strong links among users increase the speed with which videos spread. This potential also increases because the videos can be integrated into other social media, such as when the brand publishes videos from its YouTube channel on its Facebook page too. But distribution often depends on consumers, as the successful example of Evian's "Baby & Me" video from 2013 shows. In the video, adults passing a shop window see not their own reflections but a baby version of themselves, which begins to dance on joy. At the end, the brand logo appears next to the directive, "Live young." This vastly successful viral brand campaign prompted nearly 104 million clicks and was shared about 7 million times on social network sites. In addition, a version produced with Spiderman and a mini version in 2014 coincided the release of a new Spiderman movie;

regular users also have posted numerous self-interpretations online, all of which lead viewers indirectly to the original video by Evian.

Instagram is the most used photo application for mobile devices; it allows people to upload, edit, and share images within that network and on Facebook, which purchased the site in 2012, around two years after its founding. Meanwhile, around 300 million people use the app, mainly to take pictures, but also to record up to 15-s videos, quickly and easy. Instagram works with hashtags and can address individual members with an @ sign, as is well-known due to Twitter. Users can draw attention to images featuring their friends, public figures, or brands. With its emotionally loaded images and visual storytelling, this relatively new platform is ideal for brand management. The majority of users are young (under 29 years; cf. Duggan et al. 2015), so Instagram can help brands trying to reach younger target audiences. The pictures also tend to bring joy, attract attention, and evoke emotions or memories. Effective brand-related uses of Instagram thus should be less about any dull or repetitive presentation of a brand's products and more about gathering as many users or followers as possible and encouraging them to publish pictures of the products to signal their attachment to the brand.

Social Entertainment

The third zone of social media is aligned with fun and entertainment. Game sites, virtual worlds, and other communities for entertainment (e.g., music and art platforms) are some of the available instruments. The range of games is the fastest growing area in social media (cf. Tuten and Solomon 2014).

Social games are played exclusively on social networks. A prominent example is Farmville on Facebook, which allows users to run their own farm, visit the farms of friends, and gamble or interact with them. Other types of games are played on consoles that connect to the internet, such as Xbox Live with Kinect. Users of these consoles can challenge other players worldwide and then share their gaming success in their social networks. Any game that allows players to connect with others or share achievements on the internet is a social game. The range and very high level of involvement of players in these games suggests their potential benefits for brand management. Brands can develop games targeted to their ideal customers or else take part in existing, successful games by placing their brand in a sort of virtual product placement. In producing its PGA Tour Golf games, EA Sports features popular golfers, which once meant Tiger Woods, wearing clothing and equipment by his sponsor Nike, but more recently has featured Rory McIlroy (cf. Tuten and Solomon 2014).

Spotify, Deezer, and Pandora are well-known **music services**. These providers allow users to listen to music without having bought it previously. Music from different labels and a wide range of genres is available; after creating a profile, users can also save their individual playlists. These streaming service become instruments of social media when they enable users to follow the activities of others or create collective playlists, log into Facebook, and indicate which song they are listening to at the moment. However, streaming services are not without controversy. Artists, which also can be seen as brands, suffer financially. The revenue per song streamed is greater than that for songs played on the radio, but the proceeds from these services are still far less than those from CD sales by a singer or band. Nevertheless, it makes sense for most artists to appear on the major platforms, because users who listen to similar music might discover them by browsing, recommendations by the platform, or friends. If they are sufficiently interested, these new fans might seek to experience the music live and book tickets for a concert.

Social Commerce

Instruments associated with buying and selling brands constitute the last zone of social media. Facebook appears in this zone as well, because advertising on the platform can redirect users to a brand's web store, which might lead to purchases.

  Social shopping gives customers the option to interact with others while they are shopping and seek advice. Customers also can provide feedback to retailers and brands, such as when clothing they have ordered is the wrong size (cf. Tuten and Solomon 2014). An excellent example of a stationary shopping phenomenon in social commerce is **Groupon**, a coupon site that features daily changing, location-specific deals for members. Brands offer a larger market of potential customers their products and services, at a reduced price. Existing customers also might be convinced to purchase vouchers repeatedly, which might tie them more closely to the brand. Users also share interesting offers with friends in social networks or give vouchers as gifts, thus drawing the attention of new potential buyers to the brand.

  In some sectors, such as tourism, social commerce is especially important. Travel booking increasingly takes place online. For example, in a survey of 603 adult U.S. residents with private Internet connections who travelled at least occasionally and had taken at least one trip in the past 12 months, 10% booked exclusively through travel agencies or catalogues, whereas 37% only used the Internet (cf. PhoCusWright 2013). Online booking allows consumers to look for accommodations and flights while also gathering information about the experiences and judgments of real travellers on travel **review sites**. Consumers rely more on the judgments and opinions of other customers more than on information spread by the brand (cf. Kardon 2007; Trusov et al. 2009; Lee and Youn 2009; Li and Bernhoff 2008). Therefore, review sites are among the most important contact points for customers, helping them determine which positive and negative experiences other users have had with products, services, and brands. Both positive and negative reviews influence consumers' purchasing behaviour, though negative feedback generally has a stronger influence (cf. Lee and Rodgers 2009; Sen and Lerman 2007). **TripAdvisor** allows critiqued restaurants, hotels, cities, or regions to respond directly to users and interact with them; it also gives companies a widget they can install on their corporate websites. Recent reviews published on TripAdvisor also can be integrated onto the brand's homepage (cf. TripAdvisor 2015). Such openness ensures that these ratings can be seen even by people who do not visit the review site.

  In selecting social media platforms for brand management, the specifics of each must be considered. For example, less UGC focused on brands spreads on YouTube.

On Facebook and Twitter though, content produced by consumers often features concrete judgments of brands. Although brands thus are more prominent in these UGC, such that their visibility increases and positive attitudes might result, there is also always the risk that these sites spread negative brand-relevant content (cf. Smith et al. 2012).

In summary, social media instruments can reach **high target group–specific ranges** and tend to be relatively inexpensive to implement, compared with traditional communication. That is, maintaining a business-related presence in social media and the active creation of Web 2.0 content are both less expensive than other types of media activities (cf. Arnhold 2010). However, the process and human resource costs are high, because commitment to social media demands the sustained participation of the whole enterprise. In addition to interactions between companies and consumers, interactions also take place among customers, with great opportunities for feedback. Furthermore, the design options are extensive, with very diverse possible applications that might include text, image, sound, moving images, or some combination thereof. The controllability of communication effects should be good and benefit from high degrees of interaction. But the brand lacks complete influence over concrete content. Temporal applicability is indefinite. That is, social media instruments are always available, which increases temporal flexibility.

The **informational purposes** of social media are great but limited in range and depth; social media cannot reflect the same amount of information that a corporate website does. The communication of feelings and emotions is very easy through various embodiments. Thus, links to photos and videos and direct interactions with the brand and among consumers allow for almost unlimited emotional accessibility.

4.3.3.2 Importance of Employees for Brand Communication in Social Media

For purposeful interactions in social media, brand employees must be fully engaged, because they are critical to brand performance. However, they are caught in the middle: Employees have their own personalities, but they are part of the holistic brand identity as well. Therefore, companies must motivate employees to engage in brand-compliant behaviour, without making them jump through too many hoops. They must be trained to act on the behalf of the brand, though some personal capacity is required to establish intense online interactions with high-value customers, based on their needs. Furthermore, it is the responsibility of the company to ensure the consistent appearance of the brand across various communication channels and brand touch points. Therefore, appropriate structures must be established to ensure successful brand management in social media.

Companies adopt different strategies to organize activities in social media. Perhaps the easiest approach assigns all responsibility to one of the company's existing departments. Coordinating communication activities often is the job of marketing or communication departments (cf. Schögel and Mrkwicka 2011). However, because of its multidisciplinary potential, social media often require some interdepartmental structures, such as by involving employees from various areas or building a central social media department to coordinate an enterprise-wide social media presence.

Involving all employees in social media communication means that the brand can leverage their interdisciplinary know-how. Dell has trained more than 1000 social media experts (cf. Greve 2011), and PepsiCo established a specific department to screen and test of new digital concepts, as well as ensure the "digital fitness" of its employees through internal training (cf. Blader 2011). The German food producer FRoSTA encourages its staff to be active in social media, so employees from different departments (e.g., production, marketing, consumer service, research and development, public relations) and management contribute to the company's blog (cf. Arnhold 2010; FRoSTA 2012).

Other companies establish **separate departments** to handle social media activities. A substantive task is holistic brand management that can guarantee a cohesive brand identity in social media. To ensure that employees behave in brand-compliant ways in interactions with consumers on social media, professional, internal brand management is required.

As described in Sect. 3.1.1, internal brand management has three targets: brand knowledge, brand commitment, and brand citizenship behaviours. To achieve these outcomes, companies use various instruments. For example, **brand-oriented human resource management** involves staff intercourse with social media. The fast pace of this medium means that responses are expected in real time, so interminable internal review or approval processes would obstructive. In this case, flat hierarchies and quick decisions are required (cf. Schögel and Mrkwicka 2011).

Internal communication is a second field of action, designed to ensure knowledge and understanding of the brand concept at all levels and functional areas. The conditions for success thus are clear to employees, with transparent verbal and visual representations of the brand identity (cf. Maloney 2007). Furthermore, relative to the social media presence, the demands and requirements for employees' behaviour in social media must be clearly communicated. Guidelines can be beneficial, as long as they are understood as forms of assistance and orientation, not as required mandates.

The **external brand communication** also might have a positive effect on brand knowledge and brand commitment in certain conditions, such as the integration of internal and external communications, authentic brand value and employee representation, consistency between the represented and lived culture, and the effectiveness of external brand communications (cf. Piehler 2011). Transferred to social media, this means that the communicated content should be directed toward both external groups and employees. Thus, brand knowledge and brand commitment can be strengthened through external communication in social media.

Only professional internal brand management can create the conditions for successful, long-term uses of social media. Interaction competence has great importance, because it determines the quality of experiences and thus the differentiation effect of a brand's social media activities.

4.3.3.3 Brand Interaction Competence

The speed of interaction in social media increases demands for brand responsiveness and quality. The interaction competence of the brand thus must increase considerably, because this competence contributes decisively to the quality of the experience and creates a differentiation from other brands. Seven components of the interaction competence of a brand or its institution can be derived from prior literature (cf. Burmann et al. 2010):

– adequacy of the interaction
– consistency of the interaction
– relevance of the interaction
– degree of the interaction
– frequency of the interaction
– speed of the interaction

The consistency and relevance of the interaction, together with the degree of interactivity, constitute the quality of the interaction. Similarly, the length, frequency, and speed of the interaction can be summarised as the intensity of the interaction (see Fig. 4.17).

Adequacy of interaction is established only if the interaction with consumers is not solely self-purposeful but also serves to achieve the brand's objectives. The criterion of adequacy is subject to the principle of economic efficiency, and this effort contrasts with the economic result of the interaction.

The German chocolate manufacturer Ritter Sport let readers of its Ritter Sport Blog create the "Blog Chocolate," submitting suggestions for the flavour of a new chocolate bar. The best suggestion was selected and manufactured. Thus the company managed to increase users' identification with the brand while simultaneously leveraging their creativity to develop and successfully market a new product (cf. Ritter Sport 2010).

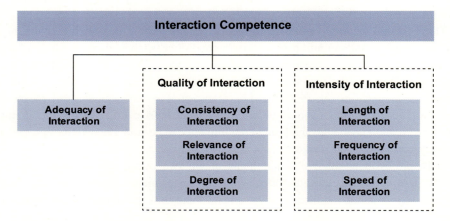

Fig. 4.17 Dimensions of interaction competence. (Source: based on Burmann et al. 2010, p. 61)

The **consistency of the interaction** presupposes that all information about present and past interactions is available to an interacting employee (cf. Belz et al. 2008). A consistent brand image can be created for consumers only if the messages in offline and online communication correspond. The direct bank ING-DiBa applies its consistent, formal brand image across different channels of communication, using an orange and blue color code, the basketball star Dirk Nowitzki as a celebrity spokesperson, and similar subject matter across television commercials, print advertisements, its website, and its Facebook page (cf. ING-DiBa 2015).

The **relevance of interaction** describes the benefits of an interaction with a brand for the consumer (cf. Burmann et al. 2010). Personal interaction, in the absence of relevance for the user, has only a small effect on brand image and purchase intentions (cf. Eilers 2014). True relevance requires solving a customer problem or handling a customer complaint. On its Twitter account @DB_Bahn, Deutsche Bahn (German Railway Company) allows passengers to contact a customer service team for any questions or problems. Responses are immediate and in real time, to help passengers when they need it. For this reason, Deutsche Bahn customers are highly motivated to interact with the brand on Twitter.

However, the football club FC Bayern Munich offers a prime example of a lack of **relevance in interaction**. The club announced that is had signed a sensational player, whose identity would be broadcast exclusively on Facebook during a live press conference. To be able to follow the press conference, fans had to "Like" the club's Facebook page and authorise its access to their basic data and profile picture. Fans expected individual customer benefits, and journalists picked up on the story, after the announcement appeared on the club's homepage. But at the press conference, the club announced that each individual fan was the "sensational new signing"—a tactic that fans and media representatives perceived very negatively, as if the club did not take them seriously and failed to appreciate their needs. Disappointed users generated complaints on the Facebook page, which then spread through Twitter and other channels (cf. Lerch 2012).

If a brand fails to offer consumers a relevant benefit, they are likely to reject any interaction. On the Facebook page of the Deutsche Bank, reactions to the brand's posts are rather scarce, and users are not permitted to publish their own posts. That is, only comments in response to posts by Deutsche Bank are possible (cf. Deutsche Bank 2015). Facebook users use this comment function to express negative opinions, often having nothing to do with the post, likely because they cannot publish their own posts. Unfortunately, this example is not an isolated one; a KEYLENS Management Consultants study of German customers' social media expectations, 61% of those surveyed (N = 1000) declared that companies failed to ensure the relevance of their social media presence (cf. Keylens 2011).

The **degree of interactivity** can span several levels (ascending order, from low to high interactivity): passivity, feigned interactivity (e.g., browsing an online catalogue), instrumental interactivity (e.g., ordering online), and interpersonal interactivity (personal dialogue). With increasing interactivity, the interaction competence of the brand increases, ceteris paribus. Vodafone leaves it to its customers to determine their degree of interactivity; on the brand's website, they can order online or watch interactive videos and read instruction manuals to configure their devices, but they can also participate in forum discussions and ask questions in live chats (cf. Vodafone 2015).

The intensity of interaction between the brand and its consumers can increase mutual trust. This aspect includes the **length and frequency of the interaction**. It also depends on whether the interactions are standardised or individualised. With greater individual-isation, the intensity of the interaction between the consumer and brand increases (cf. Jost-Benz 2009). The **speed of interaction** is also relevant for personal interactions in social media. However, sooner is not necessarily better. In one empirical study analysing two brand-driven Facebook fan pages, the effect of the speed of interaction on users' sat-isfaction was less than expected. Only when response times exceeded 24 h did they harm user satisfaction significantly (cf. Eilers 2014).

4.3.3.4 Importance of the Brand Experience for Communication in Social Media

Differentiated experiences inform brand management, because the demand for experi-ential consumption has increased significantly (cf. Freundt 2006). However, the posi-tive effects of brand experiences can emerge only if the experience matches the brand identity and thus is perceived as authentic by consumers. Brakus et al. (2009) provide evidence of the importance of brand experiences for a brand's success by noting their direct impacts on both customer satisfaction and brand loyalty. High degrees of interac-tion, multimedia formats, and the active involvement of users in creating content repre-sent several ways to generate brand experiences for consumers.

> **Brand experiences** are individual sensory impressions, feelings, and perceptions, causey by brand-related stimuli at brand touch points (cf. Brakus et al. 2009)

Brand experiences comprise the following components, either alone or in combination (Schmitt 2009):

- Sensory experiences
- Affective experiences
- Cognitive experiences
- Behavioural experiences
- Social experiences

Sensory experiences are responses to consumers' senses, namely, sight, hearing, touch, taste, and smell. A brand experience affects purchase behaviours more when more senses are addressed (cf. Schmitt and Mangold 2005; Weinberg and Diehl 2001). A multi-sense approach provides more comprehensive and more compelling experiences, thus contributing to intensive experiences and perceptions of a brand message, as well as to effective storage of these messages in long-term memory (cf. Springer 2008).

A key criterion for success is the combination of cognitive consistency and sensory variety. In other words, the brand experience for consumers must always be brand specific, clearly identifiable, new, and innovative (cf. Schmitt and Mangold 2005; Springer 2008). The holistic sense must match the brand's positioning. Multi-sensual brand management should entail several elements: colours and shapes for optics, sound and music as auditory elements, materials and texture for the haptic sense, smells as olfactory elements, and taste as a gustatory element. To ensure consistency between classical and online brand management, there is a need for good fit between sensory experiences in social media and multi-sensual approaches offline (cf. Springer 2008). To design the brand message, it is necessary to decide what senses can be addressed and how.

Affective experiences awake feelings within consumers. The aim is to prompt positive emotions in as many contact situations as possible (cf. Schmitt 1999). For example, social networks can provide high levels of fun during the interaction between the user and brand (cf. Springer 2008), as Red Bull does. Its various interactive applications and games on its Facebook page allow users to create their own aircraft and fly a virtual Red Bull parkour for example. It also provides links to videos and pictures of fun and action sports (cf. Red Bull 2015).

Cognitive experiences are the third component, and they address consumers' intellect. Benefits accrue to consumers through creative integration (cf. Schmitt 2003), perhaps as a result of interactions within communities (cf. Algesheimer and Herrmann 2005). Competitions initiated by brands in communities stimulate intellectual discussions and therefore create cognitive experiences. The interaction occurs primarily through comments and other users' assessments of the UGC. For example, the brand Labello allows fans of its Facebook page or website to create their own flavours and packaging designs, using the "Delicious Designer" function. By "Liking" submitted ideas, other users can vote for their favourite taste and the best design (cf. Labello 2015).

Behavioural experiences imply a change in consumers' behaviours. A company or other users might suggest alternative uses of the brand, and the internet can document these uses in the form of videos or pictures. Thus, imitation is simplified for other users (cf. Schmitt and Mangold 2005; Prahalad and Ramaswamy 2004). The brand thus remains up-to-date and is able to offer new ideas and alternative usages. Several online communities offer creative possibilities for using brands and their products. Rezeptwiese.de is an online community for baking and cooking enthusiasts, supporting exchanges of recipes, sponsored by the German food manufacturer Dr. Oetker. Both the brand and the users prepare new creations constantly, including existing ingredients in creative ways and adjusting recipes in new and various forms (cf. Dr. Oetker 2015).

Finally, **social experiences** include aspects of all four previous modules. They enable consumers to interact with others, develop a sense of belonging, and strengthen their social identity. Thus, they embed individual experiences in a social environment (cf. Schmitt 1999). Through this shared experience, consumers can satisfy their need for social recognition and self-expression, which can result in a high degree of customer loyalty and stronger relationships between the brand and its customers (cf. Schmitt 2009). In a social media context, social experiences are intensely conveyed through communities. User networking, both with the brand and with other users, affects their sense of belonging and provides important benefits. These social interactions strongly influence the development of long-term relations (cf. Schmitt and Mangold 2005), as the Harley-Davidson community demonstrates. These community members gain the possibility of expressing their identification with the brand and establishing relationships with other riders.

Taking these findings into account, the relationship among interaction competence, quality of experiences, and the growth of earnings is depicted in Fig. 4.18. High interaction competence has a positive effect on the quality of the brand experience in social media. If the subjective experience features high quality, psychographic targets such as customer satisfaction and brand loyalty will be influenced positively, which has a positive effect on the economic success of a brand.

4.3.3.5   Social Media's Success Factors

To use social media expediently in identity-based brand management, a brand must consider several success factors, in addition to the instruments (and various platforms) depicted previous. It must be clear at all levels, in all departments, and in all management settings just how important social media is for the own company and how it affects both the business model and the work of employees. It only makes sense to grapple in depth with implementation decisions and take further actions when these considerations have been addressed. In the course of these considerations, it is important to adjust internal structures to match the dynamism of the internet, the on-going global interconnections, and the changed usage behaviour of costumers (cf. Hau and Theobald 2011).

Social media aim to increase brand awareness. Intensive interactions with consumers gives brands opportunities to differentiate themselves from competitors, and the influence of social media on consumers' attitudes often is high. In comparison with classical communication, social media tends to have greater influences on purchase and re-purchase intentions. Yet most companies fail to use social media professionally or with an identity-based approach. Thus, in addition to setting communication goals, companies need to define **relevant target groups** for each instrument, to ensure the transmission of relevant benefits. The success of these activities must also be demonstrated in social media, for which purpose clear and operational objectives are necessary. Their achievement can be captured in the context of control.

Two additional success factors for social media are **authenticity** and **transparency**. If a brand is perceived as authentic in its social media activities (such that the brand's behaviour is determined by its identity, not external influences), consumers should be willing to enter into relations with the brand through interactions (cf. Schallehn 2012). Transparency primarily affects appearances in social media. The brand and its employ-

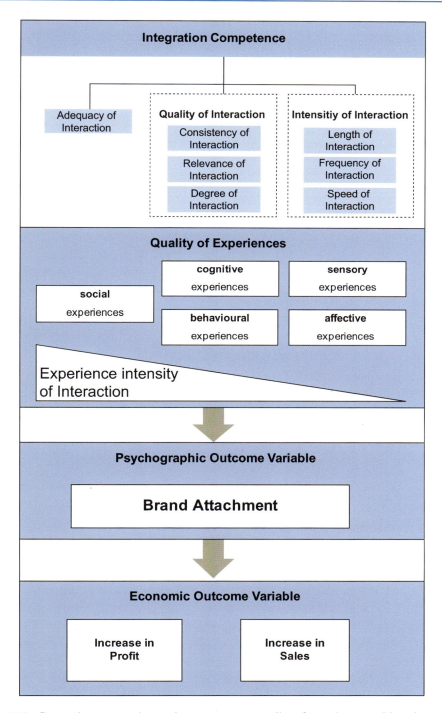

Fig. 4.18 Connections among interaction competence, quality of experience, and brand success. (Source: based on Burmann et al. 2010, p. 61)

ees must be recognizable. Trying to influence opinions and communication in social media without identification as a brand representative can cause strong negative reactions among users once they discover the attempt and thus harm the brand in the long term.

Social media also offer brands new opportunities to get in touch with customers and clients. This form of contact is particularly important for companies without direct sales and that hand over selling responsibilities to third parties (e.g., fast moving consumer goods brands). A **clear brand identity** thus is of great importance. Customers participate in interactions with brands if they recognize their brand identities and can identify with them. In a study of social media usage, and Facebook in particular, the most important reasons users (n = 2000) became fans of a brand on Facebook was to support good brands (cf. Keylens 2012). Their willingness to take a stand for a brand implies a high level of identification, which can be achieved only if the brand identity is clearly communicated and embraced by the company.

Another success factor is whether the offered **benefit** is attractive for consumers. The company must succeed in providing the consumer with a relevant benefit through its social media activities. If social media simply provide another channel to publish public relations messages or undifferentiated advertisement, it may result in negative demand reactions (cf. Arnhold 2010).

A **united brand story** must be told across various channels. The brand forms the foundation for communication, but there is also a need for the different channels to define their own communication objectives. The brand value must be translated into messages that have been adjusted for each channel. There is no additional benefit for the consumer if all online and social media activities are identical, such that users receive the same message, over and over again (Seidel 2014).

Finally, the **integration** of social media activities with the brand's other communication and corporate strategies is another significant success factor. A company that adopts a traditional image in classical media should not try to adopt a cutting-edge approach or impression. Rather, it should convey a consistent brand image to consumers and use social media to achieve economic success in the long term.

4.3.3.6 Performance Measures of Social Media

Both research and practice are still in their infancy with regard to performance measures for social media. New metrics and tools are being developed in rapid succession. They seek to take advantage of the latest technological innovations and provide insights into the interaction between the brand and consumers (cf. Eilers 2014). However, the simple transmission of traditional indicators of contacts on social media must be reviewed critically. The complexity of social media makes it difficult to compare social and traditional media. Therefore, there is no consensus about the suitability of any measurement method for evaluating the success of social media activities thus far. As examples, this section reviews two approaches to measuring the performance of social media briefly.

KEYLENS Management Consulting, a strategic consultancy from Germany, uses a benchmarking system that collects metrics of various brand objectives, then sets them in comparison with competitors' metrics. The consultancy believes that evaluations of social media that rely solely on the number of fans and followers fall short. These indicators can only give basic information about the number of generated contacts, because they include users without any sustained interest in the brand, who only started to follow it or became a fan out of a temporary impulse. An attractive contest or interesting features can increase the number of participants, regardless of whether they have a real interest in the brand. Therefore, isolated examinations of fans or followers cannot indicate the type of connection between a brand and its users. In addition, available services (e.g., "fanslave") allow brands to buy followers and fans.

A more detailed assessment of a contact requires consideration of the degree of interaction, including the amount of time and effort a user invests in the relationship with the brand. Moreover, a willingness to recommend something to close friends is an important benchmark of the attractiveness of brands in social media.

Accordingly, KEYLENS takes such requirements into account (cf. Fig. 4.19). Its benchmarking funnel compresses indicators into three stages: "attract," "engage," and "evangelize." For each platform, it captures specific parameters. The number of fans and followers on Facebook and Twitter appear in the "attract" stage, supporting evaluations of how well known the brand is in social media and how often it is visited. In the "engage" stage, the measure pertains to the degree of interaction. On Facebook, the number of Likes is assessed relative to the number of fans, and the number of comments is observed. A willingness to recommend ("evangelize" stage) is measured on Twitter

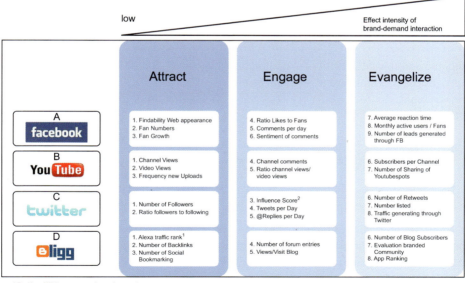

Fig. 4.19 KEYLENS benchmarking system. (Source: Lampe and von Keyserlingk 2011, p. 876)

using retweets or on YouTube by the number of shares. Then, all these collected variables are investigated relative to the matching variables for competitive brands. With this approach, brands can determine their own status quo, then evaluate it in comparison with competitors (cf. Lampe and von Keyserlingk 2011).

A similar approach is suggested by Hoffman and Fodor (2010). Their goal is to connect the evaluation of activities in social media not with investments by the company but rather with investments by consumers. Accordingly, their indicators are based on visit frequency, the number of comments, and the time a user spends on the social media site (Table 4.2). They avoid establishing any direct relation between activities in social media and sales figures, for several reasons. First, sales figures measure only immediate, short-term success. However, social media activities entail long-term relations between customers and the brand. Second, sales figures only measure quantitative value, not the qualitative value of social media. Therefore, they propose measuring social media performance according to three categories of objectives: brand awareness, brand engagement, and word of mouth. Depending on the platform, the three objectives entail various key performance indicators (KPI). Brand awareness is measured as the number of fans or installed applications. Brand engagement relies on metrics such as the number of comments in social networks. Therefore, the brand can determine how much it motivates users to communicate with the brand through social media. Whether users act as "brand ambassadors" and share their positive brand attitudes with their personal network is assessed in the third, word-of-mouth stage. The number of shares in a social network serve as an indicator.

These methods attempt to determine the influence on brand sites by measuring the degree of user participation, which also constitutes engagement. However, brand engagement is a behavioural outcome variable, so additional psychographic factors are missing. As explained in Sect. 3.1.2, **brand attachment** is an especially important psychographic outcome variable for identity-based brand management. Kleine-Kalmer (2015) accordingly proposes a brand page attachment measure (see also Park et al. 2010, as a cross-industry construct to measure the attachment of Internet users to brand pages on social networks).

> **Brand page attachment** reflects the strength of the bond connecting the brand page with the user (Park et al. 2010, p. 2).

In a 2014 empirical study, 590 participants from Germany were surveyed and asked about brands from three branches: automotive, FMCG and restaurant chains (cf. Kleine-Kalmer 2015). To participate, they had to have an active Facebook account and follow at least one of 55 brand pages specified for the study. Figure 4.20 represents the results. In all three branches, brand page attachment exerted a powerful effect on various outcome variables, such as user activity, intentions to maintain a connection to the brand,

Table 4.2   Indicators of the success of social media activities

Social media application	Brand awareness	Brand engagement	Word of mouth
Blogs	• Number of unique visits • Number of return visits • Number of times bookmarked • Search ranking	• Number of members • Number of RSS feed subscribers • Number of comments • Amount of user-generated content • Average length of time on site • Number of responses to polls, contests, surveys	• Number of references to blog in other media (online/offline) • Number of reblogs • Number of times badge displayed on other sites • Number of "likes"
Online communities	• Number of page views • Number of visits • Valance of posted content	• Number of relevant topics/threads • Number of individual replies • Number of sign-ups	• Incoming links • Citations on other sites • Offline references to the forum or its members • In private communities: pieces of content (photos, discussion, videos); chatter pointing to the community • Number of "likes"
Photo- and video-communities	• Number of videos or photos • Valence of video/photo ratings	• Number of replies • Number of page views • Number of comments • Number of subscribers	• Number of embeddings • Number of incoming links • Number of references in mock-ups or derived work • Number of times republished in other social media and offline • Number of "likes"
Microblogging	• Number of tweets about the brand • Valance of tweets • Number of followers	• Number of followers • Number of @replies	• Number of retweets

(continued)

Table 4.2 (continued)

Social media application	Brand awareness	Brand engagement	Word of mouth
Social networks	• Number of members/ fans • Number of installs of applications • Number of impressions • Number of bookmarks • Number of reviews/ ratings and valance	• Number of comments • Number of active users • Number of "likes" on friends' feeds • Number of user-generated items (photos, threads, replies) • User metrics of applications/widgets • Impressions-to-interactions ratio • Rate of activity (how often members personalize profiles, bios, links, etc.)	• Frequency of appearances in timelines of friends • Number of posts on wall • Number of reposts/ shares • Number of responses to friend referral invites

Hoffman and Fodor (2010), p. 44

and willingness to share demographic or personal information with the brand. Kleine-Kalmer thus confirmed that brand page attachment largely determines user behaviours across industries.

This construct therefore offers high predictive power regarding the active participation of users, such as creating content on the brand page or disseminating information through word of mouth. Users who are strongly associated with a brand page participate more actively than users who are less bonded. Therefore, brand page attachment has greater explanatory power for user behaviour than more widely used methods, such as measures of attitude toward a brand page. This finding underlines the importance of building emotional bonds between consumers and the brand, whether through brand pages in social networks or other social media instruments (cf. Kleine-Kalmer 2015).

Managers in turn must address the factors that influence brand page attachment. Kleine-Kalmer (2015) identifies three determinants: social interactions, infotainment, and economic incentives. **Social interactions** in this context have the strongest effect, so brand pages should encourage interactions among users of the page. **Infotainment** is a combination of information and entertainment; in addition to information about a brand, users want to be entertained. Finally, attachment to the brand page can be increased by providing **economic incentives**, such as draws, coupons, or discounts, because users regularly visit brand pages that repeatedly create such advantages for them (cf. Kleine-Kalmer 2015).

Facebook is the largest and most popular social network worldwide, with more than 1 billion active users (cf. Facebook 2015). In Germany, nearly one-quarter of all

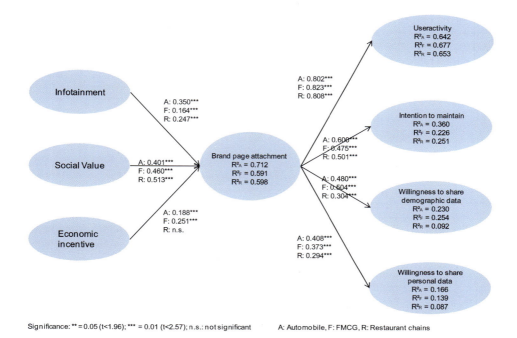

Fig. 4.20 Outcome variables and determinants of brand page attachment. (Source: Kleine-Kalmer 2015)

Internet users and almost half of users 14–19 years of age are fans of some brand or its brand page (cf. Bitcom 2013). Therefore, it stands to reason that Kleine-Kalmer (2015) included this social media channel in developing a tool to measure success. Her approach to brand page attachment provides an excellent basis for further research to develop measurement methods that apply more specifically to other social media instruments.

References

Adjei, M. T., Noble, S. M., & Noble, C. H. (2010). The influence of C2C communications in online brand communities on customer purchase behavior. *Journal of the Academy of Marketing Science, 38*(5), 634–653.

Algesheimer, R., Borle, S., Dholakia, U. M., & Singh, S. S. (2010). The impact of customer community participation on customer behaviors: An empirical investigation. *Marketing Science, 29*(4), 711–726.

Algesheimer, R., & Herrmann, A. (2005). *Brand Communities - Grundidee, Konzept und empirische Befunde*. In F.-R. Esch (Ed.), *Moderne Markenführung - Grundlagen. Innovative Ansätze. Praktische Umsetzungen* (4th ed., pp. 747–764). Wiesbaden: Gabler.

ARD-ZDF. (2014). *ARD-ZDF Onlinestudie 2014*. http://www.ard-zdf-onlinestudie.de/fileadmin/Onlinestudie_2014/PDF/0708-2014_Eimeren_Frees.pdf. Last visit: May 07, 2015.

Arnhold, U. (2010). *User-generated branding (UGB)—An exploration of a new field of study focusing on the effectiveness of participatory communication programmes.* Wiesbaden: Gabler.

Bandura, A. (1977). *Social learning theory.* Englewood Cliffs, NJ: Prentice-Hall.

Bass, B. M. (1985). *Leadership and performance beyond expectations.* New York, NY: Free Press.

Bass, B. M. (1990). From transactional to transformational leadership: Learning to share the vision. *Organizational Dynamics, 18*(3), 19–31.

Batt, V. (2013). *Qualität der Internen Markenführung.* Wiesbaden: Gabler.

Beck, K. (2010). Soziologie der Online-Kommunikation. In W. Schweiger & K. Beck (Eds.), *Handbuch Online Kommunikation* (pp. 15–35). Wiesbaden: VS Verlag für Sozialwissenschaften.

Belz, C., Schögel, M., & Arndt, O. (2008). Grenzen technologie-gestützter Kundeninteraktion. In C. Belz, M. Schögel, O. Arndt, & V. Walter (Ed.), *Interaktives Marketing - neue Wege zum Dialog mit Kunden* (pp. 3–20). Wiesbaden: Gabler.

Bender, G. (2011). *Die Marketingrevolution in Zeiten von Web 2.0 – Herausforderungen und Chancen für ein neues beziehungsaktives Kundenmanagement.* In B. Hass, G. Walsh, T. Kilian (Eds.), *Web 2.0: Neue Perspektiven für Marketing und Medien, 2* (pp. 143–156). Aufl., Berlin: Springer.

Bijmolt, T. H. A., Leeflang, P. S. H., Block, F., Eisenbeiß, M., Hardie, B. G. S., Lemmens, A., et al. (2010). Analytics for customer engagement. *Journal of Service Research, 13*(3), 341–356.

Bitkom. (2013). *Internetnutzung Privatpersonen.* http://www.bitkom.org/files/documentes/Abb09_Internetnutzung_Privatpersonen.jpg. Last visit: July 24, 2013.

Blader, R. F. (2011). *Harnessing the power of social media.* Speech at the CMO-Circle Munich. November 17, 2011.

Bleier, A., & Eisenbeiß, M. (2015). Personalized online advertising effectiveness: The interplay of what, when, and where. *Marketing Science* (in print).

Brakus, J. J., Schmitt, B. H., & Zarantonello, L. (2009). Brand experience—What is it? How is it measured? Does it affect loyalty? *Journal of Marketing, 73*(3), 52–68.

Brexendorf, T., Tomczak, T., Kernstock, J., Henkel, S., & Wentzel, D. (2012). Der Einsatz von Instrumenten zur Förderung von Brand Behavior. In T. Tomczak, F.-R. Esch, J. Kernstock, & A. Herrmann (Eds.), *Behavioral Branding: Wie Mitarbeiterverhalten die Marke stärkt* (3rd ed., pp. 337–371). Wiesbaden: Springer Gabler.

Bruhn, M. (2015). *Kommunikationspolitik: Systematischer Einsatz der Kommunikation für Unternehmen* (8th ed.). Munich: Vahlen.

Büllingen, F. (2010). Wie geht es weiter nach DSL? Entwicklungsperspektiven der Versorgung mit Breitband-Internet. In D. Klumpp & W. Schulz (Eds.), *Netzwelt-Wege, Werte, Wandel* (pp. 63–77). Berlin: Springer.

Burmann, C., & Arnhold, U. (2008). *User generated branding: State of the art of research.* Berlin: LIT.

Burmann, C., Eilers, D., & Hemmann, F. (2010). *Bedeutung der Brand Experience für die Markenführung im Internet.* Working paper No. 46 of the Chair of innovative Brand Management and Marketing (LiM) of the University of Bremen.

Burmann, C., Kleine-Kalmer, B., & Hemmann, F. (2014). Vermittlung von Markenerlebnissen durch die Nutzung von Big Data. *Marketing Review St. Gallen, 1,* 56–67.

Burmann, C., & Piehler, R. (2013). Employer branding vs. internal branding—Ein Vorschlag zur Integration im Rahmen der identitätsbasierten Markenführung. *Die Unternehmung, 67*(3), 223–245.

Burmann, C., & Zeplin, S. (2005). Building brand commitment: A behavioural approach to internal brand management. *Journal of Brand Management, 12*(4), 279–300.

Burmann, C., König, V., & Meurer, J. (2012). *Identitätsbasierte Luxusmarkenführung: Grundlagen – Strategien – Controlling.* Wiesbaden: Springer Gabler.

Burns, J. M. (1978). *Leadership.* New York: Harper Perennial Modern Classics.

Deutsche Bank (2015). Facebook page of Deutsche Bank. https://www.facebook.com/Deutsche-Bank. May 12, 2015.

De Chernatony, L., Cottam, S., & Segal-Horn, S. (2006). Communicating services brands' values internally and externally. *Service Industries Journal, 26*(8), 819–836.

Deshpandé, R. (1983). Paradigms lost: On the theory and method in research in marketing. *Journal of Marketing, 47*(4), 101–110.

Duggan, M., Ellison, N.-B., Lampe, C., Lenhart, A., & Madden, M. (2015). *Demographics of key social networking platforms.* http://www.pewinternet.org/2015/01/09/demographics-of-key-social-networking-plattforms-2. Last visit: February 19, 2015.

Eilers, D. (2014). *Wirkung von Social Media auf Marken – Eine ganzheitliche Abbildung der Markenführung in Social Media.* Wiesbaden: Springer Gabler.

eMarketer. (2013). *Social networking reaches nearly one in four around the world.* http://www.emarketer.com/article/social-networking-reaches-nearly-one-four-around-world/1009976#Ve1R72mxm6r3ScR1.99. Last visit: August 20, 2013.

Esch, F.-R., Fischer, A., & Strödter, K. (2012). Interne Kommunikation zum Aufbau von Markenwissen bei den Mitarbeitern. In T. Tomczak, F.-R. Esch, J. Kernstock, & A. Herrmann (Eds.), *Behavioral branding: Wie Mitarbeiterverhalten die Marke stärkt* (3rd ed., pp. 101–120). Wiesbaden: Springer Gabler.

Facebook. (2015). *Stats 2015.* http://newsroom.fb.com/company-info. Last visit: May 07, 2015.

FedEX. (2014). *I am FedEX.* https://www.iamfedex.com. Last visit: April 21, 2014.

Freundt, T. C. (2006). *Verhaltensrelevanz emotionaler Markenimages – eine interindustrielle Analyse auf empirischer Grundlage.* Wiesbaden: Dt. Univ.-Verlag.

FRoSTA. (2012). *FRoSTA-Blog.* http://www.frostablog.de. Last visit: May 04, 2012.

Gardner, W. L., & Avolio, B. J. (1998). The charismatic relationship: A dramaturgical perspective. *Academy of Management Review, 23*(1), 32–58.

George, W. R., & Berry, L. L. (1981). Guidelines for the advertising of services. *Business Horizons, 24*(4), 52–56.

Gilly, M. C., & Wolfinbarger, M. F. (1998). Advertising's internal audience. *Journal of Marketing, 62*(1), 69–88.

Greve, G. (2011). Social CRM – ganzheitliches Beziehungsmanagement mit Social Media. *Marketing Review St. Gallen, 5,* 16–21.

Hartmann, K. (2010). *Wirkung der Markenwahrnehmung auf das Markencommitment von Mitarbeitern: Eine empirische Untersuchung der Wirkung von Markenimage, interner Kommunikation und Fit zwischen persönlichen und Markenwerten auf das Commitment.* Hamburg: Dr. Kovac.

Hau, S.-M., & Theobald, E. (2011). Erfolgsfaktoren und Grenzen der Markenführung im Internet. In E. Theobald & P. T. Haisch (Eds.), *Brand Evolution* (pp. 127–149). Wiesbaden: Gabler.

Hausschildt, J., & Salomo, S. (2011). *Innovationsmanagment* (5th ed.). Munich: Vahlen.

Heinemann, G. (2014). *Der neue Online-Handel: Geschäftsmodell und Kanalexzellenz im E-Commerce.* Wiesbaden: Springer Gabler.

Henkel, S. (2008). *Werbung als Verhaltensvorbild für Mitarbeiter: Eine empirische Untersuchung am Beispiel UBS.* Hamburg: Dr. Kovac.

Henkel, S., Tomczak, T., & Jenewein, W. (2012). Werbung als Verhaltensvorbild für Mitarbeiter. In T. Tomczak, F.-R. Esch, J. Kernstock, & A. Herrmann (Eds.), *Behavioral branding: Wie Mitarbeiterverhalten die Marke stärkt* (3rd ed., pp. 443–467). Wiesbaden: Springer Gabler.

Henkel, S., Wentzel, D., & Tomczak, T. (2009). Die Rolle der Werbung in der internen Markenführung. *Marketing ZFP, 31*(1), 43–56.

Heun, T. (2014). Die Erweckung des Verbrauchers – Zum Nutzen von Marken im Zeitalter digi-
taler Medien. In S. Dänzler & T. Heun (Eds.), *Marke und digitale Medien* (pp. 33–48). Wiesbaden: Springer Gabler.

Hoffman, D. L., & Fodor, M. (2010). Can you measure the ROI of your social media marketing?
MIT Sloan Management Review, 52(1), 41–49.

Iltgen, A., Künzler, S. (2008). *Web 2.0 – Schon mehr als ein Hype.* In C. Belz, M. Schögel, O.
Arndt, V. Walter (Eds.), *Interaktives Marketing: Neue Wege zum Dialog mit Kunden* (pp. 237–
256), Wiesbaden: Gabler.

ING-DiBa. (2015). *Online-Auftritt.* http://www.ing-diba.de. Last visit: March 25, 2015.

Jandura, O., & Kranowski, V. (2015). Digital natives vs. digital immigrants—fruchtbares
empirisches Konzept für die Kommunikationswissenschaft oder populärwissenschaftliche Fik-
tion? *Publizistik, 60,* 63–79.

Jost-Benz, M. (2009). *Identitätsbasierte Markenbewertung - Grundlagen, theoretische Konzeptualisierung und praktische Anwendung am Beispiel einer Technologiemarke.* Wiesbaden: Gabler.

Kaiser, T. (2009). *Top Platzierungen bei Google & Co.* Göttingen: Business Village.

Kardon, B. (2007). They're saying nasty things. *Marketing News, 41*(20), 30.

Keylens. (2011). *Kundenerwartungen im Social Web.* Düsseldorf.

Keylens. (2012). *Social Media in der Ernährungsindustrie.* Düsseldorf.

Kleine-Kalmer, B. (2015). *Managing brand page attachment—An empirical study on facebook
user's attachment to brand pages* (to date unpublished dissertation).

Kollmann, T. (2013). *Online-Marketing, Grundlagen der Absatzpolitik in der Net Economy* (2nd
ed.). Stuttgart: Kohlhammer.

Kreutzer, R. T. (2014). *Praxisorientiertes online-marketing* (2nd ed.). Wiesbaden: Springer Gabler.

Krogh, H. (2010). *Seat-Chef Muir spricht Klartext über Probleme der spanischen VW-Marke.*
http://www.automobilwoche.de/article/20100513/NACHRICHTEN/100519972/seat-chef-muir-
spricht-klartext-uber-probleme-der-spanischen-vw-marke#.VE4sxfl5PHQ. Last visit: October
27, 2014.

Labello. (2015). *Labello "Delicious Designer".* http://www.labello.de/entertainment/flavor-creator.
Last visit: May 12, 2015.

Lammenett, E. (2012). *Praxisorientiertes Marketingwissen.* Wiesbaden: Springer Gabler.

Lampe, T., & von Keyserlingk, A. (2011). „Brennglas" social media benötigt strategisches Funda-
ment. *Versicherungswirtschaft, 12,* 875–877.

Larkin, T. J., & Larkin, S. (1996). Reaching and changing frontline employees. *Harvard Business
Review, 74*(3), 95–104.

Laux, H., & Liermann, F. (2005). *Grundlagen der Organisation: Die Steuerung von Entscheidungen als Grundproblem der Betriebswirtschaftslehre* (6th ed.). Berlin: Springer.

Lee, M., & Rodgers, S. K. M. (2009). Effects of valence and extremity of eWOM on attitude
toward the brand and website. *Journal of Current Issues and Research in Advertising, 31*(2),
1–11.

Lee, M., & Youn, S. (2009). Electronic word of mouth (eWOM). *International Journal of Advertising, 28*(3), 473–499.

Lerch, H. (2012). *FC Bayern München blamiert sich auf Facebook.* http://www.stutt-
garter-zeitung.de/inhalt.social-media-fc-bayern-muenchen-blamiert-sich-auf-face-
book.12251234-80b4-425b-86bb-57a14d2e2104.html. Last visit: May 04, 2012.

LG. (2012). *Der Fahrstuhltest: IPS-Monitore von LG sind zum Fürchten realistisch.* http://www.
lgblog.de/2012/10/23/der-fahrstuhltest-ips-monitore-von-lg-sind-zum-furchten-realistisch. Last
visit: August 28, 2013.

Li, C., & Bernhoff, J. (2008). *Groundswell: Winning in a world transformed by social technologies.* Boston: Harvard Business Press.

Maloney, P. (2007). *Absatzmittlergerichtetes, identitätsbasiertes Markenmanagement: Eine Erweiterung des innengerichteten, identitätsbasierten Markenmanagements unter besonderer Berücksichtigung von Premiummarken*. Wiesbaden: Gabler.

Meffert, H., Burmann, C., & Kirchgeorg, M. (2015). *Marketing: Grundlagen marktorientierter Unternehmensführung*. Wiesbaden: Springer Gabler.

Michelis, D. (2014). *Der vernetzte Konsument*. Wiesbaden: Springer Gabler.

Morhart, F. M., Herzog, W., & Tomczak, T. (2009). Brand-specific leadership: Turning employees into brand champions. *Journal of Marketing, 73*(5), 122–142.

Müller, A. (2012). *Symbole als Instrumente der Markenführung – Eine kommunikations- und wirtschaftswissenschaftliche Analyse unter besonderer Berücksichtigung von Stadtmarken*. Wiesbaden: Gabler.

Munzinger, U., & Wenhart, C. (2012). *Marken erleben im digitalen Zeitalter*. Wiesbaden: Springer Gabler.

Nerdinger, F. W., von Rosenstiel, L. (1999). Die Umgestaltung der Führungsstrukturen im Rahmen der Implementierung des Internen Marketing. In M. Bruhn (Ed.), *Internes Marketing: Integration der Kunden- und Mitarbeiterorientierung; Grundlagen - Implementierung – Praxisbeispiele* (2nd ed., pp. 175–190). Wiesbaden: Springer Gabler.

Oetker, Dr. (2015). *Rezeptwiese*. www.rezeptwiese.de. Last visit: May 12, 2015.

O'Reilly, T., Milstein, S., Bombien, V., Pahrmann, C., & Pelz, N. (2013). *Das Twitter-Buch* (3rd ed.). Cologne: O'Reilly.

Pälike, F. (2000). Die Manager-Marke kommt! Persönlichkeit ist ein Added Value. *Absatzwirtschaft, 43*(Sondernummer Oktober), 16–18.

Park, C. W., MacInnis, D. J., Priester, J., Eisingerich, A. B., & Iacobucci, D. (2010). Brand attachment and brand attitude strength: Conceptual and empirical differentiation of two critical brand equity drivers. *Journal of Marketing, 74*(6), 1–17.

Pattloch, A., & Rumler, A. (2013). Kommunikation 2.0: Von Push zu Pull. In G. Hofbauer, A. Pattloch, & M. Stumpf (Ed.), *Marketing in Forschung und Praxis* (pp. 275–286). Berlin: uni-Edition.

PhoCusWright. (2013). *Special travel weekly report 29*. Juli 2013. http//:www.travelweekly.com. Last visit: May 06, 2015.

Piehler, R. (2011). *Interne Markenführung – Theoretisches Konzept und fallstudenbasierte Evidenz*. Wiesbaden: Gabler.

Piehler, R., Hanisch, S., & Burmann, C. (2015). Internal branding—Relevance, management, and challenges. *Marketing Review St. Gallen, 32*(1), 52–60.

Pleil, T., & Zerfaß, A. (2014). Internet und Social Media in der Unternehmenskommunikation. In A. Zerfaß & M. Piwinger (Eds.), *Handbuch Unternehmenskommunikation* (pp. 731–753). Wiesbaden: Springer Gabler.

Prahalad, C. K., & Ramaswamy, S. (2004). Co-creation experiences—The next practice in value creation. *Journal of Interactive Marketing, 18*(3), 5–14.

Prensky, M. (2001). Digital natives, digital immigrants. *On the Horizon, 9*(5), 1–6.

Punjaisri, K., Evanschitzky, H., & Wilson, A. (2009). Internal branding: An enabler of employees' brand-supporting behaviours. *Journal of Service Management, 20*(2), 209–226.

Red Bull. (2015). *Facebook-Seite von Red Bull*. www.facebook.com/redbull. Last visit: May 13, 2015.

Ritter Sport. (2010). *Ritter Sport Blog-Schokolade – von euch, mit euch, für euch*! http://www.ritter-sport.de/blog/2010/12/13/ritter-sport-blog-schokolade-mit-euch-von-euch-fur-euch-2. Last visit: October 27, 2014.

Rowley, J. (2004). Online branding. *Online Information Review, 28*(2), 131–138.

Sammerl, N. (2006). *Innovationsfähigkeit und nachhaltiger Wettbewerbsvorteil – Messung – Determinanten – Wirkungen*. Wiesbaden: Gabler.

Schallehn, M. (2012). *Marken-Authentizität - Konstrukt, Determinanten und Wirkungen aus Sicht der identitätsbasierten Markenführung*. Wiesbaden: Springer Gabler.

Schau, H. J., Muniz, A. M., & Arnould, E. J. (2009). How Brand Community Practices Create Value. *Journal of Marketing 73*(5), 30–51.

Schmitt, B. (1999). Experiential marketing. *Journal of Marketing Management, 15*(1–3), 53–67.

Schmitt, B. (2003). *Customer experience management—A revolutionary approach to connecting with your customers*. Weinheim: Wiley.

Schmitt, B. (2009). Customer experience management. In M. Bruhn, F.-R. Esch, & T. Langner (Eds.), *Handbuch Kommunikation* (pp. 697–711). Wiesbaden: Gabler.

Schmitt, B., & Mangold, M. (2005). *Customer Experience Management als zentrale Erfolgsgröße der Markenführung*. In F.-R. Esch (Hrsg.), *Moderne Markenführung – Grundlagen. Innovative Ansätze. Praktische Umsetzungen* (4. Aufl. S. 287–304). Wiesbaden: Gabler.

Schmidt, H. J., Kilian, K. (2012). Internal Branding, Employer Branding & Co.: Der Mitarbeiter im Markenfokus. *Transfer Werbeforschung & Praxis, 58*(1), 28–33.

Schmidt, J.-H. (2013). *Social media*. Wiesbaden: VS Verlag.

Schögel, M. (2012). *Distributionsmanagement. Das Management der Absatzkanäle*. Munich: Vahlen.

Schögel, M., & Mrkwicka, K. (2011). Communication shift—Chancen und Herausforderungen aus Marketingsicht. *Marketing Review St. Gallen, 5*(6), 6–10.

Seidel, E. (2014). Die Zukunft der Markenidentität – Zur Kritik des Markenidentitätsmodells im digitalen Zeitalter. In S. Dänzler & T. Heun (Eds.), *Marke und digitale Medien* (pp. 363–378). Wiesbaden: Springer Gabler.

Sen, S., & Lerman, D. (2007). Why are you telling me this? An examination into negative consumer reviews on the web. *Journal of Interactive Marketing, 21*(4), 76–95.

Smith, A. N., Fischer, E., & Yongyian, C. (2012). How does brand-related user-generated content differ across youtube, facebook, and twitter? *Journal of Interactive Marketing, 26*(2), 102–113.

Spiegel Online. (2014). *Umstrittene Marketingaktion mit Shell: Lego reagiert auf Greenpeace-Kritik*. http://www.spiegel.de/wirtschaft/unternehmen/lego-beendet-spielzeug-aktion-mit-shell-nach-greenpeace-kritik-a-996299.html. Last visit: February 26, 2015.

Springer, C. (2008). *Multisensuale Markenführung - Eine verhaltenswissenschaftliche Analyse unter besonderer Berücksichtigung von Brand Lands in der Automobilwirtschaft*. Wiesbaden: Gabler.

Stanoevska-Slabeva, K. (2008). *Die Potentiale des Web 2.0 für das Interaktive Marketing*. In C. Belz, M. Schögel, O. Arndt, & V. Walter (Eds.), *Interaktives Marketing: Neue Wege zum Dialog mit Kunden* (pp. 221–236). Wiesbaden: Gabler.

Stenger, D. (2012). *Virale Markenkommunikation: Einstellungs- und Verhaltenswirkungen viraler Videos*. Wiesbaden: Springer Gabler.

Stichnoth, F. (2008). *Virtuelle Brand Communities zur Markenprofilierung - Der Einsatz virtueller Brand Communities zur Stärkung der Marke-Kunden-Beziehung*. Working paper No. 35 of the Chair of innovative Brand Management and Marketing (LiM) of the University of Bremen.

Tiago, M. T. B., & Veríssimo, J. M. C. (2014). Digital marketing and social media: why bother? *Business Horizons, 57*(6), 703–708.

Tomczak, T., Schögel, M., & Wentzel, D. (2006). Communities als Herausforderung für die Markenführung. In B. W. Wirtz & C. Burmann (Eds.), *Ganzheitliches Direktmarketing* (pp. 523–546). Wiesbaden: Gabler.

Totz, C., & Werg, F. (2014). Interaktionen machen Marken – wie die Digitalisierung Interaktionen zum Kern der Markenführung macht. In S. Dänzler & T. Heun (Eds.), *Marke und digitale Medien* (pp. 113–131). Wiesbaden: Springer Gabler.

TripAdvisor. (2015). *Willkommen in der TripAdvisor-Widget-Zentrale.* http://tripadvisor.de/Widgets. Last visit: April 20, 2015.

Trusov, M., Bucklin, R. E., & Pauwels, K. (2009). Effects of word-of-mouth versus traditional marketing: Findings from an internet social networking site. *Journal of Marketing, 73*(5), 90–102.

Tuten, T. L., & Solomon, M. R. (2014). *Social Media Marketing.* New Jersey: Prentice Hall.

Twitter. (2014). About: Company. Retrieved from https://about.twitter.com/company. Last visit: May 06, 2015.

Vallaster, C., & de Chernatony, L. (2005). Internationalisation of services brands: The role of leadership during the internal brand building process. *Journal of Marketing Management, 21*(1/2), 181–203.

Vodafone. (2015). *Vodafone website.* http://www.vodafone.de. Last visit: May 12, 2015.

von Loewenfeld, F. (2006). *Brand Communities: Erfolgsfaktoren und ökonomische Relevanz von Markengemeinschaften.* Wiesbaden: Deutscher Universitätsverlag.

vor dem Esche, J., & Hennig-Thurau, T. (2014). *German digitalization consumer report—Research report.* No. 2. Marketing Center Münster & Roland Beger Strategy Consultants.

Wallace, E., Buil, I., de Chernatony, L., & Hogan, M. (2014). Who "likes" you…and why? A typogoly of Facebook Fans. *Journal of Marketing Research, 54*(1), 92–109.

Warwitz, C. (2015). *Location-based advertising* (to date unpublished dissertation).

Watzlawick, P., Beavin, J. H., & Jackson, D. D. (2007). *Menschliche Kommunikation* (11th ed.). Bern: Hans Huber.

Weinberg, P., & Diehl, S. (2001). Aufbau und Sicherung von Markenbindung unter schwierigen Konkurrenz- und Distributionsbedingungen. In R. Köhler, W. Majer, & H. Wiezorek (Eds.), *Erfolgsfaktor Marke - Neue Strategien des Markenmanagements* (pp. 26–35). Munich: Vahlen.

Wentzel, D., Tomczak, T., & Herrmann, A. (2012). Storytelling in behavioral branding. In T. Tomczak, F.-R. Esch, J. Kernstock, & A. Herrmann (Eds.), *Behavioral branding—Wie Mitarbeiterverhalten die Marke stärkt* (3rd ed., pp. 425–442). Wiesbaden: Springer Gabler.

Wittke-Kothe, C. (2001). *Interne Markenführung: Verankerung der Markenidentität im Mitarbeiterverhalten.* Wiesbaden: Gabler.

Wunsch-Vincent, S., & Vickery, G. (2007). *Participative web and user-created content: Web 2.0, Wikis and social networking.* Paris: OECD Directorate for Science, Technology and Industry.

Xiong, L., King, C., & Piehler, R. (2013). "That's not my job": Exploring the employee perspective to becoming brand ambassadors. *International Journal of Hospitality Management, 35*(1), 348–359.

YouTube. (2015). *Statistik.* https://www.youtube.com/yt/press/de/statistics.html. Last visit: April 20, 2015.

Yukl, G. (1989). Managerial leadership: A review of theory and research. *Journal of Management, 15*(2), 251–289.

Zeplin, S. (2006). *Innengerichtetes, identitätsbasiertes Markenmanagement.* Wiesbaden: Gabler.

Identity-Based Brand Controlling

5

Contents

5.1 Internal and External Brand Performance Measurement. 235
    5.1.1 Main Features of Identity-Based Brand Controlling 235
    5.1.2 Operationalisation of the External and Internal Brand Strength 241
5.2 Customer Equity Versus Brand Equity as Key Performance Indicator
    of Brand Controlling 245
5.3 Necessity for an Identity-Based Brand Valuation Approach 245
    5.3.1 Deficits of Brand Valuation to Date in Theory and Practice. 245
    5.3.2 Requirements and Purposes of Identity-Based Brand Valuation 249
    5.3.3 Financial General Conditions of Brand Valuation 253
5.4 Systematisation of Brand Valuation Approaches. 254
    5.4.1 Financial Approaches 255
    5.4.2 Behavioural Approaches. 255
    5.4.3 Combined Approaches 259
    5.4.4 Stakeholder-Oriented Approaches 264
    5.4.5 Identity-Based Brand Valuation 268
References. 277

Structure and Learning Objectives of This Chapter

This chapter introduces brand controlling within the context of identity-based brand management. It aims to answer the following questions:

- Which tasks does identity-based brand controlling encompass?
- Which methods are available within the context of identity-based brand controlling?
- To what extent are the internal and the external perspective of identity-based brand management connected within brand controlling?
- Which current challenges does brand controlling face within the context of brand valuation and which problem-solving approaches are available?

© Springer Fachmedien Wiesbaden GmbH 2017
C. Burmann et al., *Identity-Based Brand Management*,
DOI 10.1007/978-3-658-13561-4_5

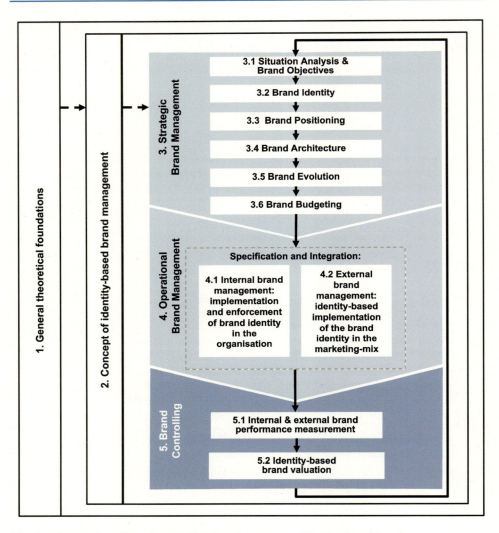

Fig. 5.1 Integration of brand controlling into the process of identity-based brand management

To this end, all areas of brand controlling within the context of identity-based brand management will be introduced; correlations will be explained and illustrated by means of examples.

Brand controlling encompasses the supply of information to and consultation of all points involved with brand management, in conjunction with a higher coordinating role to support the brand-specific planning, management and control processes within the company (cf. Meffert et al. 2015, p. 341).

The identity orientation becomes noticeable within this brand controlling in that the identity forms the content-related framework for measuring the brand performance and for the brand reporting. However, the identity orientation does not change the brand controlling process.

The brand performance measurement records, analyses and evaluates the results of the brand management. This also includes the **brand reporting system**, which provides the results generated from the **brand performance measurement** in a structured and condensed form as the basis for decision-making for the brand management (cf. Heemann 2008) (Fig. 5.1).

5.1   Internal and External Brand Performance Measurement

5.1.1   Main Features of Identity-Based Brand Controlling

For successful brand management, in terms of the business objectives, intuitive or even "spiritual brand management" as described by Gerken is inadequate (cf. Gerken 1994). A brand does not constitute an end in itself, but is used to realise business objectives. The establishment of a strong brand requires substantial investment; therefore increased professionalism is required within the context of brand management. To ensure the rationality of corporate policy, brand management also requires powerful controlling systems, which take into account both quantitative and qualitative data and which map the contribution of brand management to the result in a comprehensible manner.

The primary objective of the controlling concept used here, is the comprehensive support of the brand management with respect to optimising the result. Brand controlling encompasses system-designing and system-utilising tasks. The **system-designing function** deals with creating suitable general conditions, which facilitate coordinated decisions in the first place. The duty of brand controlling is the participation in the development and implementation of information systems, organisational guidelines and process structures, as well as planning and control instruments for the brand management. The **system-utilising function** deals with the regular control of the implementation of strategic and operational plans, as well as safeguarding the ongoing supply of information to all parties involved in the brand management. On the one hand, the brand controlling must conduct **ex-post** monitoring according to the feedback principle, by means of a stock-check of the brand management with respect to the economic, psychographic and behaviour-related factors. On the other hand, it must anticipate any target/actual deviations as an "early warning system" in terms of **ex-ante** monitoring and thus prevent them from occurring (cf. Meffert and Koers 2005).

In recent years two concepts have been in the focus of theory and practice within the field of brand controlling: **brand equity** management and **customer equity** management. Brand equity regards the brand value as a key factor, whilst customer equity represents the aggregated value of all customer relationships. To this end, all individual

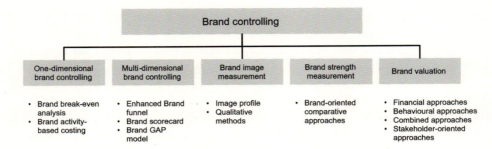

Fig. 5.2 Selected brand controlling instruments. (Source: by author, based on Tomczak et al. 2004, p. 1827)

customer relationships are first measured based on their customer lifetime value (CLV) and subsequently cumulated. The CLV is determined as a discounted value of all payment surpluses across the entire customer life cycle in in the customer relationship (cf. Breusch 2009).

The most important instruments are explained subsequently. Based on Keller (cf. 1993, 2005), Tomczak et al. (cf. 2004) differentiate the five instrument categories depicted in Fig. 5.2.

The instruments from the first category are based on findings of the costing and provide valuable information on the financial profit contributions of brands. The **brand profit contribution** describes the product profit contributions that are attributable to the brand. Brand profit contributions may have various manifestations (cf. Burmann et al. 2009). However, the utilisation of the brand profit contribution within the context of brand controlling is not plain sailing, as the division and attribution of individual business relations and transaction costs to individual brands is not always possible. Consequently, the quality of the control for individual brands is limited (cf. Tomczak et al. 2004).

Within the context of **brand activity-based costing**, the relevant cost drivers of operational processes are examined. Here, it is essential that only those cost centres are added, which are actually used in the course of the process. The objective is the activity-based attribution of brand overhead costs incurred (cf. Reckenfelderbäumer 2006). However, this is often only possible at great cost.

Multi-dimensional brand controlling is aimed at an examination of all relevant stakeholders that is as exhaustive as possible. A prevalent instrument in this category is the **enhanced brand funnel** by management consulting firm McKinsey (cf. Perrey et al. 2015). This is an easily understood instrument for determining the brand performance, from first contact to the consumer's brand loyalty (cf. Braun et al. 2003). An advantage of this instrument is the transparency and comparability between different brands (cf. Tomczak et al. 2004)

The brand funnel is based on the ascertainment of the conversion rates between the five process steps of "awareness", "familiarity", "consideration", "purchase" and

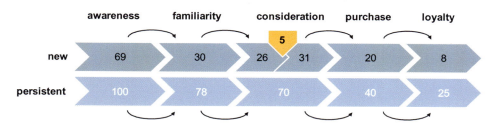

Fig. 5.3 Exemplary explanation of the enhanced brand funnel. (Source: based on Perry et al. 2015, p. 139)

"loyalty". Thus, the brand funnel draws on well-known advertising effectiveness models, such as the AIDA model (cf. Meffert et al. 2015). The brand funnel reveals between which process phases a particularly large number of potential consumers is lost. Due to a higher flexibility in the selection of information and purchase paths the steps in the process of the Customer Decision Journey (CDJ) may change. So it may be that consumers skip individual process stages, run through an earlier stage of the process several times, or go through the process as a whole more than once (cf. Perrey et al. 2015). The latter in particular is found e.g. in the context of purchasing decisions in Fast Moving Consumer Goods (FMCG). In addition, brands such as Google or Facebook change the classical decision-making process of consumers. Therefore, the Enhances Brand Funnel is not meant to be a process with fixed and defined start and end points, but rather as a "Loop" (see Fig. 5.3), which takes account of these changes.

Requirement for the successful usage of the Enhances Brand Funnel is dependable market research data. They form the basement for a reliable and resilient analysis. The first step in the Enhanced Brand Funnel can be the separation between new and existing customers, if required. In this context, new consumers are those that have never bought a product or used the service of the regarded brand before. All other customers belong to the category of existing consumers. By this separation a wide evidence base is created as part of the analysis, which is of high relevance for an accurate derivation of measures for customer acquisition and customer loyalty (cf. Perrey et al. 2015). The brand awareness for example is per definition at 100% regarding existing consumers, but is regularly lower for new consumers. In addition, two other key advantages arise by separating:

– A clear distinction between the purchase intention (I will buy the brand again) and the actual purchase behaviour (I have already bought this brand) can be made.
– It is possible to identify the driver of brand loyalty from new and existing customers separately, and to derive appropriate measures on this basis (cf. Perrey et al. 2015).

A second innovation compared to the classic funnel is the fact that new customers can now enter the decision process directly on the process stage of "consideration" (cf. Fig. 5.3). With this extension people are detected, that take a brand into consideration just before making a purchase, for example, based on a recommendation from friends or the surprising emergence of the brand in a comparison portal (yellow arrow). Such a direct entry is of importance particularly in areas where there are mostly impulsive purchases or last minute decisions (cf. Perrey et al. 2015).

A further instrument of multi-dimensional brand controlling is the **brand scorecard**. It is based on the concept of the balanced scorecard by Kaplan and Norton (1997) and is used to operationalise the brand strategy by means of monetary and non-monetary variables, which may relate to past or future performance. This procedure considers various perspectives of brand controlling through finances, consumers/market, processes and potentials (cf. Meffert and Koers 2005).

As a last instrument of this category the **brand GAP model** must be mentioned. In this model, an adjustment of the internal and external perspective is made. In the process, target and actual states are developed for both, the brand identity and the brand image. Based on these results, four gaps (GAPs) are examined. **GAP 1** shows the perception gap between the consumers' ideal expectations (target image) and the respective expectations of the employees (target identity). **GAP 2** (performance gap) examines the purely internal perspective and contrasts the target identity with the actual identity. **GAP 3** examines the differences between the current perception of the consumers (actual image) and the current self-perception of the employees (actual identity). This GAP is also referred to as communication gap. The last gap (**GAP 4**), the so-called identification gap, is present when the consumers' ideal brand expectations (target image) deviate from the actual perception (actual image) (cf. Burmann and Meffert 2005). To investigate the gaps further and to disclose the causes, the fit of individual brand management instruments and activities with the brand can be examined. This process concerns the determination of the fit to facilitate drawing conclusions with respect to the success of the instruments and measures employed, using the level of the fit (cf. Burmann et al. 2009; Schneider 2004).

The third instrument category within the field of brand controlling encompasses the approaches to measuring the brand image. **Image profiles** constitute the most well-known method in this area. Here, brands of a specific category are evaluated by consumers according to a list of specified associations. A frequent field of application for image profiles is the controlling of brand positioning. To this end, the relevant associations must first be compiled, the target group must be specified and relevant reference brands determined. When ascertaining image profiles, only those associations should be considered, which are significant for establishing brand preference and for the buying decision process, which can be influenced by brand management instruments and which contribute to the differentiation of brands. In a study from 2014 of the chair of innovative brand management of the University of Bremen the image profiles of various financial institutes were determined with 797 participants. Figure 5.4 shows the 12 image factors by which the image of all brands considered in the study were raised. The illustrated image profiles show the associations to three selected brands in a geographically defined area. For example Brand B and C are considered in this area as more "reliable" than brand A.

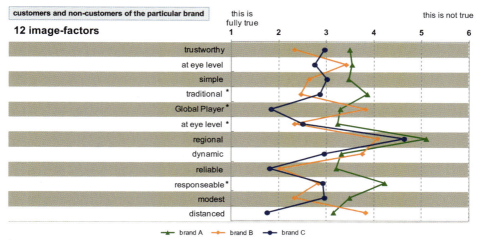

Fig. 5.4 Image profiles of selected financial institutes

Compared to qualitative measurement methods, image profiles benefit from the fact that a focus on the central associations, a representative survey and descriptive comparisons between time and enterprise are possible. Key deficits are the lack of a relevance examination of the brand associations, as well as the lack of consideration of interdependencies between the brands (cf. Tomczak et al. 2004).

In addition to this quantitative measuring instrument, there are **qualitative methods for measuring the brand image**. These methods generally provide more detailed findings about the emotional and cognitive processes that proceed when brand associations are formed. However, they usually do not provide any representative findings but are used to prepare or deepening quantitative studies (cf. Aaker 1996; Keller 2005; Schade 2012).

The fourth instrument category is comprised of methods for ascertaining the brand strength. Here, the **brand-oriented comparative approaches** are of particular importance (cf. Keller 2005). These approaches constitute comparison experiments, which examine the effects on a variable when another variable is changed. Product blind tests, which frequently reveal significant differences in the brand valuation by the consumers, are an example of this. Further fields of application are investigations of the effect brands have on the willingness to pay, as well as the brand influence on the likeability of ways and contents of communication (cf. Tomczak et al. 2004).

The fifth instrument category is the most important category within the context of brand controlling. The economic brand valuation includes "the ascertainment, diagnosis and control of the brand value" (Jost-Benz 2009, p. 20). With these brand valuation models, we can differentiate between

- financial brand valuation models,
- behavioural brand valuation models,
- combined brand valuation models and
- stakeholder-oriented brand valuation models.

These approaches and examples thereof are explained in Sect. 5.4.

As a starting point of a controlling concept requirements and target variables of brand controlling must be formulated. These can be derived from the purpose of brand controlling and must be based on the **brand targets** previously defined (cf. Sect. 3.1). In order to guarantee a meaningful illustration of the brand performance through appropriate indicators, a high quality of information and brand relevance have to be ensured in addition to validity and reliability. Therefore

- brand controlling must include both economic (core earnings indicators) and psychographic (performance drivers) variables,
- brand controlling includes both quantitative and qualitative variables,
- brand controlling has an ex-post and an ex-ante focus in equal measure,
- against the background of the identity-based brand management approach, brand controlling considers both internal variables of the statement concept of brand management (inside-out) and external variables of the acceptance concept of brand management (outside-in).

It is crucial that performance indicators integrate into one coherent system and can be used in support of a clearly defined strategy. The business objectives, which are reviewed by the brand controlling, must be derived from the corporate strategy. The development of the brand identity and, based on this, the positioning of the brand fall in line with the corporate strategy. The budgeting, which constitutes the transition to operational brand management, concludes the strategic brand management. Brand controlling is used to review the achievement of objectives, taking into account the budgeting by determining the return on marketing investment (ROMI). In order to achieve efficient, transparent and systematically optimised budgeting, systematic measurement within the context of brand controlling is essential. Here, the following four factors are particularly relevant: clear priorities and the provision of resources in the brand management, transparency with respect to the efficiency of individual measures, a high level of methodological competence regarding the measurement, as well as budget management and planning, taking into account the communication channel and the business segment (cf. Meurer and Rügge 2012). Accordingly, the integrity of all relevant control variables of the brand must be ensured. In the process, we must always consider the area of conflict between the desired integrity and the feasibility and cost effectiveness of the procurement of information. As a further requirement of a powerful brand controlling system, we should mention the currentness and sensitivity of the management and control variables.

Finally, the acceptance of the brand controlling by the employees must be ensured. For example, the degree of the achievement of target values should be set to a feasible level in order to have a motivating effect. The ascertainment of a standard of comparison for the chosen variables is meaningful for determining the targets; in particular comparative figures of the relevant strategic and operational competitors are to be used as benchmarks.

When specifying suitable performance measures of the brand controlling, it is advisable to group several indicators into a single integrated performance index (key performance indicator). Within the context of brand management, such a key performance indicator represents the brand value. The economic brand value is based on the brand strength.

5.1.2   Operationalisation of the External and Internal Brand Strength

Brand strength can be defined as the extent of a brand's relevance to behaviour for a company's external and internal reference groups (cf. Jost-Benz 2009 p. 63).

The **external brand strength** ascertains the extent of a brand's relevance to behaviour for consumers. Against the background of the identity-based understanding of this concept, the brand awareness, brand image, brand authenticity, brand trust and the brand-customer relationship are all relevant to the measurement of the external brand strength (see Fig. 5.6). The first indicator constitutes the basis for the brand image. The brand awareness is also highly relevant with respect to the internal brand strength. Therefore, a high degree of brand awareness can result in a positive impact on the employees' attitudes towards their brand. **Brand awareness** describes the consumer's ability to identify the brand and to attribute it to a product category. The manifestations of brand awareness range from the recognition to the entrenchment of a brand as the sole representative of a product category (see Fig. 5.5).

Aided brand awareness encompasses the recognition of a brand based on visual and/or acoustic stimuli and its correct attribution to a given category. The occurring brand recognition describes the weakest manifestation of brand awareness. In addition to brand recognition, **brand familiarity** ascertains the subjective feeling of being familiar with a brand. Unaided brand awareness encompasses the entrenchment of the brand in the consumer's memory. Here we distinguish between two manifestations: brand recall and top of mind awareness. In their entirety, the specified brands form the so-called "evoked set". It represents those brands that are of fundamental relevance to the consumer's buying decision.

Further variables for determining the external brand strength are shown in Fig. 5.6. Here we can ascertain the components of the subjective brand knowledge, as well as

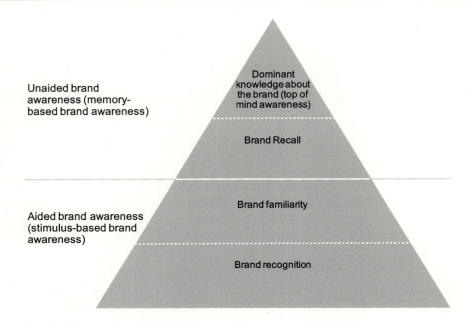

Fig. 5.5 Fundamental types of brand awareness. (Source: Aaker 1996 und Walser 2004)

the functional and symbolic brand benefit by means of the clear brand definition, the perceived brand promise and the uniqueness of the brand. The **clear brand definition** assumes that the structure of a clear brand image depends on the consistency of all associations with the brand. Therefore, the clear brand definition can be used to review to which extent the brand management succeeds in conveying the components of the brand identity in a consistent manner.

Furthermore, brand authenticity, brand trust and brand attachment should be gathered during the controlling of external brand strength (see Fig. 5.6). Measuring authenticity allows to determine whether or not a demander can detect the identity of a brand through its behaviour at the brand touchpoints. This is incredibly important for building trust towards the brand. If there is a lack of authenticity, the brand has failed to state out clearly what it stands for. By means of the measurement of trust there can be checked, if the necessary basis for transactions with a brand is present. The significance of a brand for the buyers own self (brand-self-connection) as well as the presence of a brand in the memory of the buyer (brand prominence) are captures by brand attachment. Both have a very high prognostic relevance for predicting the future purchasing behaviour of the buyer (cf. Park et al. 2010; Warwitz 2016).

The **internal brand strength** is the core of the identity-based brand value. It reflects the entrenchment of the brand within internal target groups and is an early indicator of future brand value developments. The internal brand strength represents the employees' brand identity-compliant behaviour, which is shaped by their brand identity-related knowledge, attitudes, competences and resources.

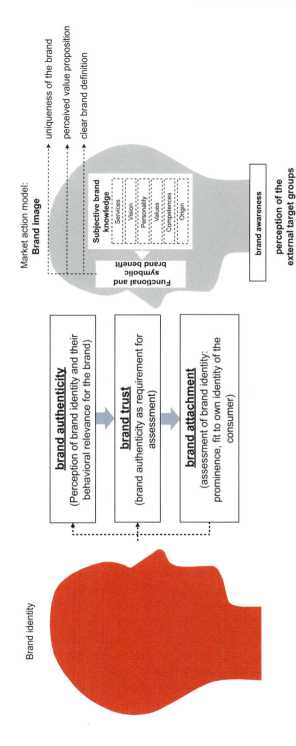

Fig. 5.6 Conceptualisation and operationalisation of the external brand strength

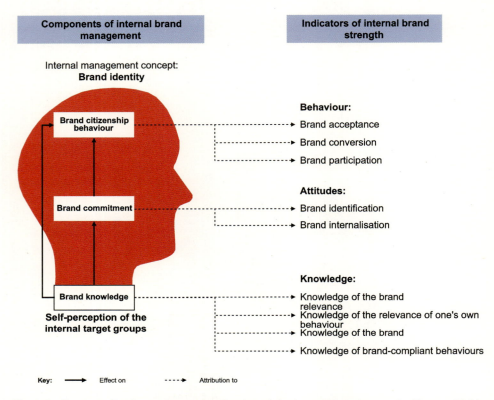

Fig. 5.7 Conceptualisation and operationalisation of the internal brand strength. (Source: Piehler 2011)

The internal brand strength can be measured using the components of the internal brand management. The brand commitment describes the brand-employee relationship. The brand citizenship behaviour ascertains the employee behaviour. As brand knowledge is a requirement for the development of brand commitment (attitude) and brand citizenship behaviour (behaviour), this component must also be considered when determining the internal brand strength (see Fig. 5.7).

The significance of the internal and external brand strength also applies to B2B markets. The brand's relevance to buying decisions in this field has been clearly verified by several studies. It varies depending on the respective product category. Whilst the ideal brand benefit is often of the greatest significance to the buying decision in the consumer goods industry, the brand's risk reduction function largely dominates in the B2B field (cf. Krause 2013). Due to the high degree of complexity and the often high level of capital expenditure, the personal contact between employees of the brand and the customer is particularly relevant in the B2B field. Krause (2013) proved that the employee is able to transfer his/her attitudes and values relating to the brand to the customer. Consequently, the employee-brand relationship has a great impact on the brand-customer relationship (cf. Krause 2013) and the purchasing behaviour of B2B consumers.

5.2 Customer Equity Versus Brand Equity as Key Performance Indicator of Brand Controlling

Within brand controlling two concepts, which were long considered as conflictual, were in focus of science and practice for the past years—brand equity management and customer equity management. The concept of customer equity emphasizes that each costumer is unique and respectively he must be observed individually (cf. Bayón et al. 2002). As a result on the side of the company, the most important costumers should be identified and supported as individual as possible. Accordingly a brand management is required, that aligns with individual customer needs. Rust et al. (2004) even demand: "We should be willing to do whatever is necessary with our brands (including replacing them with new ones) to maintain our customer relationships. Our attitude should be that brands come and go—but customers [...] remain." (Rust et al. 2004, S. 112). Therefore, brands could be arbitrarily newly created, exterminated and changed, at any time. An idea that is contrary to the identity-based brand management principles for continuity and consistency. Rush et al. missed in their statement that customers are generally linked much stronger to brands than to individual products. That is why customers switch products and services more frequently than brands. This is especially true on corporate brands and business brands, whereas Rust et al. implicitly rather think of product brands. The central questions of both fields of research differ from each other as well. While brand equity research investigated the financial value of brands, customer equity research puts the value of all customers throughout their whole lifecycle into the centre of attention.

Overall, it can be stated that differences between the two fields of research exist, but can be bridged. That is why current research approaches strive for integrated solutions. Even Rust et al. (2004) demand: "A focus on customer equity doesn't mean brand equity is unimportant. To the contrary, improving brand equity remains one of the most important marketing tasks." (Rust et al. 2004, S. 116). Instead of turning away from brand equity research they ask for a more sophisticated embodiment of the brand equity instruments in order to increase the informative value for the customer equity management. The identity-based brand management provides a good basis (cf. Sect. 5.4.5).

5.3 Necessity for an Identity-Based Brand Valuation Approach

5.3.1 Deficits of Brand Valuation to Date in Theory and Practice

The significance of brands has increased considerably not only in general, but specifically within the context of M&A transactions. Today brands are regarded as an important strategic buying motive. Companies want to increasingly distinguish themselves through strong brands vis-à-vis their stakeholders. At the same time, the establishment of a new brand is becoming increasingly difficult and expensive, particularly in mature markets.

This increases the value of existing, established brands and the incentive to acquire them. Accordingly, Buchan/Brown comment at an early stage: "It goes without saying that the motivation for companies to grow through acquisition has frequently arisen from the strategic requirement to establish leading positions in their chosen markets by controlling national and international brands." (Buchan and Brown 1989). This trend is supported by the fact that in the course of focussing on core competences, many brand portfolios are harmonised and unsuitable brands are divested. Consequently, the acquisition or sale thereof often triggers an M&A transaction.

In addition to the significance of brands as a buying motive, their relevance as an operational asset has also increased greatly in most industries. Both result in the fact that the goodwill often represents the essential part of the purchase price for a target company. For instance, Farquhar et al. (1990) estimate that when Kraft Foods was acquired by Philipp Morris, approx. 90% of the 12.9 billion US dollars paid were apportioned to the brand. A study by Markenverband and GfK in 2011 showed that 53% of the interviewees assessed the current significance of brand valuation for a company as great (cf. Markenverband et al. 2012). Therefore, what increasingly comes to the fore is the most precise assessment possible of the monetary brand value.

The great interest in brand valuation, both in theory and practice, is also a result of the barely manageable multitude of brand valuation approaches. Today, there are more than 300 different brand valuation approaches (cf. Amirkhizi 2005). The ramifications can be illustrated using the example of the TANK AG study. Here, Hanser et al. (2004) revealed that the existing brand valuation models lead to greatly differing results with respect to the valuation of brands. For the first time, they managed to conduct a transparent comparison of different brand valuation methods with respect to the same valuation object, using the same information for all brand valuation providers. In spite of a consistent data basis, the results of the German valuation institutions involved delivered a difference in the value of the fictitious brand TANK AG totalling EUR 784.9 million (see Fig. 5.8).

The considerably differing brand values are the result of a very heterogeneous understanding of how the brand value should be quantified. This is primarily a result of the fact that the **theoretical foundation of brand management** was previously often **lacking**. Due to this lack and therefore highly varying notions of the brand as the item to be valued, a barely manageable **multitude of indiscriminately developed, incompatible brand valuation models with an extremely limited validity have developed**. Here, the theoretically founded concept of identity-based brand management provides a way out (Burmann et al. 2007). On the basis of this concept, it is for the first time possible to integrate the actual sources of the economic brand equity, the resources and the competences of the brand, into the valuation. Therefore the identity-based brand valuation exceeds the level of a "valuation of the façade" and looks at the actual substance of a brand, which is neglected by all other brand valuation approaches.

The better part of existing brand valuation models is limited to considering a brand's effects on the market. However, in addition to this, an extension to the control level is of great relevance in order to facilitate adjustments within the brand management.

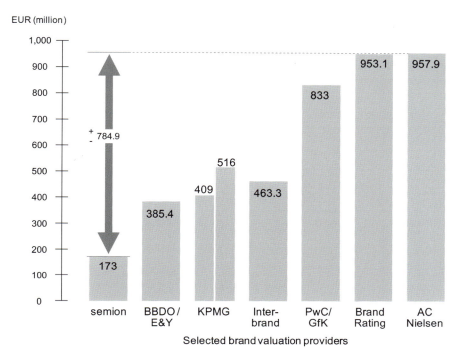

EUR (million)

Fig. 5.8 Economic valuation of the fictitious brand TANK AG. (Source: closely based on Hanser et al. 2004, p. 226 et seq.)

According to the identity-based brand management approach, this required the ascertainment of the internal and external brand strength. The following arguments show that the mere examination of the external brand strength is insufficient:

– **Increased currentness of the brand value**: All previous brand valuation methods are based on historic information and forecasts derived from this. Only the integration of the internal brand strength facilitates an up-to-date stock-check of the brand strength, as it ascertains the resources and competences required for the brand management, as well as the knowledge, attitudes and behaviour of the employees. In particular against the background of corporate mergers, an identity-based brand valuation can be extremely beneficial, as the employees' attitude towards the brands of their company can be vital for the success of a merger (cf. Fairfield-Sonn et al. 2002).
– **Internal brand strength as a direct control variable**: In all behavioural and combined brand valuation models, the brand image constitutes the basis for the valuation. However, from the company's point of view, the brand image can be controlled neither directly nor in the short-term. It arises only as the result of the employee behaviour and market developments. In contrast, the brand identity constitutes a basis for action that can be used by the company for the direct strategic and operational control of a brand.

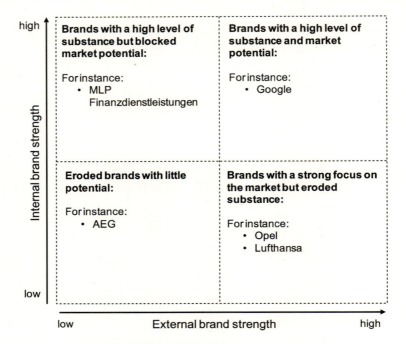

Fig. 5.9 Internal and external brand strength as the foundation of identity-based brand valuation

 – **Internal brand strength as the basis for the brand potential value**: To date, the consideration of brand potentials and future brand options has often been neglected in the brand valuation. However, a well-founded assessment of the brand potentials is only possible if the employee behaviour and the brand identity are taken into account in the process.

The following examples highlight the necessity for an examination that is differentiated according to internal and external brand strength. For this purpose, the dimensions of internal and external brand strength were contrasted. In the resulting four-field matrix, the four basic types of brand strength are differentiated (see Fig. 5.9).

1. **Brands with a high level of substance but blocked market potential**: Brands in this category have a high level of internal brand strength. The employees of these brands exhibit a higher-than-average brand commitment and brand identity-compliant behaviour. Nevertheless, this category is characterised by a low level of external brand strength. Such a situation is frequently observed with young brands. Highly motivated employees are faced with limited resources. Established brands can also be assigned to this category. Possible causes for a low level of external brand strength include the selection of the wrong distribution strategy or scandals in the brand's history. They impede the market acceptance and thus have a negative impact on the brand value. The MLP brand can be mentioned as an example of this category.

2. **Brands with a high level of substance and market potential**: This category is characterised by distinctive internal and external brand strength. The brand is classified as particularly strong by its employees and consumers alike. On the one hand, this shows a high level of substance of the brand, which is primarily due to the great commitment of its employees. On the other hand, on the basis of the high degree of external brand strength values, this indicates a great growth potential of the brand. The Google brand can be pointed out as an example of this.

3. **Brands with a strong focus on the market but eroded substance**: This category consists of those brands whose internal strength is only poorly developed compared to their external strength. Whilst brands in this category still appear strong and accepted in the market externally, their substance is already damaged. This is particularly the case if, due to internal mismanagement, the brand commitment and the brand citizenship behaviour are poorly developed. For instance, the Opel brand could be assigned to this category; whilst in certain target groups it still has a good image, which is relevant to behaviour, it is internally "emaciated" due to years of mismanagement (cf. Jahn et al. 2012). Lufthansa is to be allocated to this category as well. Here, a lack of internal brand management competence is apparent, for instance in the switch to "contract worker crews" and the disregard for suggestions for improvements by the employees to rectify quality issues. However, Lufthansa is still living off its quality image that was established over many years (cf. Machatschke 2012).

4. **Eroded brands with little potential**: This category is characterised by a lack of internal and external brand strength. Here we can often observe significant discrepancies between the communicated and actual behaviour of the brand. Such a situation is, for instance, observed with the AEG brand (cf. Manager magazin 2005).

All in all Fig. 5.9 illustrates that the internal brand strength makes an important contribution to the creation and maintenance of a valuable brand and to the success of a company. In a similar fashion, Ailawadi et al. (cf. 2003) also alluded to this using the term **"brand health"**, but without converting their analyses into a brand valuation approach. A comprehensive empirical study of the effect relationship between the internal and external brand strength has not been carried out as yet. The identity-based brand management approach provides a suitable basis for this.

5.3.2 Requirements and Purposes of Identity-Based Brand Valuation

A second reason for the previously unconvincing attempts at a brand valuation was, for many years, the lack of clear **requirements of a meaningful brand valuation**. Here the "Arbeitskreis Markenbewertung" (brand valuation task force) within the Markenverband (brand association) took a great step towards the adoption of universal principles for monetary brand valuation. From the perspective of identity-based brand management, these must be supplemented with three further requirements (see No. 11–13 in Fig. 5.10).

No.	Principle	Source
1.	Consideration of the purpose of the valuation and of the weighting function	
2.	Consideration of the brand type and function	
3.	Consideration of the protection of trademarks	
4.	Consideration of the brand and target group relevance	
5.	Consideration of the current brand status based on representative data of the relevant target group	Brand Valuation Forum (2006)
6.	Consideration of the brand potential and the economic lifetime of the brand	
7.	Isolation of brand-specific payment surpluses	
8.	Consideration of a capital value oriented technique and an appropriate discount rate	
9.	Consideration of brand-specific risks (market and competitive risks)	
10.	Traceability and transparency	
11.	Consideration of the company's internal and external brand value determinants	Based on Jost-Benz (2009)
12.	Consideration of behavioural and financial brand value determinants	
13.	Consideration of customer equity	

Fig. 5.10 Principles of monetary brand valuation

The first principle of monetary brand valuation describes the **consideration of the purpose of the valuation and of the valuation function**. According to this, a methodology that is appropriate for the purpose is to be used (see Fig. 5.11). Here we can distinguish between a companies' external and internal purposes (cf. Jost-Benz 2009). With the external purposes, the focus is on the calculation of a monetary brand value as the valuation function, whilst with internal purposes it is on the calculation of behavioural performance indicators. External purposes of a valuation include the ascertainment of acquired brands in the balance sheet, the determination of brand purchase prices, the calculation of brand licences and the specification of claims for damages. In contrast, an internal consideration focuses on the diagnosis and control of brands and on the personnel management. With an internal consideration, the monetary determination takes a back seat and behavioural brand valuation aspects come to the fore.

The second principle demands the **consideration of the brand type and function**. The term "brand type" includes the development of the brand based on its type (service, product), its geographical scope (regional, national, international) and its focus within the brand architecture (individual brand, family of brands, umbrella brand or corporate brand). The term "brand function" is understood as the characteristics of a brand with which value can be added to the company. In its nature, the brand function can be divided into four groups: the identification, communication, differentiation and quality function. The identification function describes the clear identification of the originator.

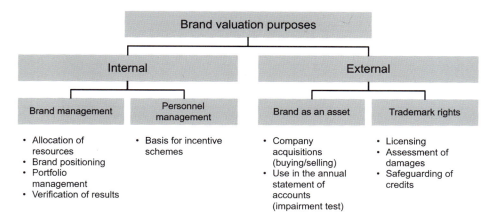

Fig. 5.11 Purposes of brand valuation. (Source: based on Jost-Benz 2009, p. 26)

The communication function concerns the activation of the consumer's brand knowledge. The differentiation function describes the differentiation of the brand from its competitors. The quality function is used to safeguard the consistent quality of the product or service. In general, identity-based brand management has no limitations with respect to the brand type. As a matter of principle, all brands can be valued. However, before the start of the valuation, a brand type must be specified in order to prevent ambiguity or errors at a later stage.

The **consideration of the protection of trademarks** (cf. Chap. 6) is the third principle of the monetary brand valuation. This point is becoming particularly controversial due to product and brand piracy, which has increased considerably in recent years (cf. APM 2012); therefore all and any legal means should be used to protect the brand and taken into consideration accordingly for the brand valuation. What also holds true for the identity-based brand valuation is that only those brands with adequate legal protection should be subjected to a valuation.

The fourth principle encompasses the **consideration of the brand and target group relevance**. The brand relevance describes the influence of the brand on the buying decision. The differentiation and definition of the target groups is the basis for the valuation of a brand. This differentiation must consider both existing business segments and potential areas of brand expansion. The brand relevance is taken into consideration in the identity-based brand valuation model by isolating the brand performance. This isolation of the brand performance must be carried out separately for each individual customer segment in order to take the target groups into account.

The **consideration of the current brand status** on the basis of the relevant target group data constitutes the fifth principle. On the one hand, this requires the ascertainment of the brand performance based on available quantitative market data. If no such information is available, it must be ascertained through representative target group surveys.

The identity-based brand valuation approach is able to fulfil this task unconditionally for the external part of the model. However, due to its innovative nature, which also draws on the company's internal perspective for the brand valuation, publicly accessible internal information is also required. On the other hand, the brand status includes the brand strength, which must be ascertained both internally and externally, in order to get a complete picture of the brand. This key aspect is only picked up by the identity-based brand valuation. This approach provides for a customer segment-specific ascertainment of the external market strength. An appropriate segmentation must also be carried out for the determination of the internal brand strength since, depending on the employee segment, the contact with the consumers and consequently the influence of the internal brand strength on the external brand strength varies. Therefore, the availability of segment-specific information is vital for a correct brand valuation.

The **consideration of the brand potential and the economic lifetime of the brand** is addressed in the sixth principle. On the one hand, this principle demands the consideration of the brand potential in relevant brand extension areas. It should be noted that only those extension areas are considered, in which a market entry is probable. The identity-based brand valuation approach meets this demand by calculating the brand potential value. The second requirement is the consideration of the brand's economic lifetime. If you take into consideration that, within the context of identity-based brand valuation, the financial calculation of the brand value is carried out based on discounted cash flows, then the specification of the economic lifetime is vital.

The following principle includes the **isolation of brand-specific payment surpluses**, which is intended to ensure that only brand-induced cash flows are incorporated in the calculation of the brand value. Methods such as the volume and price premium, hedonic prices, brand-adjusted sales and royalty relief methods have been developed for this purpose (cf. Sattler 2005). Identity-based brand valuation meets this requirement by isolating the brand performance. However, the procedure within this context is very restrictive, as the identity-based brand understanding is holistic and highly comprehensive. Therefore, frequently only few components are isolated from the company's cash flows as not brand-induced.

The aspects discussed in the eighth and ninth principles (**consideration of a capital value-oriented method and an appropriate discount rate, as well as brand-specific risks**) refer to the specification of an appropriate deduction for risk. In addition to the market and business risks, brand risks should also be covered. Information on these types of risks should therefore be available for an identity-based brand valuation. The company's weighted average cost of capital (WACC) can be used as the output variable of the appropriate discount rate. Here, the identity-based brand valuation approach considers the inflation rate as a market-specific discount factor and the WACC as a company-specific discount factor. The brand-specific risks are taken into account through the brand-specific discount factor. The latter must be guided by both the internal and external brand strength.

In the next principle of the monetary brand valuation, the **aspect of traceability and transparency**, which is neglected by most of the commercial approaches, is considered. Only if this requirement is met, can the validity, objectivity and reliability of a brand valuation approach be verified. Identity-based brand valuation has fulfilled this principle ever since the publication of the dissertation by Jost-Benz (2009).

In a nutshell, with regard to the 10 standard principles of monetary brand valuation we must acknowledge that the fulfilment of these requirements is a necessary, yet insufficient prerequisite for identity-based brand valuation. Consequently, the 10 principles of the Brand Valuation Forum must be supplemented with additional principles.

Another additional principle includes the **consideration of the customer equity** (cf. Burmann and Jost-Benz 2005; Hundacker 2005; Breusch 2009). The benefit of considering the customer equity lies primarily in the fact that all assessments regarding the significance of different customer segments are considered in this indicator. The customer equity takes on a monitoring and control function, which facilitates an evaluation as to whether the consumer behaviour induced by the brand is economically attractive (cf. Burmann 2003). This is possible due to the consideration of the costs incurred through the consumer acquisition, the cash flows generated by the consumer behaviour and the possibility of a holistic view of the consumer behaviour towards the entire brand portfolio. For instance, cross-selling effects beyond a singular brand can be examined (cf. Jost-Benz 2009). The interpretation of the customer equity, as well as the individual lifetime values of different customers contained in this value, improves the quality of the brand valuation through increased validity, reliability and objectivity of the valuation.

5.3.3   Financial General Conditions of Brand Valuation

Today the financial consideration of the brand value is of great relevance to numerous businesses. One of the main reasons is the fact that, according to a study by PricewaterhouseCoopers from 2005, by now the brand value accounts for 67% of the company value for the largest German enterprises (cf. PricewaterhouseCoopers 2006). The financial consideration of brand values is hindered by significant deviations between the provisions of the Handelsgesetzbuch (German Commercial Code) and the IAS/IFRS international accounting and financial reporting standards, as well as the lack of a generally accepted monetary brand valuation method (cf. Tafelmeier 2009).

According to German accounting legislation, acquired brands require recognition; however, internally developed brands cannot be recognised as yet (Sec. 248 II HGB—German Commercial Code). The basis of this prohibition of capitalisation of internally developed brands is a special manifestation of the principle of prudence (Sec. 252 I 4). From a legal perspective, this is due to the lack of physical substance of brands without any tangible proof of existence, a high level of uncertainty with respect to future benefits, as well as a problematic valuation (cf. Tafelmeier 2009). According to IAS/IFRS, there is also an explicit prohibition of recognising internally generated brands (cf. IAS 38.63).

This is substantiated by the fact that the costs required for establishing the brand cannot be differentiated from the costs for the development of the company (cf. IAS 38.64). In instances of business combinations and acquisitions, the purchasing company must separately put a monetary value on intangible assets within the framework of the purchase price allocation and recognise them on the acquisition date (cf. Pfeil and Vater 2002; Tafelmeier 2009).

The underlying value measure for this initial valuation is the **fair value**. The fair value corresponds to the price, at which an asset could be or has been exchanged between expert, independent business partners who are willing to enter into a contract (according to IFRS3/IAS 38 or SFAS 141 for US-GAAP). When accounting the brand values in subsequent years, we must distinguish whether the brand is limited to a certain lifetime or has an undefined useful life (cf. Meffert and Burmann 1999, p. 244 et seq.). In the first case, brands may be amortised according to plan pursuant to the useful life (cf. IAS 38). In the case of an undefined useful life, an impairment test of the brand must be performed at least once a year (cf. IAS 36 or SFAS 142 for US-GAAP). This provision for annual brand valuation increased its practical relevance to the corporate management significantly and led to a sharp growth in the market for brand reviews, including a substantial increase of appropriate service providers.

5.4   Systematisation of Brand Valuation Approaches

Brand valuation approaches can generally be categorised using a variety of different criteria. The systematisation based on their scientific origin is prevalent. According to this, we can distinguish between financial, behavioural, combined and stakeholder-oriented approaches (see Fig. 5.12).

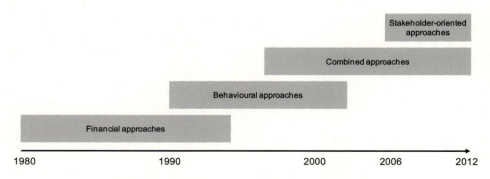

Fig. 5.12 Chronological development of brand valuation approaches. (Source: based on Jost-Benz 2009, p. 22)

5.4.1   Financial Approaches

From the early 1980s to the mid-1990s, both researchers and practitioners initially focussed on the development of financial approaches. The calculation of a monetary brand value, which is solely based on brand-induced costs and revenues, is the focus of this branch of research. Within this branch, four subcategories have been developed: the cost-oriented (cf. e.g. Kapferer 1992), price-oriented (cf. e.g. Crimmins 1992), capital market-oriented (cf. e.g. Simon and Sullivan 1993) and the future performance indicator-oriented (cf. e.g. Kern 1962) approaches.

The **cost-oriented approaches** can be differentiated into valuations that relate to past or present performance. Valuations that relate to past performance use the historic cost. Here, the brand value arises as the sum of the brand investments made in the past. Valuations relating to the present performance are guided by the replacement cost, i.e. the outlay necessary to establish a brand of equal value on the valuation date (cf. Kapferer 1992). The **price-oriented approaches** are based on the assumption that a strong brand is able to achieve a price premium in the market. Consequently, the price premium is used as the basis of the brand valuation. The **capital market-oriented methods** are based on the assumption that the value of a company in the capital market reflects, among other things, the future prospects of a brand. According to these approaches, the brand value constitutes a component of the stock price. With the **future performance indicator** and the **capitalised earnings value-oriented methods**, the brand value incorporates the added profit of the brand discounted to its present value (cf. Holtz 2012).

The strengths of the financial approaches include the simple conceptual design, the high level of transparency and the comparably low expenditure of resources (cf. Bekmeier-Feuerhahn 1998). The key weakness of these approaches is the low control potential as, due to the neglect of behavioural factors, no statement can be made regarding the causes of the monetary value (see Table 5.1, cf. Kriegbaum 2001).

With respect to the twelve requirements of a meaningful monetary brand valuation, the financial approaches also reveal numerous weak points (see Fig. 5.13).

5.4.2   Behavioural Approaches

Behavioural brand valuation approaches focus on the effects of brands on the consumer. Here, aided and unaided awareness, as well as the associations with a brand shape the so-called psychographic brand value, which is closely related to the brand strength in terms of content. Keller defines the psychographic brand value as "differential effect that brand knowledge has on consumer response to the marketing of that brand" (Keller 2003, p. 69). The most important representatives of the behavioural approaches include the Customer-Based Brand Equity model by Keller, the Brand Assessment System (BASS) by GfK, PwC and Sattler and the Brand Asset Valuator by Young & Rubicam.

The **Customer-Based Brand Equity (CBBE) model by Keller** (2013) is based on the brand knowledge. This model focuses on the brand's effects on the individual customer.

Table 5.1 Strength and weaknesses of financial valuation approaches

Method	Strength	Weaknesses
Comprehensive	– Brand value is calculated from corporate data – Simple methodology – Fast, cost-efficient calculation – Final brand value as a monetary variable	– No consideration of the consumer perspective (behavioural determinants) – No consideration of the internal brand strength
Cost-oriented methods	– Simple structure – Low expenditure	– Conclusion from past expenditure to future payments is uncertain – Neglect of situational factors – Sole focus on the past and present
Price-oriented methods	– High level of feasibility – Customised calculation generally possible – Transparent methods	– Comparison with a generic service possible only with difficulty – High brand value can also be generated without a respective price premium – Very difficult to observe overall prices, break them down into objective characteristics and to separate the brand share
Capital market-oriented methods	– Focus on the future – Direct transformation of monetary variables into brand value	– Only possible for companies listed on the stock market – Can only be executed in a meaningful manner at corporate level – Validity of the results limited due to market price fluctuations – No customer-specific findings
Future performance indicator-oriented	– Focus on the future – Direct use of monetary variables	– Estimation of future payment surpluses as element of uncertainty – Isolation of the brand-induced payment surpluses difficult

Own source, based on Gerpott and Thomas (2004), Burmann and Jost-Benz (2005)

The objective is to find out how strong an influence individual brand management measures have on the value of the brand. The following three components are of particular relevance: Differentiation (to which extent does the brand differ from a generic service), brand knowledge (is comprised of the brand awareness and the brand image) and customer responses (summarises the perceptions and responses to brand management measures). The brand value can be calculated either directly or indirectly. For the indirect calculation, we measure the brand knowledge by means of the brand awareness, as well as the brand associations and their connections with each other (cf. Sect. 5.1.2). The direct calculation deals with the measurement of the effect of the brand knowledge on the consumer behaviour. To this end, it must be ascertained experimentally to which extent the response differs between two groups if for

No.	Principle	Degree of fulfilment
1.	Consideration of the purpose of the valuation and of the weighting function	◔
2.	Consideration of the brand type and function	○
3.	Consideration of the protection of trademarks	○
4.	Consideration of the brand and target group relevance	○
5.	Consideration of the current brand status based on representative data of the relevant target group	○
6.	Consideration of the brand potential and the economic lifetime of the brand	◔
7.	Isolation of brand-specific payment surpluses	◑
8.	Consideration of a capital value oriented technique and an appropriate discount rate	◑
9.	Consideration of brand-specific risks (market and competitive risks)	◑
10.	Traceability and transparency	◕
11.	Consideration of the company's internal and external brand value determinants	○
12.	Consideration of behavioural and financial brand value determinants	○
13.	Consideration of the customer equity	○

○ not at all fulfilled   ◔ barely fulfilled   ◑ moderately fulfilled   ◕ largely fulfilled   ● completely fulfilled

Fig. 5.13 Assessment of the financial brand valuation approaches with respect to the requirements of the monetary brand valuation

one group, the brand to be examined is provided with a specific brand attribute and for the control group, a fictitious brand is associated with the same attribute (cf. Keller 1993).

The **Brand Assessment System (BASS) by GfK/PwC/Sattler** is based on the calculation of the brand value by means of two dimensions. The first dimension examines the revenue-related portion of the brand strength and is based on "hard" performance indicators. The revenue-related brand strength is calculated by means of five indicators: The brand's customer reach, number of first choice buyers of the brand, first choice value (a brand's share in the total sales that is attributable to the first choice buyers), the brand's market share and price premium. In the best-case scenario, the revenue-related brand strength is calculated using panel data. The second dimension, the emotional brand appeal, is based on the Brand Potential Index (BPI) by GfK and is divided into three sub-dimensions. The latter are ascertained by means of different indicators, which the consumer rates on a scale of 1–7, using questions. The emotional sub-dimension comprises the indicators of identification with the brand, brand likeability and brand trust. The rational part of the BPI is ascertained by means of the indicators of brand awareness, perceived quality of the brand and uniqueness. The third sub-dimension, the behaviour dimension, encompasses the willingness to recommend the brand, the purchase intention, the willingness to pay a price supplement (price premium) and the brand loyalty. During the next step, these two dimensions are compared and related to the competitors. This ascertains how strong the brand is compared to its competitors and which potentials will

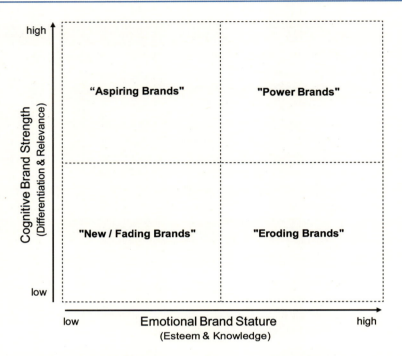

Fig. 5.14 4-field matrix of the brand asset valuator by Young & Rubicam. (Source: based on Young & Rubicam Germany 2012)

be available in the future. In conclusion, the summarised results are shown on a brand score card (cf. Högl and Hupp 2004).

The **Brand Asset Valuator by Young & Rubicam** is prevalent in practice; it is based on extensive consumer surveys. 35,000 brands were valued by 750,000 interviewed test subjects in 51 countries by 2012 (cf. BAV Consulting 2012). The brand valuation is performed in four dimensions: differentiation, relevance, esteem and knowledge. Differentiation and relevance are condensed into the brand strength, which is supposed to represent the rather cognitive strength and vitality of the brand. The other two dimensions are consolidated as the brand stature, which represents the emotional capital of the brand. The survey is carried out using 52 undisclosed criteria. For the presentation of the result, the brands are integrated into a small four-field matrix (see Fig. 5.14, cf. Young & Rubicam 2012; Kötting 2004).

The key strengths and weaknesses of the behavioural approaches are illustrated in Table 5.2.

According to this, both the diagnosis and the control of the brand value are the focus of the behavioural brand valuation approaches. In contrast to the financial approaches, this generates concrete recommendations for action for the brand management. For instance, the ascertainment of brand awareness or brand associations provides concrete clues regarding the weaknesses of the brand management. Consequently, the resulting

Table 5.2 Strength and weaknesses of selected behavioural approaches

Approach	Strength	Weaknesses
Comprehensive	– Consideration of behavioural variables – Isolation of the brand-specific performance indicators	– No specification of the monetary brand value – No consideration of the internal brand strength
Customer-based brand equity (Keller)	– Comprehensive, prevalent theoretical basis – Breakdown of individual brand strength factors – Comparison with competitors possible – Consistent focus on the consumer	– Interdependency between the variables – Feasibility of the brand value analysis (great expenditure)
Brand assessment system (BASS) (GfK/PwC/Sattler)	– Consideration of objective performance indicators (GfK panel data) – Focus on the future	– Duplicate consideration of individual variables (e.g. brand loyalty and first choice buyer) – Duplicate consideration of variables due to overlap between BPI and revenue-related brand strength – Heavy consolidation in the final stage exacerbates concrete recommendations for action – Subjectivity when ascertaining brand-specific results
Brand asset valuator (Young & Rubicam)	– Very widespread in practice – Good basis for benchmarks	– Consolidation of the data is too heavy – No specifications regarding the survey, analysis or the transfer to the matrix (52 detailed criteria remain concealed)

By author, based on Burmann and Jost-Benz (2005), Tafelmeier (2009), Ströbel (2012)

key strength is the direct transfer of brand valuation findings to a level that is relevant to action. The lack of monetary variables is a great shortcoming of the behavioural brand management approaches. The requirements of the monetary brand valuation are met only to a very limited extent by the behavioural approaches (see Fig. 5.15).

5.4.3 Combined Approaches

Based on the understanding that the isolated use of behavioural or financial approaches led to poor results, **combined brand valuation approaches** were developed, which are to some extent also referred to as "integrative brand valuation approaches" (cf. Heider

No.	Principle	Degree of fulfilment		
		CBBE	BASS	BrandAsset Valuator
1.	Consideration of the purpose of the valuation and of the weighting function	barely	barely	barely
2.	Consideration of the brand type and function	barely	not at all	not at all
3.	Consideration of the protection of trademarks	not at all	not at all	not at all
4.	Consideration of the brand and target group relevance	not at all	moderately	not at all
5.	Consideration of the current brand status based on representative data of the relevant target group	moderately	moderately	barely
6.	Consideration of the brand potential and the economic lifetime of the brand	not at all	barely	barely
7.	Isolation of brand-specific payment surpluses	not at all	not at all	not at all
8.	Consideration of a capital value oriented technique and an appropriate discount rate	not at all	not at all	not at all
9.	Consideration of brand-specific risks (market and competitive risks)	not at all	not at all	not at all
10.	Traceability and transparency	completely	moderately	barely
11.	Consideration of the company's internal and external brand value determinants	not at all	not at all	not at all
12.	Consideration of behavioural and financial brand value determinants	not at all	not at all	not at all
13.	Consideration of the customer equity	not at all	not at all	not at all

Legend: ○ not at all fulfilled · ◔ barely fulfilled · ◑ moderately fulfilled · ◕ largely fulfilled · ● completely fulfilled

Fig. 5.15 Assessment of the behavioural brand valuation approaches with respect to the requirements of the monetary brand valuation

and Strehlau 2006). The most important representatives of this category include the **Brand Valuation Model** by Interbrand, the **Brand Rating Model** by icon brand navigation and Wieselhuber & Partner, as well as the McKinsey **Brand Equity Meter**.

The **Brand Valuation Model by Interbrand** was developed in the 1980s. This approach is divided into five process steps (see Fig. 5.16). During the first step, a customer segmentation is carried out. The customer segments are later valued separately. Finally, the values of the individual segments are added and thus form the total brand value. During the second step, the brand-induced payment surpluses are isolated. To this end, the economic profit based on a 5-year forecast is used and adjusted by the not brand-induced components. Step three is used to calculate the demand factors in order to determine the brand share in the corporate assets. This involves ascertaining the brand influence on the buying decision. During the last process step, the brand strength is calculated on the basis of a competition analysis in order to determine the brand risk. This is used to specify an appropriate discount rate. To do so, the brand strength is calculated in each segment compared to the competition and to an ideal, risk-free situation (cf. Stucky 2004). The brand strength is calculated for seven dimensions (see Table 5.3)

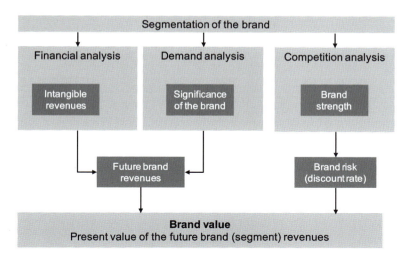

Fig. 5.16 Basic structure of the interbrand brand valuation model. (Source: by author, based on Tafelmeier 2009, p. 226)

Table 5.3 Dimensions of the brand strength in the interbrand brand valuation model

Dimension	Weighting (%)	Criteria
Market	10	Growth forecasts and dynamics, competitive structure, entry barriers, value, volume, non-market-dependent influences, market cycle etc.
Stability	15	Brand history, age, continuity of the brand management, visual appearance, substitution products, coping with past changes etc.
Market leadership	25	Market shares, market position, relative market shares, trade enforcement, product benefits, consumer image, innovation leadership etc.
Trend of the brand	10	Future developments and prospects, opportunities and risks, changes in market shares, developments of the sales volume and value, competitive trend etc.
Support of the brand	10	Quantity and quality of the brand investments, share of voice, continuity of the management, focus on the brand concept/brand personality, enforcement of the brand values, congruence of message and image, trade support etc.
Degree of internationalization	25	Representation in different geographic markets, significance within these markets, export strategy, diversification of the customer markets etc.
Legal protection	5	Type of registration, registration strategy, defence strategy, expansion of the protection area, won/lost cases etc.

By author, based on Stucky (2004, p. 443) et seq., Ströbel (2012, p. 53)

Finally, the brand value is calculated; it is based on two going concern values. The first going concern value is comprised of the discounted brand revenues within the forecasting horizon. The second partial value consists of the present value of the brand revenue of the last forecast year, adjusted at an average growth rate, for every year until the end of the assumed useful life. The brand segment value is the sum of these two values. The total brand value is the sum of all segments (cf. Tafelmeier 2009).

The **Brand Rating Model by icon brand navigation and Wieselhuber & Partner** is based on the prevalent "brand iceberg" model by icon. The brand iceberg model is a behavioural brand valuation approach, which divides the brand strength into the two dimensions of brand iconography and brand credit. Brand iconography represents the part of the iceberg that is above the water level. It is based on the appearance of the brand that is visible to the consumer and constitutes the dimensions of brand awareness, vividness of the image, subjectively perceived communication pressure, communication memorability, brand uniqueness and appeal. Therefore, brand iconography represents the current brand appearance that can be adjusted in the short-term. The hidden part of the iceberg represents the brand credit. It encompasses the emotional tie of brand and target group and is comprised of the following three dimensions: likeability, trust and loyalty. Brand credit is the long-term, sound valuation by the consumers; it is largely detached from the current brand appearance. The influence of the brand credit on the brand strength is estimated to be the greater, the older the brand is (cf. Gerpott and Thomas 2004). The brand strength is calculated based on consumer surveys. The ascertained values do not correspond to absolute numbers, but show the brand in the nine dimensions in relation to the competitive environment. In the subsequent step, the individual values are aggregated into the dimensions of brand iconography and brand credit and presented in a four-field matrix. To calculate the monetary brand value, the brand iceberg index (qualitative brand strength) is linked with the quantitative brand premium and the brand potential (see Fig. 5.17; Brand Rating 2015).

In doing so, the discounted price gap is calculated by means of the achieved price premium (Δp) and multiplied with the volume sold (q). This leads to the absurd situation that, according to the Brand Rating formula, brands without a price premium are of no economic value. The brand valuation according to Brand Rating becomes utterly absurd for brands with an aggressive pricing policy (such as Ryanair or Aldi), which are assigned a negative economic brand value pursuant to the formula in Fig. 5.17, as they have a negative price premium. In addition, the costs required for the brand's maintenance expenditure must be subtracted from the product of price premium and volume. The result is then discounted using an interest rate (i), which has been calculated using the Porter five forces analysis. This rate is composed of the risk-free interest rate and the market risk interest rate.

The Brand Future Score is the third component of the Brand Rating Model. To calculate this variable, both the brand development in the core market and the brand's extension potential are examined. On the one hand, the extension potential is based on the qualitative brand strength and on the other hand, on secondary analyses by Brand Rating. The brand's extension potential is divided into four classes—line extension, category

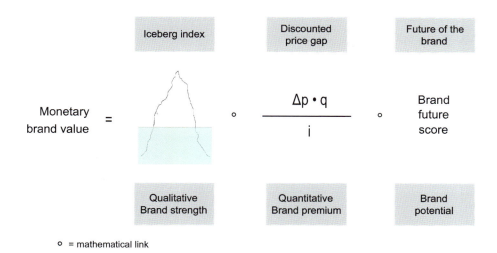

o = mathematical link

Fig. 5.17 The three components of the brand rating model. (Source: by author, based on Musiol et al. 2004, p. 386)

extension, geographic expansion and target group expansion. In addition, the appeal of the possible extension fields is evaluated. In order to assess the core market development, the price and volume development of the brand are examined compared to the total market. This is intended to ascertain whether the development is brand-induced or market-induced. Further indications of possible growth potentials are the relative brand strength and the brand uniqueness. The third component within the Brand Future Score is the legal protection of trademarks. Here the legal protection and risk of misuse are examined. These three components are condensed into the Brand Future Score and verified with respect to their plausibility by comparing them with the benchmark database (cf. Musiol et al. 2004).

The third important model within the field of combined brand valuation approaches is **the Brand Equity Meter by McKinsey**. It is based on a combination of brand equity and customer equity elements. The basis for this model is the current situation of the brand. Building on that, it attempts to ascertain the brand's customer equity. The latter, according to this approach, is composed of the following factors: revenue potential of the customer base, profitability of the services rendered, scope of the maintenance investments, marginal rate of tax and cost of capital. The customer equity is calculated using industry and corporate data. The customer equity of a brand calculated this way constitutes more than just the brand value. Therefore it is necessary to ascertain the share of brand in this customer equity. This share is determined by means of consumer surveys and consists of two factors: On the one hand, the brand's significance to all buying decisions within an industry and on the other hand, the relative brand strength in the past compared to the competition. In the survey, the brand's share in the buying decision is calculated on the basis of a constant sum scale. The brand strength is comprised of the level of awareness and the brand image, which is indexed on a flat-rate basis. The brand image is ascertained for four dimensions, which are weighted differently: emotion (50%), differentiation (25%), performance (12.5%) and trust (12.5%). The consolidation of these two components—the share of the brand in the customer equity and the customer equity of the brand—finally results in the brand value (cf. Riesenbeck and Perrey 2005).

The respective strengths and weaknesses of the selected approaches are shown in Table 5.4.

The strength of the combined brand valuation models becomes clear against the background of the purposes of the valuation. In contrast to behavioural brand valuation approaches, these models can not only be used for internal, but also for external purposes (see Fig. 5.18). However, the intersection between behavioural information and monetary variables is very problematic. Furthermore, the combined approaches only examine the consumers. Other stakeholders, such as employees, are not taken into consideration.

The requirements of the monetary brand valuation are only met to some extent by the combined approaches (see Fig. 5.19).

5.4.4   Stakeholder-Oriented Approaches

Stakeholder-oriented brand valuation approaches integrate not only consumers, but also further stakeholders into the economic valuation. An example of this category is the model of **de Chernatony** (2010), which considers both the internal and external perspective of the company. His approach aims to ascertain the "health of the brand". For this purpose, a scoring model was developed, which interviews both employees and consumers with respect to the dimensions of "brand vision", "organisational culture", "brand objectives", "brand essence" and "implementation and brand resourcing" (cf. de Chernatony 2010). These dimensions are rated on a five-point scale using a total of 51 questions, where 32 questions are aimed at the internal and 19 at the external target group. "Brand vision" examines the internal acceptance and entrenchment of the brand vision and the brand values among employees and executives. From the external perspective, the relevance of the brand values and the implementation of the brand vision are verified. The dimension of "organisational culture" is analysed only from the internal perspective and looks at the fit between the corporate culture, the brand values and the brand vision. "Brand objectives" encompass the entrenchment and appropriateness of the brand objectives and their achievement from an internal and external perspective. Within the dimension of "brand essence", the fit of the identity components, the implementation of the brand promise and the fit of brand identity and brand image are verified. The last dimension, "implementation and brand resourcing", checks the employer brand, the brand-employee relationship, the fit of organisational competences with the brand, the fit of the brand experience with the brand promise and the general relationship of external stakeholders with the brand. Finally, the valuations of the individual questions are consolidated into one overall valuation for each category by means of unweighted average values.

Table 5.4 Strength and weaknesses of selected combined brand valuation approaches

Approach	Strength	Weaknesses
Comprehensive	– Consideration of behavioural and financial variables – Isolation of the brand-specific performance indicators	– No consideration of the internal brand strength
Brand valuation model (interbrand)	– Segment-specific consideration – Focus on the future	– Subjectivity when selecting and valuating the dimensions of the brand strength, as well as with respect to the operationalisation criteria – Non-transparency during the conversion of the brand strength index into a multiplier – Offset against the earnings after taxes makes the brand value dependent on the respective tax system (lack of reproducibility at an international level)
Brand rating (icon and Wieselhuber & Partner)	– Consideration of short-term and long-term perspectives within the context of the qualitative brand strength – Simple comparison with competitors possible – Focus on the future – Universally applicable	– The calculation of the qualitative brand strength is limited to relative variables (brand X compared to the competition), therefore no universal validity – Lack of independence from brand iconography and brand credit – Lack of transparency when calculating the brand value – Only few publications on the methodology and survey quality – No consideration of tax on earnings – Consideration of the cost of equity capital instead of the weighted average cost of capital
Brand equity meter (McKinsey)	– High level of transparency and simple structure of the approach – High level of practical orientation – Can be used across different industry sectors or countries	– Assumption that the cumulated CE of all corporate brands gives the fundamental company value – Assumption that the brand influence on the buying decision is identical for all brands of an industry – Calculation of the CE without considering customer-specific data

By author, based on Gerpott and Thomas (2004), Burmann and Jost-Benz (2005), Tafelmeier (2009), Ströbel (2012)

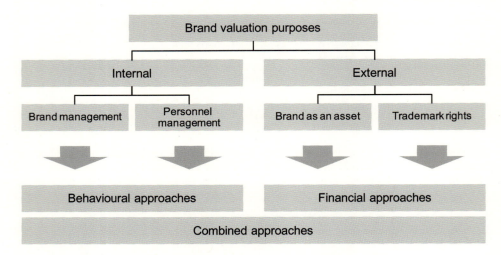

Fig. 5.18 Allocation of the brand valuation approaches to brand valuation purposes

No.	Principle	Degree of fulfilment		
		Brand Valuation Model	Brand Rating	Brand Equity Meter
1.	Consideration of the purpose of the valuation and of the weighting function	largely fulfilled	largely fulfilled	moderately fulfilled
2.	Consideration of the brand type and function	not at all fulfilled	not at all fulfilled	not at all fulfilled
3.	Consideration of the protection of trademarks	completely fulfilled	not at all fulfilled	not at all fulfilled
4.	Consideration of the brand and target group relevance	completely fulfilled	barely fulfilled	moderately fulfilled
5.	Consideration of the current brand status based on representative data of the relevant target group	largely fulfilled	barely fulfilled	moderately fulfilled
6.	Consideration of the brand potential and the economic lifetime of the brand	barely fulfilled	moderately fulfilled	barely fulfilled
7.	Isolation of brand-specific payment surpluses	completely fulfilled	completely fulfilled	completely fulfilled
8.	Consideration of a capital value oriented technique and an appropriate discount rate	barely fulfilled	barely fulfilled	moderately fulfilled
9.	Consideration of brand-specific risks (market and competitive risks)	completely fulfilled	not at all fulfilled	not at all fulfilled
10.	Traceability and transparency	moderately fulfilled	moderately fulfilled	completely fulfilled
11.	Consideration of the company's internal and external brand value determinants	not at all fulfilled	not at all fulfilled	not at all fulfilled
12.	Consideration of behavioural and financial brand value determinants	completely fulfilled	completely fulfilled	completely fulfilled
13.	Consideration of the customer equity	not at all fulfilled	not at all fulfilled	moderately fulfilled

Legend: ○ not at all fulfilled　◔ barely fulfilled　◑ moderately fulfilled　◕ largely fulfilled　● completely fulfilled

Fig. 5.19 Assessment of the monetary brand valuation approaches with respect to the requirements of monetary brand valuation

Another stakeholder-oriented approach originates from **Jones** (2005). Jones argues that the brand value develops not only in the relationship between the brand and the customer, but is the result of the brand's relationship with all relevant stakeholders, an exchange with the groups and the brand perception by these stakeholders. As generally relevant stakeholders, Jones names consumers, the public opinion, the government, NGOs, competitors, the media, distribution partners, suppliers, employees and executives. The relationship of the brand with each of these groups constitutes a part of the brand value. In order to optimise this brand value, stakeholder groups must be prioritised, their expectations determined and subsequently, these relationships must be specifically managed. The stakeholder groups are prioritised using the following four dimensions: dependency, strategic significance, currentness and appeal. Here, dependency refers to the brand's dependency on the relevant stakeholder group and any potential for changing this. The strategic significance targets the significance of the stakeholder groups for the brand competences and values. Currentness describes how acute the relationship with the group is. Here, Jones distinguishes between acute relationships, which may for instance become critical at any stage, and latent, i.e. rather dormant relationships. As the last dimension, appeal constitutes a rather qualitative valuation. This dimension ascertains to what extent the brand image appeals to the respective stakeholder group.

Following the prioritisation, the type of exchange with the individual groups must be analysed. Here, Jones distinguishes between the functional, symbolic and hedonistic manifestations. However, these three steps do not constitute a one-off procedure; they must be repeated continuously and take into account any changes in order to optimise the brand value on the basis of this. The relationship performance with reference to the individual groups forms a part of this analysis. This relationship performance is primarily influenced by the company-related communication. The latter is comprised of the leadership behaviour, success of the company, communication controlled by the company and third-party communication (for instance media reports). The relationship performance is assessed in the following categories, which represent possible results of the relationship: profitability, reputation, loyalty, synergies and political influence. During the next step, external influences must be considered. This includes political influences, macroeconomic factors and other current developments. As a result, we get the final brand value (cf. Jones 2005). The model by Jones exhibits several weaknesses; in particular the lack of information regarding any kind of measurement must be criticised. Consequently, an empirical assessment to evaluate the reliability and validity of the model cannot take place.

All in all, the comprehensive consideration of all relevant groups that drive the brand value can be named as strength of the stakeholder-oriented models. Here, a high level of influence on the brand value is attributed not only to the consumers, but in particular to the employees (cf. Jones 2005). However, despite their alleged comprehensive understanding of the brand value, these approaches have significant shortcomings. They do not explicitly take into consideration that there is an effect relationship between the (internal)

Table 5.5 Strength and weaknesses of selected stakeholder-oriented brand valuation models

Category	Strength	Weaknesses
Comprehensive	– Consideration of all relevant stakeholder groups	– No consideration of the effect relationship between internal and external brand strength – No consideration of monetary variables
De Chernatony (2010)	– Emphasis on the role of employees	– Low level of validity as only average values are analysed – No assessment of reliability and validity possible
Jones (2005)	– Valuation of stakeholder groups	– Unclear methodology – No assessment of reliability and validity possible

By author

brand strength developing with the employees and the (external) brand strength perceived by the consumers. For instance, in all existing brand valuation models, employees are not regarded as the original source of the external brand strength. Instead, this narrow understanding merely looks on employees as one of many reference groups and does not fully solve the problem of neglecting the employees, as is done in the behavioural and financial models. In addition, the lack of consideration of monetary variables must be criticised, making the stakeholder-oriented approaches unsuitable for external brand valuation purposes (Table 5.5).

The requirements of the monetary brand valuation are barely met by the stakeholder-oriented models (see Fig. 5.20).

Table 5.6 provides an overview of the strengths and weaknesses of the four different categories of brand valuation models introduced in this chapter.

5.4.5   Identity-Based Brand Valuation

5.4.5.1 Basic Structure of Identity-Based Brand Valuation

The framework of the identity-based brand valuation is based on the requirements outlined in Sect. 5.3.2 (see Fig. 5.21).

Brand management activities form the basis for the framework of the identity-based brand valuation model. All brand management activities initially only refer to the employees and executives of the brand, as only these groups of people can be controlled directly (see left-hand side of Fig. 5.21). Only then do the effects of the brand management develop inside-out (see right-hand side of Fig. 5.21).

On the internal side, first of all the self-perception of the (current or potential) employee and the brand identity are aligned. The greater the fit, the more appealing both

No.	Principle	Degree of fulfilment	
		de Chernatony (2010)	Jones (2005)
1.	Consideration of the purpose of the valuation and of the weighting function	not at all fulfilled	not at all fulfilled
2.	Consideration of the brand type and function	not at all fulfilled	not at all fulfilled
3.	Consideration of the protection of trademarks	not at all fulfilled	not at all fulfilled
4.	Consideration of the brand and target group relevance	not at all fulfilled	not at all fulfilled
5.	Consideration of the current brand status based on representative data of the relevant target group	moderately fulfilled	moderately fulfilled
6.	Consideration of the brand potential and the economic lifetime of the brand	not at all fulfilled	not at all fulfilled
7.	Isolation of brand-specific payment surpluses	not at all fulfilled	not at all fulfilled
8.	Consideration of a capital value oriented technique and an appropriate discount rate	not at all fulfilled	not at all fulfilled
9.	Consideration of brand-specific risks (market and competitive risks)	not at all fulfilled	not at all fulfilled
10.	Traceability and transparency	largely fulfilled	largely fulfilled
11.	Consideration of the company's internal and external brand value determinants	completely fulfilled	completely fulfilled
12.	Consideration of behavioural and financial brand value determinants	not at all fulfilled	not at all fulfilled
13.	Consideration of the customer equity	not at all fulfilled	not at all fulfilled

Legend:
○ not at all fulfilled ◔ barely fulfilled ◑ moderately fulfilled ◕ largely fulfilled ● completely fulfilled

Fig. 5.20 Assessment of the stakeholder-oriented brand valuation approaches with respect to the requirements of the monetary brand valuation

Table 5.6 Strength and weaknesses of the categories of brand valuation models

Category	Strength	Weaknesses
Financial approaches	– High level of transparency, simple structure – Monetary brand value	– No consideration of behavioural performance indicators – No consideration of the internal brand strength
Behavioural approaches	– Consideration of behavioural performance indicators – Consideration of the external brand strength	– No consideration of the internal brand strength – No calculation of the monetary brand value due to a lack of financial performance indicators – Frequent non-transparency and subjective assessments in the cycle of these models
Combined models	– Consideration of behavioural and financial variables	– No consideration of the internal brand strength
Stakeholder-oriented models	– Consideration of different stakeholder groups	– Insufficient consideration of employees as the original source of the brand strength – No calculation of the monetary brand value due to a lack of financial performance indicators

By author

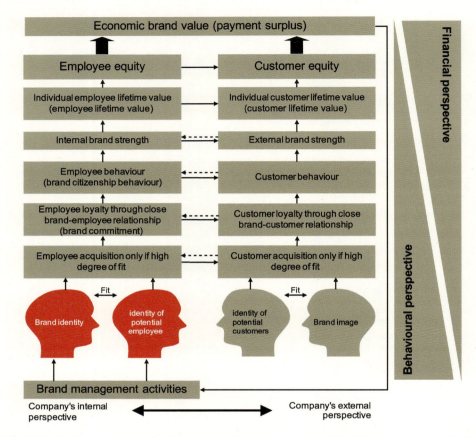

Fig. 5.21 Basic structure of the identity-based brand valuation model. (Source: based on Meffert et al. 2015, p. 832)

current and potential employees assess the (corporate) brand and the greater the likelihood of recruiting staff. The fit between brand and personal identity also determines the relationship between the brand and the employees already working for the company. This becomes particularly apparent in the employee's attitude and loyalty towards the brand (brand commitment). The latter forms the basis for the deeply brand-related behaviour of the employee (brand citizenship behaviour).

The same argument also applies to the external side of the company. According to this, the fit between the brand image and the consumer's self-concept exerts great influence on the success of the customer acquisition and has an impact on customer loyalty and the brand-customer relationship (cf. Sirgy 1982; Kleine-Kalmer 2016). The latter is responsible for the customer behaviour towards the brand (which may refer to current, potential and former customers). This argument results in internal and external brand strength.

The conversion of the behavioural brand strength into an economic brand value constitutes the second step of identity-based brand valuation. This step is particularly important from an accounting perspective. First of all, for this purpose the brand value must be divided into a present value of the brand and a brand potential value. The present value of the brand can be defined as those brand-induced and discounted payment surpluses that originate from current business segments. In contrast, the brand potential value describes those brand-induced payment surpluses, which come from potential, i.e. not currently engaged in business segments. Both values must be calculated and discounted separately (cf. Jost-Benz 2009). In addition to industry and business-specific variables, the discount rate also contains a brand strength-specific risk premium. The stronger the brand, the lower the risk premium.

In addition to calculating the brand value, the relevant customer equity segments must be taken into consideration. **Through this, the identity-based brand valuation model makes a significant contribution towards the integration of the brand value (brand equity) and the customer equity**. This model facilitates the examination of individual customer values with respect to the customer acquisition costs and the profitability of the customer behaviour. The comparison with the performed brand activities provides valuable indications with respect to the control of the brand activities. This means that the customer equity takes on a monitoring role and provides information on whether the brand-induced consumer behaviour is also appealing from an economic perspective. For the calculation of the brand value, this means that customer equity segments are to be developed that are as homogeneous as possible. Such a course of action is necessary, as different customer equity segments may exhibit different attitudes and behaviours towards the brand. In addition to the external perspective, the internal perspective must also be examined. For this purpose, the individual employee lifetime value must be calculated. This approach is comparable with the CLV calculations but, in accordance with the internal perspective, it is based on quantities of work and prices of work instead of purchase quantities and the prices of goods. Building on that, the employee equity can be calculated, which can be used as a performance indicator of internal brand management. Taking into account all aspects and based on Jost-Benz (2009), we can define the identity-based brand value as follows:

Identity-based brand value is the brand-induced payment surplus from the marketing of current brand services (present value of the brand) and potential brand services (brand potential value) with respect to one or several customer groups (cf. Jost-Benz 2009).

This model is designed as a holistic, mathematical empirical performance indicator system that, in addition to the measurement, also facilitates the control of the brand value. Consequently, it is not only the final monetary brand value, but also the behavioural interim results of the brand strength determination that is relevant to identity-based brand management (cf. Burmann et al. 2009). The first step involves the determination of the brand strength. The resulting brand strength index forms the basis for the two subsequent

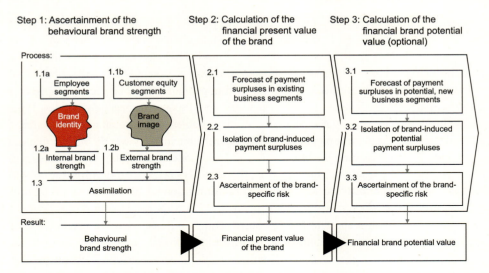

Fig. 5.22 Three steps of the identity-based brand valuation model. (Source: based on Jost-Benz 2009, p. 51)

steps: The calculation of the present value of the brand from the marketing of current services and the calculation of the brand potential value from the optional marketing of potential new services of the brand (see Fig. 5.22).

In order to ascertain the brand strength, in step 1.1a the consumers are divided into homogeneous customer equity segments according to product, market and customer equity-related determinants. This is necessary, as the attitudes, the purchasing behaviour and in particular the significance of the consumers differ. This can be illustrated using the example of a car make, which offers both small cars and premium vehicles. Here, we must assume that the customer equity segment of the buyers of small cars differs greatly from the customer segment of the buyers of premium vehicles in terms of customer equity. In addition to these customer equity segments, the present model also takes into account market and employee-specific information. Pursuant to the identity-based brand management approach, the employees are the decisive driving force of the brand value in the internal perspective of the company (step 1.1b). Here, the segmentation of the employees (for instance according to hierarchy levels or period of employment) is as necessary as the market segmentation.

In step 1.2, the brand strength is calculated. Here, the internal brand strength is measured using the brand knowledge, brand commitment and brand citizenship behaviour. The external brand strength is calculated in an integrated manner through the brand knowledge, the benefit from the brand and the long-term preference for the brand (cf. Sect. 5.1.2). It is not sufficient for the brand to exist in the consumers' knowledge alone (aided brand awareness). Furthermore, the brand benefit dimensions must be suitable for differentiation and relevant to the buying decision (cf. Sect. 3.3). The model deals with these indicators of external brand strength in comparison with relevant competitors and subsequently combines them into an external brand strength index.

In order to ascertain the entire brand strength, the internal and external brand strength must be integrated (step 1.3). The basis for this is the Balance Theory according to Heider (cf. 1958). Translated to the context at hand, this means that the internal and the external brand strength assimilate over time. Only if employees and consumers exhibit the same positive attitudes and behaviours towards a brand, can this brand be successful in the long-term. On the basis of the "mere exposure effect" we must assume that the employees are constantly influenced by the brand (cf. Obermiller 1985) and the internal brand strength therefore has a dominant impact on the assimilation process. The type of this balancing effect between the internal and external brand strength depends on the intensity of the employees' interactions with the consumers (cf. Maloney 2007): The more intensive the interaction, the faster internal and external brand strength converge. For instance, if an employee of a vulnerable brand (low level of internal brand strength, high level of external brand strength) has contact with a consumer, then it is very likely that the low level of internal brand strength, in the form of low brand commitment and brand citizenship behaviour, becomes tangible for the consumer. This causes a negative balancing effect on the external brand strength. Ultimately, the overall brand strength develops as a result of this assimilation.

The ascertained brand strength is the basis for the calculation of the financial present value of the brand. The foundation for this step is the calculation of the payment surpluses for the current services (step 2.1). This is done based on the discounted cash flow method (cf. Rappaport and Klien 1999; Riesenbeck and Perrey 2005). To isolate the brand-induced payment surpluses (step 2.2), Jost-Benz (2009) developed a method that corresponds to the keynote of identity-based brand management. In the process, a differentiated analysis of the individual buying decision determinants is carried out; its objective is to ascertain the holistic brand performance. In order to obtain the present value of the current and future brand-induced payment surpluses, it is necessary to define a discount rate that reflects the future risk of the market, company and brand (step 2.3). Such a brand-specific discount rate is essential, as the volatility of the brand-induced payment surpluses decreases with increasing brand strength. The lifetime of a brand, which must also be taken into account for this, can be roughly estimated using qualitative assessment criteria, based on publicly accessible market information (cf. Meffert and Burmann 1999).

In addition to the developments of the current services of a brand, a comprehensive brand valuation model must also consider developments based on strategic options for potentially new services (step 3). Initially, payment surpluses for previously identified potential services are ascertained (step 3.1). Based on these estimates, the brand's share in these potential payment surpluses is isolated, as is done when calculating the present value of the brand (step 3.2). The resulting brand-induced potential payment surpluses are subsequently discounted to a present value, taking into account the brand-specific risk (step 3.3). During the last step of the identity-based brand valuation, the present value of the brand and the brand potential value are added.

5.4.5.2 Calculating the Present Value of the Brand and the Brand Potential Value

The calculation of the **present value of the brand** and the **brand potential value** shall be illustrated below, using the example of a product family brand of a German technology company for the German market. This example shows that the identity-based brand valuation model fulfils all 13 brand valuation principles (cf. Jost-Benz 2009). The present value of the brand of customer segments "i" is comprised of the discounted brand-induced payment surpluses. Therefore, the cash flows (CF) of the customer segments constitute the basis for this calculation. They must be multiplied with the isolated brand performance (BP), i.e. the brand's share in the buying decision. This is necessary as only a certain share of the cash flows is attributable to the brand. Whilst the cash flows are monetary variables, the isolated brand performance is a percentage. The result of the brand-induced cash flows must subsequently be discounted over the estimated lifetime of the brand, using the discount factor (DF). As the discount factor is a percentage as well, the present value of the brand is also a monetary variable. The formula for calculating the present value of the brand is shown in Fig. 5.23.

To calculate the free cash flow, the average brand sales (ascertained on the basis of considering average past sales volumes), the brand retention expenditures (the investments necessary for the brand management), the corporate tax rate and the discount factors must all be taken into account. They are divided into market, company and brand-specific risks. Figure 5.24 shows how the cash flow can be calculated in a formal analytical way.

For 2004–2008, the net sales in the case study were between €144.6 million and €194.9 million. The expenditures incurred for the brand retention (this includes all expenditures that contribute to the brand performance) must be deducted from these

$$BPV_i = \frac{CF_i * BP_i}{DF}$$

BPV_i = Brand present value of customer segment "i"
CF_i = Cash flow of customer segment "i"
BP_i = Isolated brand performance in customer segment "i"
DF = Discount factor

Fig. 5.23 Formal analytical representation of the calculation of the present value of the brand. (Source: based on Jost-Benz 2009, p.123)

$$CF_i = \left(\begin{array}{c} \text{Ø Brand sales} \\ \text{in the previous} \\ \text{3 years} \end{array} - \begin{array}{c} \text{Ø Brand retention} \\ \text{expenditure in the} \\ \text{previous 3 years} \end{array} \right) \times (1 - \text{Corporate tax rate})$$

CF_i = Cash flow of customer segment "i"

Fig. 5.24 Formal analytical representation of the calculation of the cash flow. (Source: based on Jost-Benz 2009, p.123)

$$RP^{Brand\ strength} = Maximum\ Risk\ premium \times (1 - BS_i)$$

RP = Risk premium
BS_i= Brand strength in customer segment "i"

Fig. 5.25 Calculation of the brand strength-specific risk premium. (Source: based on Jost-Benz 2009, p.149)

Fig. 5.26 Basic structure for determining the identity-based brand potential value. (Source: based on Jost-Benz 2009, p.157)

values. This is done by using the average EBIT margin for this industry. The difference between sales and the EBIT margin provides a reliable indicator of the brand retention expenditure.

In the next step, the non-brand-induced payments must be subtracted from these interim results. To do so, the brand performance must be isolated. For this purpose, the brand performance is examined, for instance with respect to the following factors: Meeting of individual requirements, product quality, innovation competence, scope of the features, ease of use, quality of the customer service, design and the price/performance ratio.

In the third step of the calculation of the present value of the brand, the discount factors must be determined. The market-specific discount factor is guided by the rate of inflation. The company-specific discount factor is based on the cost of capital that is customary in this industry. The brand-specific discount factor results from the brand strength. Figure 5.25 shows the formal analytical calculation.

Following the calculation of the present value of the brand, the brand potential value is determined. The procedure for determining the brand potential value can be divided into six steps and is illustrated in Fig. 5.26.

Within the scope of identifying potential brand services, both internal and external perspectives must be taken into consideration. During the first step, new potential services must be identified. During the second step, the fit of these potential services with the brand must be checked.

In step 2 of the calculation of the brand potential value, the net sales of the potential brand services must be forecast. To do so, the relevant market volume must first be determined. Subsequently, a consumer survey is used to ascertain the purchasing behaviour

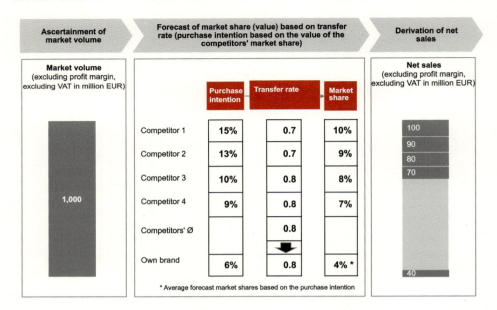

Fig. 5.27 Determining achievable net sales within the scope of the brand potential value. (Source: based on Jost-Benz 2009, p.164)

intentions towards the own brand and competitor brands, as well as the market shares of the competitors. The so-called transfer rate is calculated from these two components. If a brand achieves a 15% purchase intention and a 10% value-based brand share, this results in a transfer rate of 0.7. The average transfer rate of all examined brands in the new business segment, in conjunction with the indicated purchase intention of the consumers with respect to the own brand, is used to forecast the market share when entering a new business segment. If you relate this share to the market volume, you obtain the forecast net sales of the potential brand services (see Fig. 5.27).

In step 3 of the calculation of the brand potential value, the brand retention expenditures must be deducted from these forecast net sales. In addition to taking into account the ongoing brand retention expenditures, the market launch costs must also be estimated. In step 4, as with the calculation of the present value of the brand, the corporate taxes must be deducted from these forecast cash flows. In step 5, the brand performance is isolated. In the last step of calculating the brand potential value, the discount factor must be determined.

This chapter has demonstrated the significance of brand controlling in general and brand valuation in particular. The different purposes of a valuation render both monetary brand valuation and behavioural brand valuation vital. Against this background, the growing number of combined models must be welcomed. However, these approaches persistently neglect the internal perspective. Furthermore, the TANK AG study has shown that the different approaches result in great differences in the calculated brand

No.	Principle	Degree of fulfilment
1.	Consideration of the purpose of the valuation and of the weighting function	◐
2.	Consideration of the brand type and function	◔
3.	Consideration of the protection of trademarks	◔
4.	Consideration of the brand and target group relevance	●
5.	Consideration of the current brand status based on representative data of the relevant target group	◔
6.	Consideration of the brand potential and the economic lifetime of the brand	●
7.	Isolation of brand-specific payment surpluses	●
8.	Consideration of a capital value oriented technique and an appropriate discount rate	●
9.	Consideration of brand-specific risks (market and competitive risks)	●
10.	Traceability and transparency	●
11.	Consideration of the company's internal and external brand value determinants	●
12.	Consideration of behavioural and financial brand value determinants	●
13.	Consideration of the customer equity	●

○ not at all fulfilled   ◔ barely fulfilled   ◐ moderately fulfilled   ◕ largely fulfilled   ● completely fulfilled

Fig. 5.28 Assessment of identity-based brand valuation with reference to the requirements of monetary brand valuation

value. The efforts to standardise brand valuation by means of the formulated brand valuation requirements constitute an important step towards solving this problem. The identity-based brand valuation approach considers these requirements (see Fig. 5.28) and is the only one of the examined approaches to offer a combination of the financial and behavioural performance indicators, both in the internal and the external perspective.

References

Aaker, D. A. (1996). *Building strong brands*. New York: Free Press.
Ailawadi, K. L., Lehmann, D. E., & Neslin, S. A. (2003). Revenue premium as an outcome measure of brand equity. *Journal of Marketing, 67,* 1–17.
Amirkhizi, M. (2005). Suche nach der Weltformel. *Horizont, 6,* 3–4.
APM. (2012). Fact-sheet. http://www.markenpiraterie-apm.de/files/factsheet_16052012.pdf. Last visit: July 24, 2012.
BAV Consulting. (2012). *About us*. http://bavconsulting.com/about. Last visit: July 24, 2012.
Bayón, T., Gutsche, J., & Bauer, H. (2002). Customer equity marketing: Touching the intangible. *European Management Journal, 20*(3), 213–222.

Bekmeier-Feuerhahn, S. (1998). *Marktorientierte Markenbewertung. Eine konsumenten- und unternehmensbezogene Betrachtung*. Wiesbaden: Gabler.

Brand Rating. (2015). *Management und Kapitalisierung des Assets Marke*. http://www.marken-lexikon.com/d_texte/verfahren_brand_rating.pdf. Last visit: February 04, 2015.

Braun, M., Kopka, U., & Tochtermann, T. (2003). Promotions - ein Fass ohne Boden. *Akzente, 27*(4), 16–23.

Breusch, A. (2009). *Customer-equity-management in einem dynamischen Wettbewerbsumfeld - Konzeption und Anwendung eines customer-equity-Wettbewerbsmodells*. Wiesbaden: Gabler.

Buchan, E., & Brown, A. (1989). Brand valuation and its role in mergers & acquisitions. In: Murphy, J. (Ed.), *Brand valuation—establishing a true and fair view* (pp. 75–89).

Burmann, C. (2003). Customer equity als Steuerungsgröße für die Unternehmensführung. *Zeitschrift für Betriebswirtschaft (ZfB), 73*(2), 113–138.

Burmann, C., & Jost-Benz, M. (2005). *Brand Equity Management vs. Customer Equity Management? Zur Integration zweier Managementkonzepte*. Working paper no. 19, chair of innovative brand management (LiM), University of Bremen.

Burmann, C., Jost-Benz, M., & Riley, N. (2009). Identity-based brand equity model—development of an integrated management and measurement approach. *Journal of Business Research, 62*(3), 390–397.

Burmann, C., & Meffert, H. (2005). Managementkonzept der identitätsorientierten Markenführung. In H. Meffert, C. Burmann, & M. Koers (Eds.), *Markenmanagement – Identitätsorientierte Markenführung und praktische Umsetzung* (pp. 73–114). Wiesbaden: Gabler.

Burmann, C., Meffert, H., & Feddersen, C. (2007). Identitätsbasierte Markenführung. In A. Florack, M. Scarabis, & E. Primosch (Eds.), *Psychologie der Markenführung* (pp. 3–30). Munich: Vahlen.

Chernatony, de. (2010). *From brand vision to brand evaluation*. London: Elsevier.

Crimmins, J. C. (1992). Better measurement and management of brand value. *Journal of Advertising Research, 32*, 11–19.

Fairfield-Sonn, J. W., Ogilvie, J. R., & Delvecchio, G. A. (2002). Mergers, acquisitions and long-term employee attitudes. *Journal of Business & Economic Studies, 8*(2), 1–16.

Farquhar, P. H., Herr, P. M., & Fazio, R. H. (1990). Relational model for category extensions of brands. In M. E. Goldberg & G. Gerken (Eds.), *Die fraktale Marke*. Düsseldorf: Econ.

Gerken, G. (1994). *Die fraktale Marke*. Düsseldorf: Econ.

Gerpott, T. J., & Thomas, S. E. (2004). Markenbewertungsverfahren: Einsatzfelder und Verfahrensüberblick. *Wirtschaftswissenschaftliches Studium, 33*(7), 394–400.

Hanser, P., Högl, S., & Maul, K.-H. (2004). *Die Tank AG - Wie neun Bewertungsexperten eine fiktive Marke bewerten*. Düsseldorf: Verlags-Gruppe Handelsblatt.

Heemann, J. (2008). *Markenbudgetierung*. Wiesbaden.

Heider, F. (1958). *The psychology of interpersonal relations*. New York: Wiley.

Heider, U. H., & Strehlau, R. (2006). Markenwert-controlling. In M. P. Zerres (Ed.), *Handbuch marketing-controlling* (pp. 255–280). Wiesbaden: Springer.

Högl, S., & Hupp, O. (2004). Brand performance measurement mit dem brand assessment system (BASS). In A. Schimansky (Ed.), *Der Wert der Marke* (pp. 124–145). Munich: Vahlen.

Holtz, A. (2012). *5-Phasen-Methode der Markenbewertung*. Wiesbaden: Springer Gabler.

Hundacker, S. (2005). *Customer Equity Management bei kontinuierlichen Dienstleistungen - Konzeption, Modell und Anwendung im Mobilfunk*. Wiesbaden: Dt. Univ.-Verlag.

Jahn, T., Schneider, M. C., & Herz, C. (2012). Wie die Amerikaner eine deutsche Traditionsfirma ruinieren. *Handelsblatt*. June 8, 2012.

Jones, R. (2005). Finding sources of brand value: Developing a stakeholder model of brand equity. *Journal of Brand Management, 13*(1), 10–32.

Jost-Benz, M. (2009). *Identitätsbasierte Markenbewertung - Grundlagen, theoretische Konzeptualisierung und praktische Anwendung am Beispiel einer Technologiemarke*. Wiesbaden: Gabler.

Kapferer, J. N. (1992). *Die Marke – Kapital des Unternehmens*. Landsberg/Lech: Verlag Moderne Industrie.

Kaplan, R. S., & Norton, D. P. (1997). *Balanced scorecard: Strategien erfolgreich umsetzen*. Stuttgart: Schäffer-Poeschel.

Keller, K. L. (1993). Conceptualizing, measuring, and managing customer-based brand equity. *Journal of Marketing, 57,* 1–22.

Keller, K. L. (2003). *Strategic brand management. Building, measuring and managing brand equity* (2nd ed.). New Jersey: Upper Saddle River.

Keller, K. L. (2005). Kundenorientierte Messung des Markenwerts. In F.-R. Esch (Ed.), *Moderne Markenführung: Grundlagen – Innovative Ansätze – Praktische Umsetzungen* (pp. 1307–1328). Wiesbaden: Gabler.

Keller, K. L. (2013). *Strategic brand management: Building, measuring, and managing brand equity*. Boston: Irwin.

Kern, W. (1962). Bewertung von Warenzeichen. *Betriebswirtschaftliche Forschung und Praxis, 14*(1), 17–31.

Kleine-Kalmer, B. (2016). *Managing brand page attachment—An emipirical study on facebook user´s attachment to brand pages* (to date unpublished dissertation).

Kötting, H. (2004). Der Y&R brand asset valuator. In A. Schimansky (Ed.), *Der Wert der Marke* (pp. 720–733). Munich: Vahlen.

Krause, J. (2013). *Identitätsbasierte Markenführung im Investitionsgüterbereich - Management und Wirkungen von Marke-Kunde-Beziehungen*. Wiesbaden: Springer Gabler.

Kriegbaum, C. (2001). *Markencontrolling: Bewertung und Steuerung von Marken als immaterielle Vermögenswerte im Rahmen eines unternehmenswertorientierten controlling*. Munich: Vahlen.

Machatschke, M. (2012). Fragen Sie Franz. *Manager Magazin, 8,* 26–31.

Maloney, P. (2007). *Absatzmittlergerichtetes, identitätsbasiertes Markenmanagement: Eine Erweiterung des innengerichteten, identitätsbasierten Markenmanagements unter besonderer Berücksichtigung von Premiummarken*. Wiesbaden: Dt. Univ.-Verlag.

Manager Magazin. (2005). *AEG-Chronik – Niedergang einer Weltmarke*. http://www.managermagazin.de/unternehmen/artikel/0,2828,389986,00.html. Last visit: October 27, 2014.

Markenverband, GfK, Sattler, PwC (2012). *Praxis von Markenmanagement und Markenbewertung in deutschen Unternehmen*.

Meffert, H., & Burmann, C. (1999). Abnutzbarkeit und Nutzungsdauer von Marken. *Jahrbuch für Absatz- und Verbrauchsforschung, 45*(3), 244–263.

Meffert, H., Burmann, C., & Kirchgeorg, M. (2015). *Marketing: Grundlagen marktorientierter Unternehmensführung*. Wiesbaden: Springer Gabler.

Meffert, H., & Koers, M. (2005). Markenkannibalisierung in Markenportfolios. In H. Meffert, C. Burmann, & M. Koers (Eds.), *Markenmanagement* (pp. 297–318). Wiesbaden: Gabler.

Meurer, J., & Rügge, M. (2012). Kafka für Marketers. *Absatzwirtschaft, 7*(2012), 30–34.

Musiol, K.-G., Berens, H., Spannagl, J., & Biesalski, A. (2004). Icon Brand Navigator und Brand Rating für eine holistische Markenführung. In A. Schimansky (Ed.), *Der Wert der Marke* (pp. 370–399). Munich: Vahlen.

Obermiller, C. (1985). Varieties of mere exposure: The effects of processing style of repetition on affective response. *Journal of Consumer Research, 12*(June), 17–30.

Park, C. W., MacInnis, D. J., Priester, J., Eisingerich, A. B., & Iacobucci, D. (2010). Brand attachment and brand attitude strength: conceptual and empirical differentiation of two critical brand equity drivers. *Journal of Marketing, 74*(6), 1–17.

Perrey, J., Freundt, T., & Spillecke, D. (2015). *Power brands—Measuring—Making—Managing—Brand success*. Weinheim: WILEY-VCH.

Pfeil, O., & Vater, H. (2002). "Die kleine Unternehmensbewertung" oder die neuen Vorschriften zur Goodwill- und Intangible-Bilanzierung. *KoRe, Nr., 2,* 66–81.

Piehler, R. (2011). *Interne Markenführung – Theoretisches Konzept und fallstudenbasierte Evidenz*. Wiesbaden: Gabler.

PricewaterhouseCoopers A. G. (2006). *Praxis von Markenbewertung und Markenmanagement in deutschen Unternehmen*. Frankfurt am Main.

Rappaport, A., & Klien, W. (1999). *Shareholder value: Ein Handbuch für Manager und Investoren*. Stuttgart: Schäffer-Poeschel.

Reckenfelderbäumer, M. (2006). Prozesskostenrechnung im Marketing. In S. Reinecke & T. Tomczak (Eds.), *Handbuch marketing-controlling* (pp. 767–794). Wiesbaden: Gabler.

Riesenbeck, H., & Perrey, J. (2005). *Mega-Macht Marke. Erfolg messen, machen, managen*. Frankfurt/M.: REDLINE.

Rust, R. T., Zeithaml, V. A., & Lemon, K. N. (2004). Customer-centered brand management. *Harvard Business Review*, (September), 110–118.

Sattler, H. (2005). Markenbewertung: State-of-the-Art. *ZfB Zeitschrift für Betriebswirtschaft: Special issue, 75*(2), 33–57.

Schade, M. (2012). *Identitätsbasierte Markenführung professioneller Sportvereine – Eine empirische Untersuchung zur Ermittlung verhaltensrelevanter Markennutzen und der Relevanz der Markenpersönlichkeit*. Wiesbaden: Gabler.

Schneider, H. (2004). *Marken in der Politik, Erscheinungsformen, Relevanz, identitätsorientierte Führung und demokratietheoretische Reflektion*. Wiesbaden: Gabler.

Simon, C. J., & Sullivan, M. W. (1993). The measurement and determinants of brand equity: A financial approach. *Marketing Science, 12*(1), 28–52.

Sirgy, J. (1982). Self-concept in consumer behavior: A critical review. *Journal of Consumer Research, 9*(December), 287–300.

Ströbel, T. (2012). *Die Einflussfaktoren der Markenbewertung im Sport: eine empirische Analyse der Zusammenhänge bei Klubmarken*. Wiesbaden: Gabler.

Stucky, N. (2004). Monetäre Markenbewertung nach dem Interbrand-Ansatz. In A. Schimansky (Ed.), *Der Wert der Marke* (pp. 430–459). Munich: Vahlen.

Tafelmeier, R. (2009). *Markenbilanzierung und Markenbewertung: Analyse und Eignung von Markenbewertungsverfahren in Hinblick auf die bilanzielle Behandlung von Marken nach HGB und IAS/IFRS*. Frankfurt/M.: Lang.

Tomczak, T., Reinecke, S., & Kaetzke, P. (2004). *Markencontrolling – Sicherstellung der Effektivität und Effizienz der Markenführung*. In: Bruhn, M. (Ed.), *Handbuch Markenführung* (pp. 1821–1852). Stuttgart: Gabler.

Walser, M. G. (2004). *Brand strength: Building and testing models based on experiential information*. Wiesbaden: Dt. Univ.-Verlag.

Warwitz, C. (2016). *Location-based advertising* (to date unpublished dissertation).

Young & Rubicam. (2012). Brand asset valuator. http://young-rubicam.de/tools-wissen/tools/brandasset-valuator. Last visit: April 23, 2015.

Identity-Based Trademark Protection

6

Contents

6.1 Integral Identity-Based Trademark Protection. 282
6.2 Developing a Trademark Protection Strategy 283
6.3 Legal Trademark Protection. 284
    6.3.1 Determining the Territoriality of Trademark Protection. 284
    6.3.2 Obtaining Trademark Protection 285
6.4 Extra-Legal Trademark Protection. 285
    6.4.1 Enhancing Innovation Capabilities. 285
    6.4.2 Cooperating with Authorities 285
    6.4.3 Consumer- and Sales-Oriented Measures. 286
    6.4.4 Supplier- and Production-Oriented Measures 287
6.5 Internal Requirements for Integrated Trademark Protection 287
    6.5.1 Organisational Anchoring. 287
    6.5.2 Recourse to Local Knowledge 288
    6.5.3 Channel Monitoring 288
References. 289

"**Trademark piracy**", the practice by which unknown third parties imitate products and services by using registered trademarks, has increased since the mid-1970s. Brand piracy generated US\$ 40–80 billion at the end of the 1980s, but such sales have now increased to US\$ 800–1100 billion (cf. Keller 2015). Registered trademarks of watches and sunglasses have been plagiarised for years; pharmaceuticals, electronic devices, and capital goods are more recent but equally common victims, and sales of infringed products online continue to increase. Thus, 80% of German companies note that they have fallen victim to trademark piracy (cf. Markenverband 2008).

According to the OECD (2008), more than two-thirds of worldwide sales due to trademark piracy come from China. In the Chinese city of Kumming, an entire pirated

© Springer Fachmedien Wiesbaden GmbH 2017

C. Burmann et al., *Identity-Based Brand Management*,
DOI 10.1007/978-3-658-13561-4_6

IKEA store was opened, based on the successful concepts originated by the Swedish company, without any notion of property rights. China's easy access to production facilities and capital, the availability of skilled and low-cost human resources, and its relatively ineffective legal system support its position as the primary region for trademark piracy (cf. Keller 2015). Even in such a blatant case, IKEA's legal alternatives for fighting its Chinese copy are limited.

These increases in trademark piracy have transformed trademark protection into a key challenge for brand management. Trademarks must be protected from unauthorised use and abuse by third parties. Most prior literature has focused on legal protection (cf. e.g. Baumgarth 2004; Schröder and Ahlert 2004; Schröder 2005), but weak legal systems and a lack of sanctioning mechanisms mean that such measures are limited and ineffective in many of the countries where the majority of trademark misuse and abuse takes place (e.g., China, Russia, Thailand). Instead, an integral approach to identity-based trademark protection incorporates both legal and extra-legal measures.

This chapter addresses some key questions in this context:

– What are the tasks of trademark protection? How does an integral approach to identity-based trademark protection differ from a conventional or purely legal understanding?
– What are the criteria that determine the preferred strategy for protecting trademarks?
– Which legal actions are available to protect trademarks?
– Which extra-legal actions can be taken to provide additional protection?
– What internal conditions are required to apply an integral approach to protecting trademarks, involving both legal and extra-legal actions?

6.1   Integral Identity-Based Trademark Protection

According to the constitutive characteristics of a brand identity (reciprocity, individuality, continuity, and consistency), trademark protection aims to protect:

– the integrative relationship between a brand-managing company and its consumers against intervention by unauthorised third parties (protection of reciprocity),
– the uniqueness of one benefit bundle compared with other benefit bundles (protection of individuality),
– the essential attributes of a brand and its perceptions by internal and external target groups against influences or manipulations by third parties (protection of continuity),
– the consistency of brand management across all relevant brand touch points against influences by third parties (protection of consistency).

To implement these tasks, an integral approach to **identity-based trademark protection** is necessary.

> **Identity-based trademark protection** is the continuous protection of a trademark's benefit bundle against irritations due to legal, strategic, operative, organisational, and technological actions, to ensure maximisation of brand equity with regard to both current and future business portfolios.

While the legal understanding of trademark protection focuses on legal aspects (e.g., registration of a trademark, assertion of claims when third parties use a trademark without authorisation), identity-based trademark protection contains additional elements (cf. Keller 2015).

6.2   Developing a Trademark Protection Strategy

The concept of identity-based trademark protection requires the development of an appropriate **trademark protection strategy**. For each combination of a product and a country that might pirate the trademark, the specific need for protection has to be determined, following which the trademark holder must decide whether its trademark protection measures will focus on legal or extra-legal activities (cf. Keller 2015). To establish priority, trademark protection should reflect the "risk of plagiarism in a particular product–source country combination."

To evaluate this risk, the OECD provides the Aggregated Trade-Related Index of Counterfeiting and Piracy (ATRIC) (cf. Keller 2015). The ATRIC defines the probability of plagiarism and identifies source countries of trademark piracy. According to this index, emerging economies pose greater piracy risks. When a product–source country combination poses substantial risks, it requires more attentive trademark protection. However, this prioritisation also needs to consider the strategic relevance of each brand–country combination (cf. Keller 2015).

The decision to focus on legal or extra-legal trade protection measures is based on the degree of intellectual or industrial property right protections available (cf. Keller 2015). This country-specific degree of protection can be determined according to the Ostergard index (2000), which registers laws and their actual enforcement in a particular country. If the system supports easily enforceable trademark rights, identity-based trademark protection should concentrate on legal protection measures. If the degree of protection is low, trademark protection should instead focus extra-legal measures along the brand's value chain.

These two steps generate a four-field matrix of trademark protection, as illustrated in Fig. 6.1, which also provides an example for each trademark protection strategy.

In the following sections, we detail examples that require a greater degree of trademark protection. We divide this discussion into legal trademark protection measures, extra-legal measures, and the internal requirements for implementing such trademark protection.

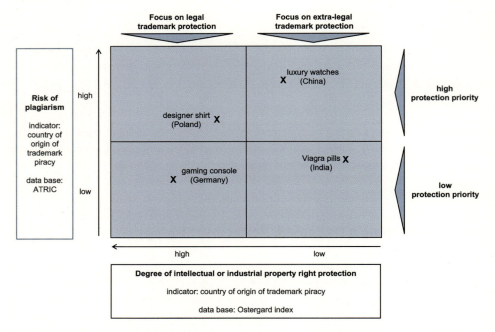

Fig. 6.1   4-field matrix of brand protection strategies. (Source: based on Keller 2015, p. 378)

6.3   Legal Trademark Protection

Legal trademark protection consists of preventive and proactive property rights policies (cf. Keller 2015). The former concentrate on defensive protection through the acquisition of trademark rights. The latter include active efforts to prevent the unauthorised registration or use of a trademark by third parties.

6.3.1   Determining the Territoriality of Trademark Protection

Registered national trademarks are valid within the territory of the country in which the trademark is registered. Due to this territorial principle, brand owners must decide in which territories they need to obtain legal trademark protection. Primarily, trademark protection should exist in the countries in which the brand is offered for sale. Trademarks also must be protected in all production locations, especially in countries that pose a higher risk of piracy. According to Keller (2015), trademarks should additionally be registered in important trade hubs (e.g., United Arab Emirates). Moreover, by obtaining property rights, future markets can be secured at an early stage. Otherwise, due to the priority principle, third parties could pre-emptively register identical or similar trademarks for identical or similar services. If unauthorised third parties were to register a trademark at an early stage, the actual owner of the trademark would be prevented from registering and launching its trademark later.

6.3.2   Obtaining Trademark Protection

If the territoriality of trademark protection involves more than one European country, or even the entire European Union, it is useful to register a community trademark. In this case, by registering a trademark at the Office for Harmonisation in the Internal Market (Trade Marks and Designs), the owner can obtain trademark protection for the EU as a whole (European Union Trademark). For territories located outside the EU, an international registration is possible. International registrations, which are based on the Madrid Agreement and Madrid Protocol, offer trademark protection for the countries that are parties to these agreements. Owners can extend a trademark that they have duly registered in a particular country (basic trademark) to several countries and thereby obtain trademark rights that extend internationally and mimic national trademark rights.

An international registration has three specific prerequisites. First, a basic trademark needs to be registered by a national trademark office (office of origin). Second, following the application for an international registration, the registration is forwarded to the World Intellectual Property Office (WIPO), which examines the requirements for an international registration. Third, the national countries in which the trademark will be valid can proclaim any grounds for refusal. Once all these criteria are met, owners can obtain trademark protection in several territories relatively easily and at attractive conditions.

6.4   Extra-Legal Trademark Protection

6.4.1   Enhancing Innovation Capabilities

If legal trademark protections are limited, companies can choose to increase their innovation capabilities. For example, the Sennheiser brand, which produces audio products such as headphones, faced the threat of Chinese piracy, distributed through Western partners. Rather than expanding legal protections, it adjusted its innovation processes with the guiding principle that it would "be so strongly innovative that competitors could not compete" (Friese et al. 2006, p. 24). With this strategy, Sennheiser responded to the low degree of protection of intellectual property rights in China, while simultaneously adding a reputation for being an "innovation leader" to its brand (cf. Keller 2015).

6.4.2   Cooperating with Authorities

Often customs or the police cannot differentiate an original product from a fake (cf. Keller 2015). Individual product attributes or safety systems (e.g., holograms, RFID chips, QR codes) can be used to address this problem. However, all information regarding these features must be clearly communicated to the authorities, to ensure that they will be able to distinguish the original from the unauthorised copy by using these symbols.

The willingness of authorities to cooperate with companies largely depends on the size and the importance of the particular trademark owner. Measures available to small- and medium-sized companies tend to be somewhat limited, especially while the safety systems remain expensive to implement. Bigger companies that use individual product attributes and safety systems are facing the problem that these labelling and tracking techniques also have been subject to plagiarism and piracy efforts (cf. Keller 2015). To successfully and sustainably implement safety features, trademark owners need to combine different systems and to ensure constant innovation in these techniques.

6.4.3   Consumer- and Sales-Oriented Measures

Consumer-oriented measures aim to increase awareness of trademark piracy and help consumers differentiate between an original and a plagiarised copy. These measures succeed best if the (unintended) purchase is connected to some form of risk for the consumer (e.g., in the case of pharmaceuticals). Labelling and tracking techniques can be used to identify the original, but communicating these signals and ensuring that consumers know how to read them requires a lot of effort. Furthermore, to identify labels such as QR codes, consumers need the relevant technical equipment (e.g., smartphones) and the associated technological expertise. Especially among older consumers, these requirements are often not fulfilled (cf. Keller 2015). Brand managers also worry that these measures might alert consumers to alternative, cheaper sources for a trademarked item, thus fostering trademark piracy (cf. Keller 2015).

Sales-related measures tend to focus on distribution channels that are at particular risk (e.g., Internet channels). Companies that hold a trademark can "flood" distribution channels with original products of lesser quality or slightly out-of-date versions (e.g., products from the previous season) at lower costs (cf. Keller 2015). This strategy also carries risks, though, especially for producers of luxury or premium trademarks. If distribution channels are flooded, consumers perceive the trademark as less exclusive, so that it might lose its competitive advantage and its appeal to consumers.

Some e-commerce shops offer tools for directly reporting cases of piracy. If the property rights can be proved (e.g., with a registered trademark), the e-commerce operator will block the plagiarised items. This move does not prevent pirates from making sales through other distribution channels, but it is necessary and appropriate to close as many channels as possible that are used to bring the products to the market.

By establishing their own exclusive distribution channels (e.g., direct distribution via the Internet or flagship stores), trademark owners can control the distribution more efficiently and thus prevent trademark piracy to a certain extent. Thus, investments in company-owned distribution channels can enhance defences against trademark piracy. Furthermore, cooperating with the owners of distribution channels that are particularly vulnerable (e.g., online retailers) may facilitate the identification and elimination of trademark piracy (cf. Keller 2015).

6.4.4   Supplier- and Production-Oriented Measures

Proactive steps in the form of certain supplier- and production-oriented measures are also possible. By identifying the key technology suppliers and entering into close cooperation with them the supply chain of the pirates can be effectively disrupted (cf. Keller 2015).

If some parts of the production process are performed by other companies (outsourcing), there is a risk that they might assist pirates in their infringements (e.g., "factory overruns"). By splitting outsourcing orders between several partners, by selecting partners in countries with a low risk of plagiarism, and by ensuring close cooperation (e.g., joint ventures), this kind of trademark infringement can largely be prevented (cf. Keller 2015).

6.5   Internal Requirements for Integrated Trademark Protection

For an effective identity-based trademark protection it is usually not sufficient to focus on single measures (cf. Keller 2015). Combining different legal and extra-legal activities can significantly increase their impact. However, integrated trademark protection is possible only if the following three key internal conditions apply.

6.5.1   Organisational Anchoring

To implement integrated trademark protection, the necessary competences have to go beyond legal trademark protection (e.g., trademark management and distribution, research and development). Keller (2015) suggests establishing a central organisational "trademark protection" unit, subordinate to the marketing or brand management departments. This organisational unit develops a trademark protection strategy (see Sect. 6.2) and a concrete project bundle (i.e., selection of legal and extra-legal measures). The organisational unit is responsible for all legal measures and coordinates the extra-legal measures. Depending on the selected protection measures, different organisational units of the company have to be integrated. For example, if the company's innovation capacity needs to be increased, the R&D, production, and trademark management departments should all be involved. If the goal is to disrupt the pirates' supply chain, the purchasing department, production, and logistics should be effectively coordinated (cf. Keller 2015).

To name an example, the international food company Nestlé maintains a central organisational trademark protection unit. All its trademark rights are grounded in the holding company, and the various national subsidiaries receive licenses to use these trademark rights. An organisational unit in the trademark-holding headquarters coordinates all trademark protection measures across the entire company. In total, 16 regional trademark protection units report to this central organisational unit (cf. Keller 2015).

6.5.2   Recourse to Local Knowledge

Another success factor for integrated trademark protection is local knowledge about the market conditions surrounding trademark piracy (e.g., distribution channels, production systems). Based on this knowledge, it is possible to predict the efficacy of individual protection measures in particular regions. Staake and Fleisch (2008) empirically demonstrated a relationship between above-average local trademark knowledge and successful trademark protection.

International Spirits Distribution (ISD) is an excellent example that illustrates the importance of local knowledge (cf. Green and Smith 2002). This producer of Scotch whisky found that their products were leading the market for strong alcoholic beverages in Thailand although they had never sold any of their products to Thailand. Several attempts to halt trademark piracy from the distance failed since the pirate companies paid higher commissions to their distribution partners than ISD was prepared to offer. However, noting the strategic relevance of this infringement, the chief executive of ISD decided to initiate local trademark protection activities. Despite criminal attacks (including shots fired on the chief executive), a local ISD presence was established, and a permanent, official anti-plagiarism unit was created. As a consequence, the fake beverages were replaced with original products, and Thailand turned into ISD's highest-revenue market.

In many cases, the need to use local knowledge can be accomplished only by integrating local responsibilities within the organisation. For example, Nestlé implemented 16 regional trademark protection units that leverage local knowledge by developing—in close cooperation with the central unit—specific trademark protection measures for each region (cf. Keller 2015).

6.5.3   Channel Monitoring

Successful trademark protection requires detailed knowledge of the extent and nature of trademark piracy (i.e., which products, which distribution channels etc.). Monitoring the Internet as an important distribution channel is highly relevant in this context, because so many pirated goods are sold online (cf. Keller 2015). A broad channel monitoring strategy (e.g., market observation, targeted test purchases) can help to determine the nature and extent of the trademark piracy. Such monitoring is very relevant for companies, for two main reasons: First, if detailed knowledge about the extent of the trademark piracy is lacking, the relevance of trademark protection might be questioned. Investments in trademark protection efforts likely will be approved by management only if the economic threats of trademark piracy are substantial, realistic, and based in factual evidence (cf. Keller 2015). Second, information gleaned through channel monitoring is necessary to define appropriate trademark protection measures (cf. Keller 2015). Only if they know the exact extent and nature of trademark piracy, can owners select appropriate, effective legal and extra-legal measures to successfully protect their trademarks.

References

Baumgarth, C. (2004). *Markenpolitik: Markenwirkungen, Markenführung, Markenforschung.* Wiesbaden: Gabler.

Friese, J., Jung, U., Röhm, T., & Spettmann, R. (2006). Intellectual property: An underestimated and undermanaged asset? *Journal of Business Chemistry, 3*(1), 42–48.

Gefälschte Marken in China. (2015). *Wohnst du noch oder kopierst du schon?* http://www. sueddeutsche.de/wirtschaft/markenpiraterie-in-china-wohnst-du-noch-oder-kopierst-du-schon-1.1127270. Last visit: January 19, 2015.

Green, R. T., & Smith, T. (2002). Executive insights: Countering brand counterfeits. *Journal of International Marketing, 10*(4), 89–106.

Keller, C. (2015). *Identitätsbasierter Markenschutz – (Re-)Konzeptualisierung im Kontext der neuen Marken- und Produktpiraterie* (to date unpublished).

Markenverband. (2008). *Identitätsschutz.* Berlin.

OECD. (2008). *The Economic impact of counterfeiting and piracy.* Paris: OECD Publishing.

Schröder, H. (2005). Markenschutz als Aufgabe der Markenführung. In F.-R. Esch (Ed.), *Moderne Markenführung: Grundlagen, Innovative Ansätze, Praktische Umsetzungen* (pp. 351–377). Wiesbaden: Gabler.

Schröder, H., & Ahlert, D. (2004). Absicherung von Marketingstrategien durch das Marketing-Rechts-Management. In M. Bruhn (Ed.), *Handbuch Markenführung: Kompendium zum erfolgreichen Markenmanagement, Strategien, Instrumente, Erfahrungen* (pp. 2471–2500). Wiesbaden: Gabler.

Staake, T., & Fleisch, E. (2008). *Countering counterfeit trade—Illicit market insights, best practice strategies, and management tools.* Heidelberg: Springer.

International Identity-Based Brand Management

7

Contents

7.1 Standardisation Versus Differentiation in International Marketing 292
7.2 Important Influences of Consumer Behaviour on Brands in International Markets 293
    7.2.1 National Culture 293
    7.2.2 Stage of Economic Development 296
    7.2.3 Socio-Demographic Characteristics 297
    7.2.4 Brand Origin 297
7.3 Strategic and Operational Aspects of International Brand Management 299
    7.3.1 Timing of Market Entry 299
    7.3.2 Positioning Brands in an International Context 300
    7.3.3 International Brand Architecture 301
    7.3.4 Specifics of Internal Brand Management in an International Context 306
References 308

The internationalisation of brands is not a special phenomenon any more. Whether in the areas of procurement, production or sales, brands seldom operate exclusively in their home market; and even if they do, they still face international competitors and need to appeal to global audiences. Since the early 1990s, the volume of international networking has increased significantly, so that even small businesses distribute their brands in foreign markets. In particular, the so-called BRIC (Brazil, Russia, India and China) nations and Eastern European countries are regarded by many companies as a "lifeline" for growth, due to their massive and positive development in recent years (cf. IMF 2014).

On the basis of these developments, the current chapter seeks to answer several pressing questions:

© Springer Fachmedien Wiesbaden GmbH 2017
C. Burmann et al., *Identity-Based Brand Management*,
DOI 10.1007/978-3-658-13561-4_7

– What are the advantages and disadvantages of a standardised versus a differentiated marketing approach for brand management?
– Which changes in consumer behaviour can be identified in different countries? How do they determine the appropriate degree of differentiation?
– What are the implications for strategic and operational brand management when it comes to implementing a successful international marketing strategy?

7.1 Standardisation Versus Differentiation in International Marketing

If a brand is distributed in more than one country, it may either be fully standardised in all countries or a market-specific approach may be adopted to address high heterogeneity (i.e. differentiation). Standardisation is based on convergence theory as initially proposed by Levitt (1983), which states that globalisation (increasing international economic activity as a result of reduced trade restrictions) will lead **"towards a converging commonality"**, i.e. towards homogenisation of consumer behaviour, implying the international standardisation of brand management. Yet modern science and practice mostly refute convergence theory (e.g. Keegan and Green 2008). Although some cross-national consumption patterns and lifestyles show up in particular population groups, no general trend towards homogenisation of consumer behaviour exists (cf. Friedmann 2006).

This even applies to everyday goods. The former CEO of Henkel, Ulrich Lehner, illustrates this point by describing the different fragrances associated with cleanliness: German consumers associate cleanliness with a lemon scent, while Spanish consumers prefer the smell of chlorine. Another point in case is hair structure which differs between Chinese and German consumers, prompting the need for a functional adaptation of the shampoo produced by Henkel for these different markets (cf. Jensen and Schlitt 2002).

Compared with trading across Europe, brand management in China or India requires more adaptation because of the greater cultural and economic heterogeneity in these countries (cf. Cheon et al. 2007; Wang 2010). Even if consumer needs were completely aligned, brand management would have to be adapted to each country to reflect local characteristics (e.g. legal framework, geography, distribution system, competitive situation). Moreover, international brands often compete against local brands, which have very good knowledge of their domestic markets, stronger customer relationships and better local networking. These disadvantages for global players increase with their degree of standardisation. Therefore, extensively standardised international marketing, as recommended by Levitt, is possible or advisable only in very rare cases.

Yet many studies still acknowledge the positive effects of standardisation, especially due to cost advantages (cf. Walter 2004; Schwarz-Musch 2013; Fuchs and Unger 2014). Furthermore, global, extensively standardised brand management can target cosmopolitan, or "global-net", consumers (cf. Cavusgil et al. 2005) who are characterised by a high level of international mobility and networking (cf. Cannon and Yaprak 2002; Riefler et al. 2012; Jin et al. 2014).

The degree of standardisation in international marketing therefore must be evaluated not only from an internal efficiency perspective but also from an external market perspective. With extensive brand standardisation, strong brands can be created, likely producing even more positive effects than might result from the cost reduction realised through globalisation (cf. O'Donnell and Jeong 2000; Zou and Cavusgil 2002; Walter 2004; Yeniyurt et al. 2013). This statement continues to provoke critical debate (cf. Fuchs and Unger 2014) because there is no recognisable, fundamental image advantage of global brands. Rather, local brands often benefit from an image advantage in that they are well-known and popular in their homeland (cf. Schilke et al. 2009; Becker 2012). For example, the global brewery Anheuser-Busch InBev builds on its extensive brand portfolio, which includes global brands (e.g. Stella Artois, Budweiser) but also more than 250 "local champions" (e.g. Hasseröder, Löwenbräu, Diebels in Germany) (cf. Anheuser-Busch InBev 2013). These local champions have a strong, identifiable local origin and often are available only in limited regional markets (cf. Becker 2012).

7.2   Important Influences of Consumer Behaviour on Brands in International Markets

7.2.1   National Culture

Despite a general consensus that "culture is the most complex and powerful influence on consumer behaviour" (cf. Cleveland and Chang 2009), the term "culture" itself is subject to many definitions. According to Kroeber and Kluckhohn (1952), culture is a common stock of knowledge shared by a group of people, which differentiates this group from other groups. Müller and Gelbrich (2004) also note that culture affects individual behaviour and provides identity and coherence for society by constructing a common social reality.

Hofstede (1980, 1993), Hofstede and Hofstede (2009) approach the construct of culture with their **pyramid of mental programming** (see Fig. 7.1). They demonstrate that, beyond the individual personality dimension, there is an acquired cultural dimension which is group-specific and produces what the authors refer to as "collective mental programming". Culture thus is "the collective programming of the mind distinguishing the members of one group or category of people from others" (Hofstede 2006). This view classifies culture as an acquired, group-specific dimension that falls between inherited universal human nature and partly inherited, partly acquired individual personality. Human nature enables us to feel; culture determines how we deal with and express these feelings (cf. Vogelsang 1999).

To assess the influence of national culture on brand management, it is necessary to operationalise it first. While an abundance of approaches is available, the most common

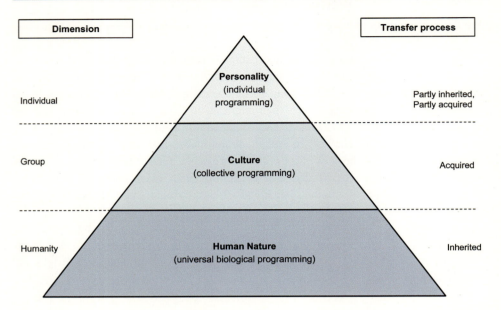

Fig. 7.1 The pyramid of mental programming. (Source: closely based on Hofstede and Hofstede 2009, p.4)

one is likely the model by Hofstede and Hofstede (2009), which operationalises culture on the basis of five dimensions (cf. Hofstede and Hofstede 2009):

1. **Individualism**, or the relationship between the individual and the collective, such as society. It defines the extent to which a culture grants priority to individual interests over collective interests.
2. **Power distance**, which refers to the relationship of the individual to authority. It indicates the extent to which an unequal distribution of power is accepted in a society, or whether a society is more "egalitarian", with a low power distance.
3. **Masculinity** describes the preference for heroism, achievement, material rewards for success and assertiveness, relative to femininity, which describes a preference for modesty, cooperation, quality of life and caring for the weak.
4. **Uncertainty avoidance** refers to a society's inherent effort to avoid uncertain, ambivalent situations.
5. **Long-term orientation** includes values such as a sense of tradition, power of endurance, perseverance or thrift.

Figure 7.2 depicts the five cultural dimensions as scored by respondents from Brazil, Germany, China, Russia and the United States. (Please note that for Russia there is no information for the long-term orientation dimension.)

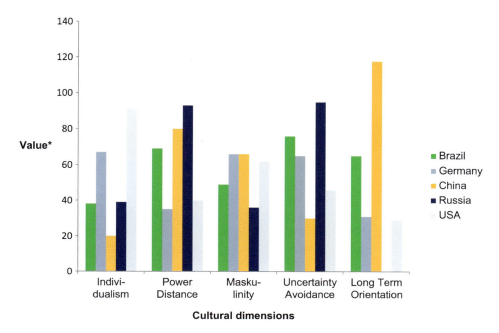

Cultural dimensions

* The higher the value of a cultural dimension, the stronger its expression.

Fig. 7.2 Hofstede's five cultural dimensions for Germany, China, Russia and the United States. (Source: by author, based on Hofstede 2001)

These five cultural dimensions affect all facets of social life. In addition to the differences, there are cultural similarities that can support some standardisation in international marketing. For example, in Germany, Great Britain, the United States and the Netherlands, power distance scores are nearly identical.

Foscht et al. (2008) demonstrated that national culture has a strong influence on brand perceptions. These authors analysed the brand perception of Red Bull in six countries (Germany, Great Britain, the Netherlands, Austria, Singapore, United States), noting that it is one of the most standardised brands of the world. Yet these authors also observed a significant difference in the evaluations of this brand's personality. In individualistic countries like the United States, it is success that shapes Red Bull's brand personality in a meaningful way. But in collectivist countries like Singapore, success has less influence on its brand personality. The authors reason that national culture thus influences the perceptions and evaluations even of consistent brand images, so that the aim of a worldwide brand image can be achieved only by internationally differentiated marketing that takes national culture into account.

In an international study on the automobile industry, Stolle (2013) also analysed the **effect of culture on brand perceptions by investigating the importance of five brand benefits** in relation to the five cultural dimensions (see Fig. 7.3). The economic utility

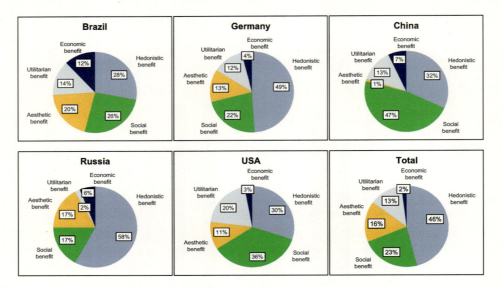

Fig. 7.3 Relevance of benefit dimensions across countries. (Source: closely based on Stolle 2013, p. 259)

of a brand has greater relevance in cultures with a comparatively strong long-term orientation (e.g. Brazil, China) than in cultures with a weak long-term orientation, likely because in the former cultures, values such as thrift are very important (cf. Knörle 2011).

As these studies show, the culturally different perception of brands limits brand standardisation. To achieve a cross-nationally consistent image, country-specific adaptations of brand management are necessary, which requires strategic flexibility (cf. Burmann 2002) and a strong knowledge of local culture. In the internationalisation process of brand management it therefore makes sense to enter culturally similar regions and countries as a first step.

7.2.2   Stage of Economic Development

The stage of economic development is reflected in macroeconomic indicators (e.g., gross domestic product (GDP) as an indicator of purchasing power, and the annual growth in GDP as an indicator of economic dynamics), which often serve as international segmentation criteria (cf. Zentes et al. 2010). Martinez and Haddock (2007) empirically verified a relationship between GDP per capita and the needs structure within a country. **With increasing purchasing power, economies pass through four stages of consumption**, which are aligned to Maslow's hierarchy of needs (cf. Maslow 1970). In an early development stage, consumers primarily struggle to survive. With increasing wealth, product quality and the satisfaction of needs become the main focus. The need for individualised products represents the final stage and is characteristic of consumers in highly developed economies (cf. Stolle 2013).

Roth (1995) derived similar results, empirically identifying an **effect of the stage of economic development on the success of brand strategies with different benefit options**. He demonstrated that a higher stage of economic development increases the success rate of brand strategies that are oriented towards non-functional benefit components. However, the assertion that non-functional benefit components are more important in highly developed countries should not be taken to mean that only functional benefit components are relevant in less developed countries. Consumers with low social status often try to gain an association with other, higher social groups by buying brands identified with them (cf. Han et al. 2010).

7.2.3   Socio-Demographic Characteristics

Socio-demographic characteristics, such as age, gender, income and educational background, drive consumer behaviour (cf. Trommsdorff 2009). A shift in the age pyramid (i.e. older age cohorts and population decline) can be observed in Western, industrialised nations, along with population growth in developing and emerging countries. Depending on a society's age pyramid, the benefits required from a brand differ. As Stolle (2013) demonstrated, **socio-demographic characteristics influence the relevance of five brand benefits for vehicle purchase decisions**. For example, for men, aesthetic benefits are significantly more important than they are for women. In accordance with Hsieh et al. (2004), Stolle has also shown that older people attach greater importance to economic benefits, whereas for younger people hedonic benefits are more important, especially when it comes to the pleasure of driving cars.

7.2.4   Brand Origin

A brand's origin is of central interest for international brand management. Claus Merbold, the former CEO of Siemens AG (who was responsible for the company's brand and image research), explains its relevance: "Every international brand needs an origin which reveals its national roots. Without attribution to a country or region, a brand cannot exist, in that it would lack substance and positioning. An international presence and a national context are not contradictions but rather premises for a successful brand policy" (cf. Merbold 1993).

From the German perspective, the seal "Made in Germany" is especially relevant. Its invention in the nineteenth century represented the birth of the so-called country-of-origin effect. On August 23, 1887, the British Parliament passed the "Merchandise Marks Act", requiring foreign producers to indicate the place of manufacture. With this regulation, the government sought to appeal to British national pride, in the hope that this would lead consumers to avoid German products and strengthen the British industry. However, in the same year, production conditions improved dramatically in

Germany, so that the label "Made in Germany" became a seal of high-quality products (cf. Hirschmann 1990). Today, many German companies integrate this seal in their marketing communication, in an effort to build a positive brand image. For example, the premium kitchen manufacturer Poggenpohl uses this seal to underline its expertise in manufacturing kitchens with perfect technology and high quality (cf. Maloney 2009). The Swatch ("Swiss Watch") brand successfully ties the Swiss tradition of producing accurate watches into its very name. In both cases, geographical origin serves as an indication of superior product quality.

Research regarding the country-of-origin (CoO) effect is prominent in international brand management (cf. Papadopoulos and Heslop 2003; Ahmed and d'Astous 2008). Since the early publications by Dichter (1962) and Schooler (1965), the influence of brand origin on brand images has been analysed in more than 1000 scientific contributions (including approximately 400 academic articles) (cf. Roth and Diamantopoulos 2009).

In 1996, Thakor and Kohli refined the CoO effect by introducing the **brand origin approach**, for two reasons. First, brands, not products, represent the relevant reference information for most consumers' purchasing behaviour. Second, it is the perceived, rather than the actual, origin that is relevant to consumers. Thus a key question centres on the "right" geographical reference for a brand. Traditional CoO research that only considers the country of production has limited value, due to globalisation trends and the relocation of production to low-wage countries. Brands such as Nike and Adidas are not perceived by buyers as Asian, even though almost all of their products are manufactured in Asia. Even the location of the corporate headquarters is rarely relevant for consumers. Although Ferrero's corporate headquarter is in Italy, the brands Kinderschokolade and Nutella are perceived as German. Becker (2012) showed that foreign brands may have problems with the consumers' identification of their geographical origins (cf. Becker 2012); only 46.9% of Indian respondents in his study identified the correct origin of foreign brands, whereas 91% correctly identified the origin of Indian brands.

Thakor and Kohli (1996) also argue that the actual origin is irrelevant because consumers associate a brand with a specific country, even if they know that the products offered by that brand are not produced there. Thus, there is no objective, formally correct origin for any brand; it is only important that the origin fits the identity of the brand. Häagen-Dazs is a good example: Reuben Mattus, living in New York and born in Poland, introduced the ice cream brand in the U.S. market in 1961. The brand name seeks to evoke the great Danish art of ice cream making to build a positive brand image, without having any factual origin in Denmark. In addition, Mattus added the outline of a map of Denmark to the company logo. Today, Häagen-Dazs enjoys a strong positioning worldwide as a premium ice cream brand (cf. Friederes 2006).

Economic research on the **influence of brand origins on purchase behaviour** mainly addresses three topics: **cognitive-functional aspects** of the brand origin ("I buy cars 'Made in Germany' because of the superior product quality!"), **affective non-functional aspects** of the brand origin ("I prefer Italian brands because I like Italy") and **normative aspects** ("I do not buy American brands because I am protesting against the data espionage by the U.S. government and the NSA") (cf. Obermüller and Spangenberg 1989; Verlegh and Steenkamp 1999).

According to a recent study spanning the automotive, mobile phone, life insurance, and beer industries, **a geographical brand origin can be a significant driver of brand image and purchasing behaviour** (cf. Becker 2012). In particular when assessing the utilitarian, aesthetic and hedonic benefits of a brand, consumers often turn to perceived brand origins. In addition to its effect on brand benefits, Becker (2012) also revealed a strong influence of brand origin on brand personality.

Whether the brand origin's influence is positive critically depends on the **authenticity of the connection between the brand's identity and its origin**. A brand positioning that emphasises its origin is recommended for brands with an identity that is strongly influenced by their geographical origin, such as watch brands that originate in Glashütte in Eastern Germany or champagne brands from the French Champagne region. In this case, geographical origin represents an essential characteristic of the brand identity and should be emphasised in all communication and considered in all key business decisions (cf. Schallehn et al. 2014).

With regard to standardisation questions, a brand origin reference must be consistent worldwide. This is also valid for internal audiences. The origin, as an essential characteristic of identity, is difficult to change, even over time. However, the intensity and the degree of detail with which the origin is communicated might need to be adapted and adjusted from country to country.

7.3   Strategic and Operational Aspects of International Brand Management

This section presents the most important decisions regarding standardised versus differentiated international brand management, including timing of market entry and positioning, as well as the appropriate design of the brand architecture. Finally, considering the importance of employees, this section will conclude with a discussion of internal brand management in an international context.

7.3.1   Timing of Market Entry

The timing of market entry is critical to market success (cf. Johnson and Tellis 2008), and two timing strategies can be differentiated: **country-specific and transnational**. With a country-specific timing strategy, the objective is to determine the best time for a market entry, whereas a transnational timing strategy seeks to determine how many countries to enter and when (cf. Meffert et al. 2010). With regard to the period of market entry, two strategic options are available: a waterfall or a sprinkler strategy (cf. Kreutzer 1989; Perlitz 2004).

A **sprinkler strategy** implies simultaneous entry into several national markets, which tends to require a standardised brand management. This strategy offers economies of scale and it also spreads market entry risks over a larger number of national markets. In contrast, in a **waterfall strategy**, the firm enters various national markets slowly and step-by-step. This strategy requires detailed advance information and a brand management approach that is adapted to the characteristics of each country. With a waterfall strategy, important country markets might get neglected or developed by competitors (cf. Meffert and Pues 2002). In a study of the automotive industry, Reibstein (2015) found that the sequence of market entries depends less on geographical distance than on the extent of cultural distance from the home market.

Regarding the timing of market entry, we can also distinguish between a pioneer and a follower strategy. In many cases, pioneers pursue a waterfall strategy, whereas followers adopt a sprinkler strategy (cf. Meffert and Pues 2002).

Pioneers benefit from a first-mover advantage, which helps them build long-term competitive advantages and defend those advantages over time. The advantages are based mainly on their early access to resources, the acquisition of local market development expertise and local relations, and the ability to skim government investment incentives (cf. Pan and Chi 1999; Johnson and Tellis 2008). **Followers**, instead, enjoy learning effects from the pioneers' efforts, so they can avoid their mistakes and imitate successful products. Follower behaviour also can improve return on investment because the pioneers have already developed the market (e.g. infrastructure). Reduced government bureaucracy and lower market entry barriers also benefit followers (cf. Holtbrügge and Puck 2008). Finally, pioneers must defend their first-mover advantages against followers in the long term, whether by establishing formal trademark protection measures (cf. Chap. 6) or difficult-to-imitate brand-customer relationships (brand attachment).

7.3.2   Positioning Brands in an International Context

To determine the degree of adaptation in international brand positioning, it is necessary to classify brand identities according to their core and extended characteristics. Strebinger (2008) stresses, in particular, the need for local enrichment of core characteristics with more extended characteristics. For the automotive industry, for example, the basic dimensions of brand positioning are the same worldwide: product quality, sheer driving pleasure, prestige, and so on. However, the actual importance of these dimensions differs widely from country to country (cf. Stolle 2013). In the United States, active and passive safety options represent evidence of brand quality; in China and Thailand, they increase the brand's prestige.

Chernatony et al. (1995) also note that consumers accept local adaptations, e.g. in communication or product policy, as long as the core characteristics of the brand remain identical. Using the example of Philadelphia cream cheese, Strebinger (2008) argues similarly: All over the world Philadelphia stands for a particularly rich, creamy consistence, a "heavenly time-out", designed especially for female consumers. These core characteristics are enriched in specific countries by extended features. The transnational consistency of the core characteristics protects the brand from dilution, which would otherwise occur by changing the extended characteristics. While Philadelphia is traditionally used as a spread in Germany, in Italy it is served mainly as an appetizer with vegetables. In North America, Philadelphia is an all-round ingredient for cooking and baking. Accordingly, the brand is offered in a very purist form in Italy, whereas there are many different flavours in Germany. Also, the package types differ clearly and are adapted to the local usage preferences. In most countries an angel in heaven is used as the communicative theme, with the angels varying according to local expectations (e.g. brunette angels in Mexico, maternal angels in Spain). Only in a few countries, the motif of the angel is not used (e.g. in the Arab world).

To achieve an ideal level of standardisation, brand managers also need to develop **central guidelines for all country markets** to define the scope of action. For example, "valuable", "innovative" and "responsible" are the core identity characteristics of the VW brand, phrased in English for all markets worldwide. In specific countries, these core characteristics are supplemented by extended characteristics. In China, the core characteristic "responsible" is supplemented by the extended characteristic "environmentally friendly". Another core characteristic of VW's brand identity is the slogan "Das Auto", written in German in every country. This standardisation emphasises the brand's German origin, which represents another core identity characteristic. Thus its German origin was a focus of communications during the launch of VW Polo in India, when a nationwide campaign referred to "German Engineering. Made for India" to highlight both its German origin and its adaptations to the Indian market (cf. Chabra 2010).

7.3.3   International Brand Architecture

The **brand architecture** of a company is laid out in three dimensions: (1) a vertical dimension that reflects the degree of brand integration in the hierarchical organisation and across brand levels, (2) a horizontal dimension related to the number of brands in a market segment and (3) a lateral dimension pertaining to the appearance of the brand relative to the brands of retailers (trade brands) and competitors. In an international context, though, these three dimensions are not sufficient and need to be supplemented by a further dimension (cf. Douglas and Craig and Nijssen 2001), that is, whether the brands of the company have a local, international (two or more national markets), supranational (transnational but not global area, such as the EU or NAFTA), or global focus (see Fig. 7.4).

For example, a company with a "Branded House" architecture may use a global corporate brand (global standardisation), or it might sell its global corporate brand in some countries, while leveraging a local business unit brand in other countries. Aldi Süd operates under its own brand name in its home market of Germany, as well as in Australia,

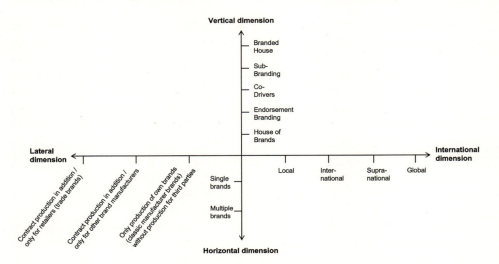

Fig. 7.4 Dimensions of brand architecture in international marketing. (Source: Burmann and Kanitz 2010, p. 41.)

Great Britain, Greece, Ireland, Slovenia, Switzerland, Hungary and the United States. However, in the Austrian market, Aldi Süd is represented by the brand Hofer. As this example shows, companies can decide whether to build a **standardised worldwide brand architecture** or adapt to the national context.

The following section focuses specifically on the international dimension of brand architecture. Subsequently, we analyse the other three dimensions, taking the degree of standardisation of international marketing into account.

7.3.3.1 International Dimension of Brand Architecture

The **four options for designing the dimensions of an international brand architecture** reflect the basic orientation of the management. Schuiling and Kapferer (2004) define **local brands** as those brands that exist only nationally (e.g. in Germany, BILD or congstar) or in a limited geographical distribution area within a country, such as a city or region (e.g. Sion Kölsch in Cologne; Dodenhof in Northern Germany). If a brand appears in at least two country markets, standardised according to the home market, it is an **international brand**. For example, Mirácoli is primarily distributed in Germany, but it is also available in Austria. For **global brands**, managers try to appeal to a worldwide, homogeneous target group with a standardised brand. If the standardisation is based not on the world market but on a transnational space (e.g. NAFTA, EU), it is a **supranational brand**. In this case, the transnational region appears homogeneous and the standardisation is aimed at its specific needs (see Table 7.1).

Levitt (1983) considered global brands a "recipe for success", but a brand portfolio that consists of just a few global brands will not be successful per se, according to the empirical data provided by Morgan and Rego (2009). As these authors show, both a

Table 7.1 How to distinguish local, international, supranational and global brands

Distribution	Target group
Local brand	Consumers of a city, an area within a country or an entire country
International brand	Primarily consumers of the domestic market, as well as consumers in a few, very similar foreign markets
Supranational brand	Consumers of a clearly defined, transnational space (e.g. NAFTA, EU, ASEAN)
Global brand	Worldwide, homogeneous group of consumers

closely based on Meffert et al. (2010, p. 150)

strategy that includes local brands and one that concentrates on a few global brands can be highly successful. Kapferer (2002, 2005) also does not consider global brand management more successful per se; rather, he predicts the **renaissance of local brands** because their culture-specific positioning and strong connection to local customers leads to superior consumer attachment to these brands. This positioning also relies on the assumption that brands must take the particular, country-specific conditions into account in order to establish themselves successfully (cf. Waltermann 1989)—an assumption that reflects consumer behaviour in the twenty-first century. That is, modern consumers exhibit increased knowledge, competence and self-confidence (mainly due to Internet availability and smartphone penetration), together with demands for sustainability, authenticity and region-specific brands (cf. Rennhak 2013). Thus, 64% of respondents to a survey stated that the notion of home has become more important in the current era of globalisation (cf. Kurbjuweit 2012).

The evaluation of the advantages and disadvantages of local and global brands in Table 7.2 includes only these two options (i.e. not international and supranational brands, which are hybrid types of the two extremes) and is based on the following criteria:

– **Realisation of differentiation advantages**: Does the selected architecture facilitate differentiated marketing? Which architecture option offers more potential for adjusting the brand positioning?
– **Realisation of standardisation advantages**: To what extent can cost savings be realised through economies of scale or scope?
– **Resource requirements**: What resources (financial and personnel) are required to implement the selected architecture?
– **Requirements for replication competence**: What are the requirements of the selected architecture, in terms of the company's ability to transfer its internally existing resources and competences in a fast, cost-efficient and effective way to a new country market (cf. Burmann 2002)?
– **Requirements for reconfiguration competence**: Does the selected architecture make high demands on the company regarding the identification and acquisition of new, country-specific resources and competences?

Table 7.2 Comparative overview of local and global brands

Evaluation criteria	Options of architecture	
	Local brand	Global brand
Realisation of differentiation benefits	High	Low
Realisation of standardisation benefits	Low	High
Resource requirements	High	Medium
Requirements for replication competence	Low	High
Requirements for reconfiguration competence	High	Low

Based on Meffert et al. (2010, p. 153)

As Table 7.2 clearly shows, the standardisation advantages of global brands are mirrored by the differentiation advantages of local brands (Strebinger 2008).

7.3.3.2 Vertical, Horizontal and Lateral Dimensions of Brand Architecture in an International Context

If organised as a Branded House, a company works in any particular national market exclusively with the corporate brand. Therefore, this architecture is suitable only if a high degree of worldwide standardisation seems realistic, with a low risk of negative feedback (for details regarding feedback in international marketing, cf. Backhaus and Voeth 2010). A Branded House architecture usually accompanies a global brand strategy.

In contrast, a "House of Brands" architecture is characterised by minimal vertical integration, so that consumers do not notice the corporate brand and instead notice and are loyal to business unit or product brands. Unlike the branded house architecture, this format allows for maximal local adaptation; in extreme cases, local brands can be introduced in each country market, which limits the amount of feedback. In an international context, this architecture is prominently represented by Anheuser-Busch InBev (see Table 7.3).

Regarding the **horizontal dimension of brand architecture** in an international context there are certain specific characteristics. For example, single-brand strategies are particularly useful for smaller country markets, whereas multi-brand strategies are beneficial in large national markets. For multi-brand strategies, the parallel use of local and global brands makes sense to satisfy consumers' different benefit requirements.

The **lateral dimension** should be determined individually for each country. For example, the importance of trade brands depends on the distribution of power in the relationship between manufacturers and retail organisations in the respective countries, as well as on the distribution structures. With strong retail organisations, manufacturers of weaker brands often have no choice but to cooperate with the retailers and produce their trade brands (cf. Koppe 2003; Sattler and Völckner 2007). Accordingly, the prevalence of trade brands is highest in Switzerland, the United Kingdom and Spain (cf. Planet Retail 2012). In these highly concentrated markets, strong retail chains dominate, with market shares well above 10%, such as Tesco in the United Kingdom (see Fig. 7.5).

Table 7.3 House of brands architecture, exemplified by Anheuser-Busch InBev

International option for brand architecture	Selected examples
Local brands	Jupiler (Belgium), Harbin (North China), Skol (Brazil)
International brands	Beck's, Leffe, Hoergaarden
Global brands	Budweiser, Corona, Stella Artois

Based on Anheuser-Busch InBev (2013, p. 61)

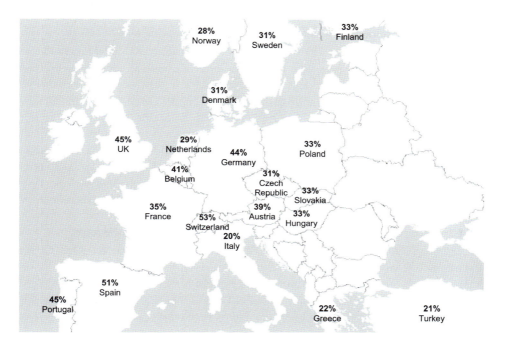

Fig. 7.5 Prevalence of trade brands (in share of turnover of all products in food retailing) in Europe. (Source: PLMA 2014)

In contrast, trade brands are relatively rare in developing and emerging countries. For example, the total proportion of trade brands in China, India and Vietnam was only approximately 10% in 2012 (cf. Planet Retail 2012). Their minimal importance in developing economies can largely be attributed to the high fragmentation of the local retail landscape. These markets are dominated not by a few large retail chains but by countless small trading firms that have a correspondingly low position of power (cf. World Economic Forum 2009). Manufacturers thus have little need to produce trade brands for retailers. In addition, consumers exhibit weak confidence in and little loyalty towards brands (cf. Planet Retail 2012). Therefore, establishing successful trade brands in developing markets will require clear communication about their positioning. A good example is Walmart's introduction of its Great Value brand in the Indian market (cf. Planet Retail 2012). In this case, the product packaging and related promotional activities highlighted selected national flags and the slogan "Trusted by millions like you the world over" in an attempt to communicate the brand's independence, its international presence and—closely linked with that—its trustworthiness. Thus, Indian consumers perceived Great Value as trustworthy and of high quality, "despite" its connection to a global company.

7.3.4   Specifics of Internal Brand Management in an International Context

Many international brand management strategies fail during implementation. A key prerequisite is employee support. Therefore, in an international context, internal brand management must be assigned very high priority. In line with internal, identity-based brand management, three areas can be identified, along with the influences imposed on them by national circumstances. First, employees in different cultures vary in their fundamental willingness to build commitment to a brand. Second, a specific brand-related style of leadership cannot be applied with equal success in every country, as the cultural dimension of power distance determines the employees' expectations regarding management style and thus their acceptance of different styles. Third, the local language and culture influence perceptions and evaluations of internal brand-related communication messages. Therefore, internal brand communication also requires country-specific adaptations.

7.3.4.1 Influence of Culture on the Strength of Brand Commitment

The extent of brand commitment exhibited by employees depends on three cultural dimensions (cf. Hofstede 2001; Felfe et al. 2006). First, employees feel more closely connected to the company and its brands and express higher normative commitment in cultures characterised by high power distance. Second, uncertainty avoidance strengthens employee commitment to the company and its brands because employees are afraid of change. Third, in collectivist cultures, brand commitment is higher than in individualistic cultures because the well-being of the group is more important in collectivist cultures, whereas people in individualistic cultures strive for self-fulfilment (cf. Clugston et al. 2000; Felfe et al. 2008). Thus, the key question for management is how to adapt their internal brand management to national traits as a means to achieve high brand commitment in different country markets. Brand-oriented leadership and internal brand communication are two important elements in this effort, as we will discuss next.

7.3.4.2 Influence of Culture on Brand-Oriented Leadership

Leadership demands social interaction (cf. Jung 2008). If social interaction involves an intercultural team, the complexity of leadership increases significantly, in line with the various individual cultural value orientations. People generally assume that others share their same cultural values and norms, so they anticipate behaviours that correspond to their own perceptions (cf. Loth 2007). Therefore, conflicts are common in intercultural

Table 7.4 Typical leadership styles in Europe

Leadership from the front (e.g. UK)	Leadership by consensus (e.g. Sweden, Finland)
• Emphasis on characteristics of the leader for the company's success • Result-oriented pragmatism • Contempt for rules and routines	• Boosting the team spirit • Open dialogue with employees • Participation of employees in decisions • Emphasis on detailed organising
Leadership from a distance (e.g. France)	Leadership towards a common goal (e.g. Austria, Germany)
• Strategic, conceptual thinking • Lack of discipline in the implementation of decisions • Inadequate communication with employees • Striving for independence	• Appreciation of expertise • Authoritarian leadership • Emphasis on rules, routines and controls

closely based on Kühlmann (2008, p. 43)

teams (cf. Brett et al. 2006). Weibler et al. (2000) showed that brand commitment among employees is higher when the culturally determined behaviours of leaders and employees are in agreement. Preferred leadership styles may differ substantially between various countries. Even in neighbouring countries, cultural influences cause significant differences in leadership style (see Table 7.4). For example, a consensus-oriented leadership style is popular in Nordic countries, but the high power distance in France means that a distant, hierarchical leadership style is preferred there.

On the whole, the culture and the resulting values of individual employees vary worldwide. The dimensions of collectivism and power distance exert a particularly strong influence on the employees' acceptance of management tools. In collectivist cultures, brand-oriented management should be implemented mainly through group events (e.g. festivals, family days), with an emphasis on common goals. Individual rewards (e.g. direct assessment, remuneration, promotion) should instead be prominent in individualistic cultures. In cultures with low power distance, employees prefer a cooperative leadership style. In cultures with high power distance, an authoritarian or paternalistic management style instead makes sense. Therefore, transnational standardisation in internal brand management efforts is very difficult.

7.3.4.3 Influence of Language and Culture on Internal Brand Communication

Internal brand communication aims to convey a consistent brand identity to all employees, which is very challenging in an international context. Thus, implementing a consistent brand identity requires extensive, uniform, employee-directed communication combined with a similar corporate culture worldwide (cf. Bruhn 2005). National languages and cultures, though, remain prominent barriers to internationally standardised internal brand communication.

Therefore, internationally oriented internal brand communication must first reflect the local language. This entails more than a mere translation of messages. It demands the in-depth consideration of national language specificities. Culture also has a decisive influ-ence on perceptions of brand communication. In an internal brand management context, brand messages will be perceived and interpreted differently in different cultures (cf. Meffert et al. 2010).

The specific design of internationally oriented internal brand communication always depends on the particular situation of the company. For example, IKEA communicates in a total of 15 languages, but Aventis (chemicals and pharmaceuticals) uses only 3. This difference stems from the heterogeneous qualifications required of their employees and the stronger regional bonds of the furniture company (cf. Bruhn 2005). As another exam-ple, in 2002 Henkel created a corporate anthem, entitled "We together", as part of its internal communication strategy, designed to strengthen its employees' sense of commu-nity and increase their identification with the company (cf. Schmidt 2007). Originally written in German, the anthem is now available in an international and several local ver-sions. The different versions account for particularities of local languages and country-specific popular music genres.

Just as in the external context, internal leadership also demands local adaptations. Only if employee behaviours and the brand promise match, can a strong brand be built.

References

Ahmed, S. A., & d'Astous, A. (2008). Antecedents, moderators and dimensions of country-of-ori-gin evaluations. *International Marketing Review, 25*(1), 75–106.

Anheuser-Busch InBev. (2013). Annual Report. http://www.ab-inbev.com/content/dam/univer-saltemplate/abinbev/pdf/media/annual-report/ABI_AR13_EN_Full.pdf. Last visit: 12. January 2015.

Backhaus, K., & Voeth, M. (2010). *Internationales marketing*. Stuttgart: Schäffer-Poeschel.

Becker, C. (2012). *Einfluss der räumlichen Markenherkunft auf das Markenimage: Kausalana-lytische Untersuchung am Beispiel Indiens*. Wiesbaden: Springer Gabler.

Brett, J., Behfar, K., & Kern, M. C. (2006). Managing multicultural teams. *Harvard Business Review, 11*, 84–91.

Bruhn, M. (2005). *Unternehmens- und Marketingkommunikation*. München: Vahlen.

Burmann, C. (2002). *Strategische Flexibilität und Strategiewechsel als Determinanten des Unternehmenswertes*. Wiesbaden: Dt. Univ.-Verlag.

Burmann, C., Halaszovich, T., & Wang, X. (2015). *Identitätsbasierte Markenführung*. Shanghai: Shanghai University of Finance and Economics Press. (in Chinese language).

Burmann, C., & Kanitz, C. (2010*). Gestaltung der Markenarchitektur – Stand der Forschung und Entwicklung eines Managementprozesses*. Working paper No. 45 of the Chair in innovative Brand Management (LiM) of the University of Bremen.

Cannon, H. M., & Yaprak, A. (2002). Will the real-world citizen please stand up! The many faces of cosmopolitan consumer behavior. *Journal of International Marketing, 10*(4), 30–52.

Cavusgil, S. T., Deligonul, S., & Yaprak, A. (2005). International marketing as a field of study: A critical assessment of earlier development and a look forward. *Journal of International Marketing, 13*(4), 1–27.

Chabra, P. (2010). "V"owing to "W"in!, in: 4Ps. *Business and Marketing, 5*(2), 32–33.

Cheon, H. J., Cho, C.-H., & Sutherland, J. (2007). A meta-analysis of studies on the determinants of standardization and localization of international marketing and advertising strategies. *Journal of International Consumer Marketing, 19*(4), 109–147.

Cleveland, M., & Chang, W. (2009). Migration and materialism: The roles of ethnic identity, religiosity, and generation. *Journal of Business Research, 62*(10), 963–971.

Clugston, M., Howell, J. P., & Dorfman, P. W. (2000). Does cultural socialization predict multiple bases and foci of commitment? *Journal of Management, 26*(1), 5–30.

de Chernatony, L., Halliburton, C., & Bernath, R. (1995). International branding: demand- or supply-driven opportunity? *International Marketing Review, 12*(2), 9–21.

Dichter, E. (1962). The world customer. *Harvard Business Review, 40*(4), 113.

Douglas, S. P., Craig, C. S., & Nijssen, E. J. (2001). Integrating branding strategy across markets: building international brand architecture. *Journal of International Marketing, 9*(2), 97–114.

Felfe, J., Schmook, R., & Six, B. (2006). Die Bedeutung kultureller Wertorientierungen für das Commitment gegenüber der Organisation, dem Vorgesetzten, der Arbeitsgruppe und der eigenen Karriere. *Zeitschrift für Personalpsychologie, 5*(3), 94–107.

Felfe, J., Yan, W., & Six, B. (2008). The impact of individual collectivism on commitment and its influence on organizational citizenship behaviour and turnover in three countries. *International Journal of Cross Cultural Management, 8*(2), 211–237.

Foscht, T., Maloles, C., Swoboda, B., Morschett, D., & Sinha, I. (2008). The impact of culture on brand perceptions: A six-nation study. *Journal of Product & Brand Management, 17*(3), 131–142.

Friederes, G. (2006). Country-of-Origin-Strategien in der Markenführung. In A. Strebinger, W. Mayerhofer, & H. Kurz (Eds.), *Werbe- und Markenforschung: Meilensteine - State of the Art – Perspektiven* (pp. 109–132). Wiesbaden: Gabler.

Friedmann, T. L. (2006). *Die Welt ist flach.* Frankfurt am Main: Suhrkamp.

Fuchs, W., & Unger, F. (2014). *Management der Marketing-Kommunikation.* Berlin u.a.: Springer.

Han, Y. J., Nunes, J. C., & Drèze, X. (2010, July). Signaling status with luxury goos: the role of brand prominence. *Journal of Marketing, 74*, 15–30.

Hirschmann, R. G. (1990). Made in Germany: Rolle und Bedeutung aus deutscher Sicht. In W. Bungard (Ed.), *Dokumenation Made in Germany: Deutsche Qualität auf dem Prüfstand* (pp. 7–16). Mannheim: Ehrenhof.

Hofstede, G. (1980). Culture's consequences: International differences in work-related values. *Nr. 5 der Schriftenreihe "Cross-cultural research and methodology series"*, Beverly Hills.

Hofstede, G. (1993). *Interkulturelle Zusammenarbeit.* Wiesbaden: Gabler.

Hofstede, G. (2001). *Culture´s consequences: Comparing values, behaviors, institutions, and organizations across nations.* Thousand Oaks: Sage Publications.

Hofstede, G. (2006). *Lokales Denken, globales Handeln: Interkulturelle Zusammenarbeit und globales Management.* München: DTV.

Hofstede, G., & Hofstede, G. J. (2009). *Lokales Denken, globales Handeln. Interkulturelle Zusammenarbeit und globales Management*, 4. Aufl. München: DTV.

Holtbrügge, D., & Puck, J. F. (2008). *Geschäftserfolg in China – Strategien für den größten Markt der Welt.* Heidelberg: Springer.

Hsieh, M.-H., Pan, S.-L., & Setiono, R. (2004). Product-, corporate-, and country-image dimensions and purchase behavior: A multicountry analysis. *Journal of the Academy of Marketing Science, 32*(3), 251–270.

IMF, (2014). *World Economic Outlook (WEO)*. International Monetary Fund.

Jensen, S., & Schlitt, P. (2002). Unternehmen Henkel: "Wir haben keine Eille". *Managermagazin, 10*, 136–140.

Jin, Z., Lynch, R., Attia, S., Chansarkar, B., Gülsoy, T., Lapoule, P., et al. (2014). The relationship between consumer ethnocentrism, cosmopolitanism and product country image among younger generation consumers: The moderating role of country development status. *International Business Review, 24*(3), 380–393.

Johnson, J., & Tellis, G. J. (2008, May). Drivers of success for market entry into China and India. *Journal of Marketing, 72*, 1–13.

Jung, H. (2008). *Personalwirtschaft* (8th ed.). München: Oldenbourg.

Kapferer, J.-N. (2002). Is there really no hope for local brands? *Journal of Brand Management, 9*(3), 163–170.

Kapferer, J.-N. (2005). The post-global brand. *Journal of Brand Management, 12*(5), 319–324.

Keegan, W. J., & Green, M. C. (2008). *Globale Marketing*. New Jersey: Upper Saddle River.

Knörle, C. (2011). *Markenloyalität in China: Kulturelle und markenbeziehungstheoretische Determinanten*. Berlin: Logos-Verlag.

Koppe, P. (2003). *Handelsmarken und Markenartikel: Wahrnehmungsunterschiede aus Sicht der Marktteilnehmer*. Wien: Service-Fachverlag.

Kreutzer, R. (1989). Markenstrategien im länderübergreifenden Marketing. *Markenartikel, 11*, 569–572.

Kroeber, A. L., & Kluckhohn, C. (1952). Culture: A critical review of concepts and definitions. Harvard University Peabody Museum of American Archeology and Ethnology Papers, 47(1).

Kühlmann, T. (2008). *Internationale Mitarbeiterführung*. Stuttgart: Kohlhammer.

Kurbjuweit, D. (2012). Mein Herz hüpft *Der Spiegel, 15*, 60–69.

Levitt, T. (1983). The globalization of markets. *Harvard Business Review, 61*(6), 92–102.

Loth, D. (2007). Missverständnisse erkennen. *Personal, 6*, 34–36.

Maloney, P. (2009). Poggenpohl - Eine Luxusmarke Made in Germany. *OSCAR.trends*, 1.

Martinez, A., & Haddock, R. (2007). The flatbread factor. In Booz Allen Hamilton. (Ed.), *Strategy + business* (No. 46). http://www.strategy-business.com. Last visit: 24 June 2009.

Maslow, A. H. (1970). *Motivation and personality* (2nd ed.). New York: Harper & Row.

Meffert, H., Burmann, C., & Becker, C. (2010). *Internationales Marketing-Management: Ein marktorientierter Ansatz*. Stuttgart.

Meffert, H., & Pues, C. (2002). Timingstrategien des internationalen Markteintritts. In K. Macharzina (Ed.), *Handbuch Internationales Management* (pp. 253–266). Wiesbaden: Gabler.

Merbold, C. (1993). *Zur Funktion der Marke. Markenartikel, 12*, 578–580.

Morgan, N. A., & Rego, L. L. (2009). Brand portfolio strategy and firm performance. *Journal of Marketing, 73*(1), 59–74.

Müller, S., & Gelbrich, K. (2004). *Interkulturelles Marketing*. München: Vahlen.

O'Donnell, S., & Jeong, I. (2000). Marketing standardization with global industries. *International Marketing Review, 17*(1), 19–33.

Obermüller, C., & Spangenberg, E. (1989). Exploring the effect of country-of-origin labels: An information processing framework. *Advances in Consumer Research, 16*, 454–459.

Pan, Y., & Chi, P. S. K. (1999). financial performance and survival of multinational corporations in China. *Strategic Management Journal, 20*(4), 359–374.

Papadopoulus, N., & Heslop, L. (2003). Country equity and product-country images: State of the art in research and implications. In S. Jain (Ed.), *Handbook of Research in International Marketing* (pp. 402–433). Northampton: Edward Elgar.

Perlitz, M. (2004). *Internationales Management*. Berlin: Ullstein.

Planet Retail. (2012). Building private label trust in emerging markets. http://www1.planetretail. net/news-and-events/rob-gregory/blogs/building-private-label-trust-emerging-markets.   Last visit: 16 Jan 2015.

PLMA. (2014). Handelsmarken heute. http://www.plmainternational.com/de/industry-news/private-label-today. Last visit: 12 Jan 2015.

Reibstein, T. (2015). *Erfolgsfaktoren internationaler Marktbearbeitungsstrategien in der Automobilindustrie – Eine Historieninventur am Beispiel der Marke Volkswagen,* to date unpublished dissertation.

Rennhak, C. (2013). Konsistent, hybrid, multioptional oder paradox? – Einsichten über den Konsumenten von heute. In M. Halfmann (Ed.), *Zielgruppen im Konsumentenmarketing: Segmentierungsansätze – Trends – Umsetzung* (pp. 177–186). Wiesbaden: Springer Fachmedien.

Riefler, P., Diamantopoulos, A., & Siguaw, J. A. (2012). Cosmopolitan consumers as a target group for segmentation. *Journal of International Business Studies 43*, 285–305.

Roth, M. S. (1995). The effects of culture and socioeconomics on the performance of global brand image strategies. *Journal of Marketing Research, 32*(2), 163–175.

Roth, K. P., & Diamantopoulos, A. (2009). Advancing the country image construct. *Journal of Business Research, 62*(7), 726–740.

Sattler, H., & Völckner, F. (2007). *Markenpolitik.* Stuttgart: Kohlhammer.

Schallehn, M., Burmann, C., & Riley, N. (2014). Brand authenticity: Model development and empirical testing. *Journal of Product & Brand Management, 23*(3), 192–199.

Schilke, O., Reimann, M., & Thomas, J. S. (2009). When does international marketing standardization matter to firm performance? *Journal of International Marketing, 17*(4), 24–46.

Schmidt, H. J. (2007). *Internal Branding: Wie Sie Ihre Mitarbeiter zu Markenbotschaftern machen.* Wiesbaden: Gabler.

Schooler, R. D. (1965). Product bias in the central american common market. *Journal of Marketing Research, 2*(4), 394–397.

Schuiling, I., & Kapferer, J.-N. (2004). Executive insights: Real differences between local and international brands: Strategic implications for international marketers. *Journal of International Marketing, 12*(4), 97–112.

Schwarz-Musch, A. (2013). Das Marketingkonzept im internationalen Umfeld. In D. Sternad, M. Höfferer, M & G. Haber (Eds.), *Grundlagen Export und Internationalisierung,* S. (pp. 111–127). Wiesbaden: Springer Gabler.

Stolle, W. (2013). *Global Brand Management: Eine konzeptionell-empirische Analyse von Autombil-Markenimages in Brasilien, China, Deutschland, Russland und den USA.* Wiesbaden: Springer Gabler.

Strebinger, A. (2008). *Markenarchitektur – Strategien zwischen Einzel- und Dachmarke sowie lokaler und globaler Marke.* Wiesbaden: Gabler.

Thakor, M. V., & Kohli, C. S. (1996). Brand origin: Conceptualization and review. *The Journal of Consumer Marketing, 13*(3), 27–42.

Trommsdorff, V. (2009). *Konsumentenverhalten* (7th ed.). Stuttgart: Kohlhammer.

Verlegh, P. W. J., & Steenkamp, J.-B. E. M. (1999). A review and meta-analysis of country-of-origin research. *Journal of Economic Psychology, 20*(5), 521–546.

Vogelsang, S. (1999). *Der Einfluss der Kultur auf die Produktgestaltung.* Köln: Fördergesellschaft Prod.-Marketing.

Walter, N. (2004). *Standardisierung des europäischen Nahrungsmittel-Marketing: eine Kausalanalyse der Determinanten und der Erfolgswirkungen einer Standardisierung des Marketing-Programms und -Managements am Beispiel der europäischen Nahrungsmittelindustrie.* München: Rainer Hampp Verlag.

Waltermann, B. (1989). *Internationale Markenpolitik und Produktpositionierung – marken-politische Entscheidungen im europäischen Automobilmarkt.* Wien: Service-Fachverlag.

Wang, J. (2010). *Brand new China: Advertising, media, and commercial culture.* Cambridge u.a.: Harvard University Press.

Weibler, J., Brodbeck, F., Szabo, E., Reber, G., Wunderer, R., & Moosmann, O. (2000). Führung in kulturverwandten Regionen: Gemeinsamkeiten und Unterschiede bei Führungsidealen in Deutschland, Österreich und der Schweiz. *Die Betriebswirtschaft, 5,* 588–606.

World Economic Forum. (2009). The next billions: Unleashing business potential in untapped markets. http://www.bcg.com. Last visit: 24 June 2009.

Yeniyurt, S., Henke, J. W., Jr., & Cavusgil, E. (2013). Integrating global and local procurement for superior supplier working relations. *International Business Review, 22*(2), 351–362.

Zentes, J., Swoboda, B., & Schramm-Klein, H. (2010). *Internationales Marketing.* München: Vahlen.

Zou, S., & Cavusgil, S. T. (2002). The GMS: A broad conceptualization of global marketing strategy and its effect on firm performance. *Journal of Marketing, 66*(4), 40–56.

Index

A

Accidental characteristics, 37
Actively accepting users, 199
Actively reading users, 199
Actively seeking users, 199
Authenticity, 218

B

Behaviour-related brand objectives, 102
Blogs, 208
Brand
   global, 302
   international, 302
   local, 302
   supranational, 302
Brand architecture, 122, 301
Brand Assessment System (BASS), 257
Brand Asset Valuator, 258
Brand attachment, 102
Brand attributes, 58
Brand authenticity, 76
Brand awareness, 29, 57, 102, 241
Brand behaviour, 28, 109
Brand benefit, 29, 58
Brand budgeting, 162
Brand citizenship behaviour, 96, 175, 270
Brand commitment, 98, 175, 270
Brand communication
   external, 183
   internal, 180
   internal (cascade), 182
   internal (central), 181
   internal (lateral), 182
Brand communication policy, 194

Brand compliance, 96
Brand consolidation, 150
Brand controlling, 234
Brand-customer relationship, 37
Brand definition, 242
Brand development, 96, 97
Brand distribution policy, 191
Branded house, 125
Brand endorsement, 96
Brand equity, 93, 235, 271
   customer-based, 255
Brand Equity Meter, 263
Brand evolution, 140
Brand experience, 28, 109, 216
   affective experiences, 217
   behavioural experiences, 217
   cognitive experiences, 217
   sensory experiences, 216
   social experiences, 217
Brand extension, 154
Brand familiarity, 241
Brand-Generated Content (BGC), 202
Brand hierarchy, 122
Brand identity, 27, 39, 106, 220
Brand image, 28, 56
Brand interaction competence, 214
Brand knowledge, 29
Brand lands, 120
Brand needs, 28, 109
Brand objectives, 93, 105
Brand offer, 55
Brand offering policy, 190
Brand-oriented human resource
   management, 184
Brand-oriented leadership, 187

© Springer Fachmedien Wiesbaden GmbH 2017
C. Burmann et al., *Identity-Based Brand Management*,
DOI 10.1007/978-3-658-13561-4

Brand origin, 45, 297
Brand page attachment, 222
Brand personality, 53
Brand Personality Scale (BPS), 53
Brand portfolio, 122
Brand positioning, 106
Brand potential value, 274
Brand price policy, 191
Brand prominence, 103
Brand promise, 28, 59, 109, 190
Brand protection, 161
Brand Rating Model, 262
Brand recall, 29, 57
Brand recognition, 29, 57
Brand-related communities, 207
Brand-related UGC, 202
Brand re-launch, 114
Brand repositioning, 114
Brand-self connection, 103
Brand story, 220
Brand strength, 241
    external, 241
    internal, 242, 247
Brand symbols, 59
Brand targets, 48, 240
Brand touch points, 26, 59, 93
Brand trust, 59, 70, 102
Brand understanding, 97, 175
Brand valuation approaches
    behavioural, 255
    combined approaches, 259
    financial, 255
    financial (capital market-oriented), 255
    financial (cost-oriented), 255
    financial (future performance
        indicator-oriented), 255
    financial (price-oriented), 255
    identity-based, 268
    stakeholder-oriented, 264
Brand Valuation Model, 260
Brand value, 51, 271
    identity-based, 271
Brand vision, 48

C
Category extensions, 156, 158
Co-branding, 145
Competence, 8

Competence-based view (CbV), 9
Competence fit, 176
Competitive advantage, 11
Conjoint analysis, 116
Consistency, 34, 73, 77, 180
Continuity, 34, 73, 77, 179
Core competences, 49
Culture fit, 179
Customer equity, 93, 235, 253, 271
Customer satisfaction, 102

D
Differentiation, 177, 292
Digital context, 195
Digital immigrants, 201
Digitalization, 195
Digital natives, 201
Dynamic Capabilities Approach, 11

E
E-commerce, 192
Economic benefits, 58
Economic brand objectives, 93
Employer brand, 149
Endorsed brand, 127
Entry phase, 185
Essential characteristics, 37
Evolutionary paths, 11
Experience orientation, 4
External brand management, 93
External target groups, 28

F
Forums, 207
Franchise agreements, 161
Functional benefit, 58

G
Gaming communities, 207

H
Hedonic benefit, 59
Homo oeconomicus, 40
Horizontal brand architecture dimension, 133

House of brands, 126
Hyper-mediality, 197

I

Identification, 99
Individual benefits, 59
Individuality, 78
Information overload, 119
Input items, 8
Inside-out perspective, 14, 26
Internal brand management, 93, 111
Internalisation, 99
Internal target groups, 27

K

Knowledge absorption, 13
Knowledge derivation, 13

L

Lateral dimension of brand architecture, 134
Line extensions, 156
Location-based advertising, 103

M

Made in Germany, 297
Market-Based View (MBV), 6
Market entry
    followers, 299, 300
    pioneers, 300
    sprinkler strategy, 300
    waterfall strategy, 300
Marketing mix, 189
Market orientation, 6
Market potential, 133
Market supply competence, 10, 49
Meta-competences, 10, 50
Metamorphosis phase, 186
Me-too strategy, 118
Microblogging services, 208
Multi-brand strategy, 133
Multi-channel, 194, 195
Multidimensional scaling, 116

N

Network-oriented interaction model, 200
Non-functional benefits, 58

O

Online communication, 196
Online communities, 206
Online promotions, 198
Operationalisation of brand identity, 178
Organisation's culture, 10
Ostergard-index, 283
Outside-in perspective, 14, 26

P

Perceived interchangeability, 3
Photo and video communities, 209
Points of difference, 118
Points of parity, 118
Pop-up stores, 139
Pre-entry phase, 185
Present value of the brand, 274
Private label brand, 22, 134, 135
Process fit, 176
Product, 190
Product and program policy, 190
Program, 190
Psychographic brand objectives, 102
Psychographic brand value, 255
Pull communication, 199
Pull principle, 182
Push communication, 199
Push principle, 182

R

Re-branding, 114
Reciprocity, 37
Reconfiguration competence, 11
Reconfiguration processes, 11
Refinement competence, 9, 49
Refinement processes, 8
Relative net advantage, 8
Replication competence, 11
Resource-based view (RbV), 8

Resource fit, 176
Retailer brand, 135
Risk reduction, 59

S
Search engine advertising, 198
Search engine optimization, 199
Self-perception, 35
Sensual-aesthetic benefit, 59
Share of wallet, 103
Single brand strategy, 133
Situation analysis, 93
Social benefits, 58
Social community, 205
Social entertainment, 210
Social media, 200
Social perception, 35
Social publishing, 207
Sport Club Brand Personality Scale (SCBPS), 54
Standardization, 292
Storing brand-related information, 57
Storytelling, 80
Structure-conduct-performance (S-C-P), 6
Structure fit, 176
Sub-brand, 127
Symbolic function, 3

T
Target groups, 218
Trademark piracy, 281
Trademark protection, 282
    extra-legal, 285
    identity-based, 283
    legal, 284
Trademark protection strategy, 283
Transformational leadership, 187
Transparency, 218
Trust function, 3
Twitter, 208

U
Unique brand experiences, 120
Unique selling proposition, 118
User-generated content (UGC), 202
Utilitarian benefits, 58

W
Web 2.0, 200
Web banners, 198
Wikipedia, 207
Wiki websites, 207

Printed by Printforce, the Netherlands